The United States, International Law, and the Struggle against Terrorism

This book discusses the critical legal issues raised by the US response to the terrorist threat. The book analyzes whether the Bush–Cheney administration's policies and practices in the so-called "war against terrorism" complied with international law, and extends that analysis to the Obama administration. Thomas McDonnell highlights specific topics of legal interest including torture, extrajudicial detentions, and the invasions of Afghanistan and Iraq, and examines them against the backdrop of terrorist movements that have plagued Britain and Russia. The book extrapolates from the actions of the USA, going on to look at the difficulties that all modern democracies face in trying to combat international terrorism.

The United States, International Law, and the Struggle against Terrorism demonstrates why current counterterrorism practices and policies should be rejected, and new policies adopted that are compatible with international law. Written for students of law, academics, and policymakers, the volume shows the dangers that breaking international law carries in the "war on terrorism."

Thomas Michael McDonnell is a Professor of Law at Pace University School of Law, USA.

Routledge Research in Terrorism and the Law

Available titles in this series include:

Forthcoming titles in this series include:

The United States, International Law, and the Struggle against Terrorism

Thomas Michael McDonnell

Routledge
Taylor & Francis Group

LONDON AND NEW YORK

This edition published in paperback in 2011

First published 2009
by Routledge
2 Park Square, Milton Park, Abingdon, Oxon, OX14 4RN

Simultaneously published in the USA and Canada
by Routledge
711 Third Avenue, New York, NY 10017

Routledge is an imprint of the Taylor & Francis Group, an informa business

© 2009 Thomas Michael McDonnell (hardback)
© 2011 Thomas Michael McDonnell (paperback)

British Library Cataloguing in Publication Data
A catalogue record for this book is available from the British Library

Library of Congress Cataloging in Publication Data
A catalog record has been requested

ISBN13: 978-0-415-48898-3 (hbk)
ISBN13: 978-0-415-78242-5 (pbk)
ISBN13: 978-0-203-86752-5 (ebk)

Typeset in Garamond
by RefineCatch Limited, Bungay, Suffolk

Printed and bound in Great Britain by
CPI Antony Rowe, Chippenham, Wiltshire

For my loving wife

Kathryn Judkins McDonnell,

forever my inspiration

Contents

Acknowledgements

Many people have helped with this book. I first wish to thank Stephen J. Friedman and Michelle S. Simon, former Dean and present Dean, respectively, of Pace University School of Law, for providing the grants to help fund the research and for encouraging me to pursue this project. I thank my colleagues at Pace University School of Law for reviewing draft chapters, specifically, Professors Adele Bernhard, James J. Fishman, Bennett L. Gershman, Vanessa H. Merton, Marie Stefanini Newman, Mark R. Shulman, Mark von Sternberg, and Gayl S. Westerman. I would like to thank Professor Louise Doswald-Beck of the Geneva Academy of International Humanitarian Law and Human Rights, Professor John E. Noyes of California Western School of Law, Professor Barbara Stark of Hofstra Law School, and Christopher G. Wren, Assistant Attorney General, Criminal Appeals Unit, Wisconsin Department of Justice, for also reviewing my drafts.

I wish to thank Pace Law School librarians Jack McNeil, Margaret Moreland, Lucie Olejnikova, and Cynthia Pittson for their valuable assistance.

I thank my research assistants, Kelly Belnick, Laura Boucher, Bari Buggé, Hannah Cochrane, Christopher DiCicco, Jesse Glickstein, Judith Murphy, William Onofry, Taylor Palmer, Jessica Rhodes-Knowlton, Zein Semaan, Katherine Sohr, Kory Salomane, Meghan Summers, and Richard Thomas for their research, editing, and cite-checking, with a special thanks to Jessica Rhodes-Knowlton, who has worked the longest with me on this project and retained her enthusiasm for the book throughout. I thank my assistant Katherine M. Frucco. My assistant Carol Grisanti, who is retiring at the end of this academic year, I wish to make special mention of, both for her sense of humor and for her sharp common sense in helping me with this and with many other projects.

A special thanks to my editor, Jessica Moody, for her invaluable assistance.

My wife, Kathryn, to whom I have dedicated this book, has been a constant source of inspiration. Her encouragement as I took on this project has made all the difference. I also wish to thank the other women in my life—my daughters Mary Louise and Ceara Clare—for their love and support. A special thanks to Ceara Clare again for keeping her music low when I was working on this project.

List of abbreviations

ACHR	American Convention on Human Rights
ADC	Arab American Anti-Discrimination Committee
ANC	African National Congress
AP I	1977 First Additional Protocol to the 1949 Geneva Conventions
AP II	1977 Second Additional Protocol to the 1949 Geneva Conventions
CAT	Convention against Torture (also, "the Torture Convention")
CEDAW	Convention on the Elimination of All Forms of Discrimination against Women
CIA	Central Intelligence Agency
CRC	Convention on the Rights of the Child
CSRT	Combat Status Review Tribunal
DTA	Detainee Treatment Act of 2005
ECtHR	European Court of Human Rights
EIT	Enhanced Interrogation Techniques
FMLN	Farabundo Martí National Liberation Front
EEOC	Equal Employment Opportunity Commission
FBI	Federal Bureau of Investigation
FLN	Front de Libération Nationale
GIA	Islamic Armed Group (Gamaa al Islamiya)
ICC	International Criminal Court
ICCPR	International Covenant on Civil and Political Rights
ICE	US Immigration and Customs Enforcement
ICJ	International Court of Justice
ICRC	International Committee of the Red Cross
ICTR	International Criminal Tribunal for Rwanda
ICTY	International Criminal Tribunal for the Former Yugoslavia
INS	Immigration and Naturalization Service
IHL	International Humanitarian Law
IRA	Irish Republican Army
KFOR	NATO's Kosovo Force
MCA	Military Commissions Act of 2006

MVD	Ministertvo Vnutrennikh Del (Ministry of Interior Affairs, Russia)
NATO	North Atlantic Treaty Organization
OAS	Organization of American States
OIC	Organization of the Islamic Conference
PAIGC	African Party for the Independence of Guinea and Cape Verde
PKK	Kurdish Workers Party
POW	Prisoner of War
SAS	Special Air Service (principal special forces unit of the British Army)
SERE	Survival, Evasion, Resistance, and Escape program
UDHR	Universal Declaration of Human Rights
UN	United Nations
UNMOVIC	UN Monitoring, Verification and Inspection Commission

Preface to the Previous Edition

This book grew out of a series of articles I had written in the months and years following September 11, 2001 out of concern over the Bush–Cheney administration's counterterrorism policies and practices, which often disregarded international law. There seemed to have been an unstated assumption that violating international law did not matter in the aftermath of a megaterrorist event like 9/11. As I probed further into the history of the West's relationship with the Arab and Muslim worlds, it became clear that the course that the administration had adopted could lead in very dangerous directions, resulting not only in strengthening rather than weakening al Qaeda and its allies, but also in undermining the moral authority of the US. As of this writing, the Obama administration appears poised to move in a markedly different direction, but events will show whether the new administration's policies and practices will match its rhetoric. Whatever the philosophical makeup Congressional leaders and the administration in power possess, they will be tempted to bend or even violate the rules, both domestic and international, in face of deadly terrorist threats. They will also be tempted (and have been) tempted to drastically change domestic rules and push for significant changes in international ones.

This book argues for a more deliberate approach. Law, both international and domestic, has been crafted over generations, if not centuries, striking a balance between security and individual and collective freedom. Similar, if not identical, threats have arisen before. The undeniable truth in the struggle against terrorism is that the US needs the help and cooperation of other governments, their intelligence and police forces, and their individual citizens to meet the threat posed by highly organized, well-financed, transnational terrorist organizations. Complying with international law and restoring the US's moral authority may be the most effective way to obtain that help. In that light, this work discusses the terrorist challenge and the legal and policy issues that the country and government are facing.

Thomas Michael McDonnell
White Plains, New York
August 2009

Preface to this Edition

It is remarkable that in less than two years so many significant developments have taken place that concern the United States and the struggle against transnational terrorism. Perhaps the three most significant are as follows: (1) the Obama administration's failure to reject wholesale the Bush-Cheney administration's counterterrorism policies and practices; (2) the popular revolts sweeping the Arab world, often referred to as the "Arab spring"; and (3) the US Navy Seals killing Osama bin Laden in Abbottabad, Pakistan.

As noted in the first edition, the Obama administration is to be commended for moving many suspected terrorists for trial in US federal court.[1] Furthermore, after a "year-long review of all detainee files," the Obama administration cleared for release over half of the 242 Guantánamo Bay prisoners still remaining when Obama took office. [2] The Obama administration has "repatriated, resettled or transferred" a third of these detainees.[3]

The Obama administration has apparently carried through on the President's inauguration day promise to end torture and cruel, degrading and inhuman treatment of detained suspected Islamic terrorists—a crucial step toward restoring the moral authority of the United States.[4] President Obama has also ordered that the infamous CIA black sites be closed.[5] In other areas of international law, the Obama administration has renewed US efforts to cooperate with the International Criminal Court. The administration also obtained a binding chapter VII Security Council resolution approving the use of force against Libya to protect the civilian population and has insisted on allies playing key leadership and combat roles, all a departure from the generally unilateral approach that had been the previous administration's hallmark, at least in its first term.

The Obama administration has also supported a significant change in policy in Afghanistan to reduce civilian casualties and damage to civilian objects. Issued in 2009 by then commander General Stanley A. McChrystal and reissued with some modifications by his successor, General David H. Petraeus, the Tactical Directive requires American and other NATO forces to go beyond the protections of international humanitarian law to avoid civilian casualties and damage to civilian property.[6] The purpose of the Directive is, if not to win the hearts and minds of the Afghan people, at least not to push them into the arms of the Taliban. As a result, far fewer civilians have been killed and many fewer Afghan homes have been destroyed at the hands of American and other NATO forces.[7]

As of this writing, the outcome of the war in Afghanistan is in doubt. Even the initial invasion raised some questions under international law because al Qaeda, not the Taliban, had attacked the US. Granted al Qaeda had received safe haven in Taliban Afghanistan, but the publicly available evidence fails to indicate that the Taliban had "effectively controlled" al Qaeda or had participated in the 9/11 attacks.[8] There are some who question the Tactical Directive and the concern about protecting Afghani civilians as an approach that prevents the US from winning the war.[9] Given Afghanistan's colonization by Britain, the Russian invasion in 1979, and the subsequent civil strife, resulting in the Taliban's creating a totalitarian religious state, an approach highly respecting the human rights of Afghanistan civilians is likely to be a more effective counterterrorism policy and practice.[10]

On the other hand, the Obama administration has failed to fulfill its promise to close the Guantánamo Bay detention facility.[11] Not only has the administration failed to do so, but has announced that it intends to detain indefinitely without trial 47 suspected Islamic terrorists.[12] The first edition criticized the Obama administration for appealing the 2009 US federal district court decision in *Maqaleh v. Gates,*[13] which had extended the right of habeas corpus to detainees who had been brought from other countries to Bagram Airbase in Afghanistan. As I feared, the Court of Appeals for the District of Columbia reversed that decision, enabling the creation of yet another legal black hole to take the place of Guantánamo Bay. Given the current make-up of the Supreme Court and Justice Elena Kagan's promise to recuse herself in all cases in which she was involved as the Solicitor General, the Court of Appeals ruling will almost certainly stand for years to come.[14]

Congress has also contributed to the violation of international law by prohibiting the use of funds from the Defense Authorization Act to transport GITMO detainees to the United States for trial and prosecution.[15] This legislation, if not found unconstitutional, in effect prohibits trying any GITMO detainee in US federal courts.[16] The legislation contributes to GITMO detainees being tried by military commissions,[17] special courts which do not comport with the Geneva Conventions.[18] The legislation also prohibits the use of federal funds to transfer any detainee to any foreign country unless certain onerous criteria are met.[19] In cases in which the Administration wishes to release a detainee, the only option is to find a country that is willing to accept that person. Congress's rigid rules will make that process—already a difficult one—increasingly hard to accomplish. Consequently, the Congressional legislation will abet prolonged, if not indefinite detention of individuals whom the Executive has concluded are entitled to freedom.

Unfortunately, the Obama administration has acquiesced in Congress's prohibiting funding to transport Guantánamo Bay detainees in the United

States. President Obama signed the bill, albeit with a signing statement asserting that the bill constituted "a dangerous and unprecedented challenge to critical executive branch authority" and that regarding transferring detainees to other countries, the legislation "could hinder the conduct of delicate negotiations with foreign countries and therefore the effort to conclude detainee transfers in accord with our national security."[20]

The administration has not subjected the defunding statute to judicial challenge. Bowing to Congress and to public opinion, Attorney General Eric H. Holder has gone back on his decision to have Khalid Sheikh Mohammed, alleged mastermind of the 9/11 attacks, tried in federal court in New York City. "KSM" will now be tried by military commission in Guantánamo Bay. As horrific as the crimes he is accused of are, the decision is disquieting because the military commissions, among other things, lack judicial independence and have not, unlike federal courts, been fully tested.[21] Moving his case to a military commission virtually guarantees a death sentence, which is probably exactly what Khalid Sheikh Mohammed wants.

The first edition praised the Obama administration for avoiding the vague, overbroad phrase "war on terrorism" or "global war on terrorism," coined by the Bush-Cheney administration.[22] Yet the Obama administration has crafted a virtually equally troubling phrase: United States being "in armed conflict with al Qaeda, the Taliban and associated forces."[23] That formulation is a bit more definite, by mentioning al Qaeda and Taliban by name, but contains the vague words, "associated forces," whoever they may be. More ominously, this formulation permits the Administration to carry out a military attack anywhere in the world—broadly employing the law of war rather than law enforcement under a human rights regime. Harold Koh, the Legal Adviser to the State Department, suggests attacks would be permissible in states that are either unwilling or unable to arrest or capture members of al Qaeda or "associated forces." Such an expansive standard for the use of military force, without more, raises serious questions under international law.

Most alarming in this regard, the Obama administration has vastly increased the deployment of weaponized drones for targeted killing of alleged Islamic terrorists, authorizing the Central Intelligence Agency to carry out such attacks in Yemen and the tribal areas of Pakistan, and the US Air Force to conduct these attacks in Iraq and Afghanistan.[24] The number of attacks the administration has authorized in Pakistan represents nearly a four fold increase over the Bush-Cheney administration. Although targeted killing may sometimes comport with international humanitarian and human rights law, it is literally an explosive counterterrorism tactic, which at best presses the bounds of international law.[25] Routinely resorting to such methods and means of warfare against religiously and nationalistically motivated terrorists leaders and groups may have the effect of making the targets of such attacks martyrs and inflame rather than dampen Islamic terrorism.[26] Such attacks may further undermine the moral authority of the United States in the eyes of

Arab/Muslim peoples. (Despite the legal label, "targeted killing," a great number of people in the affected countries view such attacks as assassinations.)

Many Americans have enthusiastically greeted the killing of Osama bin Laden, responsible for horrendous crimes against thousands of innocent civilians in the US and elsewhere. The available evidence suggests that the Navy Seals essentially carried out a targeted killing operation. Reportedly, unless bin Laden clearly surrendered, the Seals were ordered to kill him. Although, as of this writing, the facts of the raid have not been clarified, many commentators, with some exceptions, have concluded that the targeted killing operation comported with international law.[27]

The significance of bin Laden's killing will probably not be able to be definitively determined for years. Yet some research suggests that killing a religious terrorist leader is likely to strengthen rather than weaken the terrorist organization in question.[28] Such an outcome would be particularly unfortunate given that al Qaeda and its allied terrorist organizations have generally been in decline. That decline is likely due to two factors: first, al Qaeda's decision to attack other Muslims rather than directing its fire solely on the West; and, second, the Arab spring, which al Qaeda and its allies have had little to do with. The promise of obtaining genuine democracy threatens to take the air out of the extremists' balloon. So many Arab and Muslim countries have had dictatorial rulers for decades, effectively cutting off avenues of peaceful protest and preventing Islamic peoples from democratically changing their government. Since democratic channels had been eliminated, individuals with legitimate grievances could only go underground, thereby encouraging the young to join terrorist organizations. If the Arab spring bears fruit and if genuine democratic institutions can be established, there will be a decreased need to pursue illegal courses to effect change.

Given this new reality, United States and its allies should even more strictly comply with international humanitarian law and human rights law, and, to the extent possible, afford greater protections to civilians than traditional humanitarian law requires. Overacting could have the effect of reinvigorating jihadist movements and gaining them more recruits, more sympathizers, and more supporters in the Islamic world just when these extremists have grown increasingly unpopular and disrespected. Explaining the Tactical Directive, General David Petraeus told his troops in Afghanistan to fight aggressively, but he also stated: "We can't win without fighting, but we also cannot *kill* or capture *our way to victory. Moreover, if we kill civilians or damage their property in the course of our operations, we will create more enemies than our operations eliminate.*"[29] His Directive appears in direct conflict with the targeted killing weaponized drone program carried out by the CIA and by the Air Force. General Petraeus is essentially calling for virtually no civilian casualties, fairly close to what the law enforcement regime requires and in contradistinction to what drone Hellfire missiles, capable of destroying a house, typically accomplish.

In summary, the Obama administration has definitely moved towards stricter compliance with international law in the struggle against terrorism, but at the same time it has clung to many of the previous administration's counter-terrorism policies, including indefinite detention, the preference for military commissions rather than civilian courts to try alleged terrorists,[30] and the use of military rather than law enforcement as the major counter-terrorism practice. The Obama administration has even increased the use of weaponized drones for "targeted killing" far beyond the level of the Bush-Cheney years. Furthermore, Congress has been an obstacle to fashioning enlightened counterterrorism policies.

United States has thus yet to learn from the experiences of its close ally, the United Kingdom, that the surer way towards eliminating terrorist organizations is to respect international law and to reverse the American government's priorities, namely, making law enforcement the primary counter-terrorism practice and the military approach the exception. This edition continues to examine the legal and public world order challenges that the struggle against terrorism poses for the international community, for the West, and particularly for the United States.

Additional Developments since the First Edition

On page 69, the chapter notes President Obama's opposition to investigations and prosecutions of Bush administration officials for alleged illegal acts in that administration's counterterrorism practices and policies and notes that "there is increasing pressure, as of this writing, for a the very least a bipartisan investigation similar to the 9/11 Commission."

Despite President Obama's opposition, Attorney General Holder did appoint a special prosecutor in 2009 to investigate the CIA interrogators' practices.[31] As of this writing, however, no indictments or reports have been forthcoming. The Special Prosecutor refused to indict any member of the CIA for intentionally destroying 92 video recordings of waterboarding, despite their being a court order against the CIA not to destroy any evidence.[32] The failure to prosecute or at a minimum to issue a critical report is disappointing and a troubling precedent, suggesting that CIA officials have the green light to destroy damaging evidence in the future. Given the clandestine nature of their activities and the special powers the country invests in the CIA, one would have expected a much sharper response from the Special Prosecutor.

Furthermore, pressure for a bipartisan investigation or truth commission (as indicated on page 69) has now substantially subsided.

On page 81, the chapter mentions that CIA officers were being tried *in absentia* for the kidnapping from Italy of an alleged Islamic terrorist whom the CIA had extraordinarily rendered to Egypt. The trial has since been concluded and the court found 23 American CIA officers guilty of abduction.[33]

Note 65 on page 90 cites to sources suggesting that the Obama administration, to the disappointment of many, has failed to unequivocally reject extraordinary rendition of suspected Islamic terrorists to countries with poor human rights records. In a similar vein, the Obama administration has used the same arguments as the Bush-Cheney administration—preserving state secrets—in vigorously defending the Boeing subsidiary that allegedly transported detainees to CIA black sites as part of the Bush administration's extraordinary rendition program.[34]

On page 109, the chapter mentions that US federal courts were just beginning to take up the habeas corpus petitions of the Guantánamo Bay Detainees. The federal courts have granted the habeas corpus petitions of many Guantánamo Bay detainees, but that does not mean that they are automatically freed.[35] The D.C. Circuit has ruled that they are not entitled to be released into the United States.[36] Consequently, the Executive has to find a country that will accept them, generally a challenge.[37]

On pages 109 to 114, the chapter discusses trial rights of unprivileged combatants. The United States Military Commissions Act of 2006 accorded unprivileged combatants limited trial rights. The Obama adminstration sponsored the Military Commissions Act of 2009, which marks an improvement over the 2006 Act. For example, the previous Act prohibited the admissibility of statements made under torture, but otherwise permitted coerced statements not rising to the level of torture to be admitted under a totality of the circumstances test.[38] Given that the US Torture Statute adopts an exceedingly narrow definition of torture, the 2006 Act permits the admissibility of a broad range of coerced statements. On the other hand, the 2009 Act prohibits the admissibility of statements made either under torture or under "cruel, inhuman or degrading treatment." Nonetheless, military commissions even under the 2009 Act fall substantially short of the rights accorded to a defendant in a court-martial: "In particular, military commissions differ from courts-martial in which individuals have the authority to convene trials, the required pretrial procedures, the rules for admitting evidence, and the appellate processes available to the accused."[39] For example, the Military Commissions Act empowers the Secretary of Defense to "authorize 'any officer or official' to convene military commissions permit[ting] an accuser to serve as the convening authority . [a] practice . . . specifically prohibited in courts-martial. Thus, in military commissions, but not in courts-martial, the accuser may convene the proceedings and then select the officers who will serve on the commission."[40]

On page 119, the chapter indicates that the Ninth Circuit declared unconstitutional part of the Material Support Statute, the main legal weapon used in prosecuting alleged terrorists. That opinion was vacated by the Ninth Circuit sitting *en banc* and remanded to the district court. On appeal after remand, a panel of the Ninth Circuit concluded that the statute was unconstitutionally vague as applied to petitioners, who wished to provide legal training and political advocacy for the Kurdistan Workers Party and the Tamil

Tigers, two foreign terrorist organizations listed by the Secretary of State.[41] Reversing, the United States Supreme Court in *Holder v. Humanitarian Law Project*, [42] ruled that the statute was not vague as applied to petitioners and did not violate their rights under the First Amendment freedom of speech or freedom of association clauses.[43] Regardless of the merits of the case, the Supreme Court reaffirms the breadth of the material support statute, strengthening the argument to try terror offense cases in federal courts rather than in military commissions.

On page 123, the chapter states that "with the lead of the Obama administration, a counter-trend appears to be emerging [that recognizes more strictly human rights and humanitarian law principles]". Unfortunately given the Obama administration's position on so many counter-terrorism issues that resemble its predecessor's this statement concerning the Obama administration can no longer be made.[44]

On page 161, the chapter expresses concern for entrusting the CIA with the authority to carry out drone attacks.[45] The reasons given for this concern are the Agency's role in the detainee abuse scandal and its inaccurate intelligence reporting in the run-up to the war in Iraq. Additional reasons that question assigning the CIA this responsibility include its unfortunate history in conducting assassinations in the 1960s and 70s, its inherent lack of transparency as a secret service,[46] and the non-uniformed status of its officers, which render them unprivileged combatants.

Thomas Michael McDonnell
White Plains, New York
June 2011

Notes

1   Most notably, the Obama Justice Department obtained a guilty plea from the New York Times Square bomber, Faisal Shazad; the federal district court sentenced Shazad to life imprisonment. *Faisal Shazad,* N.Y. Times, Oct. 5, 2010, *available at* http://topics.nytimes.com/top/reference/timestopics/people/s/faisal_shahzad/index.html. The Administration also obtained a guilty verdict, after a jury trial, against Ahmed Ghailani, who was sentenced to life in prison. Benjamin Weiser, *Heightened Security for Former Detainee,* N.Y. Times, June 9, 2011, *available at* http://www.nytimes.com/2011/06/10/nyregion/ghailani-ex-guantanamo-detainee-is-moved-to-supermax.html. Ghailani had been imprisoned in Guantánamo Bay and was convicted for his involvement in the 1998 bombings of two US embassies in East Africa, resulting in the death of 224 people. *Id.*
2   *Report Card: Assessing the Obama Administration's Record of Compliance with the Rule of Law and Human Rights in National Security Policy,* Human Rights First, Jan. 13, 2011, *available at* http://www.humanrightsfirst.org/2011/01/13/report-card-assessing-the-obama-administrations-record-of-compliance-with-the-rule-of-law-and-human-rights-in-national-security-policy-2/
3   *Id.* Included in this group are some of the Uighars. (The 22 Uighars, captured by bounty hunters in Afghanistan but who had fled China because of their

persecution there, had been detained without trial in Guantánamo Bay since shortly after 9/11. The US had continued to detain them even after they were found not to be enemy combatants). The Obama administration has obtained offers from other countries to accept the Uighars, but has refused to permit them to be released into the United States. The D. C. Circuit has upheld the Obama administration's position that even if a detainee's habeas corpus petition has been granted, that does not give the detainee a right to be released in or to reside in the US. Kiyemba v. Obama, 555 F.3d 1022 (D.C. Cir. 2009). Upon the Obama administration's showing that all Uighars had received offers of resettlement, the Supreme Court decided to vacate the judgment. Kiyemba v. Obama, 130 S.Ct. 1235 (2010).

Many of the Uighars, however, have refused to accept the offers of resettlement. *See* Nick Baumann, *Supreme Court to Uighars-No US for You*, Mother Jones, Apr. 2011, *available at* http://motherjones.com/mojo/2011/04/supreme-court-uighurs-no. *See also* Richard M. Pious, *Prerogative Power in the Obama Administration: Continuity and Change in the War on Terrorism*, Presidential Stud. Q. 263, June 1, 2011, *available at* 2011 WLNR 11025271.

4   In his memoir, President George W. Bush admitted that he expressly approved the waterboarding of Khalid Sheik Mohammed and Abu Zubaydah. George W. Bush, *Decision Points,* 169, 170–71 (2010). *See also House Committee on the Judiciary, Majority Staff Report, Reining in the Imperial Presidency*, Jan. 13, 2009, at 114, 123.

5   Barack Obama, Exec. Order No. 13,491, § 4(a), 74 Fed. Reg. 4893 (Jan. 22, 2009). The order does permit the CIA to have "temporary holding facilities" overseas. Some have expressed concern that such facilities could—albeit for a short term of detention—permit the CIA to abuse prisoners yet again. *See Editorial: A Bush-lite Approach to Terror,* Washington Times, Jan. 30, 2009, at A22, *available at* 2009 WLNR 1813505 (quoting Christopher Anders, senior legislative counsel for the ACLU, "Our position is that the CIA should have no detention authority . . . ").

6   *See Senator Carl Levin Holds a Hearing on Operation Moshtarak in Helmand Province Afghanistan*, CQ Capital Transcripts, Feb. 22, 2010 (Department of Defense Undersecretary Michelle Fluornoy testified that President Obama's ordered an "immediate strategy review" and as part of that strategy he appointed General Stanley A. McChrystal as commander who "prioritized protecting the Afghan people over killing the enemy"), available *at* 2010 WLNR 3804516. *See also* Richard A. Oppel & Rod Norland, *New Rules Stress G.I. Limits in Fighting,* N.Y. Times, Aug. 3, 2010, (noting that General McChrystal's Tactical Directive was greeted warmly by President Hamid Karzai and by human rights groups, but disliked by American troops on the ground), *available at* http://www.nytimes.com/2010/08/04/world/asia/04petraeus.html.

7   *See, e.g.,* Hashim Shukoor, *U.N. Taliban Attacks Driving Up Afghan Civilian Casualties*, McClatchy Newspapers (noting that "[c]ivilian casualties caused by coalition and Afghan security forces fell by 30 percent during the first half of this year, to 223 deaths and 160 wounded"), Aug. 10, 2010, *available at* 2010 WLNR 15933571.

8   See chapter 12, starting on page 259, for a much fuller discussion of this issue.

9   *See, e.g.,* Tod Robberson, *BLOG: Opinion: Point Person: Michael Scheuer, former CIA bin Laden tracker*, The Daily Morning News, May 6, 2011, *available at* 2011 WLNR 8914735.

10   Obviously, such an approach does not guaranty victory. By the way, "counter-terrorism" may be the wrong term here, because the Taliban had been in power before US invasion on October 7, 2010. The administration uses the term

counter-insurgency. This again illustrates the slipperiness and vagueness of the term "terrorism" and its counterpart "war on terrorism." *See* chapter 2, pages 36 *et seq.* for a more detailed discussion of this issue.

11   The statement on page 38 that President Obama "declaring that the Guantanamo Bay detention center would be closed within a year" has thus failed to come to pass.

12   Executive Order, Barack Obama, *Periodic Review of Individuals Detained at Guantánamo Bay Naval Station Pursuant to the Authorization for Use of Military Force,* March 7, 2011, *available at* http://www.whitehouse.gov/sites/default/files/Executive_Order_on_Periodic_Review.pdf.

13   Maqaleh v. Gates, 604 F. Supp. 2d 205 (D.D.C. 2009), *rev'd*, 605 F.3d 84 (D.C. Cir. 2010).

14   Justice Kagan had argued to reverse Maqaleh when she was serving as Solicitor General, so even had she not made the pledge to recuse herself from all cases she had participated in as SG, there is little likelihood that the Supreme Court would reverse the Court of Appeals ruling. (On the other hand one never knows for certain how a justice might vote.) Recall that Justice Kagan took the place of Justice John Paul Stevens who formed part of the majority in the 5 to 4 opinion in Boumediene v. Bush, 553 U.S. 723 (2008), granting Guantánamo Bay detainees the right of habeas corpus in US federal courts. Since Maqaleh was arguing for an extension of Boumediene to Bagram, Airbase in Afghanistan, it is unlikely that he would garner more than four votes. The outcome for him would probably at best be a tie: 4 to 4, meaning that the D.C. Circuit Court's decision would be affirmed.

15   Ike Skelton National Defense Authorization Act for Fiscal Year 2011, Pub. L. No. 111–383, 124 Stat. 4137 (2010). *See* Kristine A. Huskey, *Guantánamo and Beyond: Reflections on the Past, A Present and Future of Preventive Detention,* 9 U. N.H. L. Rev. 183 (2011).

16   Ashley Pope, *Note, After Guantánamo: Legal Rights of Foreign Detainees Held in the United States*, 34, Fordham Int'l L.J. 504, 504–505 (2011). The legislation also prohibits the use of Department of Defense funds to build or modify prisons in the US for Guantánamo Bay detainees. *Id.*

17   Of course, the Obama administration could, instead of military commission, try the Taliban, al Qaeda or other unprivileged combatants by courts-martial, regularly constituted courts that comport with the Geneva Conventions. *See* Uniform Code of Military Justice, 10 U.S.C.A. §§ 802(a)(9)-(10), 802(a)(12). *See also* Brian S. McComa, *Comment, Article III by Default: Constitutional Requirements for the Capital Prosecution of Unprivileged Enemy Belligerents,* 44 U.S.F. L. Rev. 979, 984 n.29 (2010).

18   *See* chapter 6, pages 109 to 123. *See also* Daniel H. Benson, *Repeal of the Military Commissions Act,* 19, S. Cal. Rev. L. & Soc. Just. 265, 292 (2010) ("On the most basic level, the military commissions enacted by President Bush, and extended by President Obama, run afoul of the Geneva Convention of 1949, which requires that persons who are prisoners of war be tried by court-martial using the same procedures as the United States would apply in the criminal trials of its own military personnel.") That the detainees may be unprivileged rather than privileged combatants does not matter. Perhaps more importantly, the Military Commissions are a "special" court created to try a particular class of alleged offenders and therefore run afoul of Common Article 3's requirement that individuals, regardless of status, be tried by *regularly constituted* courts. For a good brief discussion of the Military Commissions Act of 2009, see Ved P. Nanda & Daniel K. Pansius, 3 Litigation of International Disputes in U.S. Courts § 14:33 (2011).

19   *See* Huskey, *supra* note 15, at 191. The legislation does not apply to individuals

who have been ordered released by a court, for example, by a federal court granting a habeas corpus petition.

20   Angie Drobnic Holan, *Obama and Congress Remain at Odds on Closing Guantánamo*, St. Petersburg Times, Jan. 12, 2011 (quoting Barack Obama's signing statement), *available at* 2011 WLNR 742517.

Apparently as part of the huge defense appropriation bill funding the wars in Afghanistan and Iraq, the President believed that he could not veto the legislation. *See* Huskey, *supra* note 15, at 193–94.

21   *See infra* notes 38 to 40 and accompanying text for a brief discussion of military commissions.

22   *See* pages 36 to 41 in chapter 2 for a fuller discussion.

23   Harold H. Koh, *Keynote Address to the American Society of International Law*, US Dep't of State, March 25, 2010, Washington, D. C., *available at* http://www.state.gov/s/l/releases/remarks/139119.htm. The statement on page 41 of chapter concerning the Obama administration's refraining from use of the term "war on terrorism" is technically correct, but does not capture the Obama administration's subsequent characterization and policy.

24   *See also* Greg Miller, *CIA Will Direct Yemen Drones*, Washington Post, June 14, 2011, at A1, *available at* 2011 WLNR 11827499.

The Obama administration has also recently authorized drone attacks in Somalia, which were carried out not by the CIA, but by the Joint Special Operations Command. *See* Mark Mazzetti & Eric Schmitt, *U.S. Expands Its Drone War Into Somalia*, N.Y. Times, July 2, 2011, at A1, *available at* 2011 WLNR 13130039.

25   *See* chapter 8, page 156 *et seq.* for a more detailed discussion of this issue.

26   Both Republican and Democratic administrations have considered the use of drones and other targeted killing operations to have been an eminently successful counterterrorism tactic, and can point to apparent success on the ground: "Of 30 prominent members of the terrorist organization [al Qaeda] indentified by intelligence agencies as targets, 20 have been killed in the last year and a half." Mark Landler & Helene Cooper, *Qaeda Woes Fuel Talk of Speeding Afghan Pullback*, N.Y. Times, June 19, 2011, at A1. *But see* Jenna Jordan, *When Heads Roll*, 18, Security Studies 719, 746 (2009), DOI: 10.1080/09636410903369068, *available at* http://cpost.uchicago.edu/pdf/Jordan.pdf (noting that empirical research indicates that killing the leaders of a religious and nationalistic terrorist organization is likely to be counter-productive).

27   *See, e.g.,* Harold Koh, the Legal Adviser to the Secretary of State, *The Lawfulness of the Operation against Osama bin Laden*, Opinio Juris Blog, May 19, 2011 (arguing, among other things, that bin Laden was a combatant who could be killed anywhere, that he constituted an imminent threat, and that he failed to surrender), *available at* http://opiniojuris.org/tag/bin-laden-killing/. *But see* Thomas Darnstadt, *Justice American Style: Was Bin Laden's Killing Legal,* Der Spiegel, May 3, 2011 (suggesting that the operation was illegal, because it occurred in a peaceful part of Pakistan territory, away from an area of armed conflict, and that human rights law demanded that a law enforcement approach be used), *available at* http://www.spiegel.de/international/world/0,1518,760358,00.html. Note that the Naval Seals 6, which carried out the operation against bin Laden, is part of the Joint Special Operations Command, discussed in notes 24 and 45.

28   *See* Jordan, *supra* note 26, at 746.

29   General David H. Petraeus, Commander NATO/ISAF, COMISAF Guidance, August 1, 2010 (emphasis added).

30   To be fair, the Obama administration did wish to try Khalid Sheikh Mohammed in federal court and bring other GITMO detainees to the United States for trial,

but the administration did not push hard against Congress and public opinion to make that happen.

31   Mark Mazzetti & Scott Shane, *CIA Abuse Scandal Detailed in Report on Detainees*, N.Y. Times, Aug. 24, 2009, *available at* http://www.nytimes.com/2009/08/25/us/politics/25detain.html

32   Ken Dilanian, *CIA avoids charges Officers won't be prosecuted over the destruction of interrogation tapes*, L.A. Times, Nov. 10, 2010, at 14, *available at* 2010 WLNR 22436102. *See also* Editorial, *Waffling on Waterboarding*, L.A. Times, Nov. 16, 2010, at 24, *available at* 2010 WLNR 22838475.

33   Rachel Donaldo, *Italy Convict 23 Americans for CIA Renditions*, N.Y. Times, Nov. 4, 2009, at A1, *available at* http://www.nytimes.com/2009/11/05/world/europe/05italy.html.

34   Mohamed v. Jeppesen Dataplan, Inc., 614 F.3d 1070 (9th Cir. 2010), *cert. denied*, 2011 WL 1832889, 79 USLW 3370 (2011). *See also* Owen Fiss, *Aberrations No More*, 2010 Utah L. Rev. 1085, 1095–96 (implicitly criticizing the Obama administration for failing to clearly disavow extraordinary rendition and for its defending Jeppesen Dataplan, *supra*, as well as resisting the suit of a victim of extraordinary rendition in Arar v. Ashcroft, 585 F.3d 559, 574–78 (2d Cir. 2009) (en banc)).

35   William Glaberson & Charlie Savage, *Secret Case Against Detainee Crumbles*, N.Y. Times, Apr. 26, 2011, at A12, *available at* http://www.nytimes.com/2011/04/27/world/secret-case-against-detainee-crumbles.html?_r=1&ref=habeascorpus.

36   *See supra* note 3, for a discussion of Kiyemba v. Obama, 555 F.3d 1022 (D.C. Cir. 2009), and its subsequent case history.

37   See supra note 3 for a discussion of the Uighars and the difficulty of finding a suitable country willing to receive them and to which they are willing to go.

38   10 U.S.C. § 948b(d). *See also* Jennifer K. Elsea, *The Military Commissions Act of 2009: Overview and Legal Issues*, Congressional Research Service, Apr. 6, 2010, at 25–26, *available at* http://www.fas.org/sgp/crs/natsec/R41163.pdf.

39   *See* Benson, *supra* note 18, at 278.

40   *Id. But see* Elsea, *supra* note 38 at 17. Elsea notes that "[i]n particular, the MCA prohibits the unlawful influence of military commissions and provides that neither the military commission members nor military counsel may have adverse actions taken against them in performance reviews." *Id.* Nevertheless, Elsea also observes: "On the other hand, it has been argued that the multiple roles assigned to the convening authority, i.e., the DOD official who decides which charges to bring, allocates resources among the parties, and then approves or disapproves the findings of the military commission, create an inherent risk of unfairness (or the perception of unfairness). *Id.* at 17–18 (citing Gregory S. McNeal, *Beyond Guantánamo, Obstacles and Options*, 103 Nw. U. L. Rev. Colloquy 29, 32 (2008) (blaming "conflicting statutory provisions" for perceived undue influence at military commissions under the MCA)).

Others variances with courts-martial include the following: "The MCA of 2009 explicitly withholds from unprivileged enemy belligerents rights against unreasonable search and seizure, protections against compulsory self-incrimination, protections against testimonial hearsay, the right to speedy trial, and the right to pretrial discovery of exculpatory evidence if deemed confidential. More troublesome is the fact that it allows the government to use confidential information against the accused without disclosure so long as it is described by generic categories." McComa, *supra* note 17, at 993 (citing 10 U.S.C. §§ 949a(b)(2), 939(d)(1)(2), 949d(d)(1)(2); 949a(b)(2), 949h, 949s, 949a(b)(3)(A)(B)(D), and 948b(d)(1)(A)).

41   The majority states that the plaintiffs also wished make a monetary contribution for the humanitarian activities of the organizations. Holder v. Humanitarian

Law Project, 130 S.Ct. 2705, 2714 (2010). Dissenting, Justice Breyer criticizes this characterization: "[T]the majority discusses the plaintiffs' proposal to 'teach PKK members how to petition various representative bodies such as the United Nations *for relief.*' *Ante,* at 2729 (quoting 552 F.3d, at 921, n. 1; emphasis added). The majority's only argument with respect to this proposal is that the relief obtained 'could readily include monetary aid,' which the PKK might use to buy guns. *Ante,* at 2729. The majority misunderstands the word 'relief.' In *this* context, as the record makes clear, the word 'relief' does not refer to 'money.' It refers to recognition under the Geneva Conventions." Humanitarian Law Project, 130 S. Ct. at 2738–39 (Breyer J., dissenting) (emphasis in original).

42   *Id.*

43   *Id.* at 2714.

44   *See* Pious, *supra* note 3 (quoting General Michael Hayden, CIA Director under President George W. Bush) (Bush's CIA director General Michael Hayden praised Obama's 'continuity' of policy, observing 'to President Obama's credit, he has used many of the tools that we used to continue to take the fight to the enemy.' He mentioned renditions to other nations for interrogation, indefinite detention of detainees, limited definition of habeas corpus rights, use of military commissions, and reliance on state secrets defenses in court proceedings.) (Citation omitted).

45   The CIA has been tasked with carrying out drone attacks in Pakistan and Yemen. The Joint Special Service Command, however, apparently has also had authority to carry out drone strikes in Yemen and carried out the recent strike in Somalia. *See supra* note 24. Authorizing the Joint Special Operations Command to carry out targeted killings, including by drone attacks, suffers from much of the same problems that authorizing the CIA to do so, because such operations are often clandestine and receive little Congressional oversight. *See, e.g.,* Barbara Barrett, *Anti-Terror Command in N.C. Flies under the Radar,* News & Observer (Raleigh NC), May 4, 2011, *available at* 2011 WLNR 8648797. *See also* W. Hays Parks, *Special Forces Wear of Non-Standard Uniforms,* 4 Chicago Journal of International Law 493 (2003). This is not to suggest that JSOC should be abolished, only that procedures be implemented to insure greater transparency and far greater congressional oversight to help make certain that Special Forces comply with international law.

46   Charlie Savage, *UN Report Highly Critical of US Drone Attacks,* N.Y. Times, June 3, 2010, *available at* http://www.nytimes.com/2010/06/03/world/03drones.html.

1 The West's colonization of Muslim lands and the rise of Islamic fundamentalism

Like locating fault lines to determine where earthquakes are apt to develop, examining the history of the affected peoples, particularly who did what to whom, helps explain the advent of terrorism perpetrated by extreme Muslim fundamentalist groups against the West and against the United States in particular. When Russian, American, or European leaders condemn Muslim terrorism and terrorists, they rarely, if ever, mention the behavior of Russia and European countries towards Muslim ones[1] in the seventeenth, eighteenth, nineteenth, and twentieth centuries. For example, in 1830, France invaded, and in 1834 annexed, Algeria. Only after a bitterly fought and bloody nine-year war of independence in which the rebels killed French civilians and targeted French bars and restaurants and the French engaged in ruthless counterterrorist methods, including torture, did General Charles de Gaulle finally accede to Algerian independence in 1962. In the 1600s, the Dutch, following the Portuguese, began the conquest and colonization of the Indonesian islands, today the most populous Muslim nation, only to give them up under intense internal and international pressure in 1949. In the late 1700s and in the 1800s, Russia annexed Tatar Crimea, the Caucasus, including Chechnya and other Central Asian Muslim nations like Azerbaijan, Kazakhstan, Kyrgyzstan, Tajikistan, Turkmenistan, and Uzbekistan. These latter six countries only achieved independence with the breakup of the Soviet Union in 1991. Chechnya, which Russia did not consider an independent state, remains under Russian rule.

Britain began the colonization of India and what is now Pakistan in the 1700s, with the activities of the government-sanctioned East India Company, only to fully colonize the Indian subcontinent in the 1800s.[2] The British left their former colony in 1947, agreeing to divide it along religious lines (Hindu and Muslim) into two bitterly separated states, India and Pakistan. Britain also had three times waged war against Afghanistan, invading in 1838 and in 1878, and fighting a rebellion in 1919.[3] To protect its hold on India and to thwart Russian influence, Britain took the Khyber Pass and other areas and installed the Afghan ruler in 1880 on the condition that Britain would run Afghanistan's foreign policy. After the 1919 rebellion, Britain recognized Afghanistan's independence. (The Soviet Union was to invade Afghanistan in

1979. In response, the US armed the Afghan Mujahideen, unwittingly helping Osama bin Laden and his organization, al Qaeda, to emerge.)

Britain invaded Egypt in 1882, retaining a colonial relationship with that country until 1954. Britain also took over as "trust territories" Muslim states from the former Ottoman Empire after the First World War, literally drawing the map establishing Iraq, as well as taking Jordan and Palestine. Britain also exploited its economic ties to Iran, obtaining in 1901 an exclusive 60-year concession to explore for oil in that country and in 1907 agreeing with Russia to divide Iran into separate spheres of influence. In addition, the European countries colonized virtually all of Africa, including the Northern African Muslim states, generally not giving them up for independence until the 1960s.

The list does not end here. Almost every Muslim country on the planet was conquered and colonized by Europeans or Russians (see Table 1.1, pp. 19–27). Most of those countries became free of the colonizer only since the end of the Second World War, with many gaining independence in the 1960s. In every Muslim country that experienced colonization, there are still substantial numbers of the populace living today who also lived under colonization. Although most Muslims living today were born after the Second World War (and even after 1980), colonization has cast a long, dark shadow.

Just as abolishing *de jure* discrimination has not eliminated *de facto* racial discrimination in the US, the simple act of becoming independent does not immediately eliminate the attitudes, customs, and institutions of either the colonizer or the colonized. After casting off the yoke of white minority rule in South Africa, the government is nonetheless finding it particularly difficult to grapple with the issues of unemployment and underemployment, economic development, and the AIDS pandemic, not to mention transitional justice. Nelson Mandela's declaration that the new South African constitution put to rest the 500 years of colonization starting with the Portuguese has not, in and of itself, made South Africa a stable or a prosperous country.

Even after independence, the colonizer often exerted inordinate influence on its former colony. The colonizer's government, its private corporations, and its religions had been operating in the former colony for decades. Even after independence, these institutions often keep on operating. Sometimes for self-interest, sometimes out of a sense of obligation, the colonizer has intervened militarily or economically or both. Sometimes, the colonizer, if not pulling all the strings as it did previously, continues to run important businesses and to provide the major source of foreign capital and investment in the former colony. Culture, language, and religion, likewise, sometimes have bound former colonizer and colony in ways that neither had foreseen.

Explaining the British tactic of controlling another country without necessarily colonizing it, historian John Darwin's words apply equally strongly to the post-colonization experience of many formally colonized states:

> [T]he British had always been prepared to secure their imperial ends—
> trade, security, influence—by the widest variety of political means, using

the inflexible and expensive method of direct colonial rule only when necessary—and often grudging the necessity. Whenever possible they preferred to influence, persuade, inveigle (by economic benefits) or frighten local rulers into cooperation with them. All this means that we cannot easily measure the extent to which British dominance over client states and colonial peoples contracted by the crude yardstick of a change in constitutional forms.[4]

Until conquest and colonization were made illegal in the last century, the story of the human race mainly consists of peoples conquering, colonizing, often enslaving and, in some cases, destroying or banishing other peoples. The Muslim Ottoman Empire itself was established through conquest and colonization. The US was established through conquest and, to a great extent, by destruction of the native population. That conquest and colonization were commonly practiced does not, however, heal the wounds they caused any faster. Furthermore, the world community's outlawing conquest and colonization has heightened the consciousness, even of peoples who were conquered and colonized before the practice was banned. Most Muslim countries were subject to colonization within 100 years of the UN Charter, the multilateral treaty, concluded in 1945, which most clearly made conquest illegal.[5] A large number of Muslim countries achieved independence in the 1960s, so the wounds caused by colonization, from the perspective of world history, remain relatively fresh.

Most Muslim countries have had difficulty in the post-colonial period meeting the fundamental needs of their people. If one excludes the oil-producing states, Muslim countries are disproportionately represented among the bottom third of countries in terms of absolute and per capita gross domestic product.[6] Non-oil-producing Muslim countries rank in the bottom third of states in terms of industrial production and in income per capita.[7]

Many of the independent post-colonial Arab and Muslim states adopted far more draconian laws and policies than the former Ottoman Empire. The Ottomans often governed on the basis of accommodation rather than absolute force. The governments of the independent Arab and Muslim states often borrowed the repressive policies and practices of the European and Russian colonizers rather than the generally more relaxed practices of the Ottoman Empire.

Few Muslim countries have a democratic form of government; most, unfortunately, are run by authoritarian regimes. Freedom House lists only three Muslim countries as "free."[8] Muslim countries also score low on Transparency International's corruption index.[9] Of the large Muslim states, Turkey may be the most democratic. It also has suffered military coups and possesses one of the worst human rights records in Europe. In attempting to gain entry into the European Union, Turkey has commendably made real reform, such as abolishing the death penalty in peacetime. Amnesty International reports, however, that Turkey is still actively prosecuting individuals under Article 301 of its penal law for "denigrating Turkishness," going so far, for example, as to criminally prosecute an attorney for uttering the word, "Kurdistan."[10] Amnesty also notes that Turkey is continuing to torture and mistreat prisoners.[11]

The literacy rate of Arab counties is 70.3 percent,[12] far behind the former Eastern bloc countries, Europe, Canada, and the US. The Arab states rate towards the bottom of countries on indices measuring freedom of speech and freedom of the press. Consequently, cultural life in these states has stagnated.

For many Muslims, it must be galling to have been passed by the West in almost every category. In the mid-1500s, the Ottoman Empire was the superpower, the unquestioned top military power in Europe, Asia, and Africa.[13] Muslim architecture was the most advanced; their mathematicians were making breakthroughs that made the rest of the world wonder.[14] Their scholars generally were the most respected in the world. Furthermore, Muslim societies were among those most tolerant of the "other." For example, Muslim Turkey welcomed the Jews after they were expelled from Catholic Spain in 1492.[15] (Jews and Christians were generally tolerated in the Ottoman Empire probably because of the teaching of the Hanafite school of Islam.)[16] Given this history, Muslims must have found it particularly humiliating to be conquered and colonized by the Europeans and Russians. It must have resembled Detroit automakers being taken over by the Japanese (and now the Italians). Furthermore, as noted above, the post-colonial experience of Muslim countries has not generally been as positive as it might have been, and certainly has not cleansed those societies of the humiliation of colonization.

1.1 The colonial experience—Egypt

As noted above, nearly every Muslim country was colonized by European countries or Russia. It might be instructive to examine the colonial experience of one such country that is probably representative of many. Egypt had been a Muslim country since 641 CE.[17] Egypt was the only Muslim country to successfully fight off the thirteenth-century Mongol invasion that so devastated the Muslim world.[18] The army of Sultan Selim brought Egypt into the Ottoman Empire after defeating the ruling Mamluks outside Cairo in 1517.[19] In 1798, Egypt, however, was conquered by Napoleon. Napoleon's conquest was short-lived. The Ottoman Turks and the British banded together and pushed the French out in 1801. One of the Turkish officers, Muhammad Ali (also known as Mehemet Ali), became the ruler of Egypt. He defeated the British in 1807, brutally confiscated the lands of rival feudal lords, persuaded the Ottoman Sultan to name him viceroy, and, of all Muslim leaders in the nineteenth century, did the most to modernize his country along European lines.[20] His modernization projects included the building of irrigation canals, the construction of shipbuilding plants, textile mills, and other factories, the creation of a huge, conscripted standing army on the European model, the cultivation of cotton, sugar cane, and other cash crops, and the imposition of tariffs on European imports to protect Egypt's nascent industries.[21] He ruthlessly impressed the peasantry into the army and into his textile mills. He also excluded the Muslim clergy, the ulama, from avenues of power.[22]

Muhammad Ali gained Egypt's *de facto* independence from the Ottoman Empire, an independence that displeased Britain. One of Ali's military campaigns threatened Constantinople. Britain and France supported the Ottoman Empire in fending off the attack and in defeating Ali. Under the terms of the Treaty of London of 1841, Ali had to give up Syria, limit his army to 18,000 troops, and ease his tariffs on British imports, an act that contributed to the failure of his efforts to establish Egyptian manufacturing.[23] This Treaty did make Ali's heirs hereditary rulers, the only viceroys in the Ottoman Empire to have gained this privilege.

Ali was uninterested in cutting a canal through the Suez. His successor, Abbas Pasha, was likewise uninterested, but upon the latter's death in 1854, Said Pasha, Ali's son, began a nine-year rule. He wanted to continue the modernization of Egypt, and happened to be a childhood friend of French diplomat and engineer Ferdinand de Lesseps, to whom he gave the concession to build the canal.[24] The latter founded the Universal Company of the Maritime Suez Canal in 1858.[25] His company, financed by French and Egyptian investors, started construction that year. Using the forced labor of thousands of Egyptian peasants, the Company completed the canal nearly 11 years later at twice the estimated cost.[26]

When the company ran into financial trouble, Said Pasha bought 44 percent of its stock. In his attempts to modernize the country, from stringing telegraph lines up the Nile to expanding the railroad and building the Suez Canal, Said Pasha had run the government into debt.[27]

Said's successor, Ismail Pasha, under the thrall of the Europeans, continued modernization projects, including greatly expanding public education, railroads, harbors, and other public works. Unfortunately, Ismail spent far beyond his and his country's means, nearly bankrupting Egypt and permitting it to fall largely into the hands of French and British creditors.[28] In 1875, the dire financial situation virtually compelled the government to sell its shares in the canal to Britain. (By 1880, 66 percent of Egypt's revenue went to pay the debt and the tribute to the Sultan.[29]) The French and English governments urged Ismail to abdicate in favor of his son Toufik. When the Ottoman Sultan agreed, Ismail was deposed, and Toufik, at 27, became the viceroy of Egypt.

Toufik did not reign independently for long. Although he tried to turn the debt crisis around, he lacked the stature to control the army. A charismatic officer, Said Ahmed Urabi, led an army revolt in 1881, which resulted in Urabi's being appointed Minister of War in 1882 and shortly thereafter the military ruler of the country.[30] Urabi set to work wresting internal control of Egypt from the French and the British, and called for the expulsion of foreigners.[31] His policies alarmed the two European powers.

Although initially opposed to the canal's construction,[32] the British considered the completed Suez Canal vital to their interests as "the highway to

India."[33] Concerned that Urabi's revolt might threaten their access to the canal, the British invaded Egypt in 1882, beat Urabi's troops with superior firepower, captured Urabi, and reinstated Toufik.[34] For the next 72 years, the British retained *de facto* if not *de jure* control of the country. Specifically, the British occupied Egypt, but permitted the Egyptian viceroy to exercise nominal authority. At the outbreak of the First World War, the British appointed their own sultan of Egypt, establishing a protectorate that lasted until shortly after that war.[35] After the protectorate ended, authority was supposedly passed to Egypt's monarchy (Ali's heir), but real power lay with the British who continued to station large troop contingents in Egypt until 1954.[36]

The colonization of Egypt had practical effects, for example, changing a diverse economy into a single commodity enterprise: "From a country which formed one of the hubs in the commerce of the Ottoman world and beyond, and which produced and exported its own food and textiles, Egypt was turning into a country whose economy was dominated by the production of a single commodity, raw cotton, for the global textile industry of Europe. By the eve of the First World War, cotton was to account for more than ninety-two percent of the total value of Egypt's exports."[37] Four-fifths of Egyptian cotton went directly to British textile mills.[38]

Some aspects of European colonization were particularly humiliating to Egyptians. For example, they were blatantly discriminated against in employment contracts. Furthermore, under a seventeenth-century agreement between the Ottoman Sultan and the French, which was ultimately applied to all Europeans, the Egyptian government had no authority to apply Egyptian laws to Europeans living in Egypt. Known as the Capitulations, this set of laws and practices enabled the Europeans to act with impunity in committing crimes and civil wrongs. The Earl of Cromer, the first British Viceroy, who was the real power in Egypt for 18 years, admitted: "At first sight, it appears monstrous that the smuggler should carry on his illicit trade under the eyes of the Custom-house authorities because treaty engagements forbid any prompt and effective action taken against him. These engagements have also been turned to such base uses that they have protected the keeper of the gambling hell, the vendor of adulterated drinks, the receiver of stolen goods, and the careless apothecary who supplies his customer with poison in the place of some healing drug."[39] Cromer defended the practice on the grounds that the Egyptian government was "bad" and that the European colonizers had to be assured they could make money without the interference of such a government.[40]

After the First World War, representatives of the Egyptian people contested Britain's holding onto Egypt. Several US members of Congress likewise objected. One of Woodrow Wilson's 14 points declared that such nations as Egypt should be free of colonization of any sort.[41] Wilson himself criticized Britain's practice of colonization. Britain and France successfully resisted all such claims. The 1920 San Remo Conference, the subsequent Treaty of Sèvres, and the League of Nations parceled out the Ottoman Empire mainly between the British and the French.[42] The creation of the mandate system in the former Ottoman Empire outraged the Arab population living in many of these lands.[43] Instead of freedom and self-government, the Arabs received another brand of colonial rule.[44]

Only Turkey had the military strength to reject the Treaty of Sèvres, which, by the way, had carved out new states of Armenia and Kurdistan, respectively. Upon Kemal Ataturk's overthrow of the Ottomon Sultan (the Caliph)[45] and his imposition of secular rule, the Allies agreed to Ataturk's demands to throw out the Treaty of Sèvres, expanding Turkey's borders and eliminating the two new states. In his zeal to establish a modern, democratic Turkey, Kemel Ataturk also persuaded the Turkish Parliament to abolish the Caliphate in 1924.[46] Although most Muslims frequently disagreed with the Caliph and the Caliph's practice of bowing to Western powers, the abolition of the religious head for Muslims was somewhat like abolishing the papacy would be for Catholics. The abolition caused dismay throughout the Muslim world, leaving Muslims feeling adrift.

In Egypt, meanwhile, a group of prominent nationalists, led by Sacd Zaghul, demanded that Britain end the protectorate and give Egypt independence. Britain responded by arresting and exiling the group to Malta in March 1919.[47] Incensed by the British response, the Egyptians revolted. The British used military force to put down the revolt, eventually killing approximately 800 Egyptians and wounding 1,400 others.[48]

Between the two world wars, nationalism in Egypt and much of the Middle East was ascendant, but little progress toward throwing off the English yoke was made. The breakup of the Ottoman Empire and the abolition of the Caliphate devastated much of the Arab and Muslim worlds, both economically and culturally. In a sense, the breakup was like creating the European Union in reverse. What had been a single though somewhat loosely bound empire, overnight became a group of new states (or at least new separately designated colonies or protectorates). Each of the newly created Arab or Muslim states all at once had foreign borders; each had its own set of tariffs, customs, and taxes. Former Ottoman Empire provinces that had little to do with one another were cobbled together to form a country (for example, Iraq was formed from three provinces of the Ottoman Empire). Others, like Transjordan, were created because of squabbles between France and Britain over Syria. Fragmenting the Ottoman Empire weakened the whole, which was France and Britain's objective,[49] since they received most of the Ottoman Empire; only Turkey's military might and its drastic drive towards modernity enabled it to escape the colonial powers' grasp.

In 1936, Britain and Egypt signed the bilateral Anglo-Egypt treaty, which supposedly formally ended the British occupation of Egypt, but also provided Egypt with a British defense guarantee against the possible invasion by the then fascist Italy.[50] Under the treaty, however, 10,000 additional British troops were moved to the Canal Zone at this time and, with the advent of the Second World War, Britain effectively occupied the country again. In the

British view, the renewed *de facto* colonization of Egypt was justified because of the threat to the Canal during the war for Allied shipping of supplies, matériel, and troops.[51]

1.2 The rise of Nasser, the secular, authoritarian military leader

As disappointment continued to sweep through the Arab world after the Second World War, all parts of the Egyptian population were agitating against British rule. Although the British had left the rest of Egypt largely alone, Britain stationed 80,000 troops in the Canal Zone. One Egyptian commentator describes the forces that led to the Egyptian Army Revolt of July 23, 1952: "The presence of British troops in the Suez Canal Zone [was] widely resented as a national humiliation."[52] In January 1952, when the British used heavy weapons against the light-armed Egyptian police, there was a national outcry. "The following day, the Black Saturday of 26 January 1952, the Cairo mobs burst out and burned the fashionable shopping centre of the city."[53] The army had to be called in to impose order.

The so-called Black Saturday was a preview of the Free Officers Revolt six months later. On July 23, 1952, some young military officers led a revolt against the monarchy and Britain. All sectors of the population from religious fundamentalists to the secularists supported the revolt. It succeeded. King Farouk left the country to become a playboy on the Riviera. Under the treaty of 1954, Britain agreed to leave the Canal to the nationalist Egyptian governments. Although the British left Egypt, the Canal continued to be run by the Suez Canal Company, which was predominantly a European company with mainly European employees in positions of importance.

After the revolt, Gamal Abdul Nasser, one of the Free Officers, was named premier of Egypt. Nasser espoused a pan-Arabian ideology, but along secular lines. Nearly four years to the day after the 1952 revolt, Nasser nationalized the Suez Canal. He offered to compensate the Canal Company shareholders, based on their share value on the French La Bourse, the French Stock Exchange, on the day before the nationalization.

The reaction of Britain and France was electric. Despite Egypt's offer to pay the European shareholders, the British and French saw the takeover as robbery of "their" Canal. They moved in the press and in the United Nations (UN) to stop the nationalization. In concert with the British and French governments, the largely European-owned Suez Canal Company took the extraordinary step of offering two years' pay to all Canal company employees to leave Egypt.[54] The Company wanted to demonstrate that Egypt could not run the Canal. The expected Egyptian failure was to serve as a pretext for invasion. Apparently, that effort was unsuccessful. Using its naval pilots and the few Egyptian pilots who worked for the Suez Canal Company, the Egyptians kept the Canal running efficiently after nearly all the foreign pilots and technical personnel pulled out.[55] The US and other members of the UN counseled that France and Britain bring their case to the International Court of Justice (ICJ). Probably knowing they would lose in the ICJ, the French and English rejected that proposal. (Egypt had met all the elements of the conservative, supposedly customary international norm of legal nationalization: it had taken the Suez for a public purpose and it offered to provide fair and adequate compensation to the shareholders.[56])

Instead, the French and the English encouraged Israel to invade Egypt and promised that they would supply air support and other matériel. On October 29, 1956, Israel invaded Egypt according to plan, and, as agreed, the French supplied air support for the attacking force and for the protection of Israel. Two days later, the Royal Air Force and the French Armée de l'Air "bombed and rocketed every conceivable target of military importance [in Egypt]: airfields and strips all the way from Delta to Luxor, harbors, railways, roads, and bridges, barracks, and assembly yards."[57] These included attacks on a military barracks in a densely populated part of Cairo and attacks coming as often as one every ten minutes "with an average of forty to fifty attacks in a day," resulting in a large loss of civilian life.[58] The Egyptians initially fought back, but later retreated from the Sinai.

Both the USSR and the US opposed the attacks on Egypt. On October 30, 1956, the US introduced a resolution in the UN Security Council, "calling on all countries to refrain from [using armed] force in the Middle East."[59] Both France and Britain vetoed the resolution. They also vetoed a Soviet resolution calling for a ceasefire and for Israel to withdraw from the Sinai.[60]

Then the USSR threatened both Britain and Israel; the US told Britain that it would not financially support the pound sterling, which for other reasons had been losing value. Dag Hammarskjöld, the distinguished UN Secretary General, offered his resignation in protest of the attacks on Egypt.[61] France and Britain backed down. The Israeli forces moved back from the Sinai, but retained access to the Straits of Tiran, to which it did not have access before the attack.

The colonial powers lost, and, even though his army was defeated, Nasser became a hero in the non-aligned world.[62] At least one commentator attributes the brisk pace of worldwide decolonization after the "Suez Affair" to the success of Nasser in nationalizing a primarily European-owned company and to the defeat of France and Britain in their attempts to retake the canal.[63]

That was probably the apogee of Nasser's fame. When the US refused to finance the Aswan Dam because Nasser had purchased military equipment from Czechoslovakia—then a Soviet satellite—Nasser turned to the USSR. The tilt towards the USSR made Nasser unpopular with the US government and the US began to move against him. On the other hand, Nasser's break with the West was exceedingly popular in the Arab world, which had been under the thumb of the European powers.[64]

In the 1960s, Nasser (and other Arab leaders) increasingly made threats to Israel; Nasser also took threatening actions: "On May 15, [1967] Nasser put the Egyptian military forces on alert and began moving them into the Sinai.

He . . . request[ed] the complete withdrawal [of the United Nations Emergency force, which patrolled on the Egypt side of the Egypt-Israeli border]. After the withdrawal, Egypt again [on May 23, 1967] closed the Strait of Tiran to Israeli ships, an action Israel said it would consider an act of war."[65] Nasser continuously talked openly of his plans to attack Israel and continuously encouraged other states to do so as well.

Israeli leaders agreed to negotiate, but the Arab leaders refused to do so. Nasser avowed on May 27, 1965 that if it came to a war "the objective will be the destruction of Israel,"[66] and although he agreed to a UN mediation of the Israeli dispute, any concessions he made were extremely limited. Nasser's stance against Israel and the UN reinforced his popularity among Arab governments.[67]

Faced with the provocative language and actions, Israel launched a preemptive attack on June 5, 1967, conquering Egypt, Jordan, and Syria, taking the Sinai from Egypt, the Gaza Strip from Jordan, and the Golan Heights from Syria. Although not expressly authorized under Article 51 of the UN Charter, a preemptive attack is probably justifiable under customary international law in narrow circumstances. The legality of such an attack is usually evaluated under the *Caroline* case, requiring that the preemptive use of force "be confined to cases in which the 'necessity of that self-defense is instant, overwhelming, and leaving no choice of means, and no moment for deliberation.' "[68] A large body of legal scholars believe that Israel was entitled under international law to make a preemptive strike because the threat was imminent ("instant" and "overwhelming") and Israel had exhausted all peaceful means to avoid the use of military force.[69]

1.3 The rise of al Banna and the Muslim Brotherhood

During the 1919 Egyptian revolt against Britain, a 13-year-old boy named Hasan al Banna went on strike with the university students, wrote anti-imperialist poetry, and saw British soldiers occupy his town near the Canal, apparently as part of their keeping the Suez Canal under their control.[70] Al Banna grew to become a religious and nationalist leader. Isaac Musa Husain explains how the First World War and its aftermath affected al Banna and helped create the movement he led:

> After the war Turkey abandoned the Caliphate, discarded the Arabic alphabet, and carried out extensive reforms. These things had profound repercussions in Egypt. The Liberals seized this opportunity to issue literature on Egypt's relations with the West, the substitution of the Western hat for the fez, the emancipation of women, freedom of thought, and the like. On the other hand, the Conservatives held these to be a departure from the fold of Islam, the message of the Koran, the name of the Caliphate, and religion in its totality. It was their opinion that Egypt had become the headquarters of the Islamic mission, the field of its

struggle, and the legal heir of its leadership. Al Banna was among those of the latter party.[71]

In 1928, in Ismailia, Egypt, al Banna founded the Muslim Brotherhood.[72] A gifted speaker and organizer, al Banna built the society into one of the most formidable organizations in Egypt, if not the Arab world. At its height, in the 1940s, the Muslim Brotherhood had over 500,000 registered members.[73] The Brotherhood ran schools, health clinics, religious classes, and other services, as well as developing a clandestine military arm. Fearing the Brotherhood's power, the Egyptian prime minister, Mahmud al Nuqrashi, in 1948, declared the organization illegal and seized its assets. Three weeks later, one of the Brotherhood's members assassinated the prime minister. This murder led to the assassination of the 43-year-old al Banna the following year, probably by an Egyptian government agent.[74]

The Muslim Brotherhood was the forerunner of those Arab–Muslim groups today, including al Qaeda, which have targeted the West for violence. Specifically, after al Banna's assassination, the Brotherhood became more militant and its views more extreme. Sayyid al Qutb became the Brotherhood's philosophical and theological prophet as well as one of the organization's leaders. A skilled writer and deep thinker, al Qutb went far beyond al Banna and called not only for a Muslim state and for the recovery of all territory once under Muslim control, but also for world conquest and the imposition of Islam as the official world government and as the sole religion for all peoples of the world.[75] After studying for a postgraduate degree at Colorado State College of Education (now University of Northern Colorado) from 1948 to 1951, al Qutb returned to Egypt with special antipathy towards the United States, its culture, and its people.

Al Qutb and the Muslim Brotherhood had crossed paths with the new government since the Free Officers' successful liberation of Egypt from Britain in 1952. Although initially supporting the government, the Muslim Brotherhood soon stood at odds with Nasser's secular state. Some members of the Muslim Brotherhood engaged in violence against state officials, including at least one assassination attempt against Nasser. Although al Qutb did not directly take part in such violence, he was tortured and imprisoned for many years. He was subsequently accused of plotting against the state and against its president. Nasser had him executed on August 29, 1966, elevating al Qutb to martyrdom status in the eyes of Islamic fundamentalists. Al Qutb's philosophical writings have become the holy writ of today's Muslim fundamentalist movements and he is said to have inspired Osama bin Laden.

Up until 1967, most Muslims looked up to Nasser, admired his pan-Arab nationalism, and his apparent modernization of Egypt. Islamic fundamentalists held relatively little power. The Israeli success in the Six Day War, however, had a devastating impact on the secular Arab governments. These governments were discredited in the eyes of their people. Because of the failure of these governments vis-à-vis Israel, domestically, the pendulum began to swing away from the secular modernizing governments epitomized by Nasser,[76] and by the Shah of Iran, to the "conservative" Muslim fundamentalists, epitomized by the Muslim Brotherhood.[77] As previously noted, there is a competition going on in the Islamic world between the "conservative" fundamentalists and the "liberal" modern secularists. In the last 40 years, we may still be witnessing the rise of fundamentalism in the Muslim world, with the possible exception of Iran. There, actual experience of living under a Muslim state has fuelled an active opposition, which, however, has not yet become strong enough to displace the mullahs.

"Conservative" fundamentalists have also been strengthened by internal domestic policies of Islamic states. Nasser, for example, ruled with an iron hand, imprisoning political opponents, torturing them, and, in some cases, executing them. He took repressive measures against the Muslim Brotherhood, which had opposed his secularizing of Egyptian society. Lawrence Wright notes that the seeds for 9/11 may very well have been sown in Egypt's torture chambers.[78]

In addition to imprisoning political opponents, Nasser muzzled the press. His apologists note that he nationalized much of the economy, establishing state socialism, and that he broke up the large manors and engaged in land reform, distributing much land to the peasants. With its grip on most institutions and on newspapers, radio, and television, however, the Nasser regime censored much and allowed little press freedom. Like most controlled economies, Egypt's suffered and declined. Once a center of culture, debate, and publishing, Cairo lost its edge, later to be taken up by Beirut because of the latter's relative openness.

1.4 Anwar al Sadat

When Nasser died unexpectedly in 1970 of a heart attack, his lieutenants became the rulers of Egypt. But Anwar al Sadat, one of the original "Free Officers" in the war of independence, took control of the country in a military coup in 1971, dismissed Nasser's lieutenants from government, and became the President of Egypt.[79] He is most noted for three things: his attack on Israel on Yom Kippur in 1973; his trip to Jerusalem in 1977; and his agreeing to the Camp David Accords in 1979. The attack on Yom Kippur caught the Israelis off guard. During this attack, the Egyptians retook the entire Sinai. The US subsequently provided military supplies to Israel, including tanks and other weapons, helping Israel take the Sinai back. These efforts led directly to the Arab oil boycott of 1973. Yet Egypt's initial success probably enabled Sadat to go to Jerusalem and to agree to the Camp David Accords.

Although Sadat had never been elected and ruled by decree, he tried to dismantle the Nasser socialist economic policy by opening up the economy to private investment and by denationalizing a significant part of the government's holdings. He also widened press freedoms far more than Nasser had done. "There was relative freedom for Egyptians to speak their minds openly on political issues; something which was hardly possible under Nasser."[80]

The openness under Sadat allowed the Muslim Brotherhood to reestablish itself. Although Sadat cracked down on extremists from both the left and the right, his non-partisan approach did little to faze the fundamentalists. In 1981, he arrested "over 1,500 religious militants," a move that outraged the fundamentalist opposition.[81] Although generally popular in Egypt, Sadat had been reviled by Muslim fundamentalists such as the Muslim Brotherhood and by the Islamic Armed Group (Gamaa al Islamiya (GIA)). They could not forgive him for recognizing Israel or for his role in the trial and execution of their ideological high priest, al Qutb. (Anwar Sadat was one of the judges who ordered al Qutb's execution.)[82] An assassin said to be closely linked to the GIA and Egyptian Islamic Jihad (al Jihad), an organization later led by Ayman al Zawahiri, killed Anwar Sadat at a parade on 6 October 1981.

Richard Bernstein of the *New York Times* notes, two men "implicated in the Sadat assassination," later came to Peshawar, Afghanistan, to struggle against the Soviet aggression there. These men were the blind cleric Omar Abdel Rahman and Ayman al Zawahiri, later to become bin Laden's right hand.[83] The latter was arrested at the age of 15 for being a member of the Muslim Brotherhood; the former was the spiritual leader of those members of al Jihad that carried out the assassination of Sadat.[84] Rahman ultimately emigrated to the US and planned the 1993 World Trade Center bombing.

Hosni Mubarak, who succeeded Sadat in 1981, ruled even more dictatorially. Mubarak remained in power as president of Egypt for over 25 years. During that period, the US has given to Egypt over $59 billion in military and civilian aid.[85] Under the Camp David Accords and the Special International Security Assistance Act of 1979 enacted to support the Israeli–Egyptian peace agreement, Egypt has received approximately the same amount of US aid as does Israel, roughly $2 billion a year.[86] Although such a payment appears benign, it probably had the effect of helping a dictatorial regime stay in power. Mubarak filled his prisons with secular opposition leaders as well as with Muslim fundamentalists from the Muslim Brotherhood. He became increasingly unpopular with his people until the 2011, popular, non-violent uprising ultimately forced him to fall from power.[87]

1.5 The US assumes the mantle of a colonial power

The US never colonized a Muslim nation. But it gradually assumed—at least for Muslims—the mantle of colonization over the Middle East, particularly after the Second World War. The US showed relatively little interest in the Middle East until American oil executives discovered oil in Bahrain and Kuwait in the 1930s.[88] From the end of the Second World War to the end of the Cold War in 1990, the US had three, sometimes conflicting and sometimes overlapping, concerns that drove its policies in the Middle East region: (1) ensuring the supply of oil; (2) supporting Israel; and (3) containing communism.[89] Given the huge amount of oil that US industry and people consume, keeping oil flowing from the Middle East to the American gas pump has concerned all US presidents since 1945. To guarantee that oil is readily available, the US has supported authoritarian regimes in the Arab world, including the House of Saud in Saudi Arabia, the Shah of Iran, and, initially, Saddam Hussein in Iraq, not to mention autocratic leaders of the tiny, oil-rich Gulf states. For most of its history, the US had been indifferent to the plight of Arab and Muslim peoples living in these countries, to their economic difficulties, and to the human rights deprivations they have had to bear.[90]

Muslims were not the only parties in the Middle East who suffered conquest, colonization, and discrimination. The US policy towards Israel stems in part from the Christian West's attitudes and conduct toward the Jewish people. The Christian West has practiced virulent discrimination against Jews for over 2,000 years. Laying the foundation for such discrimination, early Christian leaders claimed the Jewish people were collectively responsible for the death of Jesus,[91] a claim that was repeated down through the centuries by Christian clerics, not to be repudiated by the Catholic Church until 1965. Space here does not permit a recounting anything close to the amount and degree of abuse to which Christians subjected Jews; below are just some examples.[92] The Jews were expelled from England in 1290, from France in 1306, and from Spain in 1492. If not expelled temporarily or on a more permanent basis, some European cities confined Jews to ghettos. Jews were generally prohibited from participating in politics and were excluded from many professions. On their way to the First Crusade in 1096, the European soldier crusaders killed thousands of European Jews and tortured others who refused to convert to Christianity. Upon retaking Jerusalem, the Crusaders gathered all the Jews in the city, put them in a synagogue, and burned it to the ground. Jews were blamed for the Black Plague when it swept through Europe in 1348 on the totally false charge that Jews had poisoned the well water. As a result of this baseless charge "[f]rom Christian Spain to Poland, Jews were slaughtered and burnt; but the worst massacres occurred in the German Empire."[93] A century later, Tomas de Torquemada, "Grand Inquisitor" of the Spanish Inquisition, led an institution that tortured and executed thousands of Jews.[94]

The so-called blood libel, a vicious myth that Jews would kill Christian children for their blood, was another ruse for persecuting Jews. For example, in the Italian city of Trent, in 1475, Bernardino de Feltre, "a Jew-baiting Franciscan preacher," incited the community to violence when a rumor spread through out the town that a two-year-old named Simon had gone missing. Consequently, "[t]he entire [Jewish] community was arrested and subject to torture, which led to conflicting confessions. Those sentenced were promptly executed while the remaining Jews were expelled."[95] In 1582, the infant Simon was officially beatified by the Catholic Church.[96] Only after the Vatican

Council II in 1965 did Pope Paul VI revoke the beatification, remove Simon's feast day from the Church calendar, dismantle his shrine, forbid veneration of Simon, and recognize that the Jews of Trent had been wrongfully convicted and sentenced.[97]

The discrimination continued in the modern era in the "civilized" West, with, for example, the framing of Captain Alfred Dreyfus around the turn of the nineteenth century in France, the continued exclusion of Jews from private clubs and from significant employment opportunities, and the use of restrictive quotas against Jews by prestigious universities. More gravely, Jews were subjected to pogroms[98] in Russia, Ukraine, and Germany, among other countries, and suffered genocide on an almost unimaginable scale: the Holocaust during the Second World War, in which Nazi Germany murdered six million Jews.[99]

The Roman Catholic Church and other predominantly Western Christian denominations[100] have done little to atone for the hateful conduct to which their adherents subjected the Jewish people since the first century after the birth of Christ. Outside of an apology by Pope Paul II[101] and statements abhorring anti-Semitism,[102] neither the Roman Catholic Church nor other Christian denominations have made much reparation[103] to the Jewish people for the monstrous wrong that Christians have inflicted upon them.[104]

The two-millennia history of persecution of Jewry has made an overwhelmingly compelling case for a Jewish homeland, a place that would serve, at the very least, as refuge for every Jew on the planet who feels at risk of being persecuted. That the US has supported the creation of a Jewish State in the Middle East is a recognition of the suffering the Jewish people have endured through the centuries and in particular during the Nazi-inflicted Holocaust, which the US helped end.

Muslims, however, had governed the area now occupied by Israel since the seventh century CE.[105] The conquest of the Ottoman Empire in the First World War and Britain's *de facto* colonization of Palestine (as a "trust" territory) after that conflict permitted the modern state of Israel to emerge.[106] Historians indicate that the Jewish People, though at times subject to Babylonian rule, Assyrian rule, Greek rule, and Roman rule, had governed Israel for over a millennium, namely, from about 1200 BCE–1000 BCE to 135 CE.[107] In 70 CE and 135 CE, the Romans defeated Israeli uprisings. The latter uprising, called the Bar Kokhba Revolt, began in 132 CE with initial Jewish victories over the Romans, but ultimately the Romans brought in several legions from all over the empire, defeating the rebels, slaying the Israeli fighters, killing a great number of the remaining Jews, or selling them into slavery.[108] The Romans also changed the name of the province from Judea to "Syria-Palestina."[109] Rabbi Joseph Telushkin described the effect of the Romans vanquishing the Jews: "The Great Revolt of 66–70 followed some sixty years later by the Bar-Kokhba Revolt were [*sic*] the greatest calamities in Jewish history prior to the Holocaust. In addition to the more than one million Jews killed, these failed rebellions led to the total loss of Jewish political authority until 1948."[110] Thus both the Israelis and the Muslims have suffered conquest and colonization or banishment from the territory that is now Israel. This work does not attempt to resolve the conflict between Israelis and Palestinians, the vast majority of whom are Muslim, but only to observe that the forces and consequences of conquest, colonization, and banishment, both ancient and relatively recent, are very much still in play.

The third concern of the US had been stemming the tide of communism. In the fierce post-Second World War battle between the US and the Soviet Union, the Middle East was a critical geopolitical region. The US moved aggressively to ensure that the Soviet Union would not extend its influence there. Among other things, the US engineered the coup in 1953 against the elected Prime Minister of Iran, Mohammed Mossadegh, because of largely unsupported claims that he was leaning toward the communists.[111] The US reinstalled the dictatorial Shah of Iran in his place. A military junta in Iraq was likewise implicitly supporting the Soviet Union. During the Kennedy administration, the CIA again engineered a coup, ousting communist-leaning General Abdel Karim Kassem and putting in his place Abu Salam Arif of the Ba'ath Party in 1963. That ouster ultimately led to Saddam Hussein taking control of the country.

Nasser's decision to nationalize the Suez Canal came one week after the US refused to support a loan to Egypt that would have helped finance the Aswan Dam.[112] Egypt then turned to the Soviet Union for financial assistance to complete that project. Nasser's turn to the communist bloc led the US to work against him and helped solidify US support of Israel.[113]

The Islamic revolution in Iran upset the order that the US helped establish. The US support for Saddam Hussein's Iraq against Iran can be seen, to a certain extent, to fall within this context. The next major cleavage arose when Saddam Hussein invaded Kuwait. No longer considered a reliable US partner, Saddam Hussein was attacked by a broad coalition led by the US. Significantly, the repressive House of Saud requested that the US post standing troops in Saudi Arabia as a protection force against Iraq. In this instance, however, the US was not acting through intermediaries. At one point, half a million US troops were stationed on the ground in the country containing the two holiest places in Islam, Mecca and Medina.[114]

All this behavior was not lost on the Muslims. With the end of the Cold War, the counterweight to the US, Russia, was a far less significant presence in the Middle East than the former Soviet Union had been. The US had now taken the step of actually stationing troops in the holiest land of Islam. Osama bin Laden's first fatwa, in 1996, was entitled, "Declaration of Jihad against the Americans Occupying the Land of the Two Holy Places." Reading Osama bin Laden's writings, one gets the clear impression that his holy war against the US and against all Americans was triggered more by the stationing of troops in Saudi Arabia[115] than by US support of Israel.[116] The invasion of Afghanistan, and even more importantly the 2003 invasion of Iraq, further underscored, in Muslim eyes, the US assuming the familiar role of Western colonial overlord.

In short, the history of the Arab and Muslim peoples creates within them a reservoir of righteous resentment, caused primarily by the West. To be sure, the Ottoman Empire, so dominant in the sixteenth century, failed to embrace the scientific method and thus missed the industrial revolution the scientific method spawned.[117] Islam has not had a reformation as did Christianity, and thus did not have a separation of church and state or plural institutions in which freedom of speech and thought could more easily develop.[118] The wealth that industrialization and capitalism created in the West was not generally created in the Arab and Islamic world. Yet, instead of helping the Arab world, the West and Russia conquered, colonized, and exploited it. Such exploitation does not excuse those claiming to act in the name of Islam, who deliberately kill and terrorize innocent civilians. Nor did Britain's subjecting the Irish people in general and the Northern Irish Catholics in particular to continued British rule and to *de jure* discrimination excuse the Provisional Irish Republican Army from blowing up English pubs and committing other acts of violence. On the other hand, the individuals who carry out such acts cannot be dismissed as "mere" criminals or "evildoers." Yes—they are criminals— and yes—they do perpetrate acts of evil, but these often despicable deeds spring from soil that has been cultivated with hate, with conquest, with *de jure* and *de facto* discrimination, and with public humiliation of colonized peoples.

In other words, the heavy hand of history lies atop these peoples and influences what they will think and do, including a small remnant who will resort to violence. Not every people that has experienced colonization with the concomitant hatred and discrimination will necessarily give birth to a terrorist group. Not everyone who smokes a pack of cigarettes a day contracts lung cancer. Yet, it is hard to deny that conquest, colonization, and their companion, invidious discrimination, often give rise to terrorist movements.

Robert Pape, a professor at the University of Chicago, conducted research that supports this conclusion. He studied every suicide bombing from 1980 to 2003 and discovered that Muslims were neither the first nor the most extensive users of this tactic, but rather the Tamil Tigers were.[119] More importantly, he discovered that the vast majority of suicide bombings were carried out because those sponsoring the bombings believed that they were entitled to the land, the territory that another group was occupying. Pape concluded that private terrorist organizations resort to suicide bombers primarily "to compel modern democracies to withdraw their military forces from territory the terrorists consider to be their homeland."[120] If one probes into history a little, one finds that virtually all groups that sponsor suicide bombings have at least a colorable claim to the territory based on the contemporary right of self-determination. Almost every such group has likewise suffered colonization and conquest.

1.6 The counterterrorism response

When confronted with a megaterrorist event, governmental officials may be tempted to ignore the lessons of history and concentrate on getting vengeance and on achieving maximum security, regardless of cost. Their electorate will probably demand such a response. Perhaps only leaders with exceptional judgment, strength, and integrity, and with an understanding of the world and world affairs, could withstand such a political onslaught in reaction to such monstrous violence. Consequently, governmental officials, in the face of such an attack, may cast aside both domestic and international law that restricts how the government carries out counterterrorism policy. History generally shows that such an approach is not only questionable legally and morally, but also questionable practically. Here, for example, Arab and Muslim peoples have an understandable, and to a certain extent justifiable, reservoir of resentment against the West in general and against the US in particular. In other words, changing the rules may be perceived as applying a double standard to Muslims, resulting in that people supporting rather than isolating extreme fundamentalist groups that have targeted the West. Little evidence suggests that the administration in power on September 11, 2001 appreciated how violating international law might ultimately affect the reputation of the US and its ability to stem the violence wrought by al Qaeda and its allies. This edition will thus continue to explore whether international law is an obstacle or a guide in the continuing struggle against transnational terrorism.

Table 1.1 The Colonization of Countries with Large Muslim Populations[121]

Country	Controlling power	Occupation time period	Type of colonial rule	Notes
Afghanistan	Britain, Russia, and the US	1839–1919; 1953–89; 2001–present	indirect/ protectorate; occupation; occupation	Britain repeatedly tried to take control of the area occupied by Afghanistan, but never completely succeeded. Independence was declared for last time in 1919, but Soviet involvement began in 1953 at General Mohammed Daud's invite. A full-blown Soviet intervention began in 1980; they left in 1989. The US invaded in 2001.
Albania	Italy/ Germany	1939–44	occupation	Italy invaded in 1939; Germans replaced them in 1943 after Italian surrender in WWII; Germans left in 1944.
Algeria	France	1830–1962	direct	Local, non-Jewish population denied French citizenship under French rule.
Armenia	Russia	1916–18	annexed territory	Joined USSR in 1922. Independence gained in 1991.
Azerbaijan	Russia	1828–1918; 1920–91	occupation; occupation	
Bahrain	Britain	1913–71	protectorate	Prior to 1913, there was a dispute between Britain and the Ottoman Empire regarding who properly controlled Bahrain. Britain and the Ottomans signed a treaty in 1913, purportedly recognizing the independence of Bahrain, but declaring that it was to remain under British administration.
Bangladesh (East Pakistan, formally part of India)	Britain	1858–1947	direct	The idea for a separate nation to house India's Muslim population was formally introduced in 1940. Pakistan was created in 1947 after British rule ended in India. Gained independence from Pakistan in 1971.
Benin (Dahomey)	France	1894–1960	occupation	Became an overseas territory of France in 1946, then became self-governing in 1958.
Borneo (Island of Kalamatan in Malay archipelago)	Netherlands, Britain, Japan	1824–1941; 1941–45	direct; direct	After Indonesia gained independence in 1957, control of Borneo was divided between Indonesia, Malaysia, and Brunei, who all currently share control.

(Continued Overleaf)

Table 1.1 Continued.

Country	Controlling power	Occupation time period	Type of colonial rule	Notes
Bosnia and Herzegovina	Austria–Hungary, etc.	1908–45	occupation	The geographical area comprising Bosnia and Herzegovina was annexed to Austria–Hungary in 1908. In 1918 it became part of the Serb, Croat, Slovene Kingdom. In 1941 it was annexed to the Croatian state and it became part of Yugoslavia in 1945.
Brunei	Britain	1888–1984	protectorate	Occupied by Japan from 1941 to 1945. In 1963, it decided to remain a British dependency instead of joining the Malaysian Federation. A written constitution first produced in 1959 declared Islam the state religion.
Burkina Faso	France	1896–1960	protectorate	Formerly Upper Volta, it was divided between Côte d'Ivoire and French Sudan in 1932. Upper Volta was established as a separate territory in 1947 and in 1958 it became an autonomous republic within the French Community. It became Burkina Faso in 1984.
Burma (Myanmar)	Britain	1852–1948	direct	The Arakan coastal strip was ceded to British India after the Anglo-Burmese war (1824–26) and, in 1852, it was annexed as a part of British India. In 1937, Burma was separated from British India and became its own colony. The Japanese occupied the area from 1942 to 1945, but the British liberated Burma in 1945.
Cameroon	Portuguese; Netherlands; Germany; Britain and France; Britain	1520–1600s; 1600s–1884; 1884–1916; 1916–60	direct/slave trade; slave trade; protectorate; occupation/ administration	This area was divided into French and British "Administration Zones" in 1919. The League of Nations conferred mandates to Britain and France in 1922, which were subsequently renewed by the UN as "trusteeships." Self-government was granted in 1958. Southern Cameroon and the Republic of Cameroon unified in 1961; Northern Cameroon joined Nigeria.
Celebes (Indonesia)	Netherlands			This island is one of the four Greater Sunda Islands, Indonesia.

Chad	France	1913–60	direct	Sudanese "adventurer" Rabih al Zubayr ruled from 1883 to 1893. France took control in 1900 and the area became an official French colony in 1913. In 1946 it became an overseas territory.
China	n/a	n/a	n/a	None.
Comoros	France	1886–1961	protectorate	Located off the eastern coast of Africa in the Indian Ocean. In 1947, it became an "overseas territory" and was given representation in French Parliament. The Comoros were given autonomy in 1961 and they declared independence in 1975.
Côte d'Ivoire	France	1842–93; 1893–1960	protectorate; direct	This country became part of the French Federation of West Africa in 1904. In 1958, it became a republic within the French Community.
Cyprus	Britain; Turkey and Greece	1914–60; 1960–present	direct; occupation	Ruled by the Ottomans from the 1600s to 1914.
Djibouti	France	1888–1977	direct/indirect	Islam introduced here in 825 CE. France acquired the port of Obock in 1862. The French colony of Somaliland was established in the area. Ethiopia acquired what is now part of Djibouti in a 1897 treaty with France. In 1946, Somaliland became an overseas territory of France and voted to stay a part of the French Community in 1958. It voted to join the French Community in 1967.
Egypt	Britain	1882–1922; 1922–54 de facto control	protectorate (as of 1914)	Arabs conquered Egypt in 642 CE. Ottomans took control in 1517, the French invaded in 1798, and were repelled by British and Turks in 1801. The Ottomans took control again until 1882 and employed a "divide and rule" principle. Britain assumed control in 1882, then relinquished formal control in 1922. A republic was declared in 1953, but British forces and government did not really leave until 1954.
Eritrea	Italy; Britain; Ethiopia	1890–1941; 1941–62; 1962–93	direct; occupation/ trusteeship; annexed territory	Islam was introduced in 600 CE. The Ottoman empire annexed Eritrea in the 1500s. Italy occupied Eritrea from 1885 until the Italian surrender in WWII. Britain invaded in 1941 and, in 1949, the UN assigned the area to Britain as trusteeship. In 1952, the UN made Eritrea a federal component of Ethiopia.

(Continued Overleaf)

Table 1.1 Continued.

Country	Controlling power	Occupation time period	Type of colonial rule	Notes
Ethiopia	Italy	1889–96; 1935–41	protectorate; occupation	Islam was introduced in the sixteenth century. The Emperor signed a friendship treaty with Italy in 1889 and Italians interpreted this as Ethiopia conceding to protectorate status. Italy invaded in 1895. Italy recognized Ethiopian independence in 1896, but retained control and combined Ethiopia, Eritrea, and Italian Somaliland to form Italian Eastern Africa. The British helped Ethiopia regain self-control from the Italians in 1941.
Gambia	Portugal; Britain	1455–1889; 1894–1965	trading occupation; protectorate	Independence occurred in 1965; a republic was declared in 1970.
Georgia	Russia; USSR	1801–1918; 1921–91	occupation	
Ghana	Portugal; Britain	1482–1874; 1874–1957	trading occupation; direct	A republic was proclaimed in 1960.
Guinea	France	1891–1958	direct	France declared Guinea a colony separate from Senegal in 1891. In 1952, it became a part of the French West African Federation.
Guinea-Bissau	Portugal	1846–1974	direct	In 1951, it was declared a province of Portugal. The African Party for the Independence of Guinea and Cape Verde (PAIGC) declared independence on behalf of the area encompassed by Guinea-Bissau in 1973, which Portugal recognized in 1974.
India	Britain	1858–1947	direct	Britain implemented a "divide and rule" scheme here.
Indochina (Cambodia, Laos, Vietnam)	France			Home to somewhere between one half and one million Muslim Cham, an ethnic group thought to be descended from a fifteenth century kingdom in the area.
Indonesia	Netherlands	1670–1949		The Dutch colonists brought the islands of Indonesia under one government during the period of 1670–1900. In 1942, the Japanese invaded and, in 1945, they assisted independence leader Sukarno in returning from internal exile and declaring independence in 1945. The Dutch recognized Indonesian independence in 1949.

Country	Colonizer	Dates	Type	Notes
Iran	n/a	n/a	n/a	Islam introduced here in 636 CE. Iran successfully resisted occupation after WWII.
Iraq	Britain	1919–32	protectorate	Britain was awarded the country after WWI as a League of Nations mandate. An independent republic formed in 1958.
Jordan	Britain	1919–46	protectorate	British troops completely withdrew in 1957.
Kazakhstan	Russia/USSR	1731–1991	occupation	Islam was introduced here by Arab invaders in the eighth century.
Kenya	Britain	1895–1920; 1920–63	protectorate; direct	In 600 CE, Arabs began settling in coastal areas. The Portuguese tried to establish a foothold here in the sixteenth century, but were repelled. The British East African Protectorate was formed in 1895.
Kuwait	Britain	1899–1961	protectorate	This area became part of the Ottoman Empire in the seventeenth century. Kuwait became a British protectorate in 1899 out of fear of direct rule from Turkey.
Kyrgyzstan	Russia/USSR	1876–1991		Islam was introduced here by Arab invaders in the eighth century. Many sought refuge from the Russian/Soviet occupation and fled into China in 1916–17.
Lebanon	France	1920–26; 1940–41	protectorate	The French employed the "divide and rule" principle here. A League of Nations mandate granted this territory to France in 1920. The Lebanese declared an independent republic in 1926. France's Vichy government assumed control in 1940. Lebanon declared independence again in 1941 and French forces/government actually left in 1944.
Liberia	n/a	n/a	n/a	Africa's oldest republic. It was founded in 1847 with a constitution modeled on the US constitution.
Libya	Italy; France and Britain	1911–42; 1942–51	occupation	Islam was introduced into the area in 643 CE by Arab conquerors. Allied forces ousted Italians in 1942 and divided the territory between the French and the British.

(Continued Overleaf)

Table 1.1 Continued.

Country	Controlling power	Occupation time period	Type of colonial rule	Notes
Macedonia	Bulgaria; Germany; Yugoslavia	1914–18; 1939–45; 1945–91	occupation; occupation; annexed territory	Ottomans ruled from the fifteenth century to 1913. In 1913, control of the area was divided between Serbia, Bulgaria, and Greece. It joined what became Yugoslavia in 1918.
Maldives	Portugal; Netherlands; Britain	1558–73; 1600s; 1796–1965	occupation; protectorate; protectorate	Islam was introduced here in the twelfth century. The Portuguese occupied from 1558 to 1573 and the area was a Dutch protectorate during the seventeenth century. Britain took control in 1796 and the area formally became a British protectorate in 1887. The first democratic constitution was proclaimed in 1932 and independence was finally gained in 1965.
Malaysia	Britain	1826–1957	protectorate	Islam conversion began here in the fourteenth century. British settlement began in 1826 but the Japanese occupied from 1942 to 1945.
Mali	France	1898–1960	direct	This country was sometimes called French Sudan. Mali and Senegal formed the Mali Federation in 1959, then split in 1960.
Mauritania	France	1904–60	indirect/direct	French forces gained control in the 1850s. The colony was not established until 1904 and it became a part of French West Africa in 1920, administered from Senegal. In 1946, it became a French overseas territory and, in 1958, became self-governing.
Morocco	Spain; France	1884–1912; 1912–56	protectorate; indirect	Arabs invaded in the seventh century. Spain and France carved out zones of influence in 1904. It became a French protectorate in 1912, but the Spanish continued to operate their coastal protectorate and the Sultan acted as a mere figurehead.
Niger	France	1890–1960	occupation	Became an autonomous republic of the French Community in 1958.

Country	Colonizer	Dates	Type	Description
Nigeria	Britain	1851–1960	direct/ protectorate	The slave trade sent millions to the Americas in the sixteenth–eighteenth centuries. In 1809, a single Islamic state was founded in the north of what is now Nigeria. Civil wars plagued the south from the 1830s to 1886. In the 1850s, Britain established a political presence. Between 1861 and 1915, the British consolidated power and in 1922 a League of Nations mandate added part of the former German colony of Kamerun (Cameroon) to Nigeria.
Oman	Portugal	1507–1650	coastal occupation	Islam was introduced to the area in 700 CE. In 1507, the Portuguese captured the coast; they were not driven out until 1650. Though there was no real evidence of colonization by the British, Oman seemed to have close ties to Britain going back to 1913.
Pakistan (West Pakistan – formally part of India)	Britain	1858–1947	colony	The idea for a separate nation to house India's Muslim population was formally introduced in 1940. Pakistan was created in 1947 after British rule ended in India.
Palestine	Britain	1917–47	protectorate	The British employed the principle of "divide and rule" in their governance. The San Remo conference assigned the area as a protectorate to Britain.
Qatar	Britain	1916–71	protectorate	From the eighteenth century to 1867, this area was widely recognized as a dependant of Bahrain.
Saudi Arabia	n/a	n/a	n/a	Remained unoccupied.
Senegal	Portugal; Netherlands; France; Britain	1444–1677; 1588–1677; 1659–1763; 1775–1960	slave trade/ indirect; annexed	Portuguese traders landed here in the 1440s. In 1588, Dutch slave traders established a port. France established a slave-trading port in 1659 and, in 1677, it took over the Dutch port. From 1756 to 1763, the British and French fought over the area and Britain won. France regained its holdings during the American Revolutionary War (1775–83) and in 1895 Senegal became part of French West Africa. In 1946, Senegal became part of the French Union and in 1958 it became an autonomous republic as a part of the French Community.

(Continued Overleaf)

Table 1.1 Continued.

Country	Controlling power	Occupation time period	Type of colonial rule	Notes
Sierra Leone	Britain	1808–1961	colony/ protectorate	British abolitionists established a settlement in Freetown for repatriated/rescued slaves. In 1808, Freetown became a British colony and in 1896 a British protectorate was established.
Somalia	Britain; Italy	1887–1960; 1889–1960	colony/ protectorate	In 1887, Britain proclaimed this area a British protectorate. In 1888, an Anglo–French agreement defined the land area in Somalia that belonged to the respective colonial powers. Italy established a protectorate in central Somalia in 1889 and, in 1940, Italy occupied British Somaliland. The British took over Italian Somaliland in 1941 and, in 1950, Italian Somaliland became a UN Trusteeship under Italian Control. Italian Somaliland was granted internal autonomy in 1956. The British and Italian parts of Somalia became independent in 1960 and merged to form modern Somalia.
Sudan	Egypt and Britain (Eastern Sudan)/ France (Western Sudan)	1899–1956	occupation	Sharia law was imposed in 1983.
Syria	The Ottomans; France	1500–1918; 1920–46	protectorate	The Ottoman Empire ruled from 1500 to 1918. The British assisted in ousting the Ottomans and, in 1920 the San Remo conference established Syria as a French protectorate. The French employed a "divide and rule" approach to their government of Syria and agreed to independence in 1936, but maintained military and economic dominance until 1940 when Axis powers controlled the area after France fell to their control. Britain and France reclaimed control of Syria in 1941 and the French troops finally left in 1946.
Tajikistan	Russia (North)/ Emirate of Bukhara (South); USSR	1860–1900; 1921–91	occupation; annexed territory	Islam was introduced to the area by Arab invaders in the eighth century. An increase in Islamist activity occurred in 1970 and seems to have endured.

Country	Colonizer(s)	Dates	Type	Description
Tanzania	Portugal; Germany; Britain	1506–1699; 1884–86; 1886–16; 1916–61	direct; occupation; protectorate; trusteeship	The Portuguese controlled most of the East African coast from 1506 to 1699 when they were ousted by Omani Arabs. In 1884, the Germans began to acquire control of the territory. Britain and Germany later divided control of the territory: Germans got control of most of mainland Tanzania and Zanzibar became a protectorate of Britain.
Togo	Denmark; Germany; Britain/France	18th century; 1884–1914; 1914–60	coastal occupation; protectorate	The Danes occupied coastal areas throughout the eighteenth century. In 1922, the League of Nations issued mandates to France and Britain to administer the Eastern and Western parts of Togo(land), respectively. In 1956, the Gold Coast (later renamed Ghana) was added to the British territory of Togo(land).
Tunisia	The Ottomans; France	1600s–1881; 1881–1956	protectorate	Arabs conquered this area in the seventh century. The Ottoman Empire ruled from the 1600s to 1881. Tunisia became a French protectorate in 1881 and an independent republic was formed in 1957.
Turkey	Seat of the Ottoman Empire	1299–1922	occupation	Seat of the Ottoman Empire, Turkey successfully resisted occupation after WWI.
Turkmenistan	Russia/ USSR	1881–1991	occupation	Arab conquerors introduced Islam in the seventh century.
United Arab Emirates	Britain	1892–1971	protectorate	In 1820, Britain was given permission to combat piracy along the Gulf Coast. Iran occupied associated islands in November 1971.
Uzbekistan	Russia/ USSR	1865–1991	occupation	Arab conquerors introduced Islam in the seventh century.
Western Sahara	Spain	1884–1976	direct/ protectorate	Spain ruled this area directly until 1934; then, it became a Spanish province. Modern Western Sahara has been the subject of a decades-long dispute between Morocco and the Algerian-backed Polisario Front, with most of the territory remaining under Moroccan control since 1976.
Yemen	n/a	n/a	n/a	Yemen, as a country, has remained unoccupied. Aden was occupied by Britain from 1830 to 1967, but was finally unified with Southern Yemen in 1970. Northern and Southern Yemen unified in 1990.

Notes

1   By Muslim country is meant that the majority of the inhabitants are Muslims, not that the government is secular, on the one hand, or based on the Muslim religion, on the other.

2   Queen Elizabeth I gave the East India Company a royal charter in 1600 and the East India Company began its activities in the 1600s; the beginning of the British Empire in India, however, is generally dated from 1757, when Robert Clive, an agent of the company, defeated a Mughal governor in Bengal. *See* Lawrence James, The Rise and Fall of the British Empire 24–26, 127–28 (1997); Niall Fergusson, Empire: The Rise and Demise of the British World Order and the Lessons for Global Power 15, 30–32 (2004); Richard Allen & Harish Trivedi, Literature & Nation 30 (2001); Robert B. Marks, The Origins of The Modern World 129 (2006); MSN Encarta, Robert Clive, *available at* http://encarta.msn.com/encyclopedia_761560186/Robert_Clive.html.

3   Library of Congress, A Selection of Historical Maps of Afghanistan, *available at* www.loc.gov/rr/geogmap/pub/afghanistan.html (citing Afghanistan a Country Study 39–40 (Richard F. Nystrop & Donald M. Seekins eds., 1986).

4   John Darwin, Britain And Decolonisation 7 (1988).

5   *See* chapter 13 on colonization and self-determination for a more detailed discussion of this issue.

6   *See* United Nations Statistics Division, Per Capita GDP in US Dollars: All Countries for all Years – Sorted Alphabetically, *available at* http://unstats.un.org/unsd/snaama/dnllist.asp; International Monetary Fund, World Economic Outlook Database (October 2008), *available at* www.imf.org/external/pubs/ft/weo/2008/02/weodata/index.aspx.

7   *See* Howard J. Wiarda, The Crisis of American Foreign Policy 297 (2006); *see also* Hillel Frisch & Efraim Inbar, Radical Islam And International Security 48–49 (2008).

8   Freedom House, Freedom in the World 2009, *available at* www.freedomhouse.org/uploads/fiw09/FIW09_Tables&GraphsForWeb.pdf (last visited Mar. 27, 2009). According to the 2008 Freedom House report, three Muslim countries are "Free" and 20 more are "Partly Free." *Id*.

9   Transparency International, World Report 2008, *available at* www.transparency.org/policy_research/surveys_indices/cpi/2008

10 *Turkey*, Amnesty International Report 2008, *available at* www.amnesty.org/en/region/turkey/report-2008.

11 *Id*.

12 United Nations Development Program, Human Development Report 2007/2008 232, *available at* http://hdr.undp.org/en/media/HDR_20072008_EN_Complete.pdf.

13 David Arnold, The Age of Discovery 1400–1600 at 10 (2d edition 2002); Edward Augustus Freeman, The Ottoman Power in Europe 127 (1877).

14 One scholar explains the position of the Ottomans vis-à-vis the Europeans in the fifteenth and sixteenth centuries: "Europeans felt besieged by the richer, expansive Islamic world. . . . The Ottoman's were confident, sure of their power and cultural accomplishments. From the Ottoman perspective large parts of Europe were marginal, just as central Asia or sub-Saharan Africa was to the Victorian Englishmen." Thomas Bender, a Nation Among Nations 26 (2007).

15 1 Stanford Jay Shaw & Ezel Kural Shaw, History of the Ottoman Empire and Modern Turkey 152 (1976).

16 David Sagiv, Fundamentalism and Intellectuals in Egypt 168–69 (1995); Kaegi, *infra* note 17, at 34, 61.

17   Walter E. Kaegi, *Egypt on the Eve of the Muslim Conquest, in* 1 The Cambridge History of Egypt 34, 61 (Carl F. Petry, ed. 1998).

18   *See* Shaw and Shaw, *supra* note 15, at 8–9. That invasion had a far deadlier impact on Muslims than had the crusades. *Id.*

19   Emory C. Bogle, Islam: origin and belief 68 (1998). *See, e.g.*, Caroline Finkel, Osman's Dream: The Story of the Ottoman Empire, 1300–1923, at 110 (2006).

20   Shafik Ghorbal, The Beginnings of the Egyptian Question and the Rise of Mehemet Ali 280, 284 (1977); Karen Armstrong, Islam, a Short History 150–51 (2000).

21   Timothy Mitchell, Colonising Egypt 36–37 (1991); *see also* Jaques Berque, Egypt, Imperialism and Revolution (1972).

22   Arthur Goldschmidt Jr. & Lawrence Davidson, a Concise History of the Middle East 173–174 (8th edition 2006); Jason Goodwin, Lords of the Horizons: a History of the Ottoman Empire 296 (2003).

23   In return he, alone of all the viceroys of the Ottomon Empire, gained for his heirs the right of succession to the Egyptian viceroyship.

24   Edwin De Leon, The Khedive's Egypt; or, The old house of bondage under new masters 98–99 (1877).

25   Jimmy Dunn, *Suez Canal*, www.touregypt.net/featurestories/suezcanal.htm.

26   *Suez Canal*, MSN Encarta, http://encarta.msn.com/encyclopedia_761578705/suez_canal.html

27   De Leon, *supra* note 24, at 101–102.

28   *Id.* at 170.

29   10 William Ewart Gladstone, *The Gladstone Diaries* lxxi (1990); see also Berque, *supra* note 21 for a discussion of the debt before and after the First World War, at 291.

30   Donald Featherstone, Tel El-Kebir 1882: Wolseley's Conquest of Egypt 8–9 (1993); De Leon, *supra* note 24, at 98–99.

31   Springhall, *supra* note 35 at 88.

32   Ferdinand de Lesseps, The Suez Canal, Letters and Documents Descriptive of its Rise and Progress in 1854 to 1856 at 130–31 (1876).

33   Aside from improved communication to India, the Suez Canal opened up much more of Africa to European exploitation. See Eur, Europa Publications Staff, Africa South of the Sahara 26 (London: Routledge 2003); Featherstone, *supra* note 30.

34   Featherstone, *supra* note 30, at 6, 7. See also Gladstone, *supra* note 29, at 327. The canal, which, in the words of one commentator, had become 'the highway to India'. *Id.* 'Almost unselfconscious because . . . before the occupation was decided upon, Gladstone mentions 'the rights of bondholders' [holders of the Egyptian debt] on a par with the rights of the Sultan, the Khedive [royal viceroy of Egypt] and the Egyptian people.' at lxii. (Gladstone himself was a bondholder.)

35   John Springhall, Decolonization since 1945 at 87 (2001); *see also* Berque, *supra* note 21, at 263 (noting that 'on its own authority, it [Great Britain] rejected Ottoman sovereignty, dismissed the Khedive, imposed its Protectorate unilaterally').

36   Springhall, *supra* note 35, at 88. Bernard Reich, Political Leaders of the Contemporary Middle East and North Africa 190–91 (1990).

37   Mitchell, *supra* note 21, at 16. Mohammed Ali started the shift towards cotton as the main cash crop, but Britain took measures, largely demanding a low tariff, which prevented the growth of Egyptian industry.

38   *Id.*

39   The Earl of Cromer, *Modern Egypt* 428 (1908).

40   *Id.*

41   Erez Manela, The Wilsonian Moment 40 (2007). '[O]ther nationalities which are now under Turkish rule should be assured an undoubted security of life and an absolutely unmolested opportunity of autonomous development.' President Woodrow Wilson, Address to a Joint Session of Congress on the Conditions of Peace (Jan. 8, 1918), *available at* www.presidency.ucsb.edu/ws/index.php?pid=65405.

42   *See, e.g.*, British Mandate for Palestine confirmed by the Council of the League of Nations on 24 July 1922, 3 League of Nations O.J. 1007 (August 1922), *available at* http://avalon.law.yale.edu/20th_century/palmanda.asp.

43   *See* Berque, *supra* note 21, at 269. William L. Cleveland, A History of the Modern Middle East 163–64 (2d edition, 2000). (For the Arabs, the aftermath of the war [World War I] produced feelings of bitterness toward the western powers and a deep-seated conviction that they [the Arabs] had been betrayed'). Note after the First World War, the British supported 'Syrian unity and Iraqi independence', but refused to loosen the British grip on Egypt. *Id.* at 271.

44   Cleveland, *supra* note 43, at 161 ('[T]he mandate system was little more than nineteenth-century imperialism repackaged to give the appearance of self-determination.').

45   Tom Reiss, The Orientalist: Solving the Mystery of a Strange and Dangerous Life 117–118 (2006); see also *Ataturk and the Last Caliph, 1922–24, available at* http://faroutliers.blogspot.com/2006/08/13/ataturk-and-last-caliph-19224.htm

46   Debjani Ganguli, Rethinking Ghandi and Nonviolent Relationality 251 (2007).

47   Cleveland, *supra* note 43, at 193.

48   *Id.*

49   Dona Stewart, The Middle East Today: Political, Geographical and Cultural Perspectives 95 (2009) (noting that the Allies wanted to insure that the Ottoman Empire would never rise again).

50   P.J. Vatikiotis, The History of Modern Egypt 293 (1991).

51   Springhall, *supra* note 35, at 88.

52   Nejla M. Abu Izzeddin, Nasser of the Arabs 5 (1975).

53   *Id.* at 5–6.

54   *See* Izzeddin, *supra* note 52, at 192.

55   *Id.; see also* David Tal, The 1956 War: Collusion and Rivalry in the Middle East 104 (2001) ("The belief that Egyptian management of the canal would be either incompetent or maliciously partisan or both was not at all upheld.").

56   A decade later the United States Supreme Court refused to apply this formulation for legal nationalization because of, *inter alia*, uncertainty whether it still amounted to customary international law. *See* Banco Nacional de Cuba v. Sabbatino, 376 U.S. 398 (1964).

57   Izeddin, *supra* note 52, at 89. See also Tal, *supra* note 55, at 180 (quoting an aide to Israeli General Moshe Dayan observing the French bombing of Egyptian military bases, "The camps became an inferno.")

58   Izzeddin, *supra* note 52, at 189–90.

59   Hugh Thomas, Suez 134 (1967).

60   *See* Izzeddin, *supra* note 52, at 192.

61   Hall Gardner, American Global Strategy and the "War on Terrorism" 87 (2007).

62   Furthermore, Britain's defeat marked it as a second-rate power.

63   Izzeddin, *supra* note 52.

64   Nasser, however, continued to try to keep good relations with the United States.

65   Deborah J. Gener, One Land, Two Peoples 111–12 (1994). Richard Bordeaux Parker, The Six Day War 8–9 (1996); Christopher Gelpi, The Power of Legitimacy 141 (2002).

66 *1967: Israel launches attack on Egypt, On this Day 1950–2005*, BBC, http://news.bbc.co.uk/onthisday/hi/dates/stories/june/5/newsid_2654000/2654251.stm

67 Gelpi, *supra* note 65, at 141–42.

68 Letter from Daniel Webster to Lord Ashburton (Aug. 6, 1842), *available at* http://avalon.law.yale.edu/19th_century/br-1842d.asp.

69 Michael Walzer, Just and Unjust Wars 85 (4th edition 2006). *See also* Alan M. Dershowitz, Preemption: A Knife That Cuts Both Ways 82 (2007); Yoram Dinstein, War, Aggression and Self-Defence 192 (4th edition 2005). UN Security Council Resolution 242 requires return of occupied territories, on the one hand, and recognition and guarantees for the security of Israel, on the other. *See* chapter 13 for a more detailed discussion of this issue.

70 Musa Husaini, The Moslem Brethren 5 (1955).

71 *Id.* at 1–2.

72 *Id.* The group formed under the name, "Association of the Moslem Brethren."

73 Karen Armstrong puts the number of members in the "millions . . . by 1948." Armstrong, *supra* note 20, at 156.

74 Youssef M. Choueiri, Islamic Fundamentalism 40 (2002).

75 David Bukay, From Muhammad to Bin Laden 215–16 (2007).

76 On the other hand, the Egyptian people forgave Nasser. After the Six Day War, Nasser tendered his resignation. His people would not accept it, loudly proclaiming their loyalty to him. When he died unexpectedly of a heart attack three years later, millions came to his funeral.

77 Vatikiotis describes the aftermath of the defeat and its strengthening extreme fundamentalists:

> In fact, inter-communal conflict began to gather momentum soon after the military debacle of June 1967. It was, in a sense, one of the inevitable consequences of the disappointment with and the insecurity felt under the Nasser regime. There was steady proliferation of militant religious organizations in both the Muslim and Coptic communities, especially among university students. This process of militant religious resurgence was accelerated by Nasser's failing socialist policies followed by Sadat's pro-Western economic liberalization [policy and his alliance with rich, conservative oil-producing Arab states after 1971]. A suitable climate for religious militancy was created by both leaders, especially Sadat.

Vatikiotis, *supra* note 50, at 420–21.

78 Richard Wright, The Looming Tower 52 (2007).

79 Vatikiotis, *supra* note 50, at 414–15.

80 *Id.*

81 Vatikiotis, *supra* note 50, at 420, 424.

82 *See* Sagiv, *supra* note 16, at preface (unnumbered). *See also* Berman, *infra* notes 39–57 in chapter 10, and accompanying text for a deeper discussion of al Qutb.

83 Richard Bernstein, Out of the Blue 16 (2002).

84 *Id.*, at 40.

85 *See* Congressional Research Service, Egypt: Background and U.S. Relations 25–27 (2008), *available at* www.fas.org/sgp/crs/mideast/RL33003.pdf.

86 *See* A Framework for Peace in the Middle East Agreed at Camp David, Egypt-Isr., 17 Sept 1978, 17 I.L.M. 1466 (1978); Special International Security Assistance Act of 1979, 22 U.S.C. §§ 3401–3408 (2009).

87 Tatah Mentan, Dilemmas of Weak States 327 (2004).

88 The Gulf War and the New World Order 59–60 (Tareq Y. Ismael & Jacqueline Ismael eds., 1995).

89 *Id.*

90   One commentator notes that "[t]he tragedy of U.S.–Middle East policy is that the United States has not been celebrated for its selfless devotion to democracy, but rather it has been bitterly criticized for not showing the slightest commitment to democracy whether in Turkey, Iran[, and] country after country in the Arab and non-Arab Middle East with the sole exception of Israel." Andrew Ross & Kristin Ross, Anti-Americanism 115 (2004) (quoting Rashid Khalidi).

91   *See* Mark W.G. Stibbe, John's Gospel 109–110 (London: Routledge, 1994). Paul Johnson points out that Greek anti-Semitism predates the Christian, implying that they combined in the first century. Paul Johnson, A History of the Jews 133–34 (1987). The plain meaning of parts of John's Gospel appears directly anti-Semitic, *see* John 8.31–59. Johnson asserts that meaning was mis-interpreted but notes that passages from Matthew appear even more anti-Semitic, passages implicitly condemning Jews and their heirs to collective responsibility for Christ's death. *Id.* at 145–46. Mel Gibson's film "The Passion of the Christ" (2004), was criticized for likewise implying collective Jewish responsibility for the crucifixion of Christ.

92   For a far more complete discussion of this topic, *see* A History of the Jewish People (H.H. Benson ed., 1976); Johnson, *supra* note 91.

93   *See* Benson, *supra* note 92, at 486–87. To his credit, Pope Clement VI issued a papal bull that "contradicted the allegation . . . and argued that the Jews were suffering [from the plague] as badly as any other element of the population." Johnson, *supra* note 91, at 216. Unfortunately, the papal decree had little effect.

94   Terence Alan Morris, Europe and England in the Sixteenth Century 111 (1998); David Bridger & Samuel Wolk, The New Jewish Encyclopedia 220 (1962); Himilce Novas, Everything You Need to Know about Latino History 45 (4th edition 2008). Torquemada also played a direct role in persuading King Ferdinand and Queen Isabella to expel all Jews from Spain in 1492.

95   Benson, *supra* note 92, at 580.

96   St. Simon of Trent Blood Libel, Zionism and Israel—Encyclopedic Dictionary, www.zionism-israel.com/dic/Simon_of_Trent_blood_libel.htm.

97   *Id. See also* Documents of the II Vatican Council, *available at* www.vatican.va/archive/hist_councils/ii_vatican_council/index.htm (follow "Nostra Aetate" hyperlink); *see also* Robert Drinan, Can God and Caesar Coexist? 196–97 (2005); Richard S. Levy, Antisemitism 734 (2005).

98   Pogroms are "organized riots accompanied by murder and pillage of the Jewish community." Joseph Telushkin, Jewish Literacy 660 (1991). Between 1903 and 1906, there were 600 pogroms in Russia, prompting mass emigration to the US and to other countries. *Id.*

99   Leni Yahil, The Holocaust 43 (1991). Holocaust Memorial Museum, Holocaust Encyclopedia, *available at* www.ushmm.org/wlc/Article.php?lang=en&ModuleId=10005143 (last visited Mar. 28, 2009); International Military Tribunal, Nuremberg, Judgment of the International Military Tribunal for the Trial of German Major War Criminals: Kaltenbrunner Judgment (Sept. 30–Oct. 1, 1946), Avalon Project, www.yale.edu/lawweb/avalon/imt/proc/judkalt.htm.
      Attorney-General Hausner's Opening Speech, Session nos. 6, 7, 8 of the district court of Jerusalem in *Eichmann* trial, (*infra* note 107 in chapter 6) (Apr. 17–18, 1961), *available at* www.nizkor.org/hweb/people/e/eichmann-adolf/transcripts/Sessions/Session-006-007-008-01.htm; Attorney General v. Eichmann, 36 *International Law Reports* (*ILR*) (Dist. Ct) (1968)18; Martin Gilbert, The Holocaust: A History of the Jews of Europe During the Second World War 26, 280–85 (1985); Raul Hilberg, The Destruction of the European Jews 1321 (3d edition 2003).

100 Martin Luther also preached anti-Semitism: his writings include "On the Jews and Their Lies (1543)," which said "that rabbis should not be allowed to teach or to travel; banking and commerce should be professions closed to Jews; and, to settle the matter finally, this people ought to be expelled from German lands as France, Spain, and Bohemia had done." Gerald S. Sloyan, *Christian Persecution of the Jews over the Centuries*, The Centre for Advanced Holocaust Studies, *available at* www.ushmm.org/research/center/church/persecution/

101 At Yad Vashem, Israel's memorial to the Jews who died in the holocaust, the Pope stated, "As bishop of Rome and successor of the Apostle Peter, I assure the Jewish people that the Catholic Church, motivated by the Gospel law of truth and love, and by no political considerations, is deeply saddened by the hatred, acts of persecution and displays of anti-Semitism directed against the Jews by Christians at any time and in any place." *Pope's Address at Yad Vashem*, BBC News, Mar. 23, 2000, *available at* http://news.bbc.co.uk/2/hi/middle_east/688059.stm. In 1997, the French Catholic bishops apologized to Jews regarding the French Church's inaction during the Holocaust, stating, "Today we confess that silence was a mistake. . . . We beg for the pardon of God, and we ask the Jewish people to hear this word of repentance." Roger Cohen, *French Church Issues an Apology to Jews On War*, N.Y. Times, 1997, Oct. 1, 1997, *available at* www.nytimes.com/1997/10/01/world/french-church-issues-apology-to-jews-on-war.html.

102 Specifically, the Second Vatican Council documents state:

> True, the Jewish authorities and those who followed their lead pressed for the death of Christ; still, what happened in His passion cannot be charged against all the Jews, without distinction, then alive, nor against the Jews of today. Although the Church is the new people of God, the Jews should not be presented as rejected or accursed by God, as if this followed from the Holy Scriptures. All should see to it, then, that in catechetical work or in the preaching of the word of God they do not teach anything that does not conform to the truth of the Gospel and the spirit of Christ.
>
> Furthermore, in her rejection of every persecution against any man, the Church, mindful of the patrimony she shares with the Jews and moved not by political reasons but by the Gospel's spiritual love, decries hatred, persecutions, displays of anti-Semitism, directed against Jews at any time and by anyone.

Declaration on the Relation of the Church to Non-Christian Religions, Nostra Aetate, Proclaimed by Pope Paul VI, Oct. 28, 1965, para. 4, II Vatican Council Documents, *supra* note 97, at: www.vatican.va/archive/hist_councils/ii_vatican_council/documents/vat-ii_decl_19651028_nostra-aetate_en.html.

103 It is undeniable the Second Vatican Council initiated a far better relationship between Catholics and Jews. See *Nostra Aetate: Transforming the Catholic-Jewish Relationship*, Anti-Defamation League, Oct. 20, 2005, www.adl.org/main_Interfaith/nostra_aetate.htm. Those ecumenical efforts are to be commended. However transformative, they have, nevertheless, not come close to "wiping out" the wrong that Christians have perpetrated against Jews over 2,000 years. Cf. *Chorzow Factory Case*, 1928 P.C.I.J. (ser. A), No. 17 ("[R]eparation [under international law] must, as far as possible, *wipe out* all the consequences of the illegal act and re-establish the situation which would, in all probability, have existed if that act had not been committed.") (emphasis added).

104 After the Second World War the Allied powers and particularly, the US, did demand that the new West Germany make reparations to Jews and to Israel. Under the reparations agreement, Western Germany did make some reparations, agreeing to pay the new state of Israel $750 million in goods, and to pay $107 million into a claims fund. In addition, West Germany made individual

payments, which led to $1.7 billion being added to the Israeli economy. Itamar Rabinovich & Jehuda Reinharz, Israel in the Middle East: documents and readings on society, politics, and foreign relations, pre-1948 to the present 106 (2008).

105 The European Crusaders did defeat the Muslims in 1090 and held Jerusalem for nearly one hundred years until Saladin conquered it in 1187. Sir George W. Cook, *Saladin Takes Jerusalem from the Christians*, http://history-world.org/saladin_takes_jerusalem.htm.

106 *See* Martin Sicker, Reshaping Palestine: From Muhammad Ali to the British Mandate, 1831–1922, at 17 (1999); Beverley Milton-Edwards & Peter Hinchcliffe, Conflicts in the Middle East since 1945, at 11–12 (3d edition 2008); Dore Gold, The Fight for Jerusalem 122–23 (2007); Thomas M. Leonard, Encyclopedia of the Developing World 69–70 (2006).

107 Abraham Malamat argues that because the Egyptians lost the Battle of Kadesh in 1285 BCE, a loss that led to "loosening control" in Canaan, because Sihon, King of the Amorites, arose "shortly after" that battle, and because the Israeli tribes subsequently conquered Sihon, the Israeli victories over Canaan must have occurred some time after 1285 BCE. Abraham Malamat, *Origins and the Formative Period*, A History of the Jewish People, *supra* note 92 at 23, 55, 56. *See also* Shaye J.D. Cohen, From the Maccabees to the Mishnah 29–30 (1987). Johnson, *supra* note 91, at 44–45. Daniel Gavron, The Other Side of Despair xi (Rowman and Littlefield 2003). Note, however, that Professor Dershowitz states that the figure is 1600 years, not 1000. Alan M. Dershowitz, The Case for Israel 15, 17 (2003). *See also* TimeLine of Zionism, Israeli and Palestinian History and the Conflict, Zion-Israeli Encyclopedic Dictionary, *at* www.zionism-israel.com/zionism_timeline.htm.

108 Johnson, *supra* note 91, at 138–43.

109 A History of the Jewish People, *supra* note 92, at 334.

110 *See* Telushkin, *supra* note 98, at 134; Johnson, *supra* note 91, at 143 ("The two catastrophes of AD 70 and AD 135 effectively ended Jewish state history in antiquity.").

111 Stephen Kinzer, Overthrow: America's Century of Regime Change from Hawaii to Iraq 122 (2007). There is some evidence suggesting that though American authorities knew that Mossadegh was not a communist or even communist leaning, there was fear that should he be overthrown, communists would come to power. *Id.* Iraq had the largest communist party of all the Arab states.

112 Richard H. Immerman, John Foster Dulles 149 (1998).

113 Although the US opposition to the Anglo-French effort to retake the Canal was received positively in the Arab world, that stance was not enough to outweigh other measures taken by the US that appeared hostile to Arabs and Muslims.

114 Toby Jones, *Shifting Sands*, 85(2) Foreign Affairs, Mar. 1, 2006, 2006 WLNR 3634272 (noting from the high in Desert Storm that a "substantial presence" of US troops was maintained in Saudi Arabia until the pullout after April 2003).

115 The fatwa, however, characterizes "the enemy" as the "the American-Israeli alliance occupying the country of the two Holy Places. . . ." *Bin Laden's Fatwa*, PBS NewsHour (quoting *Al Quds Al Arab*, Aug. 1996), *available at* www.pbs.org/newshour/terrorism/international/fatwa_1996.html.

116 Robert Pape makes the further point that all the 9/11 suicide bombers came from countries where the US had stationed troops or had military bases: "My study assesses the complete set of Al Qaeda suicide attackers, the 71 terrorists from 1995 to 2004 willing to kill themselves for Osama bin Laden. More than two-thirds come from Sunni Muslim countries where the United States has tens of thousands of combat troops in Saudi Arabia, countries on the Arabian Peninsula, Turkey and Afghanistan." Robert A. Pape, *Al Qaeda Strategy{:} Target*

Europe, Int'l Herald Trib., July 12, 2005, at 7, *available at* 2005 WLNR 10892074.

Aside from Iraq and Afghanistan, the US maintains military bases in Qatar, Bahrain, Kuwait, Oman and United Emirates. Dep't of Defense, *Base Structure Report: Fiscal Year 2007 Baseline* 77–95 (2006), *available at* www.defenselink.mil/pubs/BSR_2007_Baseline.pdf. US troops are stationed in an additional 29 Muslim countries. Dep't of Defense, Active Duty Military Personnel Strengths By Regional Area and by Country (2008); *available at* http://siadapp.dmdc.osd.mil/personnel/MILITARY/history/hst0809.pdf.

117 Armstrong, *supra* note 20, at 142–46.

118 *Id.* at 157–58.

119 Robert Pape, Op-Ed., *Blowing Up an Assumption*, N.Y. Times, May 18, 2005 *available at* www.nytimes.com/2005/05/18/opinion/18pape.html (his study of all suicide bombings from 1980 to 2003, 315 total revealed that the Tamil Tigers of Sri Lanka were the biggest "instigators of suicide attacks": "This group committed 76 of the 315 incidents, more than Hamas (54) or Islamic Jihad (27).").

120 Robert A. Pape, Dying to Win 4 (2006). De Leon, *supra* note 24, at 98–99.

121 This table was prepared and written by my research assistant, Jessica Rhodes-Knowlton, A.B., Wellesley College, 2005, J.D., Pace University School of Law, 2009.

2 "The global war on terrorism"

A mislabeling of the terrorist challenge?

Right after the heinous and devastating 9/11 attacks, high ranking members of the Bush administration, including Vice-President Richard Cheney, Secretary of Defense Donald Rumsfeld, National Security Adviser Condoleezza Rice, Attorney General John Ashcroft, and President George W. Bush, himself, began using the phrases "war against terrorism" and later the "global war on terrorism."[1] These officials did not call for war on a country, on a government, or on a regime, or on insurgents or on rebels. They called for war on a thing, yet not a thing really, because terrorism itself cannot be picked up or touched or seen or destroyed. We can certainly see what individuals or groups of individuals or governments or countries can do. Here are a few examples of terrorism, mostly committed by states: (1) Turkey's murdering over 600,000 Armenians in 1915; (2) Japan's indiscriminately bombing civilians in Nanking; (3) Nazi Germany's murdering over six million Jews, gypsies and gays; (4) Stalin's murdering millions of its own citizens; (5) Pol Pot's murdering over a million of his own people; (6) the Hutus' genocidal killing of the Tutsis; (7) the Bosnian Serbs' ethnic cleansing of Muslims; (8) Serbia under Slobodan Milošević, killing, raping and expelling Albanian Kosvars in mass; and (9) the despotic Sudan regime's killing of innocents in Darfur.[2] The list goes, unfortunately, on and on, and includes, among others, non-state terrorism, the 9/11 attacks, the 3/11 Madrid attacks, the 7/7 attacks in London, the 7/11 attacks in Mumbai, and the 12/27 assassination of Benazir Bhutto in Rawalpindi in which 20 others also lost their lives.

Yet history teaches that we fight wars not against things or concepts, but against countries or governments or rebel groups. We can claim we are fighting a war against poverty or drugs or ignorance, but we know deep down that when we use such language, we are really engaging in rhetorical hyperbole—exaggeration to make a point. Few can object to such exaggeration as mere metaphor—that we are going to marshal our resources against poverty, for example, *as if* we were at war with it. But when we start believing our own exaggerated use of language or when the government intends to have these words take on a meaning far from their roots, we may find ourselves blown in dangerous directions. It has now become clear, however, that this phrase has not only become unthinkingly part of the lexicon, but also is dangerously overbroad. Grenville Byford put it aptly:

> Wars have typically been fought against proper nouns (Germany, say) for the good reason that proper nouns can surrender and promise not to do it again. Wars against common nouns (poverty, crime, drugs) have been less successful. Such opponents never give up. The war on terrorism, unfortunately, falls into the second category.[3]

Emergency measures put into effect because of the "war on terrorism" may likewise never end, and governmental officials may justify military actions that have little to do with our immediate security by invoking such a broad description of the threat.

Aside from being never ending, "the war against terrorism" describes "the enemy" so vaguely that the phrase can be trotted out to justify just about any military adventure or policy. Perhaps an example from domestic law could help show why vaguely characterizing the enemy presents dangers. In 1910, Congress passed the Mann Act (also called The White Slave Act), aimed at pimps who take foreign-born female prostitutes across state lines. Specifically, the Act prohibits "knowingly transport[ing] . . . in interstate or foreign commerce . . . any woman or girl for the purpose of prostitution . . . or for any other *immoral purpose*."[4] Congress intended the phrase "any other immoral purpose" to be limited to prostitution and other commercial vices. However, the Bureau of Investigation (the forerunner to the FBI) under William J. Burns, and then Assistant Chief J. Edgar Hoover, threatened publisher William Randolph Hearst with prosecution under the Mann Act for taking his mistress from California to Nevada and sleeping with her in a Las Vegas hotel. Yielding to the threat, the Hearst newspapers stopped publishing stories on the Teapot Dome scandal.[5] Vague statutes allow the police to cast such a big net that they can often arrest whomever they want—regardless of what the legislature may have intended or what sound public policy demands.

The vague term "war against terrorism" allowed the Bush–Cheney administration to cast too big a net. The phrase put the Democrats on the defensive and helped the administration initially convince the American people that the war against Iraq was justified. Neither before nor after the US-invasion has there been credible evidence that Saddam Hussein was behind the 9/11 attacks, and little evidence suggests that he supported al Qaeda or allied fundamentalist groups. In fact, much evidence shows, on the one hand, that the secularist Saddam Hussein had rebuffed efforts by Ayman al Zawahiri and other extreme fundamentalists and, on the other, that bin Laden hated Saddam. Saddam Hussein, however, had apparently financially supported suicide bombings in Israel, reportedly giving approximately $20,000 to each surviving family of suicide bombers. This allowed the Bush–Cheney administration to claim that Saddam Hussein supported "terrorism." (The Palestinian suicide bombers have committed crimes against humanity and should be utterly condemned for their deliberate attacks on civilians. Anyone who aids and abets such crimes, as Saddam Hussein reportedly did, should be stigmatized and, if possible, prosecuted, but labeling Hamas as the same entity as al Qaeda or as complicit with al Qaeda before the invasion of Iraq is not supported by the available evidence.)

The Bush–Cheney administration also stressed that Saddam Hussein used chemical weapons against his own people. (While knowing Saddam Hussein used poison gas against the Kurds and against the Iranians, President Ronald Reagan and then Vice-President George H.W. Bush's administration, however, continued to support Iraq in its war against Iran.) Aside from the exaggerated assertion that Saddam Hussein had weapons of mass destruction, fighting Saddam Hussein thus could technically be deemed fighting the "war against terrorism." In the run-up to the war, high administration officials constantly mentioned al Qaeda in the same breath as Saddam Hussein, implying that Saddam Hussein was behind al Qaeda. Before the war, polls indicated that most Americans erroneously believed that Saddam Hussein was behind the 9/11 attacks. When American troops entered Baghdad, reportedly they were shouting "9/11, 9/11, 9/11."[6]

An emulator of Stalin, Saddam Hussein was surely one of the most brutal dictators to walk the world's stage in the last 100 years. He murdered thousands of his own people, tortured, maimed (cut the tongues out of) countless others, started two aggressive wars, and used poison gas—a weapon that even Hitler refused to employ against troops in the field. If the US call to arms had been based on humanitarian intervention, to free the Iraqi people from a brutal tyrannical regime, that would have been a different matter. But carrying out a misleading campaign that there was incontrovertible evidence that Saddam Hussein had weapons of mass destruction and that the war on Iraq was a "war against terrorism," intending to suggest that the US was carrying out military action against al Qaeda, at the very least undercut the government's credibility both at home and abroad and limited its ability to assemble a truly broad international coalition. In Muslim eyes, the American invasion cast the US in the role not of savior, but of an occupying superpower using its military might to attempt to ensure its supply of oil and its hegemony over the Middle East.

We start with this phrase "global war on terrorism" because it has helped establish the methods the US employs to counter terrorism.[7] If the US is engaged in a global war, then it follows that the US can use its military rather than its police forces everywhere. The US can kill without warning even if we could easily arrest a suspected terrorist. The US can kill civilians as long as they fit in the expansive category of acceptable collateral damage. The US may invade and attack other countries if they somehow are against us in the "war on terrorism."[8] Despite President Bush's claims that on his watch the US did not torture and that it treated all detainees "humanely," his administration regarded suspected terrorists as possessing few, if any, legal rights and has routinely abused, if not tortured, them.

Certainly, we Americans, like all peoples, are entitled to protect ourselves, to act in self-defense, and to take affirmative action to prevent future terrorist attacks, including using the military in certain theaters and in certain circumstances. Let us not avoid the chilling fact that al Qaeda, its allied groups and followers are almost certain to strike the US mainland again.[9] But tearing out most of the pages of the rulebook and using an overarching, overly broad phrase to justify lawlessness has had such far-reaching repercussions that, rather than make us safer, has placed us in greater danger.

As of this writing, the Obama administration appears intent on taking a new approach in American counterterrorism policy and practice. President Obama, in his first act in office, declared that the Guantánamo Bay detention center would be closed within a year and that the nation's security forces, including the Central Intelligence Agency (CIA), would not engage in torture. Closing Guantánamo does have enormous symbolic importance, but the far more difficult question is what policies and practices the Obama administration will adopt toward those detained in that facility, toward those detained in other US detention facilities around the world, and toward future terrorist suspects who operate either here or abroad.

So far the record is mixed. During the presidential campaign, Barack Obama used the term, "war on terrorism." Since assuming office, he has commendably avoided the phrase. The Obama Justice Department stated that the administration is dropping the label "enemy combatant" for Guantánamo Bay detainees, a step "that seemed intended to symbolically separate the new administration from Bush detention policies."[10] Furthermore, his Justice Department has indicated that it will require a more stringent standard for providing material support for terrorism as a basis of detention, namely, "substantial support."[11] The Department's court papers states that "substantial support" would *not* permit detaining individuals at Guantánamo "who provide unwilling or insignificant support" to terrorist organizations.[12]

Furthermore, President Obama's Justice Department under US Attorney General Eric H. Holder, has had Ali Saleh Kahlah al Marri, an alleged member of an al Qaeda sleeper cell, indicted in federal court for providing material support to terrorism, entitling al Marri to legal counsel and to a civil criminal trial.[13] Arrested in the US in 2001 for fraud,[14] al Marri was transferred in 2003 from the federal courts to the Pentagon as an "enemy combatant" by the Bush–Cheney administration. He had been the only "enemy combatant held on US soil."[15] The Bush–Cheney administration held him virtually *incommunicado* in a Navy Brig, and argued it had the authority "to detain legal residents like al Marri indefinitely."[16]

The Obama Justice Department, however, adopted the Bush–Cheney Justice Department's position in *al Maqaleh v. Gates*,[17] a case brought in the Federal District Court for the District of Columbia. That case involved denominated "enemy combatants" who were taken to the US's detention facility in Bagram Air Base in Afghanistan, but who were captured in another country. The US Supreme Court, however, had held in 2008 in *Boumediene v.*

Bush[18] that Guantánamo Bay detainees were entitled to habeas corpus, despite Congress's attempt to strip them of that right. The Bush–Cheney Justice Department had argued that the district court should not extend that right to the *al Maqaleh* detainees held in Afghanistan. The district court judge, a Republican appointee, hearing the *al Maqaleh* case, ruled as follows: "Under *Boumediene*, Bagram detainees who are not Afghan citizens, who were not captured in Afghanistan, and who have been held for an unreasonable amount of time-here, over six years—without adequate process may invoke the protections of the Suspension Clause, and hence the privilege of habeas corpus. . . ."[19] The Obama administration decided to appeal this ruling, and regrettably the D.C. Circuit reversed.[20]

The district court in *al Maqaleh* observed that the Obama Justice Department dropped the "enemy combatant" label only for the Guantánamo Bay detainees, not necessarily for those detained in other US facilities abroad. Specifically in the *al Maqaleh* case, the Obama Justice Department implicitly kept the enemy combatant label: "[F]or detainees at Bagram, respondents [the Government under the Obama Justice Department] apparently adhere to the definition of 'enemy combatant' that [the Bush Justice Department] previously proposed in the habeas cases involving Guantánamo detainees."

In a filing on 13 March 2009, also in the Federal District Court for the District of Columbia, Obama Justice Department lawyers, though implying that this may not be its final position, essentially adopted the Bush–Cheney administration's arguments on Executive Power of detention. The government argued that the Executive had the power to detain suspected terrorists in Guantánamo Bay, despite nominally rejecting the "enemy combatant" label for those detainees. Although adding the "substantial" gloss in interpreting material support, the administration refused to disavow or modify the other broad language of the material support statute. In any event, "substantial" is a deliberately vague term whose meaning in a particular case could very well be in the eyes of the beholder.

As of this writing, insufficient time has passed to judge what the Obama administration's counterterrorism policies will be. The above policy choices may be the tentative steps of an administration feeling its way through the challenging legal and security questions that the struggle against terrorism poses for the US. Following the Bush–Cheney administration's policy on indefinitely detaining individuals suspected of terrorism, particularly when they are not captured on the battlefields of Afghanistan or Iraq, resembles the Bush–Cheney administration's attempt to create detention centers deliberately placed abroad to avoid the scrutiny of the courts, defense attorneys, and the rule of law. Likewise, using the broad label "enemy combatant" as a means of removing an individual from review by American courts, harkens back to the abuses of excessive executive power of the previous administration. In dealing with the terrorist threat, the risk for the Obama administration may be focusing primarily on symbols rather than on substantive change in counterterrorism policy and practice.

Notes

1 For example, the President first mentioned the term in his speech to the nation on September 11, 2001. President George W. Bush, Statement by the President in His Address to the Nation in Light of the Terrorist Attacks of September 11 (Sept. 11, 2001), *available at* www.nationalcenter.org/BushGW91101 Address.html.

  White House Press Secretary Ari Fleischer first referred to the "War on Terror" in his Press Briefing on September 15. Ari Fleischer, White House Press Sec'y, Press Briefing, Sept. 15, 2001, http://georgewbush-whitehouse.archives. gov/news/releases/2001/09/20010915-5.html.

  Dick Cheney first mentioned the "War against Terrorism" in an appearance on Meet the Press on September 16. Vice-President Richard B. Cheney, Interview on Meet the Press with Tim Russert, Sept. 16, 2001, *available at* http://georgewbush-whitehouse.archives.gov/vicepresident/news-speeches/speeches/vp20010916.html.

  President Bush referred again to the War on Terror in his September 20 address to Congress. President George W. Bush, Address to a Joint Session of Congress, Sept. 20, 2001, *available at* http://archives.cnn.com/2001/US/09/20/gen.bush.transcript.

  Donald Rumsfeld discussed the "war against terrorism's attack on our way of life" in a speech on September 27. Donald H. Rumsfeld, US Sec'y of Def., A New Kind Of War, Sept. 27, 2001, *available at* www.defenselink.mil/speeches/speech.aspx?speechid=440.

  John Ashcroft referred to the "war against terrorism" in a press briefing at FBI headquarters on September 27. John Ashcroft, Attorney General, Prepared Remarks for a Press Briefing with FBI Director Mueller, Sept. 27, 2001, *available at* www.usdoj.gov/archive/ag/speeches/2001/agcrisisremarks9_27.htm.

2 *Tamil Tigers 'Regret' Gandhi*, BBC News, June 27, 2006, *available at* http://news.bbc.co.uk/2/hi/5122032.stm. One could add to this list the US dropping atomic bombs on Hiroshima and Nagasaki, decisions that are still controversial today.

3 Grenville Byford, *The Wrong War*, Foreign Aff., July–Aug 2002, at 34, *available at* 2002 WLNR 11724647.

4 *See* Caminetti v. United States, 272 U.S. 470, 470 n.1 (1917) (quoting the Mann Act) (emphasis added).

5 *See* Thomas Michael McDonnell, *Defensively Invoking Treaties in American Courts—Jurisdictional Challenges under the U.N. Drug Trafficking Convention by Foreign Defendants Kidnapped Abroad by U.S. Agents*, 37 Wm. & Mary L. Rev. 1401, 1434 n.151 (1996) (citing Curt Gentry, J. Edgar Hoover: The Man and the Secrets (1991)).

6 Asne Seierstad, A Hundred and One Days – A Baghdad Journal 314 (Ingrid Christophersen trans., 2003).

7 The Pentagon actually decided in 2005 to drop the phrase "War on Terrorism" and replace it with "Global Struggle Against Violent Extremists." Gen. Richard B. Myers, chairman of the Joint Chiefs of Staff, stated: "If you call it a war, then you think of people in uniform as being the solution." Aside from the military, Myers noted that "'all instruments' of each nation's power need to be employed because meeting the challenge of terrorism is 'more diplomatic, more economic, more political than it is military.'" *It's a Struggle, not a War*, The Hartford Courant, July 31, 2005 at C2, *available at* 2005 WLNR 23579417. *See also* Eric Schmitt & Thom Shanker, *Bombings in London: Hearts and Minds; New Name for "War on Terror" Reflects Wider U.S. Campaign*, N.Y. Times, July 26, 2005, at A7, *available at* 2005 WLNR 11681010.

A few weeks later, however, President Bush rejected the Pentagon's approach, asserting: "Make no mistake about it, we are at war." Ruth Walker, *Defining Militancy Downward: GWOT's Next?*, The Christian Science Monitor, Aug. 12, 2005, at 18, *available at* 2005 WLNR 12646778. So also did former Secretary of Defense Donald Rumsfeld: "Some ask, are we still engaged in a war on terror? Let there be no mistake about it. It's a war." *Id.*

Despite the debate within the administration itself, the American media have stuck with President Bush's characterization, as have virtually all public officials regardless of the side of the aisle on which they sit. Note, however, that shortly after coming into office, Gordon Brown, the British Prime Minister, instructed the Foreign Office to drop using the phrase "war on terrorism." Brian Hanley, *Where's the Beef*, U.S. Naval Inst. Proc., Sept. 1, 2007, at 16, *available at* 2007 WLNR 22032479.

8　President George W. Bush's famous phrase suggests such an approach: "If you are not with us, you're against us." *See* Katerine M. Skiba Kskiba, *U.S. Security Veteran Says Help is Critical We Cannot Succeed Alone in Iraq, Brzezinski Argues*, Milwaukee J. and Sentinel, Apr. 14, 2004, at 14, *available at* 2004 WLNR 4720251 (criticizing President Bush's approach).

9　*See* Jack Goldsmith, The Terror Presidency 65 (2007).

10　*Id.*

11　Respondent's Memorandum Regarding the Government's Detention Authority Relative to Detainees Held at Guantánamo Bay at 2, In re Guantánamo Bay Detainee Litigation, Misc. No. 08-442(TFH) (D.D.C. March 13, 2009).

12　*Id.*

13　David Johnston & Neila Lewis, *U.S. Will Give Qaeda Suspect a Civilian Trial*, N.Y. Times, Feb. 26, 2009, at A1. Al Marri subsequently pleaded guilty to one count of conspiring to provide material support to a foreign terrorist organization. *Ali Saleh Kahleh al-Marri*, N.Y. Times, July 7, 2009, *available at* http://topics.nytimes.com/top/reference/timestopics/people/m/ali_saleh_kahlah_al_marri/index.html.

14　Bruce Smith, *Accused Al Qaeda operative in court after 5 years in brig*, The Boston Globe, Mar. 11, 2009, *available at* www.boston.com/news/nation/Articles/2009/03/11/accused_al_qaeda_operative_in_court_after_5_years_in_brig/

15　*Id.*

16　William Glaberson, *U.S. Won't Label Terror Suspects as "Combatants,"* N.Y. Times, Mar. 14, 2009, *available at* www.nytimes.com/2009/03/14/us/politics/14gitmo.html.

17　Al Maqaleh v. Gates, 604 F. Supp. 2d 205 (D.D.C. 2009), *rev'd*, 605 F.3d 84 (D.C. Cir. 2010).

18　Boumediene v. Bush, 553 U.S. 723 (2008).

19　Al Maqaleh, 604 F. Supp. 2d at 235.

20　Al Maqaleh v. Gates, 605 F.3d 84 (D.C. Cir. 2010), *rev'g* 604 F. Supp. 2d 205 (D.D.C. 2009). Because of a change in the composition of the United States Supreme Court, because Elena Kagan, the newest Supreme Justice, argued in favor of the Obama administration's position in the D.C. Circuit Court, and because she has decided, in any event, to recuse herself from the cases in which she participated as Solicitor General, the Court is unlikely to reinstate the district court's decision. (Boumediene was decided 5 to 4, with retiring Justice Stephens in the majority.) The Obama administration's decision to appeal the district court's opinion in al Maqaleh and the administration's failure to carry out its pledge to close the Guantánamo Bay detention facility, among other things, cast doubt on the Obama administration's commitment to turning away from the Bush-Cheney administration's discredited counter-terrorism policy and practices.

Part I

Imprisoning suspected agents of terror

3   Torture light

3.1 An ally's hand at rough interrogation of suspected terrorists

When Ireland threw off a good part of the English yoke in 1921 after well over three centuries of colonial rule, the English kept for themselves the six northern counties, the only areas in Ireland where the descendants of the original English colonists had a majority or a substantial presence.[1] Most descendants of the colonists, who were largely Protestant, continued to keep the native Irish people, mainly Catholics,[2] downtrodden in what had been their ancestors' land.[3] The Northern Catholic Irish suffered double the unemployment, generally could get only menial or low-ranking jobs, and lived in segregated neighborhoods in dilapidated houses or tenements. Well before 1921, the Protestants kept the best land for farming, leaving the rocky hill land for the Catholics.[4] The Protestants controlled banking, industry, the police, all other parts of government, and, except for the Catholic Church, almost every other institution in Northern Ireland society. Although the Catholic birth rate was much higher, the Protestant rulers counted on shutting out the Catholic Irish from decent jobs, housing, and just about everything else to prod the Catholic young to emigrate.[5] In any event, Protestant officials gerrymandered voting districts, ensuring that Catholics had only slightly more than token representation for their numbers.[6] In many ways, the plight of the Catholic minority resembled that of African-Americans in the Jim Crow South.[7]

In the 1960s, the winds of the Civil Rights Movement in the US reached Ireland.[8] Irish Catholics in Northern Ireland began to protest against the bonds of discrimination and prejudice. In 1968, the Protestant authorities and Protestant crowds and paramilitaries put down many of the peaceful protests with violence.[9] Riots broke out. Catholic youth began to throw stones at British soldiers and at the Northern Irish police. Three Protestants were killed in one riot. A new branch of the Irish Republican Army—the Provisional IRA—arose in response to what it perceived to be Protestant oppression of Catholics.[10] In 1969, the English government ordered its troops into Northern Ireland. Unfortunately, these troops "seemed either to have a

natural antipathy for the Irish or to have been indoctrinated against them."[11]
The British troops concentrated on the IRA and did little to stop the
Protestant paramilitary groups. While not committing nearly as many acts
of violence as the IRA, these groups were also growing and threatening
the peace.[12]

The IRA answered every British act of violence with one of its own. The
cycle of violence increased in frequency until the IRA was carrying out more
than one attack a day:

> In April 1971, there were 37 bombings; in May, 47; and in June, 50 such
> attacks: "Bombs were going off once or twice a day. Sniping was continu-
> ous. Military movement in Catholic areas was, if not impossible, very
> difficult without a massive buildup and the use of armored vehicles.
> Between April and August, the sniping and return of fire killed four
> British soldiers and wounded 28. Over 100 civilians had been injured
> by bombs."[13]

Because of the escalating violence, Brian Faulkner, the Prime Minister of
Northern Ireland, called for internment of IRA suspects. Internment—
imprisoning individuals without trial and holding them *incommunicado*—
had been used by the British and Northern Irish Protestant rulers against
Irish Catholics before.[14] In 1971, Edward Heath's Conservative government
granted the Protestant government's request and implemented a policy of
internment without trial for Catholics suspected of being members of the
IRA.[15] Despite the activities of Protestant paramilitaries, the British and the
Northern Irish government did not initially intern any Protestants.

The British treated the IRA suspects harshly. Specifically, the British: (1)
made them wear hoods over their faces except during interrogation; (2) forced
the suspects to stand spread-eagled in an uncomfortable position for hours;
(3) bombarded them continuously with loud noise; (4) prevented them from
sleeping; and (5) put them on a diet of bread and water.[16] Tim Coogan quotes
one such suspect who was detained and to whom a Belfast court later awarded
damages:

> After they arrested me, I was thrown into a lorry where I got a kicking [in
> the genitals]. Then I was taken to another barracks where I got another
> kicking and they took me up in a helicopter and told me they were going
> to throw me out. I thought we were hundreds of feet up but we were only
> a few feet up. They set Alsatians on me, my thigh was all torn, and they
> made me run in my bare feet over broken glass.[17]

Then, he underwent the five interrogation-preparation methods listed above.

Many of the detainees apparently turned out not to be members of the
IRA.[18] Feeling that the authorities acted arbitrarily and had discriminated
against Catholics, the Catholic community closed like a clam and refused

to cooperate with the police or with the British authorities. In addition, Catholics lined up to join the IRA.[19] Even though the British claimed to have gained some useful information from the interrogations, the Northern Ireland Chief of Police called the internment program "a disaster."[20]

3.2 The US tries rough interrogation methods

Among other things, September 11 counts as one of the greatest intelligence failures in American history. Despite some warnings from disparate voices in different agencies, US intelligence failed to connect the proverbial dots. Some assert that this failure was due to the wall that had been placed between the intelligence agencies and the Federal Bureau of Investigation (FBI).[21] Others blame the Central Intelligence Agency (CIA) and the FBI for failing to pay more attention to the terrorist threat.[22] Some blame the airlines for caring more about profit than security.[23] Others say that the Bush–Cheney administration ignored warnings from departing Clinton administration officials about the dangers al Qaeda posed.[24] Yet others say the Clinton administration could have been proactive in dealing with the terrorist threat.[25] Some argue that American intelligence agencies had downplayed so-called "human intelligence" in favor of high technology.[26]

George Tenet, the CIA Director under Bill Clinton and, for four years, under George W. Bush, admitted that the US did not have human intelligence—spies—effectively operating within al Qaeda or other extremist terrorist groups. Obtaining such intelligence is reportedly more difficult than obtaining intelligence on a foreign country, because of the nature of a trans-national terrorist organization: it operates clandestinely in numerous coun-tries, and typically adopts an elaborate cell structure.[27] The US's vaunted spy satellites help little in learning about the activities, plans and operations of such an organization.[28]

Yet the US's need for reliable intelligence has become all the greater because of the asymmetrical type of violence and warfare perpetrated by terrorist organizations. Absent advance knowledge, the Navy or the Coast Guard would have great difficulty in stopping and searching every com-mercial vessel entering US waters to find a shipping container with a nuclear device. Despite its status as a superpower, the US cannot post troops or police officers around every school, every hospital, every reservoir, every chemical plant, every nuclear power plant, every shopping center, and every other conceivable target in the country. In short, the best tactical defense against such a terrorist attack—at least from an operational perspective—is to gain "actionable intelligence" beforehand.[29]

In the absence of accurate intelligence garnered by the intelligence com-munity, US governmental authorities—the Pentagon, the CIA, the FBI, the National Security Agency, troops and officers in the field—had primarily one source for intelligence—prisoners that the US and its allies had captured or arrested. Given the stakes, it is understandable that US officials from the highest levels down claimed to possess the right to use extraordinary measures in interrogating such prisoners or at least so-called "high value" prisoners.[30]

This perceived need to interrogate prisoners also explains many of the Bush–Cheney administration's controversial counterterrorism policies. Among the major reasons put forward for establishing military tribunals and commissions for the Guantánamo Bay detainees was to prevent attorneys from advising their clients to invoke the Fifth-Amendment right to silence.[31] Neither President Bush's military commissions, nor the subsequent Military Commissions Acts of 2006 and of 2009 accords detainees Fifth-Amendment rights. This rationale—detainees potentially using the Fifth-Amendment right to silence—also probably served to justify the *incommunicado* detention of two American citizens, Jose Padilla and Yasser Hamdi, and permanent legal resident Ali al Marri. It also probably has a lot to do with the Bush–Cheney administration's argument, up until the Supreme Court's 2006 *Hamdan v. Rumsfeld* decision, that the Geneva Conventions do not apply to al Qaeda detainees and, despite some rhetoric to the contrary, to the Taliban detainees. Although the Third Geneva Convention of 1949 does not prohibit interrogation, it requires that the detaining state respect a prisoner's right only to provide basic information, namely, the proverbial name, rank, and serial number plus date of birth.[32]

The US imprisoned those it suspected of terrorism: in Guantánamo Bay, Cuba; in Abu Ghraib, Iraq; in Bagram Air Base in Afghanistan (and other sites in that country); and in the so-called CIA black sites, reportedly at the Stare Kiejkuty base in Poland and the Mihail Kogalniceanu Air Base in Romania as well as sites in Afghanistan, Thailand, and Jordan.[33] The US may have detained suspected terrorists in other American military bases around the world and off base in other countries.

3.3 Guantánamo Bay

The US invaded Afghanistan on 7 October 2001, less than a month after 9/11. With significant help from the Afghan Northern Alliance, the US forces defeated the repressive Taliban regime. The Northern Alliance captured large numbers of Taliban and al Qaeda members on the battlefield and turned them over to the US. Apparently, some individuals were turned over who were not captured on the battlefield. After questioning the captives, the US decided to send nearly 800 of them to Guantánamo Bay Naval Base. Besides those caught on or near the battlefield in Afghanistan, the US has sent other suspected terrorists arrested in other countries such as Bosnia and Thailand to Guantánamo Bay.

The so-called "high-value" prisoners, as well as others, were subject to "enhanced interrogation" methods. Some prisoners were short shackled, namely, the suspect's hands and ankles were "both shackled to a bolt in the floor, so that the suspect is in an uncomfortable fetal position."[34] Apparently, prisoners were often left in that position for hours, compelling them to urinate and defecate upon themselves.[35] Some prisoners were subjected to alternating cold and hot temperatures.[36] Some were subjected to loud noise and music so they could not sleep.[37] Some were beaten; some were sexually humiliated by female interrogators.[38] Some detainees were daubed with fake menstrual blood so they could not pray properly according to the Muslim religion.[39] Some were intimidated by unmuzzled dogs. Some of those who refused to talk were threatened with "extraordinary rendition" to states such as Jordan and Egypt with established reputations for torturing prisoners. Some were subjected to many, if not all these enhanced interrogation techniques.[40]

3.4 Abu Ghraib

The US invaded Iraq on March 19, 2003. Initially, the US appeared to have won a convincing victory over Saddam Hussein's National Guard and his regular troops. Less than a month and a half later on 1 May 2003, President Bush declared major combat over in Iraq. The declaration was premature as insurgency exploded into ongoing violence. The so-called surge and the rapprochement with the Sunni Insurgents (the "Awakening") are now credited with decreasing the violence,[41] but, as of this writing, Iraq is far from stable.[42]

As the insurgency increasingly caused greater violence and insecurity, high-level US officials called for more "actionable intelligence."[43] With few informants or live agents in positions to provide such intelligence,[44] Lieutenant General Ricardo S. Sanchez, commander of coalition ground forces in Iraq, viewed those captured or arrested as the prime source. "In part as a result of MG [Major General Geoffrey] Miller's call for strong, command-wide interrogation policies and in part as a result of a request for guidance coming up from the 519th [519th Military Intelligence Batalion] at Abu Ghraib, on September 14, 2003, General Sanchez signed a memorandum authorizing a dozen interrogation techniques beyond [Army] Field Manual 34–52 [regulating interrogations]—five more beyond those approved for Guantánamo."[45] The US had been capturing a considerable number of suspected insurgents, placing them in detention centers including Saddam Hussein's notorious prison, Abu Ghraib. The shocking pictures that appeared in the media in April 2004 do not require further description here, except to say that their publication caused an outcry and demands for the investigation of the Bush–Cheney administration's enhanced interrogation program.

3.5 Bagram Air Base and other Afghani detention centers

Officers in charge of Bagram Air Base in Afghanistan apparently did not receive "action memos" from Secretary of Defense Donald Rumsfeld, but developed interrogation techniques on their own. In practice, however, the techniques adopted in Afghanistan mirrored those in Guantánamo Bay.

Apparently, military intelligence officers (and military contractors) moved among the theaters and also communicated with one another; the Schlesinger Report notes that "interrogators and lists of techniques circulated from Guantánamo and Afghanistan to Iraq."[46] Although Army Field Manual (FM-34–52) "served as the baseline for interrogations . . . more aggressive interrogations of detainees appears (*sic*) to be on-going."[47] The Schlesinger Report also notes that "[on] January 14, 2003, in response to a data call from the joint Staff to facilitate working group efforts, the CJT Force [Combined Joint Task Force] 180 [which commands operations in Afghanistan] for-warded a list of techniques being used in Afghanistan, including some not explicitly set out in FM 34–52. . . . The 59th Military Intelligence Battalion, a company of which was later sent to Iraq, assisted in interrogations in support of SOF [Special Operations Forces] [in Afghanistan] and was fully aware of their interrogation techniques."[48]

Detention customs and practices were thus communicated informally as well as formally. In Afghanistan, these techniques included hooding, stress positions, short shackling, darkness, limited diet, sleep deprivation, loud noise, and use of cold temperatures. The Washington Post quoted Human Rights Watch as follows: "Afghans detained at Bagram airbase in 2002 have described being held in detention for weeks, continuously shackled, inten-tionally kept awake for extended periods of time, and forced to kneel or stand in painful positions for extended periods. . . . Some say they were kicked and beaten when arrested, or later as part of efforts to keep them awake. Some say they were doused with freezing water in the winter."[49] The New York Times quotes Bagram police commander Capt. Christopher M. Beiring, saying that it was standard operating procedure "that detainees were hooded, shackled and isolated for at least the first 24 hours, sometimes 72 hours of captivity."[50] In some cases their arms were shackled to the ceiling.

At least two prisoners died under suspicious circumstances in Bagram while in US custody.[51] Two soldiers who were accused of homicide in connec-tion with the deaths were acquitted by court-martial. Several other deaths of prisoners have been reported to have occurred within Bagram.[52] Similar tech-niques and conditions were reported to have been used in other Afghan detention centers run by the US.

The Justice Department official legal memos (and other Executive memo-randa) helped set the stage for the US to use so-called enhanced interrogation techniques (EITs) abroad on those suspected of terrorist activities. High gov-ernment officials may have believed that the official legal memoranda would shield them and their subordinates from any criminal or civil liability for the enhanced interrogation program. By expressly authorizing the enhanced interrogation program, the writers of the memoranda had to assume that these interrogation techniques would be carried out. In addition, they had to foresee that some interrogators would "explore the outer boundary of the rules" and that some would go beyond what the rules the writers established permitted. Likewise, it would not be difficult to foresee that other branches would implicitly learn about the new rules and that troops down the line might believe that they had a green light to engage in such conduct.

Secretary of Defense Donald Rumsfeld issued an order in November 2002, approving rough interrogation methods in Guantánamo Bay, as well as "[t]echniques of deception [including permitting the interrogator] to identify himself as a citizen of a foreign nation or an interrogator from a country with a reputation for harsh treatment of detainees."[53] Presumably, the purpose of such deception is to implicitly threaten the detainee with torture (or possibly death) if he does not talk.

The Secretary also approved so-called "Category II techniques,"[54] including: forcing detainees to assume "stress positions like standing for a maximum of four hours"; putting detainees into solitary confinement for 30 days at a time; depriving the detainee of light and "other stimuli"; hooding the detainee; interrogating the detainee for 20 hours straight; using dogs to threaten the detainee; and stripping the detainee naked. The Secretary also approved carrying out interrogations "in an environment other than the standard interrogation booth."[55] Presumably, subjecting the detainee to cold conditions while strapped naked in a crouched position qualifies as an "environment other than the standard interrogation booth." Secretary Rumsfeld also approved one Category III technique, "use of mild, non-injurious physical contact such as grabbing, poking in the chest with the finger, and light pushing."[56] Nothing in the action memo prohibits combining these techniques on a single detainee. At the end of the action memo approving these techniques, Donald Rumsfeld wrote: "However, I stand for 8–10 hours a day. Why is standing limited to 4 hours? D.R."[57]

The International Committee of the Red Cross (ICRC) reported that some of the US facilities kept the prisoners in total or near total darkness 24 hours a day. The prisoners were often hooded, stripped naked, short shackled, hosed down, and then subjected to extreme cold. When the prisoners went on a hunger strike, US guards forcibly fed them through apparently very painful nose tubes.

The abuses carried out in Abu Ghraib appear to deviate little from those approved techniques for Guantánamo Bay. Stripping prisoners naked, a primary step in dehumanizing them in the eyes of the guards and of themselves, was expressly authorized. Using police dogs to threaten the detainee was likewise expressly authorized. Forcing prisoners to form parts of a human pyramid, while naked, could be considered putting them in "stress positions." Forcing the detainees to masturbate and using female guards to humiliate them and other tactics, while not expressly authorized, do not stray far from the loose boundaries set by the Action Memo. Furthermore, it may be hard to draw the line between the approved light assaulting of detainees and actual beatings.

The evidence suggests that some officers and interrogators who carried out the "enhanced interrogation" techniques in Guantánamo Bay were transferred to Iraq and brought the techniques with them. Secretary of State Rumsfeld withdrew his authorization of the harshest techniques three months later. Yet, customs and practices had been established. The methods apparently did not die with the Secretary's signature on a document purporting to ban them: at around the time of the deaths of two detainees in Bagram Air Base, interrogators had started to use new, aggressive techniques that had not been approved in Afghanistan. "The military's acting chief lawyer at Bagram, Lt. Col. Robert J. Cotell Jr., on Jan. 24, 2003, in a memorandum [wrote that Bagram interrogators had] adopted some of the more extreme interrogation methods that Secretary of Defense Donald H. Rumsfeld approved on Dec. 2, 2002, exclusively for use at Guantánamo Bay, Cuba."[58]

3.6 Legal analysis

International law controlling how governments may treat detainees, even detainees suspected of committing terrorist acts, can be visualized as a large oak with two main branches—human rights law and humanitarian law (the law of war). Humanitarian law does not apply in times of peace, but only in times of war. Humanitarian law generally has geographical as well as temporal limits, extending to the geographical boundaries of the conflict and possibly to the immediate neighboring states, but no farther. On the other hand, human rights law applies in peacetime and in wartime. If, however, the human rights branch and the humanitarian law branch conflict during a war, then humanitarian law (the law of war branch) will probably control.

Deciding which of these two branches controls has enormous consequences for counterterrorism policy and practice, for the individual suspects, and for the civilian population in which they reside. If the law of war controls, exceptional measures are permitted, including the right of one combatant to intentionally kill another, and the right of a combatant to inflict collateral damage on civilians.[59]

The Bush–Cheney administration argued that only one branch applies— the law of war branch—to suspected terrorists. The administration then argued that under the relevant law of war, the Third Geneva Convention of 1949, suspected Taliban fighters and al Qaeda members, and their allies and adherents are not lawful combatants and when captured lack the status of prisoners of war (POWs). As "enemy combatants," the detained suspected terrorist suspects possess few, if any, rights.

Although Bush–Cheney administration officials often alluded to the Geneva Conventions (generally arguing that they do not apply), these officials in public all but ignored two other treaties that directly bear on these issues. The two human rights conventions, the International Covenant on Civil and Political Rights (ICCPR) and the Convention against Torture (CAT), discussed above, expressly prohibit both torture and cruel, inhuman, or degrading treatment. The US is a party to both conventions and is bound thereby. Chapter 6 on Indefinite Detention and Trial Rights of Suspected Terrorists argues that alleged unprivileged combatants arrested on the battlefield possess rights under both the Third and the Fourth Geneva Conventions.[60] That chapter also discusses the possible applicability of Common Article 3 of the Four Geneva Conventions.[61] Here, however, let's assume, for argument's sake, that the Bush–Cheney administration was right in arguing that the Geneva Conventions do not apply. The question we address in this chapter is whether the foundational human rights treaties,[62] the ICCPR and the CAT, have applied to those detained in Guantánamo Bay, Abu Ghraib, Bagram Air Base, the CIA black sites, and other US detention centers, wherever located.

Article 7 of the Covenant on Civil and Political Rights expressly forbids any government from using such methods on detainees: "No one shall be subjected to torture or to *cruel, inhuman or degrading treatment.*"[63] The Covenant does provide some latitude in times of national emergency,[64] permitting countries to "derogate" from some of its obligations (to take security measures that otherwise would violate the Covenant). Even in such times, however, the Covenant expressly forbids any country from derogating from its responsibilities under Article 7.[65] That means that countries cannot engage in "cruel, inhuman or degrading treatment," even in times of national emergency, such as 9/11 arguably ushered in.

The Convention against Torture likewise prohibits states from using national emergencies or an outbreak of armed conflict as a justification for torturing detainees: "No exceptional circumstances whatsoever, whether a state of war or a threat of war, internal political instability or any other public emergency, may be invoked as a justification of torture."[66] Formed after the ICCPR, the Torture Convention implicitly references the second prong of Article 7 of the ICCPR, noting that "[t]he provisions of this Convention are without prejudice to the provisions of any other international instrument or national law which prohibit cruel, inhuman or degrading treatment. . . ." So the plain meaning of CAT endorses the ICCPR's, making Article 7 non-derogable. In other words, even during a national emergency a state party may not torture detainees *or* subject them to cruel, inhuman, or degrading treatment.

Despite the clear mandate of the two human rights treaties, the administration attacked their applicability on two fronts: first, that under the doctrine of *lex specialis*, only humanitarian law (the law of war) applies, and second, even assuming *arguendo* human rights law would otherwise apply, the ICCPR operates only within the territory of a signatory state. Since Guantánamo Bay is outside the territory of the US, the ICCPR does not apply there. Each attack is discussed in turn.

The doctrine of *lex specialis* is used to resolve a conflict between two rules of international law, namely, that the more particular rule should predominate over the more general rule. Summarizing the thoughts of renowned international law scholars Grotius and Vattel, one commentator explains the raison d'être of *lex specialis*: "(i) the special norm is [the] more effective or precise norm, allowing for fewer exceptions . . . and (ii) because of this, the special norm reflects more closely, most precisely and/or strongly the consent or expression of will of the states in question."[67] The Geneva Conventions of 1949 have been ratified by all 192 UN member states. The ICCPR and the CAT have been ratified by 167 and by 147 states, respectively. The ultimate question is whether, under the facts here, the special norms of the Geneva Conventions and other humanitarian conventions "more closely, more precisely [or more] strongly" reflect the "consent or expression of will" of these states parties than do the states parties' assent to the ICCPR and the CAT.

The most cited authority on *lex specialis* in this context is the International Court of Justice's 1996 opinion on the *Legality of the Threat or Use of Nuclear Weapons*.[68] That case was dealing with the following question: "Is the threat or use of nuclear weapons in any circumstance permitted under international law?" In the course of that opinion, the Court discussed *lex specialis* and the relationship between human rights law and humanitarian law during an armed conflict:

> The Court observes that the protection of the International Covenant of Civil and Political Rights does *not* cease in times of war, except by oper-ation of Article 4 of the Covenant whereby certain provisions *may be derogated from* in a time of national emergency. Respect for the right to life is not, however, such a provision. In principle, the right not *arbitrar-ily* to be deprived of one's life applies also in hostilities. The test of what is an arbitrary deprivation of life, however, then falls to be determined by the applicable *lex specialis*, namely, the law applicable in armed conflict which is designed to regulate the conduct of hostilities.[69]

The Court is referring to Article 6.1 of the ICCPR, which states, "No one shall be *arbitrarily* deprived of his life."[70] Consequently, under humanitarian law a uniformed soldier may purposely kill an enemy combatant during armed conflict. Such a killing during armed conflict is not "an arbitrary[] depriv-ation[] of . . . life" under Article 6.1. The Court also observes, however, that the ICCPR's protections "do[] not cease in times of war except by operation of Article 4 of the Covenant whereby certain provisions may be derogated from in time of national emergency." Most notably, Article 4 makes Article 7 of the Covenant non-derogable. Consequently, the obligation to refrain from torture *or* from inflicting "cruel, inhuman or degrading treatment" likewise "does not cease in times of war."

Such an obligation appears particularly apt under the circumstances here. Although the Bush–Cheney administration claimed that it did not torture and claimed that as a matter of policy (not as a matter of legal obligation) it was according the detainees the principle of "humanity," the practices of the administration belied these claims. Given the administration's position that the detainees lay outside the protection of the Geneva Conventions, it should properly be held to the non-derogable duties of Article 7 of the ICCPR. Other commentators have supported this position by noting that the ICCPR and the official Human Rights Committee interpretations and monitoring of the Covenant have produced a far more detailed jurisprudence on the mode and conditions of confinement to which a state may subject detainees. Consequently, human rights law is far more specific in this area than humanitarian law itself. Furthermore, it is hard to claim that the states' parties to the Geneva Conventions and to the ICCPR would have agreed that the special interpretation the administration made of the Geneva Conventions "reflects more closely, most precisely and/or strongly the consent or expression of will of the states in question" than does Article 7 of the ICCPR.

The second attack on the applicability of human rights treaties to detainees in Guantánamo Bay rests on the claim that human rights treaties apply only within a state party's own territory and do not extend beyond a state's own borders, regardless of the degree of control the state may be exercising on foreign soil. Article 2.1 of the ICCPR states as follows: "Each State Party to the present Covenant undertakes to respect and to ensure to all individuals *within its territory and subject to its jurisdiction* the rights recognized in the present Covenant. . . ." Relying on the strict conjunctive interpretation of "within its territory *and* subject to its jurisdiction," the US Government, in a reply to a United Nations Refugee Report, stated, "[T]his Article establishes that States Parties are required to ensure the rights in the Covenant only to individuals who are both *within* the territory of a State Party *and* subject to that State Party's sovereign authority."[71] The reply also relies upon apparently compelling *travaux préparatoires* (drafting history provided in the previous endnote) of the ICCPR.

The authoritative Human Rights Committee rejected the US's position, reasoning in part that some members of the UN General Assembly were concerned that excising the "within its territory" language might suggest that states have the authority to take military action in other states. The UN Committee on Human Rights has held that state agents traveling to another state to kidnap an individual and bring him or her back to the home state violate the ICCPR, reasoning that the abducted individual has been, at all relevant times, within the sending state's jurisdiction and control.[72] The Committee has similarly ruled in a case in which the Uruguayan consulate confiscated a passport in German territory.[73]

Likewise, the International Court of Justice rejected the conjunctive interpretation in the Israeli Wall case: "[W]hile the jurisdiction of States is primarily territorial, it may sometimes be exercised outside the national territory. Considering the object and purpose of the International Covenant on Civil and Political Rights, it would seem natural that, even when such is the case, States parties to the Covenant should be bound to comply with its provisions."[74] The Court further reasoned that the Human Rights Committee analysis of the *travaux préparatoires* was correct in that "in adopting the wording chosen, the drafters of the Covenant did not intend to allow States to escape from their obligations when they exercise jurisdiction outside their national territory. They only intended to prevent persons residing abroad from asserting, vis-à-vis their State of origin, rights that do not fall within the competence of that State, but of that of the State of residence."[75]

Furthermore, Manfred Nowak in his highly respected commentary on the ICCPR also expressed concern that such an approach could undermine the purpose of the ICCPR:

> When States Parties, however, take actions on foreign territory that violate the rights of persons subject to their sovereign authority, it would be *contrary to the purpose* of the Covenant if they could not be held responsible.[76]

It is 60 years since the Universal Declaration on Human Rights was unanimously adopted, over 50 years since the *travaux* the US relies upon were created, and over 40 years since the ICCPR was concluded. In that time, the world community has undergone a human rights revolution. (See chapter 6, for a more detailed discussion of the human rights revolution.) It is not tenable for the US to continue to maintain that its human rights obligations stay at home while its armed forces go abroad.

Furthermore, the highest court of the US noted in *Rasul v. Bush*, decided in 2004, that Guantánamo Bay is "a territory over which the United States exercises plenary and exclusive jurisdiction, but not 'ultimate sovereignty.' "[77] The Court ruled that those held in Guantánamo Bay had a right to pursue habeas corpus petitions in the US federal court, implicitly rejecting the Bush–Cheney administration's attempt to place the detainees in a largely law-free zone. Two years later, in *Hamdan v. Rumsfeld*, the Court rejected the President's executively created military commissions to try Guantánamo Bay detainees. In 2008, in *Boumediene v. Bush*, the Court noted that Guantánamo Bay "is no transient possession. In every practical sense Guantánamo is not abroad; it is within the constant jurisdiction of the United States."[78] The *Boumediene* Court held that the US Constitution applied to Guantánamo Bay and the detainees imprisoned there, and concluded that Congress had unconstitutionally attempted to suspend the right of habeas corpus.[79]

Although the United States Supreme Court was not deciding the precise issue here, namely, whether the ICCPR applies extraterritorially, its holding mirrors that of the Human Rights Committee and the ICJ, that for all practical purposes, Guantánamo Bay is the territory of the US, and therefore federal statutes and the US Constitution apply there. Concluding that the ICCPR applies there follows directly from the analysis finding Guantánamo Bay to be the functional equivalent of US territory.[80] Furthermore, the District Court for the District of Columbia held in 2009 that detainees brought from abroad to Bagram Air Base in Afghanistan have a right to habeas corpus in a United States federal court.[81] Again, this decision was based not on the ICCPR, but on Congressional enactment and the US Constitution, but it nevertheless suggests a broader interpretation of foundational instruments is called for.

The legal memos from the Department of Justice reveal a similar argument concerning the applicability of Article 16 of the UN Convention against Torture. That Article prohibits cruel, inhuman, or degrading treatment: "Each State Party shall undertake to prevent *in any territory under its jurisdiction* other acts of cruel, inhuman or degrading treatment or punishment which do not amount to torture . . . when such acts are committed [by or with the acquiescence of public officials.]"[82] Steven Bradbury, Assistant Attorney General with the Justice Department, in a secret memo to John Rizzo, the Senior Deputy General Counsel of the CIA, argued in 2005 that Article 16 did not apply to the CIA black sites, because they were outside the territory of the US and thus not "in any territory under [US] jurisdiction." The drafting history of Article 16 suggests a broader interpretation than that for which Bradbury argues. The first draft of the Article made the convention applicable to treatment "within [the party's] jurisdiction." Arguing that this language might apply to a state's own nationals residing in another country, France proposed the language "in any territory under its [the party's] jurisdiction." That language was ultimately adopted, and at the conference "it was stressed that 'any territory under its jurisdiction' would also cover torture inflicted aboard ships, aircrafts, and *in occupied territories.*"[83]

Although not fully supported by plain meaning analysis, the Committee against Torture has interpreted this language as applying to any place where the state has effective control. But one does not necessarily have to resort to such an interpretation. First, Congress has implicitly endorsed the extraterritorial application of the Torture Convention. The Torture Statute, enacted to fulfill US obligations under the CAT, applies *only* to acts of torture committed outside the territory of the US.[84] True, the Torture Statute only criminalizes torture, not cruel, inhuman and degrading treatment. Article 2.1 of the CAT, however, requires states "to prevent acts of torture *in any territory under its jurisdiction,*" thus using the same language concerning scope as Article 16. Secondly, the US created the extraterritorial detention centers. Centers in Iraq and Afghanistan, which the US had occupied, fall directly under the plain meaning and under the drafting history. The CIA black sites and Guantánamo Bay, the US established deliberately to avoid the reach of US courts and perhaps international law. Neither international law nor domestic law can permit a state party to avoid its domestic or international obligations by employing such an obvious artifice.[85] Lastly, as was noted above, the Supreme Court has concluded that US federal courts have the jurisdiction to hear habeas corpus petitions from Guantánamo Bay, and, for the reasons discussed above, the human rights treaties, including the Torture Convention, apply there and elsewhere.[86]

3.7 Other possible objections

In giving its advice and consent to the ICCPR, the Senate attached a reservation. A reservation is kind of a condition that departs from the exact language of the treaty text. When a country (generally called a State in international law analysis) puts a reservation on a multilateral treaty, it is saying we agree with everything in the treaty except. . . . If the reservation cuts the heart out of the treaty ("is incompatible with the object and purpose of the treaty"), then the reservation could be considered invalid. If most of the parties (other countries) to the treaty object to the reservation, it likewise could be considered invalid. Otherwise, the reservation stands and constitutes part of that state's agreement under international law.

The US Senate attached the following reservation regarding Article 7 of the ICCPR: "That the United States considers itself bound by Article 7 to the extent that 'cruel, inhuman or degrading treatment or punishment' means the cruel and unusual treatment or punishment *prohibited by the Fifth, Eighth and/or Fourteenth Amendments* to the Constitution of the United States."[87] The US probably had a good reason to attach such a reservation. Although the meaning of "torture" is somewhat clear, the type of behavior that rises to the level of "cruel, inhuman or degrading treatment or punishment" is far from it. Some might argue that imprisoning a human being is itself degrading, if not inhuman. But imprisonment alone surely could not satisfy the "cruel, inhuman or degrading" standard unless the imprisonment was grossly disproportional to the offense committed.

So we have to first determine what types of treatment or punishment of prisoners American courts have declared to violate the Fifth, Eighth, or Fourteenth Amendments. Then we can determine whether any of the conduct implicitly approved in treating prisoners in Afghanistan, Iraq, or Guantánamo Bay violates the US obligations under Article 7 of the ICCPR. Federal cases suggest that the treatment of the detainees would constitute a violation of these Amendments. The US Supreme Court has expressly stated that prison officials have the obligation under the Eighth Amendment to the US Constitution to treat prisoners humanely.

The Constitution "does not mandate comfortable prisons,"[88] but neither does it permit inhumane ones, and it is now settled that "the treatment a prisoner receives in prison and the conditions under which he is confined are subject to scrutiny under the Eighth Amendment."[89] In its prohibition of "cruel and unusual punishments," the Eighth Amendment places restraints on prison officials, who may not, for example, use excessive physical force against prisoners.[90] The Amendment also imposes duties on these officials, who must provide humane conditions of confinement; prison officials must ensure that inmates receive adequate food, clothing, shelter, and medical care, and must "take reasonable measures to guarantee the safety of the inmates."[91]

In *Helling v. McKinney*,[92] the US Supreme Court held that a prisoner may sue a prison under the Eighth Amendment for failing to accommodate his request for a smoke-free environment, given the likelihood of his suffering future ill health effects. In *Hudson v. Palmer*, the Court allowed a prisoner suit against prison officials who failed to prevent his beating and rape by another inmate. In *Wilson v. Seiter*,[93] Justice Scalia posits a hypothetical relevant to the actual treatment that some Guantánamo detainees received:

> *Some* conditions of confinement may establish an Eighth Amendment violation "in combination" when each would not do so alone, but only when they have a mutually enforcing effect that produces the deprivation of a single, identifiable human need such as food, warmth, or exercise— for example, a low cell temperature at night combined with a failure to issue blankets.[94]

Much of the debate in the Supreme Court on this issue has centered on the culpable mental state of prison officials, namely, on the one hand, whether they intentionally or recklessly deprived prisoners of humane conditions, or, on the other hand, whether these officials were just negligent or careless. For example, Justice Scalia quotes with approval Judge Richard Posner's statement:

> The infliction of punishment is a deliberate act intended to chastise or deter. This is what the word means today; it is what it meant in the eighteenth century. . . . [I]f [a] guard accidentally stepped on [a] prisoner's toe and broke it, this would not be punishment in anything remotely like the accepted meaning of the word, whether we consult the usage of 1791, or 1868, or 1985."[95]

The evidence suggests that US officials acted intentionally and with premeditation in treating the detainees in the manner set forth above. Each of the interrogation practices is set forth in the prescribed training manuals, up to and including waterboarding. The Secretary of Defense expressly approved most of the harsh interrogation techniques. The sexual humiliation that was fostered on Abu Ghraib detainees was thought up by psychologists on retainer from the Pentagon.

Justice Scalia's hypothetical indicates that failing to heat and to supply blankets to a cold prison would amount to an Eighth Amendment violation. In Guantánamo Bay, at least some detainees were put in a room where the air conditioning was deliberately set on the coldest level, the detainees were deliberately stripped naked, were deliberately strapped in chairs in uncomfortable positions, and were deliberately left in these conditions for hours. The government's conduct here far surpasses in severity the treatment that Justice Scalia indicated would violate the Eighth Amendment. In conclusion, the US official policies and practices violated Article 7 of the International Covenant on Civil and Political Rights, which forbids subjecting anyone to cruel, inhuman, or degrading treatment.

Bush–Cheney administration lawyers argued, however, that the enhanced interrogation techniques were justified by dire necessity, namely, US national security. Such necessity was absent from the above-cited cases dealing with violations of the Eighth Amendment in domestic prison cases. These attorneys argued that the US Supreme Court would have reached a different result in the above-mentioned cases had national security been at stake: "It is this paramount interest [the security of the nation] that the Government seeks to vindicate through [the] interrogation program."[96] As appealing at first glance as this argument is, it must be rejected. Article 4 of the ICCPR makes Article 7 non-derogable. Recall that Article 7 prohibits torture and cruel, inhuman, and degrading treatment. Article 4 permits states in "times of public emergency which threaten the life of the nation" to derogate from certain obligations but prohibits any derogation from Article 7. For the Bush–Cheney administration to argue that in essence because the life of the nation was threatened, it had the necessity or the right to engage in cruel, inhuman, or degrading treatment, undermines Article 4. A reservation that is "incompatible with the object and purpose of the treaty" is invalid.[97] Those Articles from which a nation State may never derogate under the ICCPR are peremptory norms, namely, super-norms. Interpreting the reservation as the Bush–Cheney attorneys do subverts the "object and purpose" of the ICCPR, rendering the reservation invalid.

Consequently, since the UK could not prevail in claiming that its rough interrogation methods in Northern Ireland comported with international law, it is unsurprising that the US, which used considerably harsher methods, has suffered a similar judgment.

Notes

1   The 1921 treaty, however, did not accord Ireland the status of an independent republic, but rather gave it dominion status like that of Canada. The treaty also required a pledge of loyalty to the Crown, conditions along with partition that led to a short Irish civil war. *See* J. Bowyer Bell, The Secret Army, The IRA, 1916–1979 at 30 (1989); Tim Pat Coogan, The IRA 27–31 (2002). According to a 1911 census although Protestants outnumbered Catholics in Ulster 891,000 to 691,000, Catholics were in the majority in some of the Ulster counties. Joseph J. Lee, Ireland, 1912–1985 at 2 (1989) (citing 1911 Census of Ireland).

2   The labels Catholic and Protestant might suggest that this was a religious struggle, but religious doctrine played little or no role. The labels more appropriately refer to differences akin to nationality. Furthermore, I do not mean to suggest that either the Catholic or the Protestant population has or had been monolithic. There were large numbers of Protestants who strongly disagreed with the discriminatory policies of the government of Northern Ireland and with the violent tactics of the Protestant paramilitaries, and there were large numbers of Catholics who strongly disagreed with Sinn Fein and with the bloody tactics of the IRA. *See, e.g.*, Hurst Hannum, Autonomy, Sovereignty, and Self-Determination 232 (rev. edition 1990).

3   Ed Moloney, A Secret History of the IRA xv (2002).

4   Hannum, *supra* note 2, at 232.

5   *Id.*

6   Moloney, *supra* note 3, at 353. Ireland v. United Kingdom, 25 Eur. Ct. H.R. (ser. A), para. 19 (1978), *available at* http://cmiskp.echr.coe.int/tkp197/view.asp?key=13921&table=F69A27FD8FB86142BF01C1166DEA398649&portal=

hbkm&action=prof&source=external-click&highlight=&sessionid=
21815621&skin=hudoc-en.

7   Hannum, *supra* note 2, at 232; *see also* Lee, *supra* note 1, at 60. *See also* Ireland v.
     United Kingdom, 25 Eur. Ct. H.R. (ser. A) at para. 19.
8   Moloney, *supra* note 3, at 62.
9   Coogan, *supra* note 1, at 333; Moloney, *supra* note 3, at 62.
10   Moloney, *supra* note 3, at 7.
11   Coogan, *supra* note 1, at 343. *See also* Lee, *supra* note 1, at 438.
12   *See* Ronald J. Terchek, *Conflict and Cleavage in Northern Ireland*, 433 Annals. Am.
     Acad. Pol. & Soc. Sci. 47, 49–50 (1977) ("Catholic agitation began to inten-
     sify and culminated in the 1968 Civil Rights Protests that met hostile and
     violent Protestant crowds. Shortly afterwards, the protests were superseded by
     rioting in the Catholic communities, the arrival of the British Army, and the
     formation of the Provisional faction of the IRA who were more militant than the
     class-oriented Official faction. Protestant paramilitary groups such as the Ulster
     Defense Association (UDA) and the Ulster Volunteer Force (UVF) were also
     increasing in strength and determination.").
13   Bell, *supra* note 1, at 380.
14   Lee, *supra* note 1, at 60. It should be noted that the Republic of Ireland also
     engaged in internment in 1939 and in 1957, interning more than 500 sus-
     pected members of the IRA. *Id.* at 223.
15   Ireland v. United Kingdom, 25 Eur. Ct. H.R. (ser. A), para. 35.
16   The European Court of Human Rights ruled that although not amounting to
     "torture," this conduct by the British authorities did "constitute[ ] a practice of
     inhuman and degrading treatment . . . in breach of Article 3 [of the European
     Convention on Human Rights and Fundamental Freedoms]." Ireland v. United
     Kingdom, 25 Eur. Ct. H.R. (ser. A), paras. 86, 168.
17   Coogan, *supra* note 1, at 439 (quoting Kevin Hannay, "one of the hooded men
     and like his father Liam a life-long Republican").
18   See Ireland v. United Kingdom, supra note 6, at para. 69 (noting that 63 of 65
     Catholics were released the day before Christmas in 1973).
19   *See* Michael P. O'Connor & Celia M. Rumann, *Into the Fire: How to Avoid Getting
     Burned by the Same Mistakes Made Fighting Terrorism in Northern Ireland*, 24 Car-
     dozo L. Rev 1680 (2003); *see also Frontline: Behind the Mask: The IRA and Sinn
     Fein* (PBS television broadcast, Oct. 21, 1997) *available at* www.pbs.org/ wgbh/
     pages/frontline/shows/ira/conflict/, [hereinafter *Frontline: Behind the Mask*]
     (quoting the Northern Ireland Chief of Police, who described the internment
     policy as "a disaster"), summary. *See also* Lee, *supra* note 1, at 437.
20   Thomas M. McDonnell, *The Death Penalty: An Obstacle to the "War against Terror-
     ism"?*, 37 Vand. J. Transnat'l L. 353, 400 n.218 (2004) (quoting *Frontline: Behind
     the Mask, supra* note 19); *see also* Paul Powers, *Civil Protest in Northern Ireland*, 9 J.
     Peace Res. 224 (1972), ("Internment without trial of suspected or actual minor-
     ity revolutionaries in August 1971 opened the final phase of the recent chapter.
     This phase featured the appearance of a sharply increased alienation of the
     minority from the regime, a further rise in desperate IRA violence, British
     paratroop repression of civilian protesters, active diplomacy by the Irish Repub-
     lic, a revival of civil disobedience, Ultra threats of counter-revolution, and the
     shift of British party politics to demand or accept a new governmental policy
     toward Northern Ireland subsystem.").
21   David Johnston, *9/11 Congressional Report Faults F.B.I.-C.I.A. Lapses*, N.Y.
     Times, July 24, 2003, *available at* www.nytimes.com/2003/07/24/us/9–11-
     congressional-report-faults-fbi-cia-lapses.html.
22   *See* James Risen, *C.I.A.'s Inquiry on Qaeda Aide Seen as Flawed*, N.Y. Times, Sept.
     23, 2002, *available at* www.nytimes.com/2002/09/23/national/23INTE.html;

Neil A. Lewis, *Agent's Role in Inquiries Is Questioned*, N.Y. Times, May 26, 2002, *available at* www.nytimes.com/2002/05/26/politics/26FBI.html

23   Jim Hall, Op-Ed., *Paying the Price for Safety*, N.Y. Times, Feb. 23, 2005, *available at* www.nytimes.com/2005/02/23/opinion/23hall.html; *see also* Eric Lictblau, *F.A.A. Alerted on Qaeda in '98, 9/11 Panel Said*, N.Y. Times, Sept. 14, 2005, *available at* www.nytimes.com/2005/09/14/politics/14terror.html. *See also* National Commission on Terrorist Attacks Upon the United States, The 9/11 Commission Report (2004), *available at* www.9–11commission.gov/report/911Report.pdf [hereinafter The 9/11 Commission Report].

24   The 9/11 Commission Report, *supra* note 23, at 348.

25   *Id.* at 346–47.

26   David Johnston, *Threats and Responses: Intelligence; Lack of Pre-9/11 Sources Is To Be Cited as a Failure Of Intelligence Agencies*, N.Y. Times, July 17, 2003, *available at* www.nytimes.com/2003/07/17/us/threats-responses-intelligence-lack-pre-9–11-sources-be-cited-failure.html?sec=&spon=.

27   *See* Amy B. Zegart, Spying Blind: the CIA, the FBI, and the origins of 9/11 at 92–93 (2007); Rohan Gunaratna, Inside Al Qaeda: Global Network of Terror 96 (2002).

28   Former CIA Director, Colonel Michal Hayden, however, recently asserted that the US now does have sound human intelligence capability against terrorist organizations.

29   The plot to blow up 10 passenger planes from London to the US falls into this category; neither scanners nor security personnel at the airport would probably have been able to stop individuals who were allegedly planning to carry on board liquids disguised as soft drinks that, when combined, can cause a fire or an explosion to take down the aircraft. John Ward Anderson & Karen DeYoung, *Plot to Bomb U.S.-Bound Jets is Foiled*, Wash. Post Foreign Service, Aug. 11, 2006, at A1; *see also* Alan Cowell, *Britain Says Two Dozen Major Terrorist Conspiracies are Under Investigtion*, N.Y. Times, Aug. 8, 2006, at A8. "Actionable intelligence" beforehand brought down the alleged plot and resulted in the arrests of most of the alleged plotters.

30   "High value" prisoners are so denominated because "of the special intelligence they are believed to possess." Douglas Jehl, *The Struggle for Iraq; Some Iraqis Held Outside Control of Top General*, N.Y. Times, May 17, 2004, *available at* www.nytimes.com/2004/05/17/world/the-struggle-for-iraq-prisoners-some-iraqis-held-outside-control-of-top-general.html.

31   Jay S. Bybee, Assistant Attorney General, *Memorandum for William J. Haynes II, General Counsel, Department of Defense: Potential Legal Constraints Applicable to Interrogations of Persons Captured by US Armed Forces in Afghanistan* (Feb. 26, 2002), *in* The Torture Papers and the Road to Abu Ghraib 144 (Karen J. Greenberg & Joshua I. Dratel eds., 2005) ("As we explain below, the Self-Incrimination Clause (and hence *Miranda*) does not apply in the context of a trial by military commissions for violations of the laws of war.").

32   Geneva Convention Relative to Prisoners of War (Geneva III) art. 17, Aug. 12, 1949 6 U.S.T. 3316, T.I.A.S. No. 3364, 75 U.N.T.S. 135, Documents on the Laws of War 2511 (3d edition Adam Roberts & Richard Guelff eds., 2003) [hereinafter Geneva III].

33   Dick Mary, Parliamentary Assembly of the Council of Europe, Secret Detentions and Illegal Transfers of Detainees Involving Council of Europe Member States: Second Report 41, 46–47 (2007) (the report also holds many Western European countries complicit in the illegal transfer of detainees, including the United Kingdom, Germany, and Italy). *See also* Scott Shane, *C.I.A. to Close Secret Overseas Prisons for Terrorism Suspects*, N.Y. Times, Apr. 10, 2009, at A9.

34 *Short Shackling*, Nation Master Encyclopedia, www.nationmaster.com/encyclopedia/Short-shackling (last visited Sept. 15, 2010).

35 Dan Eggen & R. J. Smith, *FBI Agents Allege Abuse of Detainees at Guantánamo Bay*, Wash. Post, Dec. 21, 2004, at A01, *available at* www.washingtonpost.com/wp-dyn/Articles/A14936–2004Dec20.html.

36 *See* Memorandum to Valerie E. Caproni, Federal Bureau of Investigation Office of the General Counsel, Aug. 2, 2004, *available at* www.aclu.org/torturefoia/released/FBI_5053_5054.pdf. *See also* Joseph Margulies, Guantánamo and the Abuse of Presidential Power 132–133 (2006).

37 Margulies, *supra* note 36, at 133.

38 *See 60 minutes: Torture Cover-up?* (CBS television broadcast May 1, 2005), *available at* www.cbsnews.com/stories/2005/04/28/60minutes/main691602_page3.shtml.

39 *See* Margulies, *supra* note 36, at 17.

40 *See* Association of the Bar of the City of New York, Committee on International Human Rights, Committee on Military Affairs and Justice: Human Rights Standards applicable to the United States Interrogation of Detainees, www.abcny.org/pdf/HUMANRIGHTS.pdf.

41 *See, e.g.*, General David H. Petraeus, Report to Congress on the Situation in Iraq, (Sept. 11, 2007), *available at* www.defenselink.mil/pubs/pdfs/Petraeus-Testimony20070910.pdf; Damien Cave, *Militant Group Is Out of Baghdad, U.S. Says*, N.Y. Times, Nov. 8, 2007, *available at* www.nytimes.com/2007/11/08/world/middleeast/08iraq.html?ref=us (noting that by November 2007 murders in Baghdad were down 80%, and attacks using improvised explosive devices were down 70%, from their peak before the surge). *See also* Jeffrey Lee Meyers, *Iraq*, N.Y. Times, July 1, 2009 *available at* http://topics.nytimes.com/topics/international/countriesand territories/ iraq/index.html (noting that American troops had pulled out of Iraqui cities, the first part of a phased withdrawal, but remarking that "[v]ialence may have dropped precipitously, but only from the worst levels of the past years.").

42 *See, e.g.*, Department of Defense, Measuring Stability and Security in Iraq: Report to Congress, at iv (2009) *available at* www.defenselink.mil/pubs/pdfs/Measuring_Stability_and_Security_in_Iraq_March_2009.pdf (noting that "[a]lthough . . . security achievements are increasingly positive, they remain fragile" and that "insurgents still have the capacity to conduct high-profile attacks"); Campbell Robertson, *At Least 32 Die in a Wave of Violence Across Iraq*, N.Y. Times, Mar. 23, 2009, *available at* www.nytimes.com/2009/03/24/world/middleeast/24iraq.html?n=Top/News/World/Countries%20and%20Territories/Iraq (reporting on growing instability in northern Iraq).

43 The Schlesinger Report (Aug. 2004), *in* The Torture Papers and the Road to Abu Ghraib, *supra* note 31, at 912.

44 The CIA apparently also failed to hire enough Arabic, Farsi, Pashtu speakers. Douglas Jehl, *C.I.A. Reviews Security Policy For Translators*, N.Y. Times, June 8, 2005, *available at* http://query.nytimes.com/gst/fullpage. html?res=9402E0D61338F93BA35755C0A9639C8B63&pagewanted=all (noting that there is also a shortage of Farsi and Pashtu language speakers in the CIA).

45 The Schlesinger Report, *supra* note 43, at 909, 912.

46 *Id.* at 911.

47 *Id.*

48 *Id.*

49 Joe Stephens, *Secret World of U.S. Interrogation*, Wash. Post, May 11, 2004, at A01, *available at* www.washingtonpost.com/ac2/wp-dyn/A15981–2004May10?language=printer.

50 *See* Anthony Dworkin, *Army Investigation Reveals Wide Involvement in Bagram*

Deaths, Crimes of War Project, May 20, 2005, www.crimesofwar.org/onnews/news-bagram.html (quoting Tim Golden, In U.S. Report, *Brutal Details of 2 Afghan Inmates' Deaths*, N.Y. Times, May 20, 2007, *available at* www.nytimes.com/2005/05/20/international/asia/20abuse.html).

51   *See* Human Rights Watch, Enduring Freedom 43 (2004), *available at* www.hrw.org/reports/2004/afghanistan0304/afghanistan0304.pdf. After the Supreme Court ruled that the detention of prisoners at Guantánamo was subject to judicial review, the Bush administration began sending detainees to Bagram in an effort to avoid habeas corpus requirements. Jonathan Hafetz, *Guantánamo and the "Next Frontier" of Detainee Issues*, 37 Seton Hall L. Rev. 699, 700 (2007); Tim Golden, *Bagram Detention Center*, N.Y. Times, *available at* http://topics.ny-times.com/top/reference/timestopics/subjects/b/bagram_air_ base_afghanistan/index.html (last updated April 2, 2009). However, on April 2, 2009, a federal District Court ruled that "Bagram detainees who are not Afghan citizens, who were not captured in Afghanistan, and who have been held for an unreasonable amount of time . . . without adequate process may invoke the . . . privilege of habeas corpus." Al Maqaleh v. Gates, 604 F. Supp. 2d 205, 235 (D.C. Cir. 2009). In Al Maqaleh, four detainees from Yemen, Tunisia, and the United Arab Emirates had been captured as far away as Thailand and Dubai, and held by US forces as "enemy combatants" for over six years.

52   One estimate by a former governmental official suggests about 100 detainees have died in US Detention Centers abroad, 20 to 30 of them being considered homicides by the military. *See* Daphne Eviator, *Defense Department Conceals Data on Detainee Deaths*, The Minnesota Independent, Sept. 10, 2009, *available at* http://minnesotaindependent.com/44233/defense-department-conceals-data-on-detainee-deaths#.

53   Action Memo, Office of the Secretary of Defense, Approved by Donald Rumsfeld (Nov. 27, 2002), *in* The Torture Papers and the Road to Abu Ghraib, *supra* note 31, at 237 (referring to Jerald Phifer, Request for Approval of Counter-Resistance Strategies, Department of Defense Joint Task Force 170, Guantánamo Bay, Cuba (Oct. 11, 2002) *in* The Torture Papers and the Road to Abu Ghraib, *supra* note 31, at 227–28).

54   All the approved Category II techniques are set forth here:

    (1) The use of stress positions (like standing), for a maximum of four hours;
    (2) The use of falsified documents or reports;
    (3) Use of the isolation facility for up to 30 days;
    (4) Interrogating the detainee in an environment other than the standard interrogation booth;
    (5) Deprivation of light and auditory stimuli;
    (6) The detainee may also have a hood placed over his head during transportation and questioning. The hood should not restrict breathing in any way and the detainee should be under direct observation when hooded;
    (7) The use of 20-hour interrogations;
    (8) Removal of all comfort items (including religious items);
    (9) Switching the detainee from hot rations to MREs;
    (10) Removal of clothing;
    (11) Forced grooming (shaving of facial hair, etc.);
    (12) Using detainees individual phobias (such as fear of dogs) to induce stress. *Id.*

55   The Torture Papers and the Road to Abu Ghraib, *supra* note 31, at 237 (reprinting the Action Memo signed by Donald Rumsfeld) (incorporating by reference Jerald Phifer, Request for Approval of Counter-Resistance Strategies, Department of Defense Joint Task Force 170, Guantánamo Bay, Cuba (Oct. 11,

2002), *in* The Torture Papers and the Road to Abu Ghraib, *supra* note 31, at 227–28).

56 Greenberg and Dratel, *supra* note 31, at 237 (reprinting the Action Memo signed by Donald Rumsfeld).

57 *Id.*

58 Tim Golden, *Years After 2 Afghans Died, Abuse Case Falters*, N.Y. Times, Feb. 13, 2006, *available at* www.nytimes.com/2006/02/13/national/13bagram.html? pagewanted= 1&_r=1.

59 *See* Protocol Additional to the Geneva Conventions of 12 August 1949, and relating to the Protection of Victims of International Armed Conflicts (AP I) June 8, 1977, 1125 U.N.T.S. 3, arts. 43(2), 51(5)(b). (Article 43 grants members of a party's armed forces "the right to participate directly in hostilities;" Article 53 allows the incidental killing of civilians unless that killing "would be excessive in relation to the … military advantage anticipated").

60 The Fourth Geneva Convention requires that all protected persons, which includes spies, saboteurs, and irregular combatants, "shall be treated with humanity." Geneva Convention Relative to the Protection of Civilian Persons in Time of War (Geneva IV), art. 5, Aug. 12, 1949 [hereinafter Geneva IV], 6 U.S.T. 3516, T.I.A.S. No. 3365, 75 U.N.T.S. 287.

61 Common Art. 3 expressly prohibits "cruel treatment and torture" and "outrages upon personal dignity, in particular humiliating and degrading treatment." Geneva III, *supra* note 32, art. 4.

62 Although the chapter focuses on treaty obligations, customary international law obligations are likewise applicable. *See* Restatement (3d) of Foreign Relations § 702; the Universal Declaration of Human Rights ("UDHR"); and the American Declaration of the Rights and Duties of Man, *available at* http://www.hrcr.org/docs/OAS_declaration/oasrights.html.

63 International Covenant on Civil and Political Rights, art. 7, Dec. 16, 1966, 993 U.N.T.S. 171, *reprinted in* 6 I.L.M. 368 (1967) (emphasis added) [hereinafter ICCPR].

64 *Id.*, art. 4(1).

65 *Id.*, art. 4(2).

66 Convention against Torture and other Cruel, Inhuman and Degrading Treatment, art. 3(2), Dec. 10, 1984, 1465 U.N.T.S. 85, *available at* www.hrweb.org/legal/cat.html [hereinafter CAT].

67 Joost Pauwelyn, Conflict of Norms in Public International Law 387 (2003).

68 Legality of the Threat or Use of Nuclear Weapons, Advisory Opinion, 1996 I.C.J. 226 (July 8).

69 *Id.* at 240, para. 25 (emphasis added).

70 ICCPR, *supra* note 63, art. 6.1 (emphasis added).

71 Reply of the Government of the USA to the Report of the Five UNCHR Special Rapporteurs on Detainees in Guantánamo Bay, Cuba, Mar. 10, 2006, at 29. The US government stressed that at the 1950 negotiating conference the US representative Eleanor Roosevelt proposed the "within its territory" language because the US was " 'particularly anxious' it not assume 'an obligation to ensure the rights recognized in it to citizens of countries under United States occupation.' "

72 Sergio Euben Lopez Burgos v. Uruguay, Comm. No. R.12/52, §12.3 (June 6, 1979), U.N. Doc. Supp. No. 40 (A/36/40), at 176 (1981), *available at* www1.umn.edu/humanrts/undocs/session36/12–52.htm; López Burgos v. Uruguay, No. 52/79; Lilian Celiberti de Casariego v. Uruguay, Comm. No. R.13/56, §10.3 (17 July, 1979), U.N. Doc. Supp. No. 40 (A/36/40), at 185 (1981), *available at* www1.umn.edu/humanrts/undocs/session36/13–56.htm.

73   Mabel Pereira Montero v. Uruguay, Comm. No. 106/1981, U.N. Doc. CCPR/C/
      OP/2 at 136 (1990), *available at* www1.umn.edu/humanrts/undocs/newscans/
      106–1981.html.
74   Legal Consequences of the Construction of a Wall in the Occupied Palestinian
      Territory, Advisory Opinion, 2004 I.C.J. 136, 179 (July 9).
75   *Id.*
76   Margaret Satterthwaite, *Rendered Meaningless: Extraordinary Rendition and the
      Rule of Law*, 75 Geo. Wash. L. Rev. 1333, 1363 (2007) (quoting Manfred
      Nowak, U.N. Covenant on Civil and Political Rights: CCPR Commentary
      41–42 (1993)).
77   Rasul v. Bush, 542 U.S. 466, 474 (2004).
78   Boumediene v. Bush, 128 S.Ct. 2229, 2261 (2008).
79   *Id.*
80   The Court was, however, notably silent about the reach of its opinions. For
      example, do Rasul and Boumediene also apply to detainees in Bagram Air Base
      in Afghanistan or to other detainees held around the world in US bases or
      detention centers?
81   Al Maqaleh v. Gates, 604 F.Supp.2d 205, 235 (D.C. Cir. 2009).
82   CAT, *supra* note 66, art. 16.
83   Manfred Nowak & Elizabeth McArthur, The United Nations Convention
      against Torture, A Commentary 116, para. 56 (2008).
84   *See* United States Torture Statute, 18 U.S.C.A. §§2340–2340A. Abraham D.
      Sofaer, the State Department legal advisor to the Reagan and later Bush Senior
      administrations, stated that "[t]he purpose of this reservation [the language
      equating cruel, inhuman and degrading treatment with violations of the Eighth
      Amendment to the US Constitution was to prevent any tribunal or state from
      claiming that the US would have to follow a different and broader meaning of
      the language of Article 16 than the meaning of those same words in the Eighth
      Amendment . . . . No evidence of which I am aware indicates that the reserva-
      tion was intended to enable the US to refuse to enforce Article 16 in any
      territory 'under its jurisdiction.'" Letter to Patrick J. Leahy, Committee on the
      Judiciary, from Abraham D. Sofaer, Jan. 21, 2005, Cong. Rec., S12382,
      Nov. 4, 2005. Hon. Sofaer introduced the proposed reservation to the Senate
      prior to giving its advice and consent to the CAT.
85   The five independent experts of the Commission on Human Rights rejected
      the United States' assertion that neither the ICCPR nor the CAT applied in
      Guantánamo Bay. In 2006, the CAT Committee reached a similar conclusion.
      See Nowak & McArthur, *supra* note 83, at 117, para. 57.
86   Furthermore, Article 10 of the CAT states as follows: "Each State Party shall
      ensure education and information regarding the prohibition against torture are
      fully included in the training of law enforcement personnel, civil or military,
      medical personnel, public officials and other persons who may be involved in the
      custody, interrogation or treatment of *any* individual subjected to *any* form
      of arrest, detention or imprisonment." (Emphasis added.) Article 16 makes
      Article 10, among others, apply also to cruel, inhuman, and degrading treatment.
      "[A]ny" individual subject to any form of arrest, detention, or impri-
      sonment would include those the US detains abroad in any detention center.
      Bradbury insists that Article 10 must be read together with Article 16, but doing
      so more strongly supports the Torture Committee's view, that the Convention
      reaches anywhere the state party has effective control, than the US position
      under the Bush–Cheney administration. *See* Steven Bradbury, Principal Deputy
      Attorney General, Office of Legal Counsel, U.S. Department of Justice, *Memo-
      randum for John A. Rizzo, Senior Deputy General Counsel, Central Intelligence Agency*,
      at 17 (May 30, 2005).

87 U.S. Reservations, Declarations, and Understandings, International Covenant on Civil and Political Rights, 138 Cong. Rec. S4781–01 (daily editions, Apr. 2, 1992) (emphasis added).

88 Farmer v. Brennan, 511 U.S. 825, 833 (1994) (citing Rhodes v. Chapman, 452 U.S. 337, 349 (1981)). The Bush–Cheney Justice Department argued that the Fifth Amendment "shocks the conscience" standard applies to pre-conviction mistreatment, not the Eighth Amendment. Yet it is noteworthy that Abraham Sofaer, the legal advisor to the Reagan and then Bush I administrations' State Departments spoke only of the Eighth Amendment when presenting the administration's proposed reservation to the Senate regarding the meaning of "cruel, inhuman and degrading treatment" of CAT, Article 16: "The reason for this reservation is straightforward. The formulation used by Article 16 is *ambiguous*, particularly in its reference to 'degrading treatment.' Of course, our own *8th Amendment* to the Constitution protects against cruel and unusual punishment . . . We would expect, therefore, that our Constitution would prohibit most (if not all) of the practices covered in Article 16's reference to cruel, inhuman and degrading treatment or punishment." Jamie Mayerfield, *Playing by Our Own Rules: How U.S. Marginalization of International Human Rights Law Led to Torture*, 20 Harv. Hum. Rts. J. 89, 125–26, n. 199 (2007) (quoting Convention Against Torture: Hearing Before the S. Comm. on Foreign Relations, 101st Cong. 11 (1991) (statement of Abraham D. Sofaer, former Department of State legal advisor) (emphasis added)).

89 Farmer, 511 U.S. at 833 (citing Helling v. McKinney, 509 U.S. 25, 31 (1993)).

90 Farmer, 511 U.S. at 833 (citing Hudson v. McMillian, 503 U.S. 1 (1992)).

91 Farmer, 511 U.S. at 833 (quoting Hudson v. Palmer, 468 U.S. 517 (1984)).

92 Helling v. McKinney, 509 U.S. at 35.

93 Wilson v. Seiter, 501 U.S. 294 (1991).

94 *Id.* at 304–305 (emphasis in original) (*comparing* Spain v. Procunier, 600 F.2d 189, 199 (9th Cir. 1979) (outdoor exercise required when prisoners otherwise confined in small cells almost 24 hours per day), *with* Clay v. Miller, 626 F.2d 345, 347 (4th Cir. 1980) (outdoor exercise not required when prisoners otherwise had access to dayroom 18 hours per day).

95 Wilson, 501 U.S. at 300 (quoting Duckworth v. Franzen, 780 F.2d 645, 652 (7th Cir. 1985), *cert. denied*, 479 U.S. 816 (1986)).

96 Steven Bradbury, Principal Deputy Attorney General, Office of Legal Counsel, U.S. Department of Justice, *Memorandum for John A. Rizzo, Senior Deputy General Counsel, Central Intelligence Agency*, at 29 (May 30, 2005).

97 *See* Vienna Convention on the Law of Treaties, art. 19(C), May 23, 1969, 1155 U.N.T.S. 331, *reprinted in* 8 I.L.M. 67, *available at* http://untreaty.un.org/ilc/texts/instruments/english/conventions/1_1_1969.pdf.

4 Torture heavy

A Navy Officer who was water boarded as part of survival training describes the technique as follows: "As the two men held me down [with my head lower than my legs], one [man] on each side, someone began pouring water onto the blindfold, and suddenly I was drowning. The water streamed into my nose and then into my mouth when I gasped for breath. I couldn't stop it. All I could breathe was water, and it was terrifying. I think I began to lose consciousness. I felt my lungs begin to fill with burning liquid. Pulling out my fingernails or even cutting off a finger would have been preferable. At least if someone had attacked my hands, I would have had to simply tolerate pain. But drowning is another matter."[1]

4.1 Introduction

After all that had come out about the US abuse of detainees, it did not inspire much confidence that the former US Attorney General, Michael Mukasey, claimed in 2007 that he did not know whether waterboarding to simulate drowning amounts to torture. Waterboarding attempts to produce the imminent fear that one is going to die by drowning, a fear exploited by torturers down through the ages.[2] Yet, at his nominating hearing, Mukasey, a distinguished federal judge, repeatedly insisted that he did not know the answer.

Mukasey's reluctance to call waterboarding torture might be explained by the revelation by ABC News and Associated Press (AP) that high ranking administration officials—Vice-President Richard Cheney, then National Security Advisor, Condoleezza Rice, former Secretary of Defense Donald Rumsfeld, former Secretary of State Colin Powell, former Attorney General John Ashcroft, and former CIA Director George Tenet—approved the CIA's use of waterboarding on so-called high-level detainees starting in 2002.[3] When Tenet was giving a graphic explanation of each interrogation technique to these high-level officials, Ashcroft reportedly objected, contending that high officials should only have to deal with broad questions of policy. Upon being subsequently questioned by Condoleezza Rice, Ashcroft reportedly agreed that the techniques, including waterboarding, were legal.

If these officials did, in fact, approve waterboarding,[4] they might be subject to criminal liability under both American law and international law. Recall that Britain's high court declared that Augusto Pinochet, Chile's former president, could properly be extradited to Spain for ordering that dissidents be tortured. The allegations against high Bush–Cheney administration officials might also explain the administration's insistence on provisions in the Detainee Treatment Act (DTA) of 2005 and the Military Commissions Act (MCA) of 2006, providing immunity from criminal or civil responsibility for those involved in the interrogation programs.

To be fair, the language of the DTA immunity provision seems to apply more to operational personnel and not necessarily to Bush–Cheney administration planners and policymakers.[5] Nevertheless, the ABC and AP reports indicate that high administration officials requested opinions from the Attorney General before expressly authorizing waterboarding and other "enhanced interrogation techniques." The infamous Bybee and Yoo memos, which are discussed below, take on added significance. Both memos apparently gave administration officials what they wanted. The MCA immunity provision states that "*{g}ood faith reliance on advice of counsel* should be an important factor, among others," to consider in granting immunity.[6] Did the Bush–Cheney administration have these memos in mind when insisting on the immunity provision?

Since the Nuremberg trials, and even more so since the end of the Cold War, individuals who commit war crimes or crimes against humanity face a small but greater risk that they will be subject to criminal or civil liability or both. Some scholars have specifically stated that the Justice Department Attorneys committed such crimes in issuing the opinions they did. In addition, more and more human rights organizations, including Amnesty International, Human Rights Watch, and the American Civil Liberties Union, have called for an investigation and prosecution of Bush–Cheney administration attorneys and high-level officials for war crimes and crimes against humanity. Despite President Obama's opposition to such investigations and prosecutions, there is increasing pressure, as of this writing, for at the very least a bipartisan investigation similar to the 9/11 Commission.

Whether or not the Bush–Cheney officials are ultimately prosecuted,[7] it is hard to deny that the US violated international law in the manner in which the US treated the detainees. As the previous chapter points out, the US had the obligation to ensure not only that the detainees were free from torture, but also to ensure that they were not subjected to "cruel, inhuman and degrading treatment." The Universal Declaration of Human Rights, Common Article 3 of the Geneva Conventions, Geneva Conventions III and IV,[8] the International Covenant on Civil and Political Rights, and the Convention against Torture all prohibit cruel, inhuman, and degrading treatment as well as torture. So one does not have to show that the administration tortured the detainees; it is enough to show that the Bush–Cheney administration authorized that the detainees be subject to such cruel, inhuman, and degrading treatment.[9]

Yet the Convention against Torture required the states parties to enact domestic criminal statutes punishing torture; it did not require the states to enact domestic criminal statutes to punish cruel, inhuman, and degrading treatment. Furthermore, Article 3 of the Torture Convention prohibits extraditing fugitives to states that torture. The prohibition does not extend to states that inflict "only" cruel, inhuman, and degrading treatment. The Justice Department, largely though highly technical legal argument,[10] dismissed the overwhelming treaty and customary international law prohibiting cruel and inhuman treatment. Rather, the Department fixed on the US Torture Statute,[11] which attempts to effectuate US responsibilities under the Convention; the Department failed to dispassionately examine the US obligations imposed by the Convention against Torture itself, by customary law, or by international law generally.

Before 9/11, most international law scholars would say that few principles of international human rights law were stronger than the prohibition against torture. Most of these scholars would agree that not only was the bar on torture established in treaty and customary international law, but that the bar had become a peremptory norm of international law, a "super-norm."[12] Torture is expressly prohibited by a vast array of post Second World War international instruments, including the following: the Universal Declaration of Human Rights (UDHR), the International Covenant on Civil and Political Rights (ICCPR), the Convention against Torture (CAT), the European Convention for the Protection of Human Rights and Fundamental Freedoms (European Convention), the four Geneva Conventions of 1949, the 1977 Protocols to the Geneva Conventions, the American Convention on Human Rights (ACHR), the American Declaration on the Rights of Man, the Convention on the Rights of the Child (CRC), the statutes of the ad hoc UN criminal tribunals, and the Rome Statute of the International Criminal Court.

Since the Second World War, a number of international institutions have arisen to monitor compliance with human rights, including the Human Rights Committee of the ICCPR; the Committee against Torture of the CAT; and the regional human rights regimes, namely: the Inter-American Commission of Human Rights, the American Court of Human Rights, the African Union Commission of Human Rights, and, most important of all, the European Court of Human Rights. One should add the ad hoc UN criminal tribunals and the ICC. Several non-governmental organizations have been formed that attempt to raise public awareness and public consciousness about this very basic human rights violation, for example, Amnesty International, Human Rights Watch, and the International Commission of Jurists. The International Committee of the Red Cross, one of the oldest and most respected non-governmental organizations, has continued to work to ameliorate the ravages of war and guarantee the rights of combatants and civilians in areas of armed conflict.

All the conventions prohibit a state from resorting to torture even during public emergencies such as war. Thus, the ban on torture is non-derogable.[13] One cannot deny that before 9/11 a large number of governments, particularly those from developing countries, tortured prisoners. Yet few countries, if any, would ever admit to doing so except by rogue agents[14] and virtually all agreed that torture violated international law.

Although former President W. Bush made it a refrain that the "United States does not torture," the leitmotif that the administration's memos, policies, and practices sounded have refuted that claim. The Bush–Cheney administration implicitly asserted that, yes, the US does torture and that, under the threat of transnational terrorism, torture and cruel, inhuman, and degrading treatment are justified or should be considered justified under international law. The US thus implicitly challenged the previously well-settled norm that torture was unlawful under all circumstances.

4.2 The CIA black sites

Less than a week after 9/11, the CIA sought and the President granted the authorization to establish secret prisons outside the US to interrogate particularly 'high value' members of al Qaeda and other suspected terrorists. Dana Priest states that "[s]ix days after the Sept. 11 attacks, President Bush signed a sweeping finding that gave the CIA broad authorization to disrupt terrorist activity, including permission to kill, capture and detain members of al Qaeda anywhere in the world."[15] The CIA apparently focused on establishing secret prisons to get "actionable intelligence" from the prisoners. The purpose of the program was to identify and capture the most dangerous al Qaeda members and to obtain relevant information from them to: (a) prevent future attacks; and (b) take down the terrorist organization. The sites were to be secret and to be beyond the reach of any US Court or any law generally, presumably including international law.[16] The CIA was authorized to engage in particularly harsh "enhanced interrogation techniques" (EITs) on such detainees, including the following, according to Dana Priest of the Washington Post:

> The EITs include "waterboarding," meant to simulate drowning, "water dousing," soaking detainees with water in cold rooms, prolonged stress and duress positions, liquid diets, sleep and light deprivation, noise and light bombardment, extreme isolation and other measures which are often used in combination with one another.[17]

Official legal memoranda provide additional detail on how the CIA treated its detainees. In the black sites, in addition to waterboarding, CIA interrogators used, among others, the following methods: the interrogators doused detainees with cold water from 20 minutes to an hour to bring the detainee two-thirds of the way toward hypothermia; made the detainee strip naked for long periods while making them aware that female interrogators would see the detainees nude; slammed detainees against so-called flexible walls "many times (perhaps 20 or 30) consecutively"; grabbed the detainee by the face, slapped him in the face, and slapped him in the stomach with the back of the hand; put them in dog-like crates; made the detainee stand in front of a wall for hours without moving; put the detainee in other uncomfortable stress positions; deprived the detainee of sleep for up to seven and a half consecutive days by having the detainee's hands chained to the wall or ceiling while standing on a stool to prevent him from reclining: "should the detainee begin to fall asleep, he will lose his balance and awaken, either because of the sensation of losing his balance or because of the remaining tensions of the shackles."[18] Those undergoing sleep deprivation, whether clothed or stripped naked, were made to wear a diaper. Assistant Attorney General Steven Bradbury explained its purpose: "The use of the diaper is for sanitary and health purposes; it is not used for the purpose of humiliating the detainee. . . ."[19]

The documents also reveal that Abu Zubaydah, as noted earlier, was waterboarded 83 times in August 2002 and that Khalid Sheikh Mohammed was waterboarded 183 times in March 2002. The CIA destroyed all videotapes of waterboarding. The legal opinions indicate that those subject to waterboarding were typically waterboarded numerous times over two-hour periods.

Apparently, the black sites were located in, among other countries, Afghanistan, Jordan, Poland, Romania, Thailand, and in a special facility at Guantánamo Bay Naval Base.[20] ABC reported that after sites in Eastern Europe were closed, a "North African country" agreed with the CIA to have a black site on its soil.[21] Priest notes that about 100 individuals had been interrogated at the sites, approximately 30 at a time. Detainees in such sites included, among others, Khalid Sheik Mohammed, said to be the mastermind of the 9/11 attacks, Ramzi bin al Shibh, said to be in charge of logistics, and Abu Zubaydah, initially thought to be a high ranking member of al Qaeda but now considered a relatively low level member. The CIA used both its own employees and contractors to conduct the "enhanced interrogation techniques."[22]

In 2007, the Bush–Cheney administration had claimed that approximately 10 al Qaeda operations were foiled because of the CIA's and other security services' efforts to gain actionable intelligence: "President Bush has said that 'this program has given us information that has saved innocent lives, by helping us stop new attacks.' He claims that it has contributed to the disruption of at least ten serious al Qaeda plots since September 11th, three of them inside the United States."[23] George Tenet and General Michael Hayden, past CIA directors, and former Vice-President Richard Cheney stated in 2009 that the US received valuable actionable intelligence through the black sites. Cheney justified the enhanced interrogation techniques, asserting that they "led to the arrest of nearly all al Qaeda members now in custody" and "were directly responsible for the fact that for eight years we had no further mass casualty attacks against the United States." On the other hand, former CIA Inspector

General John Helgerson contradicted Cheney's blanket assertion. Helgerson wrote the declassified but highly redacted 109 page 2004 report on the interrogation techniques at CIA black sites, saying: "We concluded, as the report states, that much valuable information came from the overall program. . . . After all I have seen, I can say that up to this day I do not know whether the particular interrogation techniques used were effective and necessary, or whether such information could be acquired using more traditional methods."[24] One of the FBI interrogators of Abu Zubaydah challenges the assertion that valuable intelligence was gained through harsh interrogation methods: "Some of the information that is cited in the memos—the revelation that Mr. Mohammed has been the mastermind of 9/11, for example, and the uncovering of Jose Padilla, the so-called dirty bomber—was gained from another terrorism suspect, Abu Zubaydah, by 'informed interrogation,' conducted by an F.B.I. colleague and me. The arrest of Walid bin Attash, one of Osama bin Laden's most trusted messengers, which was also cited in the 2005 C.I.A. memo, was thanks to a quick-witted foreign law enforcement officer, and had nothing to do with harsh interrogation of anyone. The examples [of misleading claims about the effectiveness of harsh interrogations] go on and on."[25]

4.3 Legal analysis of US obligations under the Convention Against Torture (CAT)

The CAT defines torture as follows: "[A]ny act by which *severe* pain or suffering, whether physical or mental, is intentionally inflicted on a person *for such purposes as obtaining from him or a third person information* or a confession, punishing him for an act he or a third person has committed or is suspected of having committed, or intimidating or coercing him or a third person, or for any reason based on discrimination of any kind. . . ." The Convention requires that the pain and suffering be carried out by a public official or with the consent or acquiescence of the same. The Torture Convention notes, however, that torture "does not include pain or suffering arising only from, inherent in or incidental to lawful sanctions."

The hard issue is determining what "severe" pain or suffering is. In Abu Ghraib, for example, the prisoners were subject to degrading and humiliating treatment—being stripped naked, forced to be part of human pyramids, forced to masturbate, forced to wear hoods over the faces, forced to come face-to-face with unmuzzled police dogs. But did these prisoners experience "severe" pain or suffering?

At least for this class of prisoners in Abu Ghraib, there does not seem to be a basis for claiming, in most of the cases, that they suffered *severe* physical pain. If anything, they might have experienced severe mental suffering. Webster's defines "severe" as follows: "Inflicting discomfort or pain hard to endure; sharp; afflictive; distressing; violent; extreme; as, *severe* pain, anguish, torture; *severe* cold."[26] One could certainly argue that the treatment these prisoners received qualified as "discomfort or pain hard to endure."

When giving its advice and consent to the Convention against Torture, the US Senate attached an understanding, defining what it took to be the meaning of torture under the Convention:

> That with reference to Article 1, the United States understands that, in order to constitute torture, an act must be *specifically intended* to inflict severe physical or mental pain or suffering and that mental pain or suffering refers to *prolonged* mental harm caused by or resulting from (1) the intentional infliction or threatened infliction of severe physical pain or suffering; . . . (3) *the threat of imminent death.* . . .[27]

In the Abu Ghraib case, the US could argue that the physical pain did not reach the level of 'severe' and that the 'mental suffering' did not reach the level of 'prolonged mental harm.' It is, however, certainly possible that some of the Abu Ghraib prisoners have become permanently psychologically scarred by what US officials did to them. Furthermore, the understanding indicates that the prisoner's mental suffering must stem from "the intentional infliction or threatened infliction of severe *physical* pain or suffering." Since the physical pain inflicted in most cases probably does not cross the 'severe' threshold, most of the Abu Ghraib prisoners probably cannot demonstrate that they were tortured.

An understanding is a party's interpretation; that interpretation may be incorrect.[28] Unlike a reservation, an understanding generally does not have immediate legal significance.[29] Putting it another way, "in theory understandings do not 'purport[] to exclude, limit, or modify [a] state's legal obligation.' Instead, interpretive declarations and understandings 'specify or clarify the meaning or scope attributed by the declarant to a treaty or to certain of its provisions.' "[30]

The United States' understanding appears to attempt to regain some of the arguments the US lost in negotiating the CAT. The drafting history of Article 1 of the Convention against Torture includes this proposal from the United States at the drafting conference:

> The United States, being of the opinion that torture is the most extreme form of acts of cruel, inhuman or degrading treatment, supported the inclusion of the notion of severity of pain or suffering, arguing that a requisite "intensity" and "severity" of pain or suffering was an inherent element of the offense of torture and proposing the language "*extremely* severe pain and suffering" as an alternative to mere "severe" pain and suffering as appeared in the original Swedish draft.[31]

The US's proposed language "*extremely* severe pain and suffering" was rejected and does not appear in Article 1 of the CAT. The US understanding appears to conflict with the plain language of Article 1 of the Convention against Torture. The language of the understanding requiring that mental pain or suffering "refer to prolonged mental harm" caused by "the intentional infliction or threatened infliction of severe physical pain or suffering" doubles up the actual requirement of Article 1. The Article does not require "prolonged" mental harm nor does the Article limit the manner in which severe mental pain or suffering may be inflicted. Some American soldiers are reported to have aimed an unloaded gun at a prisoner's head and pulled the trigger pretending to kill him. If the prisoner did not develop "prolonged mental harm," the soldiers would not have committed torture under the understanding, but they would be considered to have committed torture under the plain meaning of Article 1.

In negotiating the CAT, the United States also proposed a higher *mens rea* requirement, "preferring 'deliberate' and 'malicious' over 'intentional' ": "For the purpose of this Convention, the offence of torture includes any act by which *extremely* severe pain or suffering, whether physical or mental is *deliberately and maliciously* inflicted on a person by or with the consent or acquiescence of a public official."[32] This proposal was likewise rejected. The "specific intent" language in the understanding might be seen as an attempt to get in the backdoor what was initially denied the US at the negotiating conference.[33] That the US's understanding mirrors to a great extent US proposals that the conference rejected undercuts the legal validity of the understanding. Recall that, unlike a reservation[, an understanding may not "purport[] to exclude, limit, or modify [a] state's, legal obligation" under the Convention.

In defending the CIA's interrogation techniques, the legal memoranda do not focus on the CAT itself. Because the understanding is, at best, of questionable validity, US attorneys should have been more cautious in interpreting the understanding and the US Torture Statute, which essentially copies it. The starting point should have been not these two legal instruments, but Article 1 of the Convention. Severity should thus not be interpreted as "extremely severe." Likewise, the "prolonged mental harm" interpretation added to the Article should be considered suspect, and "specific intent" should be interpreted liberally.

Unsurprisingly, however, the Justice Department memos rely heavily on strict interpretations of "severe pain and suffering," "prolonged mental harm," and "specific intent." These strict interpretations were critical to the Department's justification of waterboarding as well as the other "interrogation techniques."

In formulating counterterrorism policy and practices, the administration relied little on the Department of State or even the Judge Advocate General (JAG) Corps, both of which have expertise and experience in international law.[34] Rather, the Bush–Cheney administration relied on the Justice Department attorneys whose expertise and experience generally rest in the prosecution of domestic crimes. It is hard to resist the conclusion that the administration did so because it liked what it was hearing from the Justice Department attorneys and disliked or distrusted Colin Powell's State Department and the JAG Corps.[35]

John Yoo, a young assistant US Attorney with the Justice Department's Office of Legal Counsel (OLC) and Jay S. Bybee, Assistant US Attorney and head of the (OLC), narrowly defined torture under the Convention against Torture and under the US Torture Statute: "We conclude that for an act to constitute torture as defined in Section 2340, it must inflict pain that is difficult to endure. Physical pain amounting to torture must be equivalent in intensity to the pain accompanying serious physical injury, *such as organ failure, impairment of bodily function, or even death*. For *purely mental pain* or suffering to amount to torture under [18 U.S. Code] Section 2340, it must result in *significant psychological harm of significant duration, e.g., lasting months or even years*."[36]

Furthermore, the crucial, long-held secret, Yoo–Bybee memo of August 1, 2002 asserted that "[e]ven if one were to parse the statute more finely to attempt to treat 'suffering' as a distinct concept, the waterboard could not be said to inflict severe suffering. The waterboard is simply a controlled acute episode, lacking the connotation of a protracted period of time generally given to suffering."[37] On the issue of inflicting mental suffering, Yoo and Bybee conceded that that "the waterboard constitutes a threat of imminent death."[38] However, they reiterated that "prolonged mental harm is harm of some lasting duration, e.g., mental harm lasting months or years." Reasoning that after waterboarding "relief is almost immediate" [and thus] ". . . [i]n the absence of prolonged mental harm, no severe pain or suffering would have been inflicted, and the use of these [waterboarding] procedures would not constitute torture within the meaning of the statute."[39]

Aside from defining torture narrowly, the Yoo–Bybee memo also concluded that a prosecutor would have an especially high burden in proving a torturer's intent. According to Bybee and Yoo, the "specific intent" requirement of the torture statute meant that the actor had to have the "precise" purpose of carrying out torture: "[K]nowledge alone that a particular result is certain to occur does not constitute specific intent."[40] Bybee and Yoo opined that "even if a defendant knows that severe pain will result from his actions, if causing such harm is not his objective, he lacks the requisite specific intent even though the defendant did not act in good faith."[41]

Assume, for argument sake, in the current context that a high CIA official ordered a CIA interrogator as follows: "I don't care what you do to him, get the actionable intelligence." Under the Yoo–Bybee test, that official would not be criminally responsible for torture. The high official could care less if the detainee were tortured and the victim might not have to be tortured. Consequently, the official did not have the "precise purpose" that the detainee be tortured. Yet the official knows to a high probability, if not to a practical certainty, that the detainee will be tortured. In any event, such an official should be held responsible for any torture that takes place.

The culpable mental state "specific intent" has been long criticized by the commentators, because of its chameleon-like character. The drafters of the influential Model Penal Code deliberately omitted the phrase from its culpability elements and it appears nowhere in the Code. In any event, a large body of case law concludes that "specific intent" is satisfied either when the actor acts purposely or when she knows to a "practical certainty" that a result would occur.[42] The drafters of the Model Penal Code essentially codified this case law in its redefinition of intent.

In the December 2004 memo replacing the Yoo–Bybee torture memo, the Office of Legal Counsel backed away from the Yoo–Bybee memo and quoted distinguished criminal law scholar Wayne LaFave on the meaning of specific intent:

> With crimes which require that the defendant intentionally cause a specific result, what is meant by an "intention" to cause that result? Although the theorists have not always been in agreement . . ., the traditional view is that a person who acts . . . intends a result of his act . . . under two quite different circumstances: (1) when he consciously desires that result, whatever the likelihood of that result happening from his conduct; and (2) when he knows that that result is *practically certain* to follow from his conduct, *whatever his desire may be as to that result.*[43]

The new memo relied on some broad comments from the Supreme Court in *United States v. Bailey:* "In a general sense, 'purpose' corresponds loosely with the common-law concept of specific intent, while 'knowledge' corresponds loosely with the concept of general intent. See *ibid.* [Model Penal Code § 2.02]; LaFave and Scott 201–202."[44] Unfortunately, the Court misapplied those two cited authorities, ignoring that "specific intent" can be satisfied by knowing to a practical certainty that the proscribed result will follow. Commendably, the memo notes contrary authority, namely, that "cases such as *United States v. Neiswender*, 590 F.2d 1269 (4th Cir. 1979), suggest that to prove specific intent it is enough that the defendant simply have 'knowledge or notice' that his act 'would have likely resulted in' the proscribed outcome. *Id.* at 1273." Nonetheless, the new memo appears to cling to the purpose prong.

Perhaps even more problematic is the new memo's adopting the Yoo–Bybee memo's use of "good faith" as a defense: "[I]f an individual acted in *good faith*, and *only after reasonable investigation* establishing that his conduct would not inflict severe physical or mental pain or suffering, it appears unlikely that he would have the specific intent necessary to violate sections 2340–2340A. Such an individual could be said neither consciously to desire the proscribed result, *see, e.g., Bailey*, 444 U.S. at 405, nor to have 'knowledge or notice' that his act 'would likely have resulted in' the proscribed outcome, *Neiswender*, 590 F.2d at 1273."[45]

This purported "good faith" defense appears to be a veiled mistake of law defense, which is rarely recognized. In analyzing this supposed defense, consider Assistant Attorney General Bradbury's argument in his memo to John

Rizzo, the Senior Deputy General Counsel to the CIA. Bradbury argues that although waterboarding causes an imminent threat of death, it does not cause "severe pain" or "severe suffering." Passing over the severe pain question for a moment, let us discuss severe suffering. The American Heritage Dictionary defines "severe" as follows: "1. Unsparing and harsh in treating others: *a severe taskmaster*. . . . 3. Extremely intense: *severe pain; a severe storm*."[46] It defines "suffer" as follows: "To feel or endure pain or distress," and "suffering" as "the act or condition of one that suffers."[47]

Feeling that one is drowning at a minimum amounts to "endur[ing] . . . distress." Inducing the feeling of drowning unquestionably produces an "extremely intense" reaction. Consequently, waterboarding produces "severe . . . suffering" under a plain meaning analysis. Yet Bradbury argued, like the Yoo–Bybee memo, that "enduring" distress had a time element, that waterboarding did not amount to severe suffering because one could not suffer in a minute or two; the "severe physical suffering" had to be "extreme in intensity and *significantly protracted*."[48] The dictionary definitions he cites give scant support to the "significantly protracted requirement." Likewise, the drafting history of Article 1 of the CAT does not support this interpretation. (Let us leave aside that Abu Zubaydah was waterboarded 83 times in a single month, which even Bradbury presumably would agree is "significantly protracted.")

An interrogator charged with committing torture could hardly defend by asserting that "well after investigating the degree of suffering waterboarding caused, I honestly investigated and concluded (in line with Bradbury's argument but independently of his legal opinion) that waterboarding did not amount to 'severe . . . suffering' because it only lasted a minute." The interrogator might challenge the statute for vagueness, but presumably he knew he was making the detainee feel he was drowning and that he might die. The interrogator's purpose was to make the victim feel he was drowning and he knew to a practical certainty that the victim would feel that way. That was the point of the procedure.

Whether, under the CAT, intentionally making a person experience the feeling of drowning causes "severe . . . suffering" albeit for a short span of time, is a legal question. The plain meaning and the purpose of the Convention provide an affirmative answer. The Justice Department's "good faith" defense resembles the so-called cultural defense, in which an immigrant claims that under his or her society's culture the proscribed conduct is lawful or at least not as serious an offense as United States law makes it. For example, "a young Laotian-American woman is abducted from her place of work and forced to have sexual intercourse against her will. Her Hmong immigrant assailant explains that, among his tribe, such behavior is not only accepted, but expected—it is the customary way to choose a bride."[49] Essentially, the assailant's defense is mistake of law, that he did not appreciate the gravity of these offenses in the US. Trial courts and prosecutors as a matter of discretion have often agreed upon plea bargains to lesser charges, recognizing that the culpability of the offender may be less than a similarly situated American offender. In the above-cited example, the kidnapper rapist received 120 days in jail.[50] Courts, however, have overwhelmingly rejected the cultural defense as a true defense to criminal liability.

In both the Hmong case and in the interrogator's, the defendants committed the acts necessary for the crime and purposely and knowingly committed those acts. So-called good faith about the applicability of an immigrant's cultural norms is not a defense in US courts; likewise, a so-called good faith belief that waterboarding did not amount to torture is not a defense either. In both cases, however, the defendants' "good faith" may mitigate the sentence or be the basis for a plea bargain to lesser charges as a matter of prosecutorial discretion.

Whether relying upon the legal advice of the assistant Attorney Generals provides a defense for those who carried out waterboarding is a different question. Even assuming for argument's sake that such reliance on the legal opinion of high-ranking federal prosecutors does constitute a defense for the individual interrogators (as well as for cabinet level officials who approved the techniques),[51] the underlying conduct of the interrogators remains torture within the meaning of the federal statute and the Convention. In a certain sense the reliance defense makes the initial Office of Legal Counsel's responsibility graver. But for the Office's approving of waterboarding and the other interrogation techniques, many of the abuses against detainees may never have been carried out.[52]

Yoo and Bybee (and Bradbury) would have had much more difficulty reaching the result they did if they applied the plain meaning of Article 1 of the CAT itself. Even under the understanding and statute, they engaged, as noted earlier in discussing Assistant Attorney General Bradbury's memo, in strained legal analysis. In contrast, the Committee Against Torture, charged with monitoring compliance with the CAT concluded that the following acts carried out by another country's government constituted not only cruel, inhuman, and degrading treatment under Article 16 of the CAT, but also torture under Article 1: "[R]estraining in very painful conditions, hooding under special conditions, . . . [playing] of loud music for prolonged periods, sleep deprivation for prolonged periods, threats, including death threats, violent shaking and using cold air to chill."[53] The Committee reasoned that these interrogation techniques amounted to torture: "This conclusion is particularly evident where such methods of interrogation *are used in combination*, which appears to be the standard case."[54] These techniques and their combination closely resemble the practice of the US, with the exception that more severe than any of the quoted techniques is waterboarding.[55]

In its treatment of another class of prisoners in the "war on terrorism," the US has admitted facts "that meet the restrictive definition of torture under the US understanding."[56]

4.4 Outsourcing torture

In 2003, CIA agents, apparently with the cooperation of the Italian police or Italian intelligence agents, abducted Abu Omar from Milan, put him on a CIA contracted plane in Ramstein, Germany, and eventually flew him to Cairo, Egypt. Omar was eventually released from Egyptian custody and claims he was tortured. (Egypt is known to use torture routinely as an interrogation technique.) Neither the US, nor Italy, Germany, or Egypt ever charged Omar with a crime; no Italian judge, US judge, German judge, or Egyptian judge ever reviewed his case. He was kidnapped from a Western democratic nation and brought to an authoritarian one, where the risk of his being tortured was high.

The Convention against Torture expressly prohibits such "extraordinary renditions": "No State Party shall expel, return ('refouler') or extradite a person to another State where there are substantial grounds for believing that he would be in danger of being subjected to torture." Although one might argue that Omar was not technically "returned" to Egypt, he was taken there apparently with the express purpose of being interrogated by Egyptian authorities who routinely use torture. Furthermore, the CAT details the kind of evidence that a government should consider before sending an individual to another country: In determining whether such "substantial grounds" exist, "the competent authorities shall take into account . . . the existence in the State concerned of a *consistent pattern of gross, flagrant or mass violations of human rights*."

The US Department of State Human Rights Reports for Egypt from 1999 to 2003 indicate that Egypt does engage in a "consistent pattern of gross, flagrant . . . violations of human rights." For example, the State Department's 2003 report says, "The security forces continued to mistreat and torture prisoners, arbitrarily arrest and detain persons, hold detainees in prolonged pretrial detention, and occasionally engaged in mass arrests. Local police killed, tortured, and otherwise abused both criminal suspects and other persons." The US Human Rights Reports are in agreement with the reports on Egypt from Amnesty International, Human Rights Watch, and the International Commission of Jurists.[57]

The Committee tasked to monitor state parties' compliance with the CAT interprets the "substantial grounds" clause as follows: "[T]the risk of torture must be assessed on grounds that go beyond mere theory or suspicion. However, the risk does not have to meet the test of being highly probable."[58] The US interpretation, set forth in its understanding, appears narrower: "Substantial grounds" for believing the surrendered individual would be in danger of being tortured exist "if it is *more likely than not* that he would be tortured." Given Egypt's human rights record and its reputation as a torture state, taking Omar to Egypt satisfies both the Committee's test and the "more likely than not" test, namely, that it was more likely than not that he would be tortured at the hands of Egyptian authorities.

The US has also apparently taken other suspected terrorists to states that torture, including Jordan, Tunisia, and Morocco.[59] Estimates of the number of extraordinary renditions exceed 100[60] persons.[61]

Extraordinary rendition violates other human rights treaties and may, depending on the circumstances, violate state sovereignty. Since the CIA had the cooperation of Italian law enforcement officials, the US may have had permission from the Italian authorities to operate on Italian soil. In that event, the operation would not have violated the sovereignty of Italy guaranteed by Article 2 of the UN Charter and by customary international law.

On the other hand, Italian prosecutors initiated a criminal prosecution against the Italian law enforcement officials involved in the operation and against the CIA officers who operated in Italy. As of this writing, the CIA officers are being tried *in absentia*. This unusual prosecution suggests that the US did not have formal permission to conduct the extraordinary rendition. If that is so, then the operation violated not only Omar's rights, but also Italy's state sovereignty.

Some extraordinary renditions can be considered "disappearances," a practice used by the Nazis, but perfected in Pinochet's Chile. The UN General Assembly Declaration on Enforced Disappearances defines them as follows: "[P]ersons are arrested, detained or abducted against their will or otherwise deprived of their liberty by officials of different branches or levels of government . . . followed by a refusal to disclose the fate or the whereabouts of the persons concerned . . ., thereby placing such persons outside the protection of law."[62] The United States did not usually disclose that it had detained and rendered the person to a foreign country.[63]

The horror of disappearances stem not only from the trauma to the individual disappeared, but also from the trauma to the disappeared individual's family. The individual is kidnapped and taken to a foreign place where he or she is tortured and often killed. The family often never finds out what happened to their loved one, whether he or she is alive or dead, whether he or she is hurt or physically well. The lack of closure keeps the wound forever open in the family's lives.

To this date, there have not been public reports of any death that has occurred as a result of extraordinary rendition. Yet, many renditions bear the earmarks of disappearances. Omar, for example, was kidnapped, taken to Germany, and then taken to Egypt where he or she was put in the hands of a state that routinely tortures. Neither Italy nor the US initially disclosed his whereabouts.

Note that extraordinary rendition is far more egregious than the conduct aimed at in the CAT, Article 3. That Article is aimed at typical extradition practice where a requested state is often indifferent as to what happens to the extraditee when he or she is returned to the requesting state. Article 3 wishes to ensure that requested states pay attention to what might happen when they extradite an individual to a state that tortures. Extraordinary rendition is much more deliberate and premeditated. The sending state's purpose in delivering the individual is for the receiving state to torture that person and to gather information thereby.

Aside from violating Article 3 of the CAT, extraordinary rendition violates a plethora of treaty and customary international law obligations. As David Weissbrodt and Amy Bergquist point out, the practice violates a series of Articles in the Universal Declaration of Human Rights. These include Article 3, which guarantees "life, liberty, and security of the person"; Article 5, which prohibits "torture and cruel, inhuman and degrading treatment"; Article 6, which guarantees the right of each individual "to recognition everywhere as a person before the law"; Article 8, which gives everyone "an effective remedy by competent national tribunals for acts violating fundamental rights . . ."; Article 9, which forbids "arbitrary arrest, detention or exile"; Article 10, which guarantees the right to everyone to "a fair and public hearing by an independent and impartial tribunal" for determining "fundamental rights"; Article 11(a), which grants the right "to be presumed innocent"; Article 13.1, which guarantees the right to "freedom of movement . . ."; Article 13.2, which guarantees the right of everyone "to leave any country, including his own, and to return to his country"; Article 14, which grants everyone "the right to seek and to enjoy in other countries asylum from prosecution." Most of these rights have crystallized into customary international law.

In addition to the customary law violations, intentionally delivering a person to a torture state violates a series of corresponding Articles in the ICCPR, namely Article 7, which prohibits torture and cruel, inhuman, or degrading treatment; Article 9.1, which guarantees everyone "the right to liberty and security of the person"; Article 9.2, which requires that anyone arrested be "informed, at the time of the arrest, of the reasons for his arrest and shall be promptly informed of any charges against him"; Article 9.3, which guarantees that anyone arrested "be brought promptly before a judge"; Article 9.4, which guarantees individuals detained a right to bring a petition for habeas corpus; Article 10, which provides that "all persons deprived of their liberty shall be treated with humanity and with respect for the inherent dignity of the human person"; Article 16, which requires that "everyone shall have the right to recognition anywhere as a person before the law"; and Article 22, which guarantees that "everyone shall have freedom of association with others."

Although ICCPR Articles 9 and 22 are derogable, the more important Articles for this issue, Article 7 and Article 16, are not. Article 4, the derogation Article, is intended to be limited in time and application, in any event. The bundle of rights that protect the individual from extraordinary rendition remains large, even in cases of public emergency.

Aside from the purely legal question, extraordinary rendition is immoral. Certainly, one can understand the utilitarian argument of the Bush–Cheney administration that given the enormity of 9/11, torturing individuals and using extraordinary rendition to do so is justified to safeguard Americans from another attack. Extraordinary rendition, however, is an example of Immanuel Kant's violation of a categorical moral imperative. It is using another human being only as an instrument: "Act in such a way that you treat humanity . . . always at the same time as an end and *never merely as a means*."[64]

Usually denied a lawful arrest, always denied a presentment of charges or a trial, the individual is no longer "recogniz[ed] [as] a person before the law."

Extraordinary rendition has the foul taste of a Pinochet disappearance. This evil practice stains the governmental officials who engage in it and America as a whole. Extraordinary rendition should never be used again. Yet the Obama administration is apparently continuing the practice. President Obama's Task Force on Interrogation and Transfer Policies has recommended that extraordinary rendition continue, but with stronger diplomatic assurances, a disappointing development considering the failure of diplomatic assurances to prevent torture in other cases.[65]

The US policies and practices routinely violated international norms against imposing cruel, degrading, or inhuman treatment. The available evidence indicates that the US, in some cases, has also violated its treaty and customary law obligations against directly subjecting any person to torture. The extraordinary rendition program violated almost innumerable human rights obligations, including the proscription against torture by farming out that task to other states. Yet shortly after 9/11, some legal scholars argued that the law should permit torture, at least in certain cases.

Notes

1   Richard E. Mezo, *Why It Was Called 'Water Torture,'* Wash. Post, Feb. 10, 2008, at B07.

2   Those that defend waterboarding as a legitimate interrogation technique note that it is quick and that it usually does not result in death, which by the way was the same rationale Nazi Germany intelligence officers gave to justify waterboarding and other forms of torture of Norwegian freedom fighters. As the chapter later develops neither custom nor the Convention against Torture requires that a technique be slow or that it be fatal to constitute torture.

3   Lara J. Jordan & Pamela Hess, *Sources says torture OK'd from Cheney down*, Daily Review (Hayward, CA), Apr. 11, 2008, *available at* 2008 WLNR 6954183; Jan Crawford Greenburg, Howard L. Rosenberg & Ariane de Vogue, *Bush Aware of Advisers' Interrogation Talks*, ABC News, Apr. 11, 2008, *available at* http://abcnews.go.com/TheLaw/LawPolitics/story?id=4635175&page=1. *See also Justice Department's Office of Legal Counsel: Hearing Before the Subcomm. on the Constitution, Civil Rights, and Civil Liberties of the H. Comm. on the Judiciary*, 110th Cong. (2008) (testimony of Steven G. Bradbury, Principal Deputy Assistant Attorney General, Office of Legal Counsel, U.S. Department of Justice), *available at* http://www.fas.org/irp/congress/2008_hr/olc.pdf (stating that the Bush administration allowed use of waterboarding by CIA, but defending the practice by asserting that no water entered the lungs of the individuals who were waterboarded). *See* Dan Eggen, *Justice Official Defends Rough CIA Interrogations*, Wash. Post., Feb. 17, 2008, at A03.

4   *See also* Mark Mazzetti, *Bush Aides Linked to Talks on Interrogations*, N.Y. Times, Sept. 25, 2008, at A14 (new documents reveal that then National Security Adviser Condoleezza Rice, then Attorney General John Ashcroft, then Secretary of Defense Donald Rumsfeld, and other high administration officials discussed the CIA's proposals to use harsh interrogation techniques on al Qaeda operative Abu Zubaydah in 2002.) Steven Bradbury's memorandum of May 10, 2005

relates what the CIA said to him about when waterboarding is used: "You have previously explained that the waterboard technique would be used only if (1) the CIA has credible intelligence that a terrorist attack is imminent; (2) there are 'substantial and credible indicators the subject has actionable intelligence that can prevent, disrupt or delay this attack'; and (3) other interrogation methods have failed or are unlikely to yield actionable intelligence." Steven Bradbury, Memorandum for John A. Rizzo, Senior Deputy General Counsel, Central Intelligence Agency, Re: Application of 18 U.S.C. §§ 2340–2340A to the Combined Use of Certain Techniques in the Interrogation of High Value al Qaeda Detainees, at 57 (May 10, 2005). The waterboarding of Abu Zubaydah, however, was apparently carried out against the wishes of the interrogators on the scene who had determined that he had already voluntarily furnished all the actionable intelligence he possessed. See the next chapter for a more detailed discussion.

5　The Detainee Treatment Act states in relevant part:

> (a) Protection of United States Government Personnel. In any civil action or criminal prosecution against an officer, employee, member of the Armed Forces, *or other agent of the United States Government who is a United States person, arising out of the officer, employee, member of the Armed Forces, or other agent's engaging in specific operational practices*, that involve detention and interrogation of aliens who the President or his designees have determined are believed to be engaged in or associated with international terrorist activity that poses a serious, continuing threat to the United States, its interests, or its allies, and that were officially authorized and determined to be lawful at the time that they were conducted, it shall be a defense that such officer, employee, member of the Armed Forces, or other agent did not know that the practices were unlawful and a person of ordinary sense and understanding would not know the practices were unlawful. *Good faith reliance on advice of counsel should be an important factor*, among others, to consider in assessing whether a person of ordinary sense and understanding would have known the practices to be unlawful. Nothing in this section shall be construed to limit or extinguish any defense or protection otherwise available to any person or entity from suit, civil or criminal liability, or damages or to provide immunity from prosecution for any criminal offense by the proper authorities.

Detainee Treatment Act of 2005, Pub. L. No. 109–148, § 1004 (2005) (emphasis added).

6　*See* Military Commissions Act of 2006, Pub. L. No. 109–366, § 1004(a) (2006).

7　Leaked portions of a preliminary ethics report written by the Justice Department under Eric Holder recommends that former Justice Department attorneys Bybee, Yoo, and Bradbury not be prosecuted. Their cases may be referred to bar associations for disciplinary hearings. David Johnston & Scott Shane, *Torture Memos: Inquiry Suggests no Prosecutions*, N.Y. Times, May 6, 2009, at A1, *available at* http://www.nytimes.com/2009/05/06/politics/06inquire.html

8　Common Article 3 of the Geneva Conventions, which the United States Supreme Court found applicable in Guantánamo Bay, uses somewhat different terminology, outlawing *inter alia* "cruel treatment and torture . . . outrages upon personal dignity, in particular, humiliating and degrading treatment." *See* Geneva III, *supra* note 32 in ch. 3, at art. 3. The Fourth Geneva Convention states that protected persons "shall at all times be humanely treated, and shall be especially protected against acts of violence or threats thereof and against insults and public curiosity." Geneva IV, *supra* note 60 in ch. 3, at art. 27. Furthermore,

Geneva IV states that "protected persons who are confined . . . shall during their confinement be humanely treated." *Id*. at art. 37.

9   *But see* Steven Bradbury, Memorandum for John A. Rizzo Senior Deputy General Counsel, Central Intelligence Agency, Re: Application of United States Obligations under Article 16 of the Convention against Torture to Certain Techniques that May be Used in the Interrogation of High Value al Qaeda Detainees (May 10, 2005) (arguing *inter alia* that the Convention only applies "in any territory under [the state's] jurisdiction" and does not apply to black sites in other countries over which the United States had de facto control and to which the United States deliberately transported the detainees presumably, in part, to create a legal black hole.).

10 *Id*.

11 18 U.S.C. § 2340 (2004).

12 *See, e.g.*, Restatement (Third) of Foreign Relations § 702 (1988).

13 *See* Convention Against Torture and Other Cruel, Inhuman or Degrading Treatment or Punishment, Dec. 10, 1984, 1465 U.N.T.S. 85, *reprinted in* 3 I.L.M. 1027. *See also* chapter 3, note 66 and accompanying text for additional discussion of those obligations that are not derogable.

14 Those that admitted to torturing would usually claim that the torture was unauthorized, that it was carried out by a rogue interrogator.

15 Dana Priest, *CIA Holds Terror Suspects in Secret Prisons*, Wash. Post, Nov. 2, 2005, at A01, *available at* www.washingtonpost.com/wp-dyn/content/Article/2005/11/01/AR2005110101644.html.

16 *Id*.

17 Dana Priest, *Detention and Interrogation*, Crimes of War Project, www.crimesofwar.org/thebook/detention-interr.html (last visited Sept. 23, 2010). Jane Mayer, *The Black Sites: A Rare Look Inside the C.I.A.'s Secret Interrogation Program*, The New Yorker, Aug. 13, 2007, at 47 (noting that detainees in the black sites were also placed in dog-like crates). For an official description of each EIT, see CIA Inspector General, *Special Review, Counterterrorism, Detention and Activities (September 2001–October 2003) (2003–7123–IG)*, May 7, 2004, at 15, http://luxmedia.vo.llnwd.net/o10/clients/aclu/IGReport.pdf.

18 Bradbury, *supra* note 9, at 13. In the Bybee memorandum of August 1, 2002, 11 days (or 264 hours) was the maximum that was said to be used to sleep deprive a detainee. The Bradbury memorandum of May 10, 2005, states that the maximum now is 180 hours (seven and one-half days), but after 8 hours rest, another cycle of sleep deprivation can begin. *Id*.

19 *Id*. at 14. A leaked 2007 confidential ICRC report notes, among other things, that all the detainees in the CIA black sites were held incommunicado in continuous solitary confinement, which ranged from 16 months to nearly four and a half years. ICRC Report on the Treatment of 14 "High Value" Detainees in US Custody, Feb. 2007, at 7, http://www.nybooks.com/icrc-report.pdf

20 Scott Shane, *CIA Closing Secret Overseas Sites for Terror Detainees*, N.Y. Times, Apr. 9, 2009, *available at* www.nytimes.com/2009/04/09/world/10detain.html?_r=1&hp; *see also* Priest, *supra* note 15.

21 Brian Ross & Richard Esposito, *Sources Tell ABC News Top Al Qaeda Figures Held in Secret CIA Prisons*, ABC News Dec. 5, 2005, http://abcnews.go.com/WNT/Investigation/story?id=1375123. This report may have referred to Jordan. ABC asserts that black sites began with the arrest of Zubaydah: "According to sources directly involved in setting up the CIA secret prison system, it began with the capture of Abu Zubaydah in Pakistan. After treatment there for gunshot wounds, he was whisked by the CIA to Thailand where he was housed in a small, disused warehouse on an active airbase. There, his cell was kept under 24-hour closed circuit TV surveillance and his life-threatening wounds were tended

to by a CIA doctor specially sent from Langley headquarters to assure Abu Zubaydah was given proper care, sources said. Once healthy, he was slapped, grabbed, made to stand long hours in a cold cell, and finally handcuffed and strapped feet up to a water board until after 0.31 seconds he begged for mercy and began to cooperate."

22   Noah Shachman, *Hayden Admits: Contractors Lead 'Enhanced Interrogations' at CIA Black Sites, Wired*, Feb. 2008 http://blog.wired.com/defense/2008/02/in-testimony-be.html (noting that CIA Director Hayden admitted in testimony before the Senate Foreign Relations Committee that the agency used contractors as well as its own employees to conduct the interrogations).

23   Mayer, *supra* note 17.

24   *See CIA should keep an eye on Pak{istani} nuke scientist, says Cheney*, Asian News International, Aug. 31, 2009, *available at* 2009 WLNR 16977104; *Ex-CIA Officer on Interrogation Report*, Der Spiegel, Aug. 31, 2009, *available at* http://www.spiegel.de/international/world/0,1518,646010,00.html. Furthermore, the Inspector General himself noted that waterboarding Abu Zubaydah provided "[redacted] additional [intelligence] reports." The CIA IG Report, however, fails to state that those reports apparently gave the CIA false leads. *See* Peter Finn & Joby Warwick, *Detainee's Harsh Treatment Foiled No Plots*, Wash. Post, Mar. 29, 2009, at A1. The Inspector General apparently accepted at face value the CIA's assertions that Abu Zubaydah was a top al Qaeda operative. CIA Inspector General, *Special Review, Counterterrorism, Detention and Interrogation Activities (September 2001–October 2003) (2003–7123–IG)*, May 7, 2004, at 3 n.4, *available at* http://luxmedia.vo.llnwd.net/o10/clients/aclu/IG_Report. pdf. Senior Government officials reportedly now characterize him as a jihadist travel agent or fixer, and possibly not even a member of al Qaeda. Abu Zubaydah apparently knew the key actors or at least who they were, and gave them up before he was waterboarded. Subjecting him to that measure apparently yielded little, if any, actionable intelligence. *See* Scott Shane, *Divisions Arose on Rough Tactics for Qaeda Figure*, N.Y. Times, Apr. 17, 2009, *available at* http://www.nytimes.com/2009/04/18/world/middleeast/18zubaydah.html?_r=1&   ref=global-home [hereinafter CIA Inspector General's Report]. The IG Report does note that the interrogation program, primarily of "high value detainees," yielded 3,000 intelligence reports. CIA Inspector General's Report, *supra*, para. 117. How accurate those reports are is subject to debate. *Compare* Michael Hayden & Michael Mukasey, *The President Ties His Own Hands on Terror*, Wall St. J., Apr. 17, 2009 *available at* http://online.wsj.com/Article/SB123993446103128041.html (arguing that coercive interrogation provided half the actionable intelligence the government obtained, noting that the "coercive interrogation of Abu Zubaydah" led to the capture of Ramsi bin al Shibh, which led to the capture of Khalid Sheik Mohammed, the alleged mastermind of 9/11), *with* Ali Soufan, Op-Ed, *My Tortured Decision*, N.Y. Times, Apr. 23, 2009, at A27. In this article a former FBI special agent, Ali Soufan, who had interrogated Zubaydah, noted that Zubaydah provided valuable intelligence before the harsh techniques were introduced in August 2002. Soufan implicitly criticized Captain Hayden and former Attorney General Mukasey for claiming that Zubaydah gave the information leading to the capture of Bin al Shibh, noting the latter was captured in May and Zubaydah was not waterboarded until two months later in August. Soufan also pointed out that waterboarding Zubaydah did not result in actionable intelligence. *But see* Peter Baker, *Banned Techniques Yielded 'High Value Information,' Memo Says*, N.Y. Times, Apr. 22, 2009 (quoting Adm. Dennis C. Blair, President Obama's Intelligence Director, "High value information came from interrogations in which those methods were used and provided a deeper understanding of the al Qa'ida organ-

ization that was attacking this country"). *See* chapter 5 for a more detailed discussion of this issue.

25   Ali H. Soufan, *What Torture Never Told Us*, N.Y. Times, Sept. 5, 2009 *available at* http://www.nytimes.com/2009/09/06/opinion/06soufan.html?_r=1&th&emc= th (former FBI interrogator of high value detainees criticizes claims that enhanced interrogation techniques worked and states that they actually hindered the uncovering of important intelligence). *See* chapter 5 for a more detailed discussion of this issue.

26   Webster's New International Dictionary of the English Language 2295 (2d edition unabr. 1947).

27   United States Reservations, Understandings and Declarations to the Convention against Torture, www1.umn.edu/humanrts/usdocs/tortres.html (emphasis added).

28   Unlike a reservation, another party's failure to object to an understanding has no legal effect. "It is important to bear in mind that, while an interpretative declaration that is not a reservation provides evidence of intention and understanding, it does not have the binding character of a reservation. Failure to object to another State's interpretative statement does not have any automatic legal effects." Richard Edwards, *Reservations to Treaties*, 10 Mich. J. Int'l L. 362, 372 (1989).

29   *Id.*

30   John Noyes, *The United States and the Law of the Sea Convention: U.S. Views on the Settlement of International Law Disputes in International Tribunals and U.S. Courts*, *available at* www.boalt.org/bjil/docs/Publicist01-Noyes.pdf (quoting Restatement (Third) of Foreign Relations Law of the United States § 313 cmt. G 1988).

31   Manfred Nowak & Elizabeth McArthur, The United Nations Convention Against Torture, A Commentary 37 (2008) (emphasis added).

32   *Id.* at 39.

33   As was pointed out above, the Model Penal Code's formulation of purposely and knowingly more clearly account for the *mens rea* that the "specific intent" requirement seeks to accomplish. But the understanding's mirroring of proposals that the conference rejected undercuts its legal validity.

34   For example, former President George W. Bush in his finding of February 7, 2002 relied on the Justice Department and the Attorney General that [common Article 3] of the Geneva Convention "does not apply to either al Qaeda or Taliban detainees. . . ." *Id.* at 963. He does not mention the State Department or any of the Judge Advocate Generals. *See also* Ragavan, *infra* note 35.

35   *See* Chitra Ragavan, *Cheney's Guy*, U.S. News and World Report, May 21, 2006, at 5, posted, *available at* http://www.usnews.com/usnews/news/articles/060529/ 29addington.html ("After the 9/11 attacks, the JAG officers were marginalized from decision making and the detainee treatment policies."). *See also* David Johnston & Neil A. Lewis, *Bush's Counsel Sought Ruling About Torture*, N.Y. Times, Jan. 5, 2004, *available at* www.freerepublic.com/focus/f-news/1314158/ posts (noting that current and former Bush–Cheney administration officials said that "John Yoo, a senior Justice Department lawyer [at the OLC] who wrote much of the [torture] memorandum, exchanged draft language with lawyers at the White House. . . .").

36   Jay S. Bybee, *Memorandum for Alberto R. Gonzales, Counsel to the President, Re: Standards of Conduct for Interrogation under 18 U.S.C. §§ 2340–2340A* (Aug. 1, 2002), *in* The Torture Papers and the Road to Abu Ghraib 172, 175 (Karen J. Greenburg & Joshua I. Dratel eds., 2005), *available at* www.humanrightsfirst.org/us_law/etn/gonzales/memos_dir/memo_20020801_ JD_%20Gonz_.pdf#search=%22bybee%20memo%20pdf%22.

37   Jay S. Bybee, Memorandum for John Rizzo Acting General Counsel of the

Central Intelligence Agency, Interrogation of al Qaeda Operative, at 11 (Aug. 1, 2002), *available at* http://www.fas.org/irp/agency/doj/olc/zubaydah.pdf

38   *Id.* at 15.

39   *Id.* The Rome Statute of the ICC makes subjecting detainees to "torture" or to "inhuman" or "cruel treatment" a war crime. Although the US is not a party to the Rome Statute of the ICC, four countries in which the CIA had black sites have been parties (Poland ratified December 12, 2001; Jordan and Romania both ratified on April 11, 2002; and Afghanistan acceded to the ICC in February 2002. The ICC came into force on July 1, 2002). Furthermore, although Jordan, Romania, and Afghanistan have signed Article 98 agreements with the US, promising not to extradite American citizens to the ICC, Poland has not entered into such an agreement with the US. The conduct element set forth in the ICC Elements of Crimes document tracks the Torture Convention definition. "The perpetrator inflicted *severe* physical or mental pain or suffering upon one or more persons." ICC, Elements of Crimes, art. 8(2)(c)(i)-4 *available at* http://www.icc-cpi.int/NR/rdonlyres/9CAEE830-38CF-41D6-AB0B-68E5F9082543/0/Element_of_Crimes_English. pdf (War Crime of Torture) (emphasis added). Conspicuously absent from the ICC conduct element are the terms "prolonged mental harm" and the "threat of imminent death" of the US understanding. Likewise absent from the *mens rea* ICC element is any mention of "specific intent." Even assuming for argument sake that the US understanding were valid, it would thus not have limited international criminal liability in the four above mentioned countries after July 1, 2002.

40   Bybee, *supra* note 36.

41   *Id.*

42   *See, e.g.*, People v. Velasquez 606 P.2d 341, 346 (Cal. 1980), *vacated on other grounds*, 448 U.S. 903 (1980); Schmidt v. State, 951 P.2d 23, 25 (Mont. 1997); State v. Bolton, 896 P.2d 830, 855 (Ariz. 1995).

43   Daniel Levin, Acting Assistant Attorney General, Memorandum for James B. Comey, Deputy Attorney General, Re: Legal Standards Applicable Under 18 U.S.C. §§ 2340–2340A, at 16 (Dec. 30, 2004), http://74.125.95.132/custom?q=cache:ZPpx7wr_wZUJ:news.findlaw.com/hdocs/docs/terrorism/dojtorture123004mem.pdf+Justice+Department+Dec.+30,+2004+Memo+on+U.S.+Torture+Policy+for+Deputy+Attorney+General+James+B.+Comey&cd=3&hl=en&ct=clnk&gl=us&client=pub-7407478729887929 (quoting 1 LaFave, Substantive Criminal Law, § 5.2(a), at 341) (emphasis added) [hereinafter Levin, Legal Standards Memo] *see also* Pierre v. Attorney General of the United States, 528 F.3d 180, 196 (3d Cir. 2008) (*en banc*) (Rendel, J., concurring).

44   United States v. Bailey, 444 U.S. 394, 404 (1980).

45   Levin, Legal Standards Memo, *supra* note 43, at 16.

46   American Heritage Dictionary 1123 (2d College Edition 1985) (emphasis in the original.)

47   *Id.* at 1215–16.

48   Bradbury, *supra* note 4, at 26.

49   Sanford H. Kadish, Stephen J. Shulhofer & Carol S. Steiker, Criminal Law and its Processes, Cases and Materials 289 (8th edition 2007) (quoting Doriane Lambelet Coleman, *Individualizing Justice Through Multiculturalism: The Liberal's Dilemma*, 96 Colum. L. Rev. 1093, 1093 (1996)).

50   *Id.*

51   *See* Kadish et al., *supra* note 49, at 280–81 (citing United States v. Levin, 973 F.2d 463, 468 (6th Cir. 1992); Commonwealth v. Twitchell, 416 Mass. 114, 617 N.E.2d 609 (1993); Jeffrey F. Ghent, Annotation, *Criminal Law: "Official Statement" Mistake of Law Defense*, 89 A.L.R.4th 1026 (1991)).

52   The second memorandum rejected the standard for specific intent that the Yoo–Bybee memorandum had adopted. The larger point here, however, is that

by adopting a faulty good faith defense even the second memorandum provided prospective interrogators authorization to continue to carry out a wide range of harsh practices, including waterboarding.

53   Nowak & McArthur, *supra* note 31, at 56.

54   *Id.* (quoting The Committee Against Torture, Report, A/52/44, § 257) (emphasis added).

55   Bradbury, *supra* note 4, at 59 ("Although this is a difficult question that will depend on the particular detainee, we do not believe that the use of these techniques *in combination* as you [an unidentified CIA official] have described them would be expected to inflict 'severe physical pain or suffering' within the meaning of the statute[,] 18 U.S.C. § 2340(j).") (emphasis added).

56   *See* The Torture Papers and the Road to Abu Ghraib, *supra* note 36, at 228.

57   U.S. Dept. of State, 1999 Country Reports on Human Rights Practices: Egypt, *available at* www.state.gov/g/drl/rls/hrrtpt/1999/408.htm. U.S. Dept. of State, 2000 Country Reports on Human Rights Practices: Egypt, *available at* www.state.gov/g/drl/rls/hrrpt/2000/nea/784.htm; U.S. Dept. of State, 2001 Country Reports on Human Rights Practices: Egypt, *available at* www.state.gov/g/drl/rls/hrrpt/2001/nea/8248.htm; U.S. Dept. of State, 2002 Country Reports on Human Rights Practices: Egypt, *available at* www.state.gov/g/drl/rls/hrrpt/2002/18274.htm; U.S. Dept. of State, 2003 Country Reports on Human Rights Practices: Egypt, *available at* www.state.gov/g/drl/rls/hrrpt/2003/27926.htm.; Amnesty International Report 2007: Human Rights in Arab Republic of Egypt, *available at* www.amnesty.org/en/region/egypt/report-2007; Amnesty International Report 2008: Human Rights in Arab Republic of Egypt, *available at* www.amnesty.org/en/region/egypt/report-2008; Human Rights Watch: World Report 2007: Egypt, *available at* www.hrw.org/legacy/englishwr2k7/docs/2007/01/11/egypt14701.htm; Human Rights Watch: World Report 2007: Egypt, *available at* www.hrw.org/legacy/englishwr2k8/docs/2008/01/31/egypt 17595.htm; International Commission of Jurists: Egypt – Attacks on Justice 2000, *available at* www.icj.org/news.php3?id_Article=2567&lang=en; International Commission of Jurists: Egypt – Attacks on Justice 2002, *available at* www.icj.org/news.php3?id_Article=2658&lang=en. US State Department Human Rights Reports, Egypt, 2003, at: http://www.state.gov/g/drl/rls/hrrpt/2003/27926.htm.

58   *General Comment No. 01: Implementation of Article 3 of the Convention in the context of Article 22* :. 21/11/97. A/53/44, annex IX, CAT General Comment No. 01. (General Comments).

59   Other countries to which the US reportedly rendered terrorist suspects include Egypt, Pakistan, Uzbekistan, and Morocco. *See* "Foreign Policy Aspects of the War Against Terrorism" – the Fourth Report of Session 2005–06 by Great Britain: Parliament: House of Commons: Foreign Affairs Committee. *Fact Sheet Extraordinary Rendition*, ACLU, Dec. 6, 2005, www.aclu.org/safefree/extraordinaryrendition/22203res20051206.html [hereinafter ACLU]. Noting "In the words of former CIA agent Robert Baer: 'If you want a serious interrogation, you send a prisoner to Jordan. If you want them to be tortured, you send them to Syria. If you want someone to disappear – never to see them again – you send them to Egypt." *Id. See also* Olenka Frenkiel, *Shedding Light on CIA Mystery Flights*, BBC News, May 23, 2007 (mentioning Uzbekistan, Morocco, Egypt, and Syria as receiving countries for extraordinary renditions).

60   Some estimate that about 150 persons had been "extraordinarily rendered" by 2005. *See* ACLU, *supra* note 59; Jane Mayer, *Outsourcing Torture*, The New Yorker, Feb. 14, 2005, *available at* www.newyorker.com/archive/2005/02/14/050214fa_fact6.

61   The practice of extraordinary rendition was not begun by the Bush–Cheney administration, but rather by the Clinton administration. Ass'n of the Bar of the City of N.Y., Torture by Proxy: International and Domestic Law Applicable to "Extraordinary Renditions" (2004). *See also* James Silken & Peter M. Norman, *Jack Bauer and the Rule of Law: The Case of Extraordinary Rendition*, 30 Fordham Int'l L.J. 535 (2007).

62   Declaration on the Protection of All Persons from Enforced Disappearances, G.A. Res. 47/133, at 207, UN GAOR, 47th Sess., Supp. No. 49, U.N. Doc. A/ RES/47/133 (Dec. 18, 1992).

63   David Weissbrodt & Amy Bergquist, *Extraordinary Rendition: A Human Rights Analysis*, 19 Harv. Hum. Rts. J. 123, 123 (2006). Weissbrodt and Bergquist recount the following case:

> In December 2003, Kuwaiti-born German national Khaled el Masri boarded a bus in his home of Ulm, Germany, to travel to Skopje, Macedonia. When he arrived at the Macedonian border on December 31, Macedonian police took him off the bus, confiscated his passport, and detained him for three weeks. On January 23, 2004, a jet with tail number N313P, registered to Premier Executive Transport Services, a CIA front-company, arrived in Macedonia from the island of Majorca. El Masri was driven to the Skopje airport, where he was handed over to CIA officials. Men wearing black masks and black gloves beat him, cut off his clothes, and then injected him with drugs. He was then placed on the airplane and flown, first, to Baghdad, and then to Kabul. When he arrived in Afghanistan, U.S. officials interrogated him and held him in solitary confinement for nearly five months. In May 2004, he was flown back to Central Europe and released near a checkpoint on the Albanian border, on the order of U.S. Secretary of State Condoleezza Rice. His detention was apparently a case of mistaken identity. When el Masri returned home to Germany, he learned that his wife and children had gone to stay with her family in Lebanon; his wife thought he had abandoned the family.

Id. at 123–24.

See also Scott Shane, Stephen Grey, & Margot Williams, *CIA Expanding Terror Battle under Guise of Charter Flights*, N.Y. Times, May 31, 2005 *available at* www.nytimes.com/2005/05/31/national/31planes.html?pagewanted=all (noting CIA's attempts to hide the air operations). *See* Amnesty International, *Off the Record, U.S. Responsibilities for Enforced Disappearances in the War on Terror*, at 4 (2007), http://www.chrgj.org/docs/OffRecord/OFF_THE_RECORD_FINAL. pdf.

64   Immanuel Kant, Groundwork for the Metaphysic of Morals 29 (1795) (Jonathan Bennett trans., 2005), *available at* www.earlymoderntexts.com/pdf/ kantgw.pdf.

65   *See* David Johnson, *Rendition to Continue, but With Better Oversight*, N.Y. Times, Aug. 25, 2009 at A8, *available at* 2009 WLNR 16547211. *See also* Exec. Order No. 13491, 74 Fed. Reg. 4893 (Jan. 22, 2009) (stating that "[t]here shall be established a Special Task Force on Interrogation and Transfer Policies . . . to review interrogation and *transfer* policies."), (emphasis added), *available at* http:// www.whitehouse.gov/the_press_office/EnsuringLawfulInterrogations.   Charlie Savage, *To Critics, New Policy Looks Like Old*, N.Y. Times, July 1, 2009, *available at* http://www.ny.times.com/2009/07/02/US/02gitmo.html. Aside from questionable Executive action, federal courts have refused to recognize claims of individuals whom US officials have allegedly wrongfully "extraordinarily rendered" to states such as Syria and Egypt that routinely torture prisoners. *See, e.g.,* Arar v. Ashcroft, 585 F.3d 559 (2d Cir. 2009) (*en banc*), *cert. denied*, 130 S. Ct. 3409 (2010).

5 The allure of the "ticking time bomb" hypothetical

Shortly after 9/11, a group of distinguished American law professors argued for the permissibility of torture in certain circumstances. Harvard law professor Alan Dershowitz argued that in the "ticking time bomb" scenario, governmental interrogators should be required to seek a "torture warrant" to permit the interrogators to torture the "ticking time bomb" terrorist.[1] He wrote that a decision to torture should not be left to the individual interrogator, but that a court should have to authorize an extreme interrogation device. Professor Dershowitz criticizes Judge Aharon Barack of the Israeli Supreme Court who, writing for the court, rejected the government's request for advanced authorization to torture a so-called ticking-time-bomb terrorist. The court reasoned that the necessity doctrine—the unavoidable choice of evils—might operate as a defense in a criminal prosecution of an interrogator, but, absent express legislation, could not authorize interrogators to torture.[2] Professor Dershowitz argued that this position puts interrogators in an unfair position and lets responsibility for the momentous decision whether to torture fall too far down the official pecking order.[3] He contended that judicial supervision would ensure society's protection and that the extreme remedy of torture would be used only in exceptional circumstances.

Former University of Chicago Law Professor and Seventh Circuit Court of Appeals Judge Richard Posner has likewise asserted that responsible leaders must permit torture in narrow circumstances. He criticized Professor Dershowitz's approach, however, as unduly expanding the use of torture: "If rules are promulgated permitting torture in defined circumstances, some officials are bound to want to explore the outer bounds of the rules. *Having been regularized, the practice will become regular.* Better to leave in place the formal and customary prohibitions but with the understanding that they will not be enforced in extreme circumstances."[4]

Expanding upon Judge Posner's argument, Professor Oren Gross of University of Minnesota writes that in "the truly exceptional cases[,]" such as that of the ticking-time-bomb terrorist, the interrogator may engage in "official disobedience" (similar to civil disobedience) by torturing such an individual. The interrogator would thus face the possibility of criminal prosecution (and possibly, demotion or dismissal as well). The interrogator's acts, however, could be implicitly ratified by an exercise of prosecutorial discretion not to prosecute; in the event of a prosecution, by the jury engaging in jury nullification; or, if a conviction results, by the Executive exercising the clemency power. Rather than establish a special rule for hard cases (or at least the hard case of the ticking-time-bomb terrorist), Judge Posner and Professor Gross let the existing pressure releases in the system resolve the problem.[5]

Professor Dershowitz in turn criticizes Professor Gross's position, arguing that "[i]f these horrible practices continue to operate below the radar screen of accountability, there is no legitimation, but there is continuing and ever expanding *sub rosa* employment of the practice." Professor Dershowitz argues that a decision of this magnitude (whether to torture) should not be left to the discretion of low-level officials, but should be made by the country's duly constituted courts. For his part, Judge Posner criticizes Professor Dershowitz's torture warrant proposal as providing an inadequate "check on executive discretion" and reasons that a "warrant is issued in an *ex parte* proceeding, and usually the officer seeking the warrant has the choice of judges or magistrates from whom to seek it."[6] In summary, Professor Dershowitz opts for a legal procedure to authorize torture; by contrast, Judge Posner and Professor Gross opt for an extralegal one.

All of these authorities presuppose the genuine possibility of the ticking-time-bomb terrorist and either implicitly or explicitly authorize torturing that individual. Undoubtedly, the ticking-time-bomb hypothetical appears superficially compelling. After all, if torturing a single person could have stopped 9/11, how could torture in that situation not be justified? In moral terms, would not preventing the death of nearly 3,000 human beings outweigh the wrong involved in torturing a single individual? In legal terms, would not the principle of necessity—of the unavoidable choice of evils—mandate torture, or at least excuse an interrogator for torturing?

Closer examination of the ticking-time-bomb terrorist scenario, however, undermines the potential reality of this hypothetical and the argument that flows from it. In deconstructing the ticking-time-bomb hypothetical, Professor Henry Shue of Oxford shows that it posits an idealized set of facts and either removes or ignores inconvenient but inevitable facts as well as consequences of either implicitly or explicitly permitting torture.[7]

As Professor Shue notes, the hypothetical presupposes four critical facts: (a) that the authorities have the right person, *namely*, an actual ticking-time-bomb terrorist; (b) that this person will provide accurate information; (c) that the information will be timely; and (d) that, because of the unusual confluence of the first three suppositions, torture will be rare.[8]

Particularly in the initial stages of an investigation, however, evidence is rarely clear or free of doubt: "A 'fact' may have a life of its own. From the perspective of an appellate judge after a case has been tried and the evidence has been sifted by another judge, a particular fact may be as clear and certain as a piece of crystal or a small diamond. A trial lawyer, however, must often deal with mixtures of sand and clay. . . ."[9] (Presumably, the ticking-time-bomb terrorist would just have been arrested or captured; otherwise, the expected information would likely not be timely.) As a practical matter, interrogators (analogous to trial lawyers in the initial stages of a case) will generally have little evidence about whether a recently captured individual is in fact a ticking-time-bomb terrorist. When terrorist organizations such as al Qaeda construct elaborate cell structures,[10] few participants in the terrorist organization will possess much actionable intelligence, let alone be a ticking-time-bomb terrorist. Presumably, reasonable advocates of torture would not endorse torturing a person *on the mere chance* that the person knows a ticking-time-bomb's location. They presumably would require much more than a preponderance of the evidence to justify torturing someone and would instead demand at least near-certainty that the individual is in fact the ticking-time-bomb terrorist. Analytically, a decision to torture resembles a decision to carry out the death penalty: death is different, and so is torture, at least from other noncapital punishments. If we decide to torture a putative ticking-time-bomb terrorist, we should ensure that the tortured person is in fact the ticking-time-bomb terrorist with at least the same degree of certainty that the person we execute is in fact the individual who committed the heinous crime for which he was convicted. As a practical matter, interrogators rarely possess such knowledge with the requisite degree of certainty.

Moreover, some of the targets of torture under the ticking-time-bomb scenario will have probably undergone torture previously at the hands of repressive regimes under which they lived. For example, Ayman al Zawahiri, bin Laden's chief of staff, was tortured by Egypt after his arrest for complicity in the assassination of Anwar Sadat. Hence, such individuals may be less likely to give in under torture and may even provide convincing disinformation. The experience might also make them psychologically even more determined to resist and disinform than they would be if only "classroom trained" to endure torture.

The US armed forces train even relatively low-level personnel (SEALS, Rangers, etc.) in torture resistance. If we think people can be trained to resist torture (as our efforts imply we do), then no reason exists to suppose that terrorist organizations cannot succeed in the same way. If training includes some kind of "controlled collapse" to the torture (*namely*, convincing the torturer that the torture has worked and then deliberately providing disinformation), torture may increase rather than decrease the risks of obtaining inaccurate information and therefore decrease rather than increase security. In effect, they are two sides of the same coin: whether torture resistance is learned through "real world" experience or in a training environment, the outcome is essentially the same—less security.

More fundamentally, is there any reason to assume (or believe) the authorities can actually distinguish good information from bad information in deciding at the outset whether they have identified a ticking-time-bomb terrorist, especially when they are operating under pressure and conditions of uncertainty?[11] In light of what we saw in the run-up to the Iraq invasion, can we be reasonably sure that governmental officials will honestly assess whatever information they do have? In a sense, there is really a fifth assumption at work: the integrity of the intelligence gatherers. The campaign for going to war in Iraq does not provide much support for the validity of that assumption, either.

Beyond the rarity of capturing and identifying the ticking-time-bomb terrorist, "rare torture" proponents presuppose that the ticking-time-bomb terrorist will provide accurate information as a result of torture. Professional interrogators, however, generally say that torture does not usually yield reliable intelligence.[12] Despite the impression created by Jack Bauer and the innumerable episodes of *24*, most people are willing to say anything to end torture,[13] which means telling the torturer whatever the tortured person believes the torturer wants to hear.[14] Moreover, those in the upper echelons of terrorist organizations—the people most likely to possess actionable intelligence—will generally be trained in countertorture techniques and will more likely provide prepared stories rather than the truth. Using traditional interrogation methods is a far surer way of obtaining actionable intelligence than carrying out torture or cruel, inhuman, and degrading treatment.

False information likely obtained as a result of torture provided one of the justifications for the 2003 American invasion of Iraq. Ibn al I-Shaykhal-Libi had helped run al Qaeda training camps in Afghanistan.[15] After his capture in that country in 2001, the CIA "extraordinarily rendered" him to Egypt in 2002.[16] Almost certainly interrogated under torture by the Egyptians, he confessed that beginning in December 2000, Saddam Hussein's Iraq trained al Qaeda members to use chemical and biological weapons.[17] Al Libi's "confession" made its way into Secretary of State Colin Powell's UN Security Council speech justifying the invasion of Iraq.[18] Powell referred to al Libi, "not by name, but as 'senior al Qaeda official' who ran an al Qaeda terrorist camp."[19] Al Libi later recanted, saying he made up the story while the Egyptians tortured him.[20] In 2004, the CIA withdrew the intelligence based on this confession.[21,22]

When Abu Zubaydah was arrested in Pakistan in 2002, he was described as a high-level al Qaeda operative. He was taken to a CIA black site and ultimately waterboarded 83 times. Under waterboarding, he gave out all kinds of information about al Qaeda plots and sent the CIA running around the world to investigate them. "In the end, though, not a single significant plot was foiled as a result of Abu Zubaydah's tortured confessions, according to former senior government officials who closely followed the interrogations."[23] These officials now believe that Zubaydah was never a high-level al Qaeda operative at all, but more like a travel agent for extremist Islamic Fundamentalists who wanted to attend a training camp.[24]

Beyond the "accurate information" assumption, the ticking-time-bomb hypothetical embraces a "timely torture" assumption: that torturing the individual will yield accurate information in time to prevent the bomb from exploding. This facet of the hypothetical necessarily assumes other members of the terrorist cell or terrorist group would remain unaware that the ticking-time-bomb terrorist was missing or arrested, for if the members of the cell or group knew of the absence, they would abort a plan they knew or had good reasons to know the authorities had uncovered. Even if the terrorist cell or a group acts irrationally and decides to run the risk, the authorities would have only a small window in which to (a) identify the ticking-time-bomb terrorist and (b) obtain accurate information from him to defuse the bomb.

Professor Shue points out the rarity of all these circumstances coalescing.[25] Superficially, this rare coalescence appears to dovetail with the implicit contention of Professors Gross and Dershowitz, and Judge Posner that torture will be rare. Professor Shue argues, however, that this idealized dimension of the ticking-time-bomb hypothetical sanitizes real, inescapable facts. When a government implicitly or explicitly authorizes torture, a bureaucracy will inevitably arise to carry it out. Moreover, governments will not want to employ incompetent torturers; competence in torture will require training of, practice by, and evaluation of prospective certified torturers. Professor Shue compares the "moderate" position on torture to imagining an alcoholic who has just a couple of drinks a night.[26] In reality, the alcoholic will either drink excessively or abstain completely. There is no real moderate position. "One can imagine rare torture, but one cannot institutionalize rare torture."[27]

Of course, a "rare torture" proponent could contend that torturing suspected terrorists is justified if any actionable intelligence could be gleaned, even if the torture does not lead to the ticking time bomb—essentially, an adaptation of Vice-President Richard Cheney's "one percent doctrine."[28] While that position now lies outside the hypothetical, a regime of "institutionalized rare torture" would soon expand to embrace that position, meaning that torture will become a routine tactic, not the rarity Professor Gross and others posit. Interrogators will rarely have clear and convincing evidence that they have the right person or that their subject has provided accurate and timely information to defuse the ticking bomb. We cannot realistically expect that interrogators, acting under pressure and conditions of uncertainty, will wait for the ideal conditions before torturing or inflicting cruel, inhumane, and degrading treatment.[29] For example, the CIA Inspector General asserted that "enhanced interrogation techniques" yielded considerable actionable intelligence, but concluded that the techniques did not uncover "any imminent" plots or ticking time bombs.[30]

In instituting "enhanced interrogation," the US adapted its counter-interrogation program used to train US forces likely to fall into hostile hands. In effect, the Pentagon turned a defensive training program for US personnel into an offensive program targeting detainees in the war on terrorism.[31] Called "Survival, Evasion, Resistance, and Escape" (SERE), the program was originally intended for "special mission units, sensitive reconnaissance operations personnel, military attachés, and others designated high risk of capture personnel" by repressive regimes.[32] The program was based on interrogation techniques used by North Korea and Communist China on prisoners of war in the Korean War. The SERE program, now redirected for training US interrogators, includes waterboarding, described as follows:

> WATERBOARD: Subject is interrogated while strapped to a wooden board, approximately 4'×7'. Often the subject's feet are elevated after being strapped down and having their torso stripped. Up to 1.5 gallons of water is slowly poured directly onto the subject's face from a height of 12–14 inches. In some cases, a cloth is placed over the subject's face. It will remain in place for a short period of time. Trained supervisory and medical staff monitors the subject's physical condition. However, no student will have water applied a second time. *This tactic instills a feeling of drowning* and quickly compels cooperation (typical conditions for application: to instill fear and despair, to punish selective behavior).[33]

The precise number of detainees who were waterboarded is not known. Michael Hayden, the former Director of the CIA, admitted in 2008 that the CIA had waterboarded three al Qaeda members—Khalid Sheik Mohammed, Abd al-Rahim al-Nashiri, and Abu Zubaydah—while they were held in CIA black sites in 2002 and 2003.[34] There have been reports of additional cases of waterboarding.[35] A dozen CIA agents reportedly were trained in waterboarding and other "enhanced interrogation techniques."[36]

At first glance, the ticking-time-bomb hypothetical appears so convincing that it can seduce even a reasonable person inclined to respect human rights. But this seduction arises from the facility with which the hypothetical makes seemingly reasonable the first step toward a full-fledged torture program. The ticking-time-bomb hypo is the camel's nose under the tent. Just as beginning a witch hunt inevitably leads to finding witches (and, not coincidentally, torturing them), a camel's nose under the tent soon leads to a camel-filled tent—unless, of course, the tent-minder carefully battens the tent to keep out the nose from the start. Stripping the ticking-time-bomb hypothetical of its seductive quality and demystifying its superficial sleekness exposes the true significance of this justification and, perhaps, forestalls the finding of witches and the tending of camels.

5.1 The experience of other countries with torture

The US is certainly not the first country to use torture. Most countries have tortured their opponents at one time or another. Chapter 3 explored the UK's use of cruel, degrading, and unusual punishment on suspected IRA members and the effects of that treatment on the IRA and the Northern Irish Catholic community. France was one of the first Western democracies and colonial powers to experience "modern terrorism." From 1954 to 1962, Algerian rebels from Front de Libération Nationale (FLN), seeking to free Algeria from France's colonial grip, carried out a ruthless campaign directed at the

French civilian population. The rebels targeted French restaurants, bars, clubs, schools, and other civilian places, killing thousands of civilians.[37]

Reacting to the explosion of violence, the French adopted an official policy and practice of torturing suspected Algerian rebels. As Dr. Rita Maran has explained, the second-class status of native Algerians under French rule helped legitimize the torture program.[38] The primary method was to inflict electric shock to the genitals, but water torture, beating Muslim prisoners and stripping them naked, and raping female prisoners were reportedly common.[39] French leaders and military and police officers rarely used the term "torture" to describe their interrogation techniques. Instead, they described the techniques as "effective methods" or "unaccustomed method" or "long established practice."[40] One French general justified torture by declaring that the torture methods were not nearly as painful as those employed by other countries' police forces, adding that he had actually tried the torture techniques on himself.[41]

France's policy and practice of torture violated at least one treaty and brushed against other international instruments France had signed or approved. In 1951, France ratified the Geneva Conventions of 1949; consequently, the Geneva Conventions applied throughout the Algerian conflict. Controlling in armed conflicts "not of an international character," Common Article 3 of the four Geneva Conventions prohibits "cruel treatment and torture . . . [and] outrages on personal dignity, in particular humiliating and degrading treatment. . . ."[42] The French, however, denied that Common Article 3 applied, claiming that, despite having caused at least 300,000 casualties,[43] the violence was an internal matter and did not rise to the level of armed conflict.[44]

Aside from Common Article 3, the Universal Declaration of Human Rights prohibits torture and cruel, inhuman, and degrading treatment. France joined a unanimous UN General Assembly in voting for the Declaration in 1948. While not yet having crystallized into custom at the time of the conflict, the Universal Declaration of Human Rights presumably reflected France's view on torture. As a founding member of the Council of Europe, France participated in drafting the European Convention for the Protection of Fundamental Rights and Freedoms ("the European Convention"), which prohibits "torture and inhuman and degrading treatment." The European Convention came into force in 1953 (a year before the conflict began), with France as one of the original signatories.[45] Although France did not ratify the European Convention until 1974, the Vienna Convention on the Law of Treaties (which largely codifies customary international law) requires signatories who have not yet ratified a treaty "to refrain from acts which would defeat [its] object and purpose. . . ."[46]

One commentator suggests that torture was initially effective in the Algerian conflict: "The French interrogation techniques used during the Battle of Algiers did turn out some short term positive results since the uprising of the Arabs in Algiers was suppressed within a seven month period."[47] Whatever the early French tactical successes, however, the torture program inflamed the Algerian population: "The use of torture embittered many fence-straddling Muslims and drove them into the arms of the FLN."[48] France ultimately lost the Battle of Algiers.

Although using techniques not nearly as severe as the French in Algiers, the Bush–Cheney policies and practices frequently mimicked the French policies that failed in Algeria. From using euphemisms to describe torture ("enhanced interrogation techniques" here, "unconventional methods" there) to coming up with specious reasons why the Geneva Conventions did not apply, to claiming (rightly but unconvincingly) that their interrogation techniques were not as egregious as those adopted by some other countries, to justifying their extreme measures as necessary for security, both governments appear to have similarly overreacted. In both cases, the notion of necessity, bolstered by arguments such as the ticking-time-bomb hypothetical, rationalized the descent into regularized torture.

Notes

1   Alan Dershowitz, *Tortured Reasoning, in* Torture 257, 263 (Sanford Levinson ed., 2004).
2   HCJ 5100/94, 4054/95, 6536/95, 5188/96, 7563/97, 7628/97, 1043/99 Public Committee Against Torture in Israel and others v. Israel and others [1999] 7 BHRC 31, para. 38.
3   *Id.*
4   Richard A. Posner, *Torture, Terrorism, and Interrogation, in* Torture, *supra* note 1, at 291, 296 (emphasis added). For a good discussion of this debate, see Steiner, Alston and Goodman, International Human Rights in Context 243–51 (2008). The CIA Inspector General's Report suggests that some CIA agents and contractors explored the "outer boundary of the rules" by, among other things, threatening a detainee with a power drill, conducting mock executions, pretending to load a pistol inches from the detainee's head, threatening to torture and rape a detainee's family members, threatening to kill a detainee's children, and closing (putting pressure on) a detainee's carotid artery. CIA Inspector General's Report, *supra* note 24 in ch. 4, at paras. 90, 92, 94, 97, 166, 169, 178, 184, 185, 187, 217.
5   I am indebted to Professor José Alvarez of New York University School of Law for his exceptionally lucid discussion of these issues in a presentation made while visiting Pace University School of Law in 2006.
6   *See* Torture, *supra* note 1, at 296.
7   Henry Shue, *Torture in Dreamland*, 37 Case W. Res. L. Rev. 231, 233 (2006), excerpts from which are reprinted with the permission of Case Western Reserve Law Review.
8   *Id.*
9   Nix v. Whiteside, 475 U.S. 157, 190 (1986).
10 Richard Wilson, Human Rights in the 'War on Terror' 7 (2005).
11 I am indebted to my friend Chris Wren, Assistant Attorney General with the State of Wisconsin, for suggesting this and the preceding argument.
12 *See* Philip N.S. Rumney, *Is Coercive Interrogation of Terrorist Suspects Effective? A Response to Bagaric and Clarke?*, 40 U.S.F. L. Rev. 479 (2006). Michael Scheuer, who worked in the Bin Laden unit in the White House, declared that the

information obtained under torture is not generally reliable: "[Scheuer] would have used it if it worked, but in his experience he had found that insurgents are trained to hand out disinformation, and the intelligence you get from torturing them is either dubious or wrong." *Commentary: Counterinsurgency and Torture*, U.S. Federal News, July 28, 2008. See also "Press Release, Human Rights First, Top Interrogators Declare Torture Ineffective in Intelligence Gathering (June 24, 2008)," www.humanrightsfirst.org/media/etn/2008/alert/313/index.htm.

For a contrary view, note that my friend Michael A. Newton, former professor at the Judge Advocate General's School and now at Vanderbilt School of Law, argues that the interrogators often can cross-check the information the detainee is providing under torture with others and other sources to determine if it is accurate. The CIA Inspector General noted that interrogators "frequently use[] the information from one detainee, as well as other sources, to vet the information of another detainee. Although lower-level detainees provide less information than the high value detainees, information from these detainees has on many occasions . . . [provided] the information needed to probe the high value detainees. . . ." Steven Bradbury, Deputy Assistant Attorney General, Office of Legal Counsel, Department of Justice, Memorandum for John A. Rizzo, Senior Deputy General Counsel, Central Intelligence Agency, Re: Application of United States Obligations Under Article 16 of the Convention Against Torture to Certain Techniques that May Be Used in the Interrogation of High Value of al Qaeda Detainees, at 9 (May 30, 2005). *See also* Alan M. Dershowitz, Why Terrorism Works: Understanding the Threat, Responding to the Challenge 137 (2002) (noting that although torture does not always work, it sometimes works). *See* ch. 5, note 24 and accompanying text, for a discussion of the efficacy of harsh interrogation methods.

13   *See* Interview by Frontline with Sgt. Roger Brokaw, Interrogator (Sep. 24, 2005), *available at* www.pbs.org/wgbh/pages/frontline/torture/interviews/brokaw.html:

> **[Q.] Now, as an experienced interrogator, does it work to punch people around? Does it work to be coercive? [A.]** I don't think so. I think you're going to get more disinformation and, you know, lies. Because when you're hurting somebody, they want to stop the pain, so they're going to tell you something. And if you got, you know, 100 detainees and you torture them all, and maybe only one of them is a real insurgent, you know, maybe you'll get some information from that guy. But the other ones are probably going to lie about something, turn in their neighbor or something, you know, just to stop the pain. Yeah, I think in the long run, you're going to get less information or reliable information from torture than you would by other means.

14   *See* Rumney, *supra* note 12, at 490–91.

15   Evan Thomas & Michael Hirsh, *Torture, The Debate over Torture*, Newsweek, Nov. 21, 2005, at 26, *available at* 2005 WLNR 18458606.

16   Douglas Jehl, *The Reach of the War: Intelligence, Qaeda-Iraq Link U.S. Cited is Tied to Coercion Claim*, N.Y. Times, Dec. 9, 2005, at A1, *available at* 2005 WLNR 19792105.

17   *Id.*

18   Thomas & Hirsch, *supra* note 15.

19   *Id.*

20   Jehl, *supra* note 16, at A1.

21   *Id.* The New York Times suggests that even before the war began in March 2003, government officials doubted al Libi's "confession": "A classified Defense Intelligence Agency report issued in February 2002 that expressed skepticism

about Mr. Libi's credibility on questions related to Iraq and Al Qaeda was based in part on the knowledge that he was no longer in American custody when he made the detailed statements, and that he might have been subjected to harsh treatment, the officials said. They said the CIA's decision to withdraw the intelligence based on Mr. Libi's claims had been made because of his later assertions, beginning in January 2004, that he had fabricated them to obtain better treatment from his captors." *Id.*

22   Of course, sometimes torture can provide accurate information. The Philippines tortured Abdul Hakim Murad in 1995. "His interrogators reportedly beat him so badly that most of his ribs were broken; they extinguished cigarettes on his genitals; they made him sit on ice cubes; they forced water down his throat so that he nearly drowned." Peter Maas, *The World: Torture, Tough or Lite; If a Terror Suspect Won't Talk, Should He Be Made To?*, N.Y. Times Week in Review, Mar. 9, 2003, at 4, *available at* http://query.nytimes.com/gst/fullpage.html?res= 9A07E3DC1E3FF93AA35750C0A9659C8B63&partner=rssnyt&emc=rss. He eventually told his torturers about an al Qaeda plot to blow up 11 passenger airliners and assassinate the Pope. The fundamental question remains, however: whether institutionalizing torture, given its inherent flaws, will ultimately protect or harm society. *Id.*

23   Peter Finn & Joby Warrick, *Detainee's Harsh Treatment Foiled No Plots*, Wash. Post., Mar. 29, 2009, at A01, *available at* www.washingtonpost.com/wp-dyn/ content/Article/2009/03/28/AR2009032802066.html. The useful information Zubaydah did provide, for example, names of al Qaeda members, were provided before he was waterboarded. *Id.*

24   *Id. But see* Hayden & Mukasey, *supra* note 24 in ch. 4 (asserting that Abu Zubaydah "sometimes derided as a low-level operative of questionable reliability, but who was in fact close to KSM and other senior al Qaeda leaders").

25   Shue, *supra* note 7, at 233.

26   *Id.* at 238.

27   *Id.*

28   Ron Suskind, The One Percent Doctrine: Deep Inside America's Pursuit of Its Enemies Since 9/11, 62 (2006). The "one percent doctrine" mandates that if there is a one percent chance that something may occur, it is to be treated as a certainty. *Id.*

29   Regarding the interrogations of Abu Zubaydah, one official described the pressure from high echelons of government as "enormous": "They couldn't stand the idea that there wasn't anything new," the official said. "They'd say, 'You aren't working hard enough.'" There was both a disbelief in what he [Zubaydah] was saying and also a desire for retribution – a feeling that "He's going to talk, and if he doesn't talk, we'll do whatever." Finn & Warwick, *supra* note 23, at A01.

30   CIA Inspector General's Report, *supra* note 24 in ch. 4, at 88, para. 217. *See also* Karen J. Greenberg, The Torture Debate in America 114–15 (2005); Scott Shane, *Inside a 9/11 Mastermind's Interrogation*, N.Y. Times, June 22, 2008, *available at* www.nytimes.com/2008/06/22/washington/22ksm.html? pagewanted=1.

31   Dave Keyes, *Recognize the Truth about Waterboarding*, Greenwich Time (Conn.), Jan. 13, 2007, at 1, *available at* 2007 WLNR 22439774.

32   *Torture and Cruel, Inhuman and Degrading Treatment of Detainees: The Effectiveness and Consequences of 'Enhanced' Interrogation: Hearing Before the Subcomm. on the Constitution, Civil Rights, and Civil Liberties of the H. Comm. On the Judiciary,* 110th Cong. 22–28 (2007) (testimony of Malcolm Nance, former instructor at the US Naval Survival, Evasion, Resistance, and Escape Training School).

33   S. Comm. on Armed Services, 110th Cong., Inquiry into the Treatment of

Detainees in U.S. Custody (Comm. Print 2008), *available at* http://armed-services.senate.gov/Publications/Detainee%20Report%20Final_April%2022%202009.pdf. See *Inquiry into the Treatment of Detainees in U.S. Custody, Report of the Senate Armed Services Committee*, Nov. 20, 2008.

34 *US: Hold Torturers Accountable*, U.S. Fed. News, Feb. 5, 2008, *available at* 2008 WLNR 2542559; Aamer Madhani, *U.S. Confirms Waterboarding Use*, Chi. Trib., Feb 6, 2008, *available at* 2008 WLNR 2238895.

35 *Black Arts of 'Terror Gulag' Revealed, CIA agents leak interrogation tactics*, Belfast Telegraph, Dec. 2, 2005, *available at* 2005 WLNR 19541182.

36 Hayden justified the use of waterboarding: "'We used [waterboarding] against these three detainees because of the circumstances at the time,' Hayden said. 'There was the belief that additional catastrophic attacks against the homeland were inevitable. And we had limited knowledge about Al Qaeda and its workings.'" *Id.* (citing ABC as the source for this point).

37 The FLN killed an estimated 2,700 Europeans and 16,300 native Algerians up through March 19, 1962. Todd Sheppard, *The Invention of Decolonization: The Algerian War and the Remaking of France* 44 (2006). Estimates of total casualty figures vary. The 300,000 figure apparently includes both combatants and civilians; civilian numbers ranging from 200,000 to as high as 600,000, Matthew White, Secondary Wars and Atrocities of the Twentieth Century, *available at* http://users.erols.com/mwhite28/warstat3.htm#Algeria.

38 Rita Maran, Torture: The Role of Ideology in the French-Algerian War 4 (1972).

39 James D. LeSuer, *Torture and Decolonization of French Algeria: Nationalism, 'Race' and Violence During Colonial Incarceration, in* Colonial and Post-Colonial Incarceration 166–68 (Graeme Harper ed., 2001).

40 Maran, *supra* note 38, at 98. *See also,* Jim House & Neil MacMaster, Paris 1961, at 56 (2006).

41 Maran, *supra* note 38, at 25, 102 (citing General Jacques Massou, who "ordered and approved torture during the Battle of Algiers").

42 Geneva Convention Relative to the Protection of Civilian Persons in Time of War art. 3(a), (c), Aug. 12, 1949, 6 U.S.T. 3516, 75 U.N.T.S. 287 [hereinafter, "Fourth Geneva Convention"].

43 The French estimated a total of 350,000 casualties; the FLN originally estimated 300,000 but raised that figure to 1.5 million. *Algerian War of Independence*, KnowledgeRush Encyclopedia, http://knowledgerush.com/kr/encyclopedia/Algerian_War_of_Independence/.

44 Maran, *supra* note 38, at 9.

45 "Summary of the Treaty." Convention for the Protection of Human Rights and Fundamental Freedoms, Nov. 4, 1950, ETS No. 005, *available at* http://conventions.coe.int/Treaty/en/Summaries/Html/005.htm. *See also* Maran, *supra* note 38, at 9–10.

46 Vienna Convention on the Law of Treaties art. 18, May 23, 1969, 1155 U.N.T.S. 331, *reprinted in* 8 I.L.M. 679. The Vienna Convention was concluded in 1969 and entered into force in 1988. Consequently, it was not binding law between 1954 and 1962. The Convention, however, including Article 19, is declaratory of custom. *See also* Jan Klabbers, *How to Defeat a Treaty's Object and Purpose Pending Entry into Force: Toward Manifest Intent*, 34 Vand. J. Transnat'l L. 283, 288 (2001).

47 Gerald Grodan, *The Case of the French Torture Techniques in the Battle of Algiers*, Associated Content, Sept. 19, 2008, www.associatedcontent.com/Article/1036192/the_case_ of_the_french_torture_techniques_pg3.html?cat=37.

48 Maran, *supra* note 38, at 97. *See also* Robert Imre, T. Brian Mooney, & Benjamin Clarke, Responding to Terrorism: Political, Philosophical, and Legal Perspectives 110 (2008).

6 Beyond locking 'em up and throwing away the key?

Indefinite detention, habeas corpus, and the right to a fair trial

Calling the threat a "war on terrorism" permitted policy makers in the Bush–Cheney administration, the Justice Department, and the Pentagon to argue that rather than illegally holding al Qaeda, Taliban, and other terrorist suspects without trial, the US had been employing the right of a nation during time of war to detain enemy combatants until "the cessation of active hostilities."[1] Although at first that seems to make sense, the argument runs into a rhetorical and legal quagmire. Terrorism, whether perpetrated by states or non-state actors, is a stratagem that has been employed throughout history; consequently, the "war against terrorism" may never "cease." Aside from the abuse and torture already discussed, the US had gone beyond indefinitely detaining such individuals. The US had refused for months to release the names of all persons detained, a tactic reminiscent of the Pinochet regime in Chile. The US had initially denied virtually all the detainees the right to counsel and had otherwise held them *incommunicado*.[2]

The Barack Obama adminstration has moved to undo some of the abuses of detainees under the Bush–Cheney administration. Whatever the ideological makeup of the government, however, transnational terror organizations challenge Western democracies to keep their ideals in the face of what may seem unimaginable threats to national security. This chapter discusses indefinite detention, the international law governing the right to trial, and the current debate on balancing civil liberty against security.

The mantra of the Bush–Cheney administration was that international terrorism was new, that the laws of war were not designed for such a threat, that in the words of former Attorney General Alberto Gonzalez, the law of war, the Geneva Conventions, were quaint. History teaches a different lesson. First, let us define terrorism as intentionally attacking civilians to advance a political, social, or religious end.[3] Note that this definition embraces both state and non-state terrorism. Second, from recorded history, the world has seen states, tribes, private groups, and individuals deliberately killing or wounding civilians for political purposes. During the American Revolution, Patriots murdered, summarily executed, tarred and feathered, whipped, or otherwise terrorized a large number of Tory civilians, a slice of American history that gets left out of the history textbooks.[4] Maximilien Robespierre, the leader of the French Committee of Public Safety, instituted a reign of terror in France after the revolution, sending thousands to the guillotine without a fair trial.[5] The Viet Mingh in the 1950s and 1960s targeted civilians and local civilian officials to destabilize South Vietnam.

In the relatively recent past, Western countries have dealt with a group of private individuals who engaged in a series of acts of violence that bears an uncanny resemblance to al Qaeda, its allies, and its sympathizers. The late nineteenth century and the early twentieth century saw the rise of the anarchist movement. With vague dreams of a utopian socialist state, individual anarchists around Europe and the US committed acts of violence, terrorizing several European countries and even, for a time, the US.[6] Like al Qaeda, the anarchists were loosely organized; they responded more to the same ideas than to the orders of a particular individual. "Between the two groups [the intellectual anarchist visionaries and those who killed others because of that vision] there was no contact."[7] Anarchists were responsible for assassinating six heads of state in the two decades before the First World War,[8] including US President William McKinley. One of their adherents assassinated the Archduke of Austria, plunging the world into the Great War, the First World War.[9]

For the most part, Europeans treated the anarchists as criminals, not warriors. Trial was expeditious; punishment was swift and harsh.[10] In late April 1919, anarchists mailed 30 pipe bombs to prominent US officials, including five senators, two governors, two members of Congress, and Supreme Court Justice Oliver Wendell Holmes, Jr.[11] Except for one that blew off the hands of a maid, all the bombs were discovered in time to prevent them from exploding. A few days later, however, eight bombs planted by anarchists did go off in the homes of other prominent Americans, seriously damaging, for example, the home of A. Mitchell Palmer, the new Attorney General of the US.[12] Convinced of a coming communist revolution against America and aided by his chief assistant, J. Edgar Hoover, Palmer conducted massive sweeps of immigrants in eight cities in the US. Thousands of immigrants were picked up without arrest warrants or probable cause and were detained without trial for months.[13] Palmer asserted that those immigrants who were detained were communists and anarchists, stating: "How the Department of Justice discovered upwards of 60,000 of these organized agitators of the Trotsky doctrine in the United States is the confidential information upon which the Government is now sweeping the nation clean of such alien filth."[14]

Most of the immigrants were ultimately released, but about 250 were, with little due process, deported to Russia. Palmer and Hoover's approach, particularly their concentrating on immigrants, not US citizens, was a prelude to the Bush–Cheney administration's handling of those suspected of committing or planning to commit terrorist acts after 9/11.[15] Even Palmer, however, did not assert he was engaged in a war against anarchism. Nonetheless, he and Hoover employed tactics that today violate basic principles of due process and international law.

6.1 The human rights revolution

In the nearly 90 years since the First World War ended, the planet has undergone a human rights revolution. That revolution has stemmed in part from the abuses of the victors in the First World War, abuses that led directly to the Second World War, and to the atrocities carried out by Nazi Germany, Imperial Japan, and other countries. This revolution found a legal voice first in the founding of the League of Nations in 1919 and more strongly in the establishment of the United Nations (UN) in 1945.

The drive toward greater respect for human rights continued with the UN General Assembly's issuing of the Universal Declaration of Human Rights in 1948, and the adoption of a plethora of multilateral human rights declarations and treaties including the following: the Genocide Convention in 1948, the European Convention for the Protection of Human Rights and Fundamental Rights in 1950, the Refugee Convention in 1951, the Declaration on Granting Independence to Colonial Countries and Peoples in 1960, the International Convention on the Elimination of all Forms of Racial Discrimination in 1966, the International Covenant on Civil and Political Rights (ICCPR), the International Covenant on Economic, Social and Cultural Rights (both adopted in 1966), the Convention on the Elimination of All Forms of Discrimination against Women (CEDAW) in 1979, the Convention against Torture and Other Cruel Inhuman or Degrading Treatment of Punishment in 1984, the Convention on the Rights of the Child in 1989, the Declaration on the Protection of all Persons from Enforced Disappearance in 1992, the Rome Statute of the International Criminal Court in 1998, and the Declaration on the Rights of Indigenous Peoples in 2007.[16]

Aside from the treaties themselves, new international institutions have emerged to foster human rights, including the European Court of Human Rights, the European Court of Justice, the Organization of American States' Inter-American Commission of Human Rights, the Inter-American Court of Human Rights, the Organization of African Unity, the African Commission on Human and People's Rights, the African Court on Human Rights and People's Rights, the European Union, the Council of Europe, and the UN Human Rights Council. Furthermore, special committees have been created to monitor compliance with the major human rights treaties, namely, the UN Committee on Human Rights, which monitors states' performance under the ICCPR; the UN Committee on Economic, Social and Cultural Rights, which monitors that Convention; the Committee against Torture, which monitors state compliance with the Torture Convention; the UN Committee on CEDAW; and the UN Committee on the Convention on the Rights of the Child.[17]

6.2 Advances in humanitarian law

Aside from provoking a human rights revolution, the two World Wars, especially the latter, brought about significant advances in the law of war ("humanitarian law"). The four Geneva Conventions of 1949 were a direct response to Nazi Germany's abusing prisoners of war and civilians in occupied territories. Responding to abuses during Vietnam, Korea, Japan's invasion of China, and air combat in the Second World War, the 1977 First Additional Protocol to the Geneva Conventions strengthened the protections for civilians in the actual conduct of armed conflict. These developments were followed by a series of treaties limiting the types of weapons that can be used legally, including the Ottawa Landmines Convention and the Convention outlawing blinding laser weapons.

6.3 UN Security Council as human rights and humanitarian law monitor

Particularly since the end of the Cold War and the demise of the Soviet Union, the UN Security Council has monitored many, if not all, disputes involving human rights and humanitarian law violations. The Security Council has, on countless occasions, called on specific countries to respect human rights and humanitarian law and has increasingly imposed sanctions.[18] Even during the Cold War, the Security Council imposed sanctions on then Southern Rhodesia and apartheid South Africa for their gross human rights violations, including systematically discriminating against the African majority, and for blatantly denying African people within their borders the right to self-determination.[19]

Frequently, states committing humanitarian law violations also commit human rights violations. The UN Security Council's controversial sanctions on Saddam Hussein's Iraq stemmed mainly from humanitarian law violations (Iraq's aggression in invading and attempting to annex Kuwait), but also human rights violations (Iraq's depradations against the Kurds, the Shia, and any who opposed that regime). Human rights probably played a major part in the Security Council's imposing sanctions on Afghanistan, Haiti, and Rwanda. Humanitarian law violations perhaps played a more major role in imposing sanctions on Liberia and Sierra Leone. Yet the latter two countries contained factions and groups that likewise violated human rights law.

The Security Council's establishment of the ad hoc tribunals can, to a great extent, be considered an exercise in promoting human rights and respect for humanitarian law. All these courts, for example, authorize the prosecution of individuals for committing genocide and crimes against humanity. These are essentially human rights crimes. All the tribunals also authorize the prosecution of individuals for war crimes. These tribunals now include the International Criminal Tribunal for the former Yugoslavia, the International

Criminal Tribunal for Rwanda, the Special Court for Sierra Leone, the Special Tribunal for Lebanon, and the Extraordinary Chambers in the Courts of Cambodia.[20]

6.4 Indefinite detention and detention without trial

After 9/11, one can understand the attractions of indefinite detention for those charged with guaranteeing the security of the nation. Indefinite detention prevents suspected terrorists from rejoining their colleagues, from sharing information with them, and from carrying out additional acts of terrorism. Indefinite detention might be perceived as helping security forces obtain "actionable intelligence" from the detainee and might deter others from engaging in terrorist activities. In the "global war on terror" one more terrorist is taken from the "enemy."

Furthermore, giving suspected terrorists lawyers and trials will, according to this argument, stop the flow of actionable intelligence. Informants may have to testify. Terrorist minnows could be killed or pressured by terrorist sharks. The fabric of intelligence gathering shown to be at best threadbare by 9/11 itself will be further torn. Consequently, suspects need to be kept indefinitely and given what amounts to cursory hearings at best.

Neither domestic law nor international law is deaf to security needs. The absolute approach taken by the Bush–Cheney administration, however, collided with international law and practice. Human rights law and the law of war (humanitarian law) permit detention without trial for a limited period of time. What they forbid is indefinite detention. The system of bail generally has an element of preventive detention. Although technically bail should be granted as long as the evidence shows the defendant will present herself at trial, generally courts either refuse to set bail or set bail very high in cases where the defendants are accused of a very serious crime or have otherwise exhibited dangerousness. A departure from the stated rule but probably reflecting actual practice was the Federal Bail Reform Act, which expressly permitted judges to consider a defendant's dangerousness in setting bail. In any event, the period of detention without trial ends when the defendant receives a trial. In the US, defendants denied bail generally receive a trial within a year of being charged.[21]

Likewise, the Third Geneva Convention of 1949 allows a state to detain a prisoner of war without trial until hostilities cease. Prisoners of war are entitled to a hearing if their status as a prisoner of war is in doubt, but are otherwise entitled neither (a) to be charged with an offense (other than for a war crime) nor (b) to be released. The drafters of the Third Geneva Convention presumably believed that wars would have a beginning and an end. Consequently, prisoners of war would not be indefinitely detained by the other power.

As noted at the beginning of this chapter, however, the Bush–Cheney administration made two broad assertions: first that the US is involved in a global war on terrorism and second that not only do members of terrorist organizations and their allies (such as allegedly are the Taliban) not qualify as prisoners of war under the Third Geneva Convention, but also the US, just as with prisoners of war, is entitled to detain these individuals without trial until "the cessation of hostilities." There are many problems with these assertions, but let us just discuss the last point. As noted elsewhere, "terrorism" is so vague that the war on terrorism may never cease. The term "war on terrorism" does not name a particular party that the US is at war with. Is the opposing party al Qaeda, the Iraqi insurgency, the Taliban, Muslim extremists generally, or anyone who engages in the stratagem of terrorism, killing and wounding civilians? Given the breadth of the phrase and its potentially unending duration, these individuals have been (as of this writing) indefinitely detained in Guantánamo Bay, Bagram Air Base, and in other United States foreign detention centers.[22]

The Bush–Cheney administration implicitly argued that upon being detained, al Qaeda members and their allies fell into a legal black hole, covered neither by the Geneva Conventions nor by customary international law. The authoritative ICRC commentary to Geneva Conventions, however, explains:

> [E]very person in enemy hands must have some status under inter-national law: he is either a prisoner of war and, as such, covered by the Third Convention, a civilian covered by the Fourth Convention, or again, a member of the medical personnel of the armed forces who is covered by the Convention . . . [t]here is no intermediate status; nobody in enemy hands can be outside the law.[23]

The Geneva Conventions, therefore, cover individuals who engage in hostilities, but who do not qualify for prisoner of war status. The Fourth Geneva Convention considers saboteurs and spies and persons "under definite suspicion of activity hostile to the occupying power" to be "civilians."[24] That class of individuals includes "irregular combatants."[25] Aside from requiring that the Power treat such individuals "with humanity," Article 78 of the Fourth Geneva Convention permits the occupying power to intern such individuals without trial "for imperative reasons of security." The Fourth Convention requires the internment to be regularly reviewed, generally every six months. The plain meaning and drafting history of Article 78 and related Articles 41 and 42 demonstrate that these sections intended to keep internment as short as possible and certainly did not authorize indefinite detention.

The Fourth Geneva Convention expressly applies to international armed conflict, such as exists in Afghanistan and Iraq. The law is less clear regarding non-international armed conflict. Common Article 3 of the Geneva Conventions does not expressly deal with indefinite detention. Likewise, the 1977 Additional Protocol II to the Geneva Conventions of 1949 does not specifically set out the duties of a state dealing with insurgents or other non-uniformed combatants. Most states viewed such conflicts as internal matters where their domestic law governed the rights of insurgents. States typically have treated insurgents as criminals, charging them with a criminal offense, trying them, and often sentencing them to long prison terms if not actually executing them.

Because human rights law is more detailed and specific regarding the obligations of parties to a non-international armed conflict, under the principle of *lex specialis*, human rights law should play a large role, if not control, the rights and obligations of governments and individuals in that type of conflict. Furthermore, non-derogable human rights obligations should apply regardless of the nature of the conflict. Although Article 9 of the ICCPR prohibiting arbitrary arrest and detention *is* derogable, the "public emergency which threatens the life of a nation" is contemplated as requiring a high threshold and lasting a short time. The drafters of the ICCPR did not contemplate that the public emergencies would last indefinitely.[26] True, the ICCPR drafting history indicates that making Article 9 derogable was *not* an oversight.[27] But since 1966 when the ICCPR first became open for signature, international institutions have strengthened Article 9 rights and specifically the right of habeas corpus. First, the official UN Human Rights Committee charged with monitoring compliance with the ICCPR has narrowly construed the Article 4 on derogation: "Measures derogating from the provisions must be of an exceptional and temporary nature."[28] The UN Human Rights Committee spoke specifically to the right of habeas corpus: "In order to protect non-derogable rights, the right to take proceedings before a court to enable the court to decide without delay on the lawfulness of detention, must not be diminished by a State party's decision to derogate from the Covenant."[29]

Second, sister human rights bodies dealing with generally similar derogation provisions have recognized the non-derogable nature of the right of habeas corpus. Interpreting the American Convention of Human Rights,[30] the Inter-American Court of Human Rights has held habeas corpus is a non-derogable right, explaining, "[H]abeas corpus performs a vital role in ensuring that a person's life and physical integrity are respected, in preventing his disappearance or the keeping of his whereabouts secret and in protecting him against torture or other cruel, inhumane, or degrading punishment or treatment."[31] Likewise, the European Court of Human Rights (ECtHR) has narrowly construed derogations from habeas corpus (Article 5, European Convention for the Protection of Fundamental Rights and Freedoms). For example, the ECtHR held that Turkey detaining an alleged member of the Kurdish Workers Party (PKK) for 14 days without affording him the right to appear before a magistrate violated the European Convention, even in the presence of a recognized public emergency.[32]

Furthermore, Article 7 of the ICCPR expressly prohibits torture and cruel, inhuman, and degrading treatment. Article 7 is non-derogable. Although it would be hard to demonstrate that indefinite detention amounted to torture,

Vincent Proulx notes that indefinite detention may constitute "cruel, inhuman and degrading treatment": "It is no secret that long-term incommunicado detention, in itself, engenders devastating psychological damage."[33] Cut off from families and friends, locked up in some cases for over seven years without being charged, and suffering from worrying about the uncertainty of their fate (there have been over 30 suicide attempts), Guantánamo detainees, at least before the 2008 *Boumediene* ruling, and detainees in America's other foreign prisons could make out a strong case for being subject to "cruel, inhuman and degrading treatment" on this ground.[34]

Ashley Deeks did a study of the state practice concerning indefinite detention, examining among others, Kosovo Force (KFOR) policies in Kosovo, the UK, the US, Israel, and Sierra Leone.[35] She found that most countries, even those confronting terrorist organizations, established discrete time limits, and often used the criteria of Article 78 of the Fourth Geneva Convention.

US detention policies under the Bush–Cheney administration, under the Detainee Treatment Act (DTA), and under the Military Commissions Act of 2006 (MCA), expressly withheld the right of *habeas corpus* from Guantánamo Bay detainees and other detainees the US held abroad. The DTA contained a narrow right of appeal to the D.C. Circuit Court of Appeals from CSRT (Combat Status Review Tribunal) hearings, but detainees still had no right to a trial. Consequently, both the Bush–Cheney administration and Congress established a regime of indefinite detention that violated international law.

In *Boumediene v. Bush,*[36] a sharply divided US Supreme Court found, in 2008, the Military Commissions Act unconstitutional for attempting to strip Guantánamo Bay detainees of their right to habeas corpus. The federal courts are just, as of this writing, beginning to address the habeas petitions made after *Boumediene* by Guantánamo Bay detainees.[37] The Obama administration has signaled a dramatic change in policy, but the precise contours of that policy have not, as of this writing, been revealed.[38] Even assuming, however, that the Obama administration either releases the Guantánamo Bay Detainees or brings them promptly to trial in the federal court, this issue may reappear. There is every likelihood, unfortunately, that there will be additional terrorist attacks on the US mainland.[39] There could very well be renewed pressures to adopt Bush–Cheney administration-like policies. For all the reasons set forth here, such pressures must be strongly resisted.

6.5 Trial rights

6.5.1 *Privileged and unprivileged combatants and the right to trial*

The human rights revolution has touched both humanitarian law and state practice and has narrowed the virtually unlimited power of states in dealing with rebels and others who commit crimes against civilians and against civilian buildings and other civilian objects. Understanding the legal regime first requires an analysis of the humanitarian law that applies to privileged combatants and the separate legal rules that apply to unprivileged combatants, what the Bush–Cheney administration called "unlawful enemy combatants." The Third Geneva Convention of 1949 grants combat immunity to privileged combatants. A uniformed soldier, for example, who kills enemy combatants during an armed conflict, is immune from prosecution for murder, unless the enemy had laid down their arms beforehand. If a privileged combatant, however, killed enemy combatants after they had surrendered and given up their weapons, the privileged combatant could be tried and convicted of a war crime. According to the Third Geneva Convention, the privileged combatant would be entitled to trial before a regularly constituted court and to all trial guarantees granted to the military force that captured the privileged combatant. During armed conflict, the trial can be carried out by a military court-martial rather than a civilian court as long as the military court-martial would have jurisdiction over its own troops for committing the same offense.[40]

The trial rights of unprivileged combatants to an international armed conflict are set forth initially in Article 5 of the Fourth Geneva Convention of 1949 and later more directly in Article 75 of the 1977 Additional Protocol I (AP I) to the 1949 Geneva Conventions.[41] Article 5 of Geneva IV states in pertinent part that when in a party's own territory or in territory occupied by a party, "an individual *protected person*[42] is detained as a spy or a *saboteur*, or as a person under definite suspicion of *activity hostile to security of {the State or} the Occupying Power* . . . [such individual] shall nevertheless be treated with humanity and in case of trial shall *not* be deprived of the rights of *fair and regular trial* prescribed by the present Convention."[43] Unprivileged combatants are unquestionably engaged in activities "hostile to the security of the State." They are directly akin to "saboteurs." The authoritative commentary written in 1957 by Pictet notes that, as indicated above, while perhaps "surprising," the Convention protects individuals "deliberately acting outside the laws of warfare." Pictet explains as follows:

> It might have been simpler to exclude [unprivileged combatants] from the benefits of the Convention, if such a course had been possible, but the terms espionage, sabotage, *terrorism*, banditry and intelligence with the enemy, have so often been used lightly, and applied to such trivial offences . . . that it was not advisable to leave the accused at the mercy of those detaining them.[44]

Although unprivileged combatants may be initially interned, they are entitled to a "fair and regular trial" as "prescribed by" the Convention. During the plenary session at Geneva in which Article 5 was debated, Mr. Sinclair, the UK representative, spoke, without contradiction, about the critical nature of the trial rights for such individuals: "Those who were responsible for the framing of Article 3A [Article 5 in the final version of Geneva IV] were quite satisfied that there could on *no account* be any possible occasion upon which anybody, *whatever act they did*, could not have a *fair trial* and this is why the provision in question was put in. . . ."[45] Articles 64 through 76 detail the fair trial rights of those accused under the Geneva IV. Among other rights, the accused are entitled to prompt notice "of the particulars of the charges preferred against them"; to be brought to trial "as rapidly as possible"; to present evidence "necessary to their defense," including the right to call witnesses; to counsel of their own choosing; the right to counsel visits "freely"; the right to assigned counsel under certain circumstances; the right to an interpreter; the right to appeal if convicted; the right against being convicted on the basis of *ex post facto* laws; notification to the accused's country of the charges; and the right of the accused's nation to send a representative to observe the trial.[46]

Significantly, Article 76 requires that protected persons, including unprivileged combatants, "be detained in the occupied country, and if convicted they shall serve their sentences therein."[47] Consequently, the Fourth Convention prohibited the US from transferring those captured or arrested in Afghanistan to Guantánamo Bay. According to Geneva IV, those individuals should have been kept in Afghanistan, charged and tried there, and, if found guilty, made to serve their sentence in that land.

In addition to Article 5 of the Fourth Geneva Convention, Article 75 of AP I sets forth more directly and specifically the trial rights of unprivileged combatants to an international armed conflict.[48] Article 75 states that "persons who are in the power of a Party to the conflict and who *do not benefit from more favourable treatment under the Conventions* [the four Geneva Conventions of 1949] or under this Protocol shall be treated humanely in all circumstances and shall enjoy, as a minimum," the following rights:

1. To be tried by "an impartial and regularly constituted court";
2. To be "informed without delay of the particulars of the offence alleged";
3. To not be tried for an *ex post facto* offense;
4. To receive a presumption of innocence;
5. To not be "compelled to testify against himself or to confess guilt";
6. To have the right to "examine . . . the witnesses against him and to obtain the attendance and examination of witnesses on his behalf";
7. To not be subject to double jeopardy; and
8. To have "the judgment pronounced publicly" and to "be advised" of his or her rights to appeal, the time-limits to exercise such rights, and to "other [available] remedies."[49]

Because individual members of al Qaeda and its allied groups have been characterized as unprivileged combatants in connection with the conflict in Afghanistan, they would fall under Article 5 of Geneva IV and under the customary rules set forth in AP I, Article 75. As such, they would be entitled to the fair trial guarantees set forth above.[50]

The Geneva Conventions of 1949 have been ratified by all 192 member states of the UN. The US ratified the Geneva Conventions, including the Fourth Geneva Convention, in 1955.[51] The US Senate attached no reservations relevant here in giving its advice and consent to the Conventions. Consequently, the US is bound by Geneva IV and it applies to all US operations overseas that constitute international armed conflict. Geneva IV thus applies in Afghanistan and Iraq and also to individuals captured and arrested in those conflicts and taken elsewhere, namely, those unprivileged combatants and others taken to Guantánamo Bay, Bagram Air Base, and other US detention centers around the world.

The US, however, has taken a different approach to the 1977 AP I to the Geneva Conventions of 1949. The First Additional Protocol has been widely ratified, achieving 170 state parties as of May 2011.[52] The US, however, has not ratified the Protocol. President Ronald Reagan refused to submit the AP I to the Senate because the AP I has an Article widening the definition of privileged combatant to include individuals not wearing uniforms but who are carrying their arms openly.[53] President Reagan believed that this broader definition would cover terrorists and thus opposed the AP I. The US, however, has generally approved of most of the other Articles of AP I. Relevant here, the US had acknowledged that, before 9/11, Article 75 had crystallized into customary international law.[54] So the US has been obligated under both Geneva IV and under customary international law to provide unprivileged combatants the trial rights set forth above.

6.6 Outside international armed conflict

The analysis does not, however, necessarily end here. Geneva IV and AP I apply to *international* armed conflict, namely "to all cases of declared war or of any other armed conflict which may arise between two or more of the High Contracting Parties [States (countries) that have ratified AP I]."[55] Geneva IV and the customary law rules of AP I would apply to the war in Afghanistan, which was begun by the US, with a coalition of other states, invading that country on October 7, 2001. Geneva IV and the customary law rules of AP I would also apply to the war in Iraq, for the same reason. On the other hand, individuals who commit terrorist crimes outside of an armed conflict or outside of an *international* armed conflict do not fall under the customary rules of AP I or under Geneva IV (except for Common Article 3).

So, for example, suspected al Qaeda members arrested in Bosnia hardly fit within the definition of being apprehended in the midst of an "international armed conflict." The question then is whether the rights accorded to so-called unprivileged combatants to an *international* armed conflict (under Geneva IV and under custom (AP I, Article 75)) disappear in the absence of such a conflict. More modern developments in human rights law help provide the answer to that question.

One could characterize the "war on terrorism" as a non-international armed conflict. If terrorist crimes are carried out by private groups and not sponsored by states, then there is no conflict between two or more states. There may be a conflict between one state and one or more terrorist organizations. The Bush–Cheney administration essentially accepted this characterization, which, by the way, is still the subject of debate. That administration then argued that detained suspected terrorists fell into a legal black hole: They were not covered by Geneva III because they did not wear uniforms. They were not covered by Geneva IV, the Civilian Convention, because they were combatants, not civilians.[56] They were not covered by AP I because, among other reasons, the conflict did not reach international status within the meaning of that convention. Furthermore, said the Bush–Cheney administration, these individuals were not protected by Common Article 3 of the four 1949 Geneva Conventions. In relevant part, Common Article 3 states, "In the case of armed conflict *not* of an international character *occurring in the territory of one of the High Contracting Parties, each Party* shall be bound to apply at a minimum, the following provisions . . . (1)(d) [prohibiting] the passing of sentences and the carrying out of executions without previous judgment pronounced *by a regularly constituted court affording all the judicial guarantees which are recognized as indispensable by civilized peoples.*"[57] The administration argued that since that Article was aimed at civil wars, Common Article 3 did not apply.

It is hard to deny that the drafters of Common Article 3 originally intended that the Article cover civil wars, primarily. The use of the term "not of an international character occurring in the territory of *one* of the High Contracting Parties" suggests that the conflict would "occur" inside "one" state.[58] The language does not readily lend itself to include a non-state transnational terrorist organization operating in more than one state. On the other hand, the language does not expressly limit itself to civil wars, and the authoritative commentary of the International Committee of the Red Cross points out "that the scope of application of the Article must be as wide as possible."[59] Presumably, if the drafters intended to make such a limitation, they could have done so. Furthermore, the commentary suggests that Common Article 3 provides a ground floor level of guarantees that operate in all armed conflict regardless of the label.[60] The International Court of Justice in *Nicaragua v. United States* made the same observation, noting that Common Article 3 sets forth a "minimum yardstick" applicable to all conflicts.[61] The Appellate Chamber of the International Criminal Tribunal for the former Yugoslavia so held in the *Prosecutor v. Tadic* case, noting that under current interpretations of Common Article 3 "the character of the conflict is irrelevant."[62] Lastly, the US Supreme Court implicitly agreed with the previous two tribunals, ruling in *Hamdan v. Rumsfeld* in 2006 that the "conflict" with al Qaeda can be characterized as a conflict under Common Article 3.[63]

Common Article 3 is not as specific as either Geneva IV, Articles 64–76, or AP I, Article 75. Instead of the list of guarantees enumerated above, Common Article 3 requires that individuals be tried "by a regularly constituted court," which provides "all the judicial guarantees which are recognized as indispensable by civilized peoples." Despite language in the Military Commissions Act to the contrary, military commissions in response to 9/11 probably do not amount to a "regularly constituted court." A regularly constituted court suggests one that is pre-existing and not formed to try a particular person or a particular group of individuals. On this point the US Supreme Court observed in *Hamdan v. Rumsfeld*:

> While the term "regularly constituted court" is not specifically defined in either Common Article 3 or its accompanying commentary, other sources disclose its core meaning. The commentary accompanying a provision of the Fourth Geneva Convention, for example, defines "regularly constituted" tribunals to include "ordinary military courts" and "definitely excludes all special tribunals[.]"[64]

The US Supreme Court concluded that "regularly constituted" would embrace civilian courts and military courts-martial but not military commissions established by the Executive.[65] A plurality of the US Supreme Court also discussed the second relevant phrase in Common Article 3: "All the judicial guarantees which are recognized as indispensable by civilized peoples." The *Hamdan* plurality concluded that "indispensable" judicial guarantees in Common Article 3 are now taken to mean the guarantees contained in Article 75 of AP I.[66]

6.7 Human rights law

Aside from the trial rights recognized by humanitarian law, the ICCPR contains widely agreed-upon trial guarantees. The ICCPR contains most of the same guarantees contained in Article 75 of AP I, including the presumption of innocence, the right to be promptly informed of the charges, the right to speedy trial, the right to be present at one's own trial, the right to counsel, the right to cross-examine opposing witnesses, and to be able to "obtain the attendance" of his or her own witnesses, the right not to be compelled to testify against oneself or to confess guilt, the right to an appeal, and the right against *ex post facto* laws being the basis of criminal charges.[67] The ICCPR adds some rights, namely, (1) "[t]o have adequate time and facilities for the preparation of his defense. . . ."; (2) "[t]o have the free assistance of an interpreter" if necessary, and (3) to have a right of compensation for wrongful conviction.[68]

The ICCPR does have a derogation provision, giving states parties some latitude for public emergencies. Specifically, Article 4 of the ICCPR does permit states to derogate from some of their obligations in "times of public emergency, which threatens the life of the nation. . . ."[69] There are, however, certain rights from which a state may never derogate. Even in times of emergency, such as in times of war, a state must still guarantee the following: (a) the right against being arbitrarily deprived of one's life, (b) the right against being subject to torture or to cruel, inhuman, or degrading treatment or punishment, (c) the right against being held in slavery or being required to perform compulsory labor, (d) the right against being convicted under an *ex post facto* law, and (e) the right to freedom of thought, conscience, and religion.[70]

Conspicuously absent from the list of non-derogable rights, however, is the right to a fair trial in non-capital cases. The official Human Rights Committee that is expressly charged under the ICCPR with monitoring states parties' compliance with the Covenant has responded to this apparent lacuna in the list of non-derogable rights:

> As certain elements of the right to a fair trial are explicitly guaranteed under international humanitarian law during armed conflict [presumably referring to Common Article 3 and to Article 75 of AP I] the Committee finds no justification for derogation from these guarantees during other emergency situations.[71]

The Committee concluded that during times of public emergency, fundamental requirements of fair trial "must be respected," that the accused is entitled to the presumption of innocence, that individuals may be tried for a criminal offense only by "a court of law," and that detainees are entitled to have a court decide their habeas corpus petitions "without delay."[72]

Responding to the argument about the challenge of international terrorism, the Inter-American Commission on Human Rights did issue a report on post 9/11 trial rights of suspected terrorists: "[M]ost fundamental fair trial requirements cannot justifiably be suspended under either international human rights law or international humanitarian law. These protections therefore apply to the investigation, prosecution and punishment of crimes, including those relating to terrorism, regardless of whether such initiatives may be taken in time of peace or in times of national emergency, including armed conflict. . . ."[73] The Inter-American Commission issued an order for precautionary measures against the US for failing to provide Article 5 tribunals to determine the status of those held at Guantánamo Bay.

The US vigorously objected to the Commission's action, arguing that humanitarian law as set forth in Geneva III was outside the competence of the Commission and that the US had (by Presidential order) determined that all the Guantánamo Bay detainees were unprivileged combatants and thus not entitled to be treated as prisoners of war. The US argued that since the Taliban (and al Qaeda) fighters had not worn uniforms, they did not sufficiently distinguish themselves under Article 4 of Geneva III. The US also argued that such detainees were not civilians within the meaning of Geneva IV, but nonetheless could be held until hostilities ceased just as POWs can be held. The Commission later noted, however, that some of the individuals detained in Guantánamo Bay were not captured on the battlefield, but rather in Bosnia and Pakistan. The Commission implied that such individuals were taken outside of armed conflict and thus fell squarely within the mandate of the Declaration of the Rights of Man, the OAS resolution that provides the Commission's jurisdiction over the US.[74]

We can draw from both the Commission's and the US's arguments. The US Supreme Court ultimately backed the Commission's request that the US conduct Geneva III, Article 5 hearings.[75] The US's arguments about the Commission's competence may have been sound regarding the capture of individuals on the battlefields of Afghanistan—though many argue that the US put forth an overly broad interpretation of the *lex specialis* principle.[76] Yet it is undoubtedly true that in international armed conflict, a state may try unprivileged combatants by military courts-martial, a regularly constituted court, provided that all the guarantees set forth in Geneva IV, Article 5, 64–76 and AP I, Article 75 are granted to the defendant.[77] Common Article 3 presumably permits using military courts-martial ("regularly constituted courts") to try individuals involved in non-international armed conflict.

Military tribunals themselves, however, have to comply with human rights standards. For example, in addition to the guarantees referred to in the previous paragraph, the ECtHR has required its 47 member states to insure that military courts-martial are independent and impartial and give the appearance of being independent and impartial.[78] The Court invalidated a court-martial in which the convening officer appointed the prosecutor, the defense counsel, the president of the courts-martial, and all its members and was superior to and in the direct chain of command to all the participants.[79] The UN Human Rights Committee has also underscored the necessity of judicial impartiality and independence, including in courts-martial.[80]

Let us now dispose of the easier argument first. Those unprivileged captured on the battlefield in Afghanistan or Iraq are entitled to the guarantees of Geneva IV, Articles 5, 64–76 and to the customary international law rights of Article 75 of AP I, but they are not entitled to a civilian trial. They may not be tried by special courts (such as military commissions), but rather a regularly constituted court, such as a military court-martial. Of course, the US or any other country could provide them civilian trials, but international law does no so require.

A more difficult issue is posed by individuals detained abroad but outside a war zone. For example, let us examine the cases of the six Algerians who were detained in Bosnia and taken to Guantánamo Bay (as pointed out by the Inter-American Commission of Human Rights). Unless one accepts the Bush–Cheney administration's characterization of a global war against terrorism, these individuals were not arrested, detained, or captured in an armed conflict at all. Assuming they are *not* being charged for crimes committed in a war zone such as Iraq or Afghanistan, these individuals fall outside of the law of war (humanitarian law) and fall squarely within the human rights law regime as set forth in Article 14 of the ICCPR.

Although some might argue the distinction is artificial given the highly advanced technology of communications and advanced weaponry, geography matters. The law of war is by its nature exceptional. Under this body of law, a combatant may be immune from criminal prosecution for deliberately killing a human being even when not acting in self-defense. Under this body of law, hundreds or thousands of innocent civilians can be killed or wounded as long as the combatants were aiming at a military objective and the civilian casualties were not clearly anticipated to be disproportional to the importance of that military objective. Under this body of law, so-called dual use military objects can be destroyed even if the military use is secondary and the civilian one primary. Electrical grids, oil refineries, oil wells, bridges, all can be targeted under such a rationale. Letting a nation state attack a suspected terrorist any place on earth creates greater instability than security. Such broad authority would suggest that the US, Russia, China, India, North Korea, or Iran, for example, can send its agents to any country it wishes and carry out military operations in the name of combating terrorism. Such cannot be the law.

Consequently, those individuals who are arrested for committing terrorist offenses outside of war zones should be tried not by military courts-martial, but by civilian courts.[81] The ECtHR underlined this rule in two notable cases involving Turkey. In the first case, the Court held that Turkey had violated the international law trial rights of a Turkish national who was accused of inciting a separatist movement by passing out leaflets.[82] There, the ECtHR found the trial court lacked the necessary independence under Article 6.1 of the European Convention[83] because there was one military judge in the three-judge trial panel with two civilian judges. The second case involved the infamous Abdullah Ocalan, the head of the PKK, arguably the most violent contemporary terrorist organization the world had seen before the advent of al Qaeda. (One of the PKK's strategies was to kill Turkish school-teachers.) In the middle of Ocalan's trial, a civilian judge replaced the sole military judge on the three-judge panel. The ECtHR, however, held that this change was not enough, that the case had to be retried because the presence of the military judge, though part of the trial, gave the appearance and the fact of a lack of judicial independence.[84]

If one were to accept the *Hamdan* court's characterization of the "conflict" with al Qaeda as a non-international armed conflict and if one were to accept the Bush–Cheney administration's characterization of the global war on ter-rorism, then international law would require, at a minimum, trials by a regu-larly constituted court, namely, by military courts-martial.[85] Military com-missions would not qualify. As pointed out earlier, however, that "global war on terrorism" characterization has been rejected by many nations, including Britain, the US's closest ally.[86]

As a practical matter, adopting the distinction between arresting or captur-ing individuals for crimes committed in war zones and arresting individuals for crimes committed outside of war zones is workable. Individuals captured in Afghanistan and Iraq for committing terrorist offenses are thus within the jurisdiction of US courts-martial. Individuals captured outside of these or other war zones are within the jurisdiction of civilian courts, namely in US federal courts. Most likely, the largest number of individuals would be captured in war zones and thus be subject to military courts-martial with all the attendant rights thereto. Questions of security of judges, prosecutors, and jurors become far less compelling when dealing with military rather than civilian trials. Furthermore, military courts-martial are generally far more knowledgeable of humanitarian law than civilian courts. Consequently, these tribunals are fairly well equipped to handle and manage these types of cases. On the other hand, the question of judicial independence is a real one, given the hierarchical nature of the military and the powers the Executive holds over military judges serving without life tenure. Nevertheless, military courts-martial have a long history and are generally considered independent tribunals. Of course, the US could elect to provide these individuals with civilian trials, a matter which is discussed below.

6.8 Special national security courts

Some commentators have opposed the use of federal courts for trying those charged with committing terrorist crimes. Instead, they argue that the US should establish national security courts for individuals charged with terrorist offenses. Glenn Sulmasy, Judge Advocate of the Coast Guard, for example, argues for establishing national security courts for the following reasons. First, the 'so-called war against terrorism' is a hybrid between war and law enforcement,' and thus requires a hybrid court; second, applying law-enforcement procedures to combat operations contradicts the warrior ethos and deleteriously affects combat operations; third, the law of war requires specialist judges who know humanitarian law; fourth, national security courts would be better equipped without making exorbitant expenditures to ensure the security of judges, prosecutors, defense, counsel, witnesses, and jurors; and fifth, national security courts minimize the potential for "eroding our standards" in other cases.[87]

Matthew Waxman, who served in the Justice Department during President George W. Bush's second term, poses the following hypothetical question: what about the case where "there is a reasonable basis to believe that a person [a suspected terrorist] is dangerous, but not enough evidence to persuade a court beyond a reasonable doubt that the person is guilty?"[88] As with many hypothetical cases, one has to be quite careful to make sure the hypothetical case is not misleading, namely, that antiseptically stating the hypothetical does not drain so much blood from the real cases that one loses a full appreciation of the truth facing American interrogators and other counterterrorism interrogators throughout the world. Waxman's question will be answered first, followed by a response to Sulmasy's arguments.

6.9 The material support statute

Federal prosecutors have an impressive array of tools to obtain criminal convictions of suspected terrorists. Although quite dull sounding, the material support statute has been the federal prosecutors' major weapon in the legal battle against terrorism and essentially addresses the situation Waxman highlights.[89] A species of a conspiracy offense, the material support statute imposes a punishment of up to 15 years or life if a death occurs for anyone who aids individuals carrying out terrorist offenses or supports a listed foreign terrorist organization, even if the donor did not intend to aid terrorism or to strengthen the violent wing of the listed organization. The statute eliminates the "purposely" *mens rea* usually required for conspiracy and the general requirement for aiding and abetting that the aided offense be carried out.[90] Material support includes giving "any . . . service," a fairly broad description that could include pizza delivery persons[91] and baby sitters; "material support" likewise includes giving "expert advice or assistance," which may include attorneys who represent accused terrorists at trial.[92] Attending a terrorist training camp (giving of oneself as "personnel"[93]) falls within the heartland of the statute as does joining the terrorist organization or helping, even remotely, to finance it. John Walker Lindh pleaded guilty under this statute and was sentenced to 20 years in prison for joining the Taliban.[94] The evidence, however, did not indicate that Lindh ever fought against US troops or intended to fight the US.

Civil libertarians have criticized the material support statute for being overbroad. Professor David Cole described the material support statute as follows:

> Under this law it would be a crime for a Quaker to send a book on Gandhi's theory of nonviolence—a "physical asset"—to the leader of a terrorist organization in hopes of persuading him to forgo violence. Indeed, the Quaker would have no defense even if he could show that his efforts had succeeded in convincing the group to end its violent ways. Similarly, if this law had been on the books in the 1980s, the thousands of Americans who donated money to the African National Congress (ANC) for its lawful political struggle against apartheid would face lengthy prison terms, because during those years the ANC was designated as a terrorist organization by our State Department.[95]

Presumably responding to this concern, Joan Donoghue, then Acting Legal Adviser to the State Department, stated, as noted in chapter 2, that the Obama administration would require "substantial" support rather than just any support before prosecuting an individual under the material support statute.[96] The Obama administration's first filing in federal court regarding the Guantánamo Bay detainees likewise used the term "substantial" support.[97] While an improvement over the original enactment, the word "substantial" is vague and may not give an individual fair warning of support that crosses the line from legality to illegality.

The Ninth Circuit declared part of the statute unconstitutional.[98] Other courts have declared unconstitutional language that would permit prosecuting an attorney for representing the organization and giving legal advice to the organization and its high officers. Congress amended the material support statute to eliminate some of the problems identified by the courts, but created some additional problems.[99] The statute remains broad. Anyone who gives just about anything to someone who is committing or planning to commit a terrorist offense or to listed foreign terrorist organizations, with a few limited exceptions, may be prosecuted. Although at first glance such an objective appears reasonable, the statute also applies to individuals who never intended that any terrorist crime be carried out, potentially covers minor acts of aid, and carries a heavy maximum sentence.

Many commentators have defended the statute as being "a kind of criminal early-warning and preventive-enforcement device designed to nip the risk of terrorist activity in the bud."[100] Another defender puts it this way: "The first priority of the government in fighting terrorism is prevention. The material support statute is an essential tool in the war on terror because it allows federal prosecutors to bring a case before any acts of terrorism have been committed."[101]

Regardless of what one thinks of the statute's merits, the material support statute is unquestionably the new so-called darling in the prosecutor's nursery, at least when it comes to prosecuting suspected terrorists. It has been used in virtually every prosecution for terrorist offenses. It is easy to convict an individual for violating it. On the other hand, one could construct a hypothetical where the information was gleaned from the defendant by torture or by cruel, inhuman, or degrading treatment. Even in such a case where the defendant's confession or incriminating statements should be suppressed, there will probably be other evidence available to convict that person under the material support statute. If there is not sufficient evidence, one wonders what makes our security personnel so sure that the individual in fact is a dangerous terrorist.

Furthermore, federal prosecutors possess an array of other statutes that individuals who commit terrorist offenses often run afoul of. For example, individuals bent on carrying out terrorist crimes often violate other criminal laws, such as forging passports, stealing credit cards, and infringing immigration statutes and regulations.[102] Prosecutors can and should avail themselves of these kinds of criminal charges against individuals who are carrying out or conspiring to carry out terrorism offenses.

In answering Waxman's hypothetical case, namely where the interrogator is reasonably sure that the individual suspected terrorist is highly dangerous but where there is insufficient admissible evidence to garner a conviction, Richard Zabel and James Benjamin, former federal prosecutors, state as follows:

> Given the breadth of the federal criminal code, the energy and resource-fulness of law enforcement agents and federal prosecutors, and the fact that terrorists, by definition, are criminals who often violate many laws,

we believe it would be the rare case indeed where the government could not muster enough evidence to bring a criminal charge against a person it believes is culpable.[103]

Sulmasy raises a challenging objection to using civilian courts, namely, the security threat posed by a terrorist organization to civil judges, prosecutors, defense counsel, juries, and witnesses. A well-financed terrorist organization like al Qaeda and its allied organizations do pose a genuine threat to the federal court system. The answer, however, is not automatically to turn to military tribunals for all terrorism offenses or to create special national security courts. First, approximately 90 percent of all criminal cases are resolved through plea bargains, not trials. Second, US courts have extensive experience in dealing with organized crime and with other groups of violent individuals. State and federal courts have used the device of anonymous juries, witness protection, protective custody, the material witness statute, and other tools to protect the individual actors in the criminal justice system.[104] Most of those arrested or captured would probably be taken from a war zone such as Iraq and Afghanistan and only a small remnant would be arrested outside of such war zones. At least so far, that has been the apparent pattern that the US has followed.[105] Most arrests (or captures) have taken place in Afghanistan and Iraq, with a few in neighboring countries such as Pakistan. Since those taken in war zones can properly be tried by military courts-martial, the number of individuals charged with terrorist offenses is unlikely to overwhelm the federal court system.

Sulmasy also objects to Article III federal courts and presumably also to military courts-martial because of the exclusionary rule, that is, that such law enforcement procedures "contradict the warrior ethos" and harm combat operations. Under some circumstances, US courts will suppress physical evidence and a defendant's confession or incriminating statements under the Fourth and Fifth Amendments to the United States Constitution, respectively. Sulmasy notes that it would be absurd to expect American troops to provide Miranda warnings in battlefield situations to captured terrorist combatants or, even more preposterous, to obtain a search warrant before attacking and entering an individual's home in a foreign land where terrorists or terrorist activity is indicated. There are two answers to his objections: first, the US Supreme Court has not recognized the extraterritorial application of the Fourth Amendment.[106] Second, Zabel and Benjamin maintain that the "public security" exception to Miranda would apply to battlefield arrests; namely, that the need for information for security purposes would trump Miranda and that ruling would not apply to such arrest.[107] In any event, battlefield arrests would fall within the jurisdiction of military courts-martial and would not require trial by civilian courts.

6.10 Post 9/11

The megaterrorist events of 11 September 2001 were not only domestic crimes, but crimes against humanity, international offenses. In the words of the Supreme Court of Israel in the *Eichmann* case, such offenses "constitute acts which damage vital international interests; they impair the foundations and security of the international community. . . ."[108] In the aftermath of 9/11, many other countries besides the US enacted antiterrorism laws. For example, the UK, which had already enacted among the most stringent antiterrorism laws because of IRA terrorism, passed even tougher post 9/11 and 7/7 laws, the Prevention of Terrorism Act 2005[109] and the Terrorism Act 2006.[110] The Canadian Parliament enacted the Anti-Terrorism Act in 2001.[111] In June 2002, the Australian Parliament passed a number of antiterrorism laws with "sweeping" effects.[112] In 2006, Germany amended a statute passed in hysteria of the Red Army Faction terrorism, allowing *incommunicado* detention of alleged terrorists for up to 30 days.[113] In general, these statutes broadened the grounds for convicting an individual for terrorist offenses and gave the police the right to hold suspected terrorists *incommunicado* for some extended, limited period of time. The trend is disturbing. In particular, countries that have experienced terrorism perpetrated by private actors often responded with draconian measures, which have often later been regretted by people of the state in question. India took an actual step in this direction, repealing in 2004 its 2002 antiterrorism law enacted in the wake of 9/11.[114] Unfortunately, after the 2009 Mumbai attacks, India reenacted many repressive provisions of its former anti-terrorism law.

The question that needs to be addressed is whether international law pertaining to the right against indefinite detention and the right of trial has changed since the megaterrorist event that took place on that date. As has been discussed elsewhere, the UN Security Council issued two resolutions shortly after 9/11; in its resolution of 14 September 2001, the Security Council condemned the attacks and reiterated the right of individual and collective self-defense. In its much more detailed policymaking resolution of 27 September 2001, the Security Council, acting under its chapter VII powers, required all states to actively prosecute terrorists, to stop terrorist financing, to exchange information, and to take measures to prevent terrorists from obtaining haven in any state. Other than cautioning states not to let terrorists abuse political asylum, the resolutions say nothing about the rights of individuals suspected or charged with terrorist offenses.

As a matter of state practice, the US did not comply with Geneva IV or with the customary norms codified in Article 75 of AP I. First, individuals captured in Afghanistan and later in other parts of the world were transferred to Guantánamo Bay, Cuba. They were held *incommunicado* for years; many detainees were subject to cruel and inhuman treatment, if not torture, and—until the US Supreme Court so ordered—they were not informed of the charges against them or given a hearing of any kind. The CSRT hearings were instituted to comply with Article 5 of Geneva III. That Article requires that the state holding detainees in armed conflict has to have a "competent tribunal" establish their status, for example as POWs or as unprivileged combatants. The CSRTs were set up after the US Supreme Court's decision in *Rasul*.[115] The US took the position that alleged terrorists in Guantánamo Bay could be held just like POWs until hostilities cease. Furthermore, the Bush–Cheney administration initially established military commissions, granting the accused far fewer rights than either federal courts or military courts-martial. After the US Supreme Court in *Hamdan* held that the President had exceeded his power in setting up the military commissions, the 2006 Republican Congress, in its waning months, passed the Military Commissions Act, largely duplicating the Military Commission structure that the President had established.

One cannot deny a post 9/11 trend limiting the rights of those suspected of terrorist offenses. The Bush–Cheney administration led this trend with its controversial detention policies. Those defending those policies could argue that a new customary norm is evolving limiting both the human rights and the humanitarian law rights of suspected terrorists. Yet, with the lead of the Obama administration, a counter-trend appears to be emerging, recognizing that the foundational principles both of the Geneva Conventions of 1949 and their two protocols and the human rights norms established in the human rights revolution reflect more closely the values of the world community. In addition, the UN General Assembly approved, in December 2006, a resolution for the "Protection of Human Rights and Fundamental Freedoms While Countering Terrorism" and, in December 2007, an anti-Torture resolution.[116]

Furthermore, there are real risks for the US and other countries that appear to be disregarding established humanitarian law and human rights law. There is an increased perception in the Islamic World that the West is applying a double standard to Muslims. Despite occasional calming rhetoric to the contrary, the restrictive counterterrorism laws are principally aimed at Muslims suspected of committing terrorist offenses and not at individuals from other groups that have carried out such acts. These statutes and counterterrorism practices have fomented appreciable resentment in the Islamic World, fueling recruitment for Muslim extremist groups and prompting greater financial and moral support in the Muslim world for such groups.

Consequently, the US and other democratic countries would do well to observe humanitarian law and human rights law. In the twentieth century, the world experienced more violence, more killings and wounding than in any previous century. Through dint of that experience, the international community has created laws and institutions that attempt to ensure security on the one hand and basic human protections for civilians and for the world's peoples, on the other. Although far from perfect, these efforts have advanced the world far beyond empire states, *de jure* racial and national origin discrimination, and unlimited aggressive war that marked more than the first half of the twentieth century. Such advances should not now be lightly set aside.

Notes

1   Convention relative to the Treatment of Prisoners of War (Geneva III), Aug. 12, 1949, 6 U.S.T. 3316, T.I.A.S. No. 3364, 75 U.N.T.S. 135, *available at* http://www.icrc.org/ihl.nsf/FULL/375?OpenDocument [hereinafter Geneva III].
2   *See* Charles H. Brower II, *Nunca Más or Déjà Vu*, 47 Va. J. Int'l L. 525, 527 n.45 (2007).
3   This definition reflects the definition of terrorism set forth in the Convention for the Suppression of Terrorist Financing: "Any other act intended to cause death or serious bodily injury to a civilian, or to any other person not taking an active part in the hostilities in a situation of armed conflict, when the purpose of such act, by its nature or context, is to intimidate a population, or to compel a government or an international organization to do or to abstain from doing any act." International Convention for the Suppression of the Financing of Terrorism art. 2.1(b), G.A. Res. 109, U.N. GAOR, 54th Sess., Supp. No. 49, U.N. Doc A/54/49 (Vol. I) (1999), S. Treaty Doc. No. 106–49 (2000), 39 I.L.M. 270 (2000), *adopted* Dec. 9, 1999, *entered into force* Apr. 10, 2002, *available at* www1.umn.edu/humanrts/instree/financingterrorism.html.
4   William R. Polk, Violent Politics, a History of Insurgency, Terrorism & Guerilla War from the American Revolution to Iraq 8, 12–19 (2007).
5   Ruth Scurr, Fatal Purity: Robespierre and the French Revolution 7 (2006).
6   I am indebted to Professor Detlev Vagts, who suggested this parallel at a meeting of the American Branch of the International Law Association.
7   Barbara W. Tuchman, The Proud Tower 63 (1966).
8   *Id.*
9   *Causes of World War I*, Eastern Michigan State University Wiki, http://historywiki.emich.edu/index.php?title=Causes_of_World_War_I.
10   August Vaillant, a French national, was tried and sentenced in a single day for throwing a bomb into the French parliament, which wounded many members of parliament but did not kill anyone. Tuchman, *supra* note 7, at 91–92.
11   *Luigi Galleani*, Nation Master Encyclopedia, www.nationmaster.com/encyclopedia/Luigi-Galleani; *1919 Anarchist Bombings*, Nation Master Encyclopedia, www.nationmaster.com/encyclopedia/1919-United-States-anarchist-bombings.
12   *Luigi Galleani*, Nation Master Encyclopedia, *supra* note 11.
13   J. Edgar Hoover, *The Palmer Raids*, http://law.jrank.org/pages/12220/Hoover-J-Edgar-Palmer-Raids.htm.
14   A. Mitchell Palmer, *The Case Against the Reds*, 63 Forum 173 (1920), *reprinted in* World War I At Home: Readings on American Life, 1914–1920, at 185–89 (David F. Trask comp., 1969), *available at* http://chnm.gmu.edu/courses/hist409/palmer.html.
15   David Cole observes that although Palmer and Hoover purposely targeted immigrants because they were more vulnerable and had fewer rights, some of the repressive practices after having been established against immigrants were then extended to US citizens. David Cole, *Enemy Aliens*, 54 Stan. L. Rev. 953 (2002).
16   Other human rights treaties and declarations since the Second World War include the following: the Convention on the Political Rights of Women in 1953, the ILO Convention Protecting Indigenous Populations in 1957, the Optional Protocol to the ICCPR also in 1966, the Refugee Protocol in 1967, the Declaration on Territorial Asylum also in 1967, the American Convention on Human Rights in 1969, the Universal Declaration on the Rights of Peoples in 1976, the European Convention on the Suppression of Terrorism in 1977, the African Charter on Human Rights and Peoples' Rights in 1981, the Siracusa

Principles on the Limitation and Derogation Provisions in the International Covenant on Civil and Political Rights in 1984, the Inter-American Convention to Prevent and Punish Torture in 1985, Declaration on the Right to Development in 1986, ILO Convention Concerning Indigenous and Tribal Peoples in 1989, Declaration on the Rights of Persons Belonging to National or Ethnic, Religious and Linguistic Minorities in 1992, Declaration on the Elimination of Violence against Women in 1993, Inter-American Convention on the Forced Disappearance of Persons in 1994. *See* Weston, Falk & Charleston, Treaty Supplement (1997).

17   The International Labor Organization, which was established in 1919, has worked to improve labor rights throughout the world. The ILO became the first specialized agency of the United Nations in 1946. *See* International Labor Organization, www.ilo.org/global/About_the_ILO/lang--en/index.htm.

18   Christopher C. Joyner, *United Nations Sanctions after Iraq, Looking Back to See Ahead*, 4 Chi. J. Int'l L. 329, 333 (2003) "Throughout its history, the Security Council invoked collective sanctions as enforcement actions under chapter VII only in fourteen cases: Afghanistan (1999–); Angola (1993–); Ethiopia and Eritrea (2000–2001); Haiti (1993–1994); Iraq (1990–2003); Liberia (1992–); Libya (1992–2003); Rwanda (1993–); Sierra Leone (1997–); Somalia (1992–); South Africa (1977–1994); Southern Rhodesia (1966–1979); Sudan (1996–2001); and the former Yugoslavia (1992–2002)." The Security Council has subsequently issued sanctions against the Democratic Republic of the Congo, the Ivory Coast, Iran, and North Korea. The Security Council has also sanctioned individuals, for example, freezing the assets and prohibiting the international travel of 10 top North Koreans involved with that country's nuclear weapons program. Colum Lynch, *UN Security Council Sanctions 10 in North Korea*, Wash. Post, July 17, 2009, *available at* http://www.washingtonpost.com/wp-dyn/content/article/2009/07/17/AR2009071602417.html.

19   The Security Council has imposed sanctions on many other occasions in order to prevent threats to the peace. Redressing human rights violations often, but not always, was a part of the Council's rationale in issuing sanctions. Examples include sanctions on Saddam Hussein's Iraq, sanctions on Angola, sanctions on Libya for failing to turn over individuals suspected of carrying out the Pan Am 103 bombing over Lockerbie. Critics of the Security Council have argued that sanctions have been overbroad, hurting innocent civilians while leaving the repressive leadership and ruling faction of the sanctioned country untouched. *See Sanctions*, Global Forum Policy, www.globalpolicy.org/security/sanction/theindex.htm.

20   The creation of the International Criminal Court is yet another reaffirmation of the world community's attempt to increase respect for both human rights and humanitarian law. As of this writing, 110 states have ratified the Rome Statute of the Criminal Court.

21   *Bureau of Justice Statistics*, U.S. Department of Justice, Office of Justice Programs, at: http://bjs.ojp.usdoj.gov/index.cfm?ty=pbdetail&iid=1558.

22   Decisions of the United States Supreme Court guaranteeing the right of habeas corpus and the announced Obama administration policy to close Guantánamo were thought to signal an end to indefinite detention. President Obama, however, has indicated that his administration will indefinitely detain a number of individuals: "[T]here may be a number of people who cannot be prosecuted for past crimes, but who nonetheless pose a threat to the security of the United States." Peter Finn, *Obama Endorses Indefinite Detention Without Trial For Some*, Wash. Post, May 22, 2009, *available at* http://www.washingtonpost.com/wp-dyn/content/article/2009/05/21/AR2009052104045.html.

23   *See* Rory T. Hood, *Guantánamo and Citizenship: An Unjust Ticket Home?*, 37

Case W. Res. J. Int'l L. 555, 563 (2006) (quoting Commentary on Geneva Convention IV of 1949 Relative to the Protection of Civilian Persons in Times of War 4 (Jean Pictet ed., 1958) [hereinafter Commentary on Geneva IV]).

24   *Id.*

25   *Id.*

26   Marc J. Bossuyt, Guide to the *"Travaux Préparatoires"* of the International Covenant on Civil and Political Rights 85–95 (1985).

27   *Id.*

28   UN Human Rights Committee (HRC), *General Comment No. 29, Article 4, States of Emergency*, para. 2, U.N. Doc. CCPR/C/21/Rev.1/Add/11 (Aug. 31, 2001) [hereinafter Human Rights Committee].

29   *Id.*, para. 16.

30   The US is not a party to the American Convention on Human Rights, but it is a signatory to the American Declaration on the Rights of Man.

31   Judicial Guarantees in States of Emergency (Arts. 27(2), 25 and 8, American Convention on Human Rights), Advisory Op. OC-9/87, Inter-Am. Ct. H.R. (ser. A) No. 9 (Oct. 6, 1987) (quoting Habeas Corpus in Emergency Situations (Arts. 27(2), 25(1) and 7(6), American Convention on Human Rights), Advisory Op. OC-8/87, Inter-Am. Ct. H.R. (ser. A) No. 8, at para. 35 (Jan. 30, 1987)).

32   Aksoy v. Turkey, App. No. 21987/93, 23 Eur. H.R. Rep. 553 (1996). There the Court took "account of the unquestionably serious problem of terrorism in South-East Turkey and the difficulties faced by the State in taking effective measures against it. However, it is not persuaded that the exigencies of the situation necessitated the holding of the applicant on suspicion of involvement in terrorist offences for fourteen days or more in incommunicado detention without access to a judge or other judicial officer." *Id.*, para. 84. The Court implied that a state that provides more vigorous human protections than Turkey might receive a wider margin of appreciation. Yet the court clearly disapproves of providing a blank check to states that assert the right to derogate from their Article 5 obligations. *Id.*, para. 76 (citing Brannigan and McBride v. United Kingdom, 17 Eur. H.R. Rep. 539 (1993).

33   Vincent-Joel Proulx, *If the Hat Fits Wear it, If the Turban Fits, Run for your Life, Reflections on the Indefinite Detention and Targeted Killing of Suspected Terrorists*, 56 Hastings L. J. 801, 820 (2005).

34   *Id.* at 821.

35   Ashley Deeks, *Administrative Detention in Armed Conflict*, 40 Case W. Res. J. Int'l L. 403 (2009).

36   Boumediene v. Bush, 553 U.S. 723.

37   *See* Kiyemba v. Obama, decided Feb. 18, 2009 by the DC Circuit, concerning the Uighurs. There, the D.C. Circuit Court of Appeals reversed the district court's order that mandated the release into the United States of 17 Uighurs held in Guantánamo Bay, Kiyemba v Obama, 555 F.3d 1022 (D.C. Cir. 2009).

        Later, a *certiorari* petition to overturn the D.C. Circuit's ruling in Kiyemba was granted by the U.S. Supreme Court, Scotus Blog at www.scotusblog.com/wp/wp-content/uploads/2009/04/kiyemba-petition-final-4-6-09.pdf. On April 7, 2009, the D.C. Circuit Court of Appeals reversed the district court, rejecting the Uighurs *habeas* petition for 30 days notice before being transferred to a country that might subject them to torture. Kiyemba v Obama, 561 F.3d 509 (D.C. Cir. 2009).

38   In its filing of March 13, 2009 in the Federal District Court of the District of Columbia, the Obama Justice Department used reasoning very similar to that of the Bush Justice Department in arguments supporting the Executive's power to detain individuals in Guantánamo Bay. *See* Respondent's Memorandum

Regarding the Government's Detention Authority Relative to Detainees Held at Guantánamo Bay, In re: Guantánamo Bay Detainee Litigation, Misc. No. 08-442(TFH) (March 13, 2009).

39 Joshua S. Goldstein, The Real Price of War 21–22 (2004).

40 *See* Geneva III, *supra* note 1, art. 102, *in* Documents on the Laws of War 283 (Adam Roberts & Richard Guelff eds., 3d edition, 2005). Note that some commentators argue that the word "combatant" is a term of art, meaning "privileged combatant." Those that are unprivileged are civilians who enjoy no combat immunities, and who may be targeted when they directly participate in hostilities and may be charged for their crimes. These commentators criticize the term "enemy combatants" as confusing, overly broad, and redundant.

41 1977 Geneva Protocol I Additional to the Geneva Conventions of 12 August 1949, and Relating to the Protection of Victims of International Armed Conflicts, June 8, 1977, 1125 U.N.T.S. 3–608 [hereinafter AP I], *in* Documents on the Laws of War, *supra* note 40, at 422 *et seq.*

42 "Protected person" is defined as "persons . . . who, at any given moment and *in any manner whatsoever*, find themselves, in case of *conflict or occupation*, in the hands of a Party to the conflict or Occupying Power of which they are not nationals." Geneva IV, *in* Documents on the Laws of War, *supra* note 40, at 302–03. "Protected persons" of Geneva IV thus are limited to civilians who keep out of the conflict.

43 Geneva IV, *supra* note 42, art 5, *in* Documents on the Laws of War, *supra* note 40, at 301, 303 (emphasis added). The article does not expressly accord the detained individual a right of trial. Pictet was concerned about the very circumstance, noting in his authoritative commentary:

> The Article, as it stands, is involved – one might even say, open to question. It is an important and regrettable concession to State expediency. What is most to be feared is that widespread application of the Article may eventually lead to the existence of a category of civilian internees who do not receive the normal treatment laid down by the Convention but are detained under conditions which are almost impossible to check. It must be emphasized most strongly, therefore, that Article 5 can *only* be applied in individual cases of an *exceptional* nature, when the existence of specific charges *makes it almost certain that penal proceedings will follow*. This Article should never be applied as a result of mere suspicion.

Commentary on Geneva IV, *supra* note 23, art. 5 (emphasis added).

44 *Id.* Given the practices of the Bush–Cheney administration regarding the treatment of and attempted denial of habeas corpus rights to those allegedly suspected of carrying out terrorist offenses, Pictet's words that it was "not advisable to leave the accused at the mercy of those detaining them" seem prophetic.

45 IIB Final Record of the Diplomatic Conference of Geneva of 1949, 380 (2004) (emphasis added).

46 Geneva IV, *supra* note 42, arts. 65–76, *in* Documents on the Laws of War, *supra* note 40, at 323–27.

47 Geneva IV, *supra* note 42, art. 76, *in* Documents on the Laws of War, *supra* note 40, at 326–27.

48 AP I, *supra* note 41, *in* Documents on the Laws of War, *supra* note 40, at 422 *et seq.*

49 *Id.*, art. 75 (emphasis added).

50 Under Article 4 of the Third Geneva Convention, they might be considered "militia" associated with Talban Afghanistan. That Article requires that they distinguish themselves from the civilian population, by, for example, wearing

uniforms. It is undisputed that al Qaeda members and adherents failed to wear uniforms. Consequently, they are not prisoners of war and may be characterized as unprivileged combatants.

51　Geneva Conventions of 1949, Ratifications, Accessions, and Successions, ICRC, www.icrc.org/web/eng/siteeng0.nsf/html/57JN3H.

52　*See* Table of Ratifications, ICRC, www.icrc.org/IHL.nsf/WebSign?Read Form&id=470&ps=P.

53　*See* AP I, *supra* note 41, art. 44.3 (extending combatant and prisoner of war status to individuals who "carr[y] [their] arms openly: (a) during each military engagement, and (b) during such time as [they are] visible to the adversary while [they are] engaged in a military deployment preceding the launching of an attack in which [they] are to participate.").

54　*ICRC reactions to the Schlesinger Panel Report*, International Committee of the Red Cross, ICRC, http://icrc.org/Web/Eng/siteeng0.nsf/html/64MHS7 (citing Michael J. Matheson, *The United States Position on the Relation of Customary International Law to the 1977 Protocols Additional to the 1949 Geneva Conventions*, 2 Am.U.J. Int'l L. & Pol'y 419, 419–31 (1987)). Pictet, Commentary on Geneva IV, *supra* note 23, art. 75.

55　*See* AP I, *supra* note 41, art. 1.3, *in* Documents on the Laws of War, *supra* note 40, at 244 (stating that AP I applies to international armed conflict as defined in Common Article 2 of the Geneva Conventions of 1949). *See* Geneva III, art. 2, *supra* note 1.

56　The plain meaning and drafting history of Article 5 of Geneva IV belies this claim, specifically indicating that saboteurs and others "hostile to the security of the State" are protected persons within the meaning of Geneva IV, but with more limited rights. *See supra* notes 23–25, 40–44 and accompanying text. Thus such individuals are "civilians" within the meaning of the Fourth Geneva Convention of 1949, who can be targeted when they "direct[ly] participate[]" in the hostilities, can be detained for security reasons, and can be prosecuted for their crimes. They, however, may not be tortured or denied humane treatment and are provided full trial rights.

57　Geneva III, *supra* note 1, art. 3, *in* Documents on the Laws of War, *supra* note 40, at 244, 245 (emphasis added).

58　Pictet, *supra* note 23, Commentary on Geneva IV, *supra* note 23, at Common Article 3, *available at* http://www.icrc.org/IHL.nsf/COM/375-590006?Open Document.

59　*Id.*

60　*Id.*

61　Specifically the Court states as follows: "There is no doubt that, in the event of international armed conflicts, these rules also constitute a minimum yardstick, in addition to the more elaborate rules which are also to apply to international conflicts; and they are rules which, in the Court's opinion, reflect what the Court in 1949 called 'elementary considerations of humanity.'" Case Concerning Military and Paramilitary Activities in and Against Nicaragua (Nicaragua v. United States), 1986 I.C.J. 14, para. 218 (June 27).

62　Prosecutor v. Dusco Tadic, Case No. IT-94-1-AR72, Appeals Chamber Judgment, para. 102 (Oct. 2, 1995), *available at* http://www.mpil.de/shared/data/pdf/vrstraf0910_090911.pdf.

63　United States v. Hamdan, 548 U.S. 557, 632 (2006).

64　*Id.* (citing Geneva Convention IV Commentary 340 ("defining the term 'properly constituted' in Article 66, which the commentary treats as identical to 'regularly constituted' ")).

65　United States v. Hamdan, 548 U.S. at 633.

66　*Id.* at 632. Note, however, that Justice Kennedy, concurring, disagreed about the applicability of Article 75 of AP I, noting that the US had not ratified that treaty. *Id.* at 654.

67 International Covenant on Civil and Political Rights, art. 14, Dec. 16, 1966, 993 U.N.T.S. 171, *reprinted in* 6 I.L.M. 368 (1967) [hereinafter ICCPR].

68 *Id.*, art. 14.

69 *Id.*, art. 4.1.

70 *Id.*, arts. 4.2, 6, 7, 8.1, 8.2, 11, 15, 16, and 18. The ICCPR also prohibits derogation from the obligation not to imprison an individual for failing to fulfill a contractual obligation. *Id.* arts. 4.2, 11.

71 Human Rights Committee, *supra note* 28, para. 16.

72 *Id.*

73 Henry J. Steiner, Philip Alston & Ryan Goodman, International Human Rights In Context 379 (2008) (quoting Report on Terrorism and Human Rights, Inter-American Commission on Human Rights, Oct. 22, 2002, *available at* www.cidh.org/Terrorism/Eng/toc.htm). I am indebted to Professors Steiner, Alston and Goodman for gathering many of the original documents cited in this chapter, which are contained in their excellent casebook, *International Human Rights in Context*, which is fully cited above.

74 American Declaration on the Rights and Duties of Man, O.A.S. Res. XXX, adopted by the Ninth International Conference of American States (1948), *reprinted in* Basic Documents Pertaining to Human Rights in the Inter-American System, OEA/Ser.L.V/II.82 doc.6 rev.1 at 17 (1992), *available at* http://www1.umn.edu/humanrts/oasinstr/zoas2dec.htm.

75 Article 5 of Geneva III requires that in case of doubt, individuals who are captured or detained by a military force have a right to have their status (as POWS or unprivileged combatants, for instance) determined by a "competent tribunal."

76 Recall the discussion of *lex specialis* in chapter 3.

77 Responding to the counterterrorism practices of the US after 9/11, the Inter-American Commission of Human Rights in an official report noted as follows:

> During armed conflicts, a state's military courts may also try privileged and unprivileged combatants, provided that the minimum protections of due process are guaranteed. . . . Although the provisions of international humanitarian law applicable to unprivileged combatants, including Article 75 of Additional Protocol I, do not specifically address the susceptibility of such combatants to trial by military courts, there appears to be no reason to consider that a different standard would apply as between privileged and unprivileged combatants. In any event, the standards of due process to which unprivileged combatants are entitled may in no case fall below those under Article 75 of Additional Protocol I.

Inter-Am. C.H.R., Report on Terrorism and Human Rights, OEA/Ser.L/V/II/116, doc. 5 rev. 1 corr. para. 232 (Oct. 22, 2002), *available at* www.cidh.org/Terrorism/Eng/toc.htm.

78 *See* Findlay v. United Kingdom, App. No. 110/1995/616/706, 24 Eur. H.R. Rep. 221 (1997). In Findlay, the officer who convened the court-martial appointed all the actors: the prosecutor, the defense attorney, the president, and the other members of the court-martial. All the actors were subordinate to the convening officer. The convening officer had the power to confirm the judgment of the tribunal as well as dissolve the tribunal at any time. In finding the court martial violated Article 6.1 of the European Convention, the Court reasoned as follows: "Since all the members of the court-martial which decided Mr. Findlay's case were subordinate in rank to the convening officer and fell within his

chain of command, Mr. Findlay's doubts about the tribunal's independence and impartiality could be objectively justified." *Id.*, para. 76. The Court further noted that the convening officer's power to ratify the judgment and his "power to vary the sentence imposed as he saw fit" was "contrary to the well-established principle that the power to give a binding decision which may not be altered by a non-judicial authority is inherent in the very notion of 'tribunal' and can also be seen as a component of the 'independence' required by Article 6, para.1." *Id.*, para 77 (citations omitted).

See also Grieves v. United Kingdom, 2003-XII Eur. Ct. H.R. para. 81 (holding the combination of appointing a regular naval officer as prosecutor who was subject to general evaluation based on his performance as a prosecutor instead of a prosecutor from the judge advocate's office and the "absence of a full-time PPCM [Permanent President of Courts-Martial], with no hope of promotion and no effective fear of removal and who was not subject to report on his judicial decision-making (the *Cooper* judgment, § 118) deprives naval courts-martial of what was considered, in the air-force context, to be an important contribution to the independence of an otherwise *ad hoc* tribunal").

79 *Id.*
80 UN Human Rights Committee (HRC), *General Comment No. 32, Article 14, Right to equality before courts and tribunals and to a fair trial,* U.N. Doc. CCPR/C/GC/32 (Aug. 23, 2007).
81 *See* Richard B. Zabel & James J. Benjamin, Jr., *In Pursuit of Justice—Prosecuting Terrorism Cases in the Federal Courts,* Human Rights First, May 2008, *available at* www.humanrightsfirst.org.
82 Incal v. Turkey, 1998-IV Eur. Ct. H.R. 1547.
83 Article 6.1 of the European Convention for the Protection of Fundamental Rights and Freedoms provides as follows: "In the determination of his civil rights and obligations or of any criminal charge against him, everyone is entitled to a fair and public hearing within a reasonable time by an independent tribunal established by law."
84 Ocalan v. Turkey, App. No. 46221/99, Eur. Ct. Hum. Rts., para. 114, Mar. 12, 2003, *available at* http://www.unhcr.org/refworld/docid/3e71a9d84.html. Note, however, that five judges dissented, including the President of the Court.
85 Note that the American Declaration on the Rights of Man prohibits creation of subsequently created special courts: "XXVI. Every accused person is presumed to be innocent until proved guilty. Every person accused of an offense has the right to be given an impartial and public hearing, and *to be tried by courts previously established in accordance with pre-existing laws,* and not to receive cruel, infamous or unusual punishment." (Emphasis added.)
86 Jonathan Freeland, *Who is Gordon Brown?,* 54 New York Review of Books, no. 16, Oct. 25, 2007, *available at* www.nybooks.com/Articles/20703.
87 Glen Sulmasy, Presentation on National Security Courts, International Law Weekend Conference, American Branch of the International Law Association, New York City (Oct. 19, 2008).
88 Matthew Waxman, Presentation on National Security Courts, International Law Weekend Conference, American Branch of the International Law Association, New York City (Oct. 19, 2008).
89 The material support statute has two distinct parts: The first, section 2339A (West 2010), targets anyone who provides support to another who is committing a terrorist offense. The second, section 2339B (West 2010), targets anyone who provides material support to a listed foreign terrorist organization.

Section 2239A provides as follows:

(a) **Offense.**—Whoever provides material support or resources or conceals or disguises the nature, location, source, or ownership of material support or resources, knowing or intending that they are to be used in preparation for, or in carrying out, a violation of section 32, 37, 81, 175, 229, 351, 831, 842(m) or (n), 844(f) or (i), 930(c), 956, 1114, 1116, 1203, 1361, 1362, 1363, 1366, 1751, 1992, 2155, 2156, 2280, 2281, 2332, 2332a, 2332b, 2332f, or 2340A of this title, section 236 of the Atomic Energy Act of 1954 (42 U.S.C. 2284), section 46502 or 60123(b) of title 49, or any offense listed in section 2332b(g)(5)(B) (except for sections 2339A and 2339B) or in preparation for, or in carrying out, the concealment of an escape from the commission of any such violation, or attempts or conspires to do such an act, shall be fined under this title, imprisoned not more than 15 years, or both, and, if the death of any person results, shall be imprisoned for any term of years or for life. A violation of this section may be prosecuted in any Federal judicial district in which the underlying offense was committed, or in any other Federal judicial district as provided by law.

(b) **Definitions.**–As used in this section–

(1) the term "material support or resources" means any property, tangible or intangible, or service, including currency or monetary instruments or financial securities, financial services, lodging, training, expert advice or assistance, safe houses, false documentation or identification, communications equipment, facilities, weapons, lethal substances, explosives, personnel (1 or more individuals who may be or include oneself), and transportation, except medicine or religious materials;

(2) the term "training" means instruction or teaching designed to impart a specific skill, as opposed to general knowledge; and

(3) the term "expert advice or assistance" means advice or assistance derived from scientific, technical or other specialized knowledge.

18 U.S.C.A. § 2339(A) (West 2010).

Section 2339B provides in relevant part as follows:

Whoever knowingly provides material support or resources to a foreign terrorist organization, or attempts or conspires to do so, shall be fined under this title or imprisoned not more than 15 years, or both, and, if the death of any person results, shall be imprisoned for any term of years or for life. To violate this paragraph, a person must have knowledge that the organization is a designated terrorist organization (as defined in subsection (g)(6)), that the organization has engaged or engages in terrorist activity (as defined in section 212(a)(3)(B) of the Immigration and Nationality Act), or that the organization has engaged or engages in terrorism (as defined in section 140(d)(2) of the Foreign Relations Authorization Act, Fiscal Years 1988 and 1989).

18 U.S.C.A. § 2339B (West 2010).

90 Norman Abrams, *The Material Support Terrorism Offenses: Perspectives Derived from the (Early) Model Penal Code*, 1 J. Nat'l Security L. 5, 11 (2005).

91 *Id.*

92 *See* Holder v. Humanitarian Law Project, 130 S. Ct. 2705 (2010) (rejecting constitutional challenge to the material support statute by individuals interested in providing designated terrorist organizations "expert advice" and "training" in international law and in peaceful political advocacy). *See* Alan F. Williams, *Prosecuting-Website Development under the Material Support to Terrorism*

Statutes: Time to Fix What's Broken, 11 N.Y.U. J. Legis. & Pub. Pol'y 365 (2007–2008) (criticizing federal prosecutors for charging a website designer under the material support statutes).

93 The material support statute, however, originally used the language "providing personnel"; it did not clarify that oneself could be the personnel that one is providing. The amended statute does so clarify.

94 Chris Francescani & Ellen Davis, *John Walker Lindh's Family Seeks Reduced Prison Sentence for Son*, ABC News, Apr. 4, 2007, *available at* http://abcnews.go.com/US/LegalCenter/Story?id=3008889&page=3.

95 David Cole, *The New McCarthyism: Repeating History*, 38 Harv. C.R.-C.L. L. Rev. 1, 9–10 (2003).

96 Joan Donoghue, Acting Legal Adviser, speaking before the Annual Meeting of the American Society of International Law, Washington, D.C. (Mar. 26, 2009) (attended by the author).

97 *See* Respondent's Memorandum Regarding the Government's Detention Authority Relative to Detainees Held at Guantánamo Bay, supra note 38.

98 Humanitarian Law Project v. Mukasey, 509 F.3d 1122 (9th Cir. 2007). *See also* the previous decision in the same case: Humanitarian Law Project v. Ashcroft, 309 F. Supp. 2d 1185 (C.D. Cal. 2004) (finding material support statute unconstitutional), *vacated upon considering subsequent congressional amendment*, Humanitarian Law Project v. United States Dep't of Justice, 393 F.3d 902 (9th Cir. 2004). *See also* United States v. Amawi, 545 F. Supp. 2d 681 (N.D. Ohio 2008) (distinguishing Humanitarian Law Project v. Mukasey, "because § 2339A [applicable in *Amawi*, unlike § 2339B [applicable in HLP v. Mukasey], requires that whoever provides the prohibited training, service and/or expert advice and assistance must do so 'knowing and intending that they are to be used in preparation for, or in carrying out, a violation' of one of statute's enumerated criminal offenses").

99 The Intelligence Reform and Terrorism Prevention Act amended 18 U.S.C.A. § 2339A and § 2339B.

100 *See* Abrams, *supra* note 90, at 7; Brian P. Comerford, Note, *Preventing Terrorism by Prosecuting Material Support*, 80 Notre Dame L. Rev. 723 (2005).

101 Comerford, *supra* note 100, at 725–26.

102 Richard B. Zabel & James J. Benjamin, Jr., *In Pursuit of Justice—Prosecuting Terrorism Cases in the Federal Courts*, Human Rights First, May 2008, at 6, *available at* www.humanrightsfirst.org.

103 *Id.* at 8.

104 In addition, federal prosecutors have long made use of motions to reduce sentences of co-felons who provide material assistance, namely, those co-conspirators who provide evidence for the prosecution. Although individuals who do testify against their co-conspirators may face retaliation for doing so, the justice system has had long experience with organized crime and street gangs, where potential jurors and witnesses have faced similar risks.

105 *But see* Clive Stafford Smith, Eight O'Clock Ferry to the Windward Side (2007) (suggesting that many more Guantánamo Bay detainees than indicated were arrested or captured in countries other than Afghanistan).

106 *See* United States v. Verdugo-Urquidez, 494 U.S. 259 (1990).

107 Similar objections, such as the duty to provide exculpatory evidence to the defense, can be answered relatively easily. *See* Zabel and Benjamin's exhaustive study of this subject for a much more detailed response than can be offered within the limits of the single chapter here. Furthermore, if the arrest takes place on a battlefield and the parties are in a state of armed conflict, then the Geneva Conventions would require that the detainee be tried there. The Fourth Geneva Convention prohibits the detainee being transported out of that country

and into the United States for trial. See chapter 6 for a more detailed discussion of this issue.

108 State of Israel v. Eichmann (1961), available at: www.nizkor.org/hweb/people/e/eichmann-adolf/transcripts/Appeal/Appeal-Session-07-03.html.

109 Christina C Logan, Comment, *Liberty or Safety Implications of the USA Patriot Act and the U.K.'s Anti-Terror Laws on Freedom of Expression and Freedom of Religion*, 37 Seton Hall L. Rev. 863, 864, 864 n.5 (2007) ("Prevention of Terrorism Act, 2005, c. 2 (Eng.), available at: www.opsi.gov.uk/acts/acts2005/50002–a.htm.").

110 *Id.* at 864 n.14 ("The Terrorism Act 2006 received Royal Assent on March 30, 2006. Press Release, Home Office, Terrorism, ID Cards and Immigration Bills Become Law (Mar. 30, 2006), available at: www.homeoffice.gov.uk/about-us/news/new-acts").

111 Jay Mykytiuk, *Behind Closed Doors: Troubling Indications of Overbroad Secrecy in Anti-Terrorist Legislation in United States and Canada*, 2 Sw. J.L. & Trade Am. 477 (2006). *See also The USA's Patriot Act and Canada's Anti-Terrorism Act, Key Differences in Legislative Approach*, The Library of the Parliament, Mar. 31, 2006, *available at* www.parl.gc.ca/information/library/PRBpubs/prb0583-e.htm#footnote2.

112 Michael Head, *Counter-Terrorism' Laws: A Threat to Political Freedom, Civil Liberties and Constitutional Rights*, 26 Melb. U. L. Rev. 666 (2002).

113 Anna Oehmichen, *Incommunicado Detention in Germany: An Example of Reactive Anti-Terror Legislation and Long Term Consequences*, 9 German L.J. 855 (2008).

114 Anil Kalhan, Gerald P. Conroy, et al., *Colonial Continuities: Human Rights, Terrorism, and Security Laws*, 20 Colum. J. Asian L. 93 (2006).

115 Rasul v. Bush, 542 U.S. 466 (2004). There, the Court held as follows: "In the end, the answer to the question presented is clear. Petitioners contend that they are being held in federal custody in violation of the laws of the United States. No party questions the District Court's jurisdiction over petitioners' custodians. Section 2241, by its terms, requires nothing more." *Id.* at 483 (citations omitted).

116 *See* G.A. Res. 61/171, U.N. Doc. A/RES/61/171 (Dec. 19, 2006) and G.A. Res. 62/148, U.N. Doc. A/RES/62/148 (Dec. 18, 2007), respectively. The Obama administration's first filing in federal court regarding the Guantánamo Bay Detainees was a little disappointing, since it reiterated the Executive's power to hold such individuals outside the civil court system. See *supra* note 38 and accompanying text for more discussion of this issue. That filing was expressly preliminary and we will have to see how the administration's policies develop in this area.

Part II

Stopping terrorists on the ground

7 Acceptable "collateral damage"?

Taking innocent life in conducting the "war on terrorism"

Russian troops were slaughtered in the initial ill-conceived, poorly coordinated attack on Grozny, the Chechen capital, an attack that started on New Year's Eve, 1994.[1] Ultimately, the Russians relied primarily on air strikes and artillery against Grozny, inflicting thousands of civilian casualties. Ironically, most of the civilians were ethnic Russians, who had no place to flee to, rather than Chechens. Before the assault, most Chechens had fled the city to stay with relatives.

Aside from the attacks on Grozny, the Russians operated in the country-side, where the Chechen fighters were believed to be hiding.[2] The Russian "Internal Troops" from the Ministerstvo Vnutrennikh Del—Ministry of Interior Affairs ("MVD"), then offered take-it or leave-it deals with leaders of villages suspected of harboring the Chechen fighters: Get rid of the fighters or we will destroy your village. A Russian Deputy who witnessed the destruction of one such village described the "pacification," killing the civilian inhabitants and laying waste to the village, as a tactic to terrorize the population.

There are significant dangers in calling the struggle against terrorism a "war": although prohibiting either side from targeting civilians, as the Russians have done in their so-called pacification campaign, the law of war makes large numbers of civilians vulnerable to attack as "collateral damage" if enemy combatants or other enemy military assets lie nearby. The right to inflict collateral damage distinguishes the law of war from human rights law. The first obligation of municipal police is to safeguard the citizenry; only in the most extreme circumstances may the police intentionally kill a civilian and they may generally do so only when that person is imminently threatening to harm others.

The rule on collateral damage evolved as a balance between the rule of discrimination, on the one hand, and military necessity, on the other. Before the Renaissance, a conquering army would generally rape the women of the vanquished city, slay all captured enemy soldiers, and kill all the civilians— the remaining men, women, and children—or take them or some of them as slaves. With the Renaissance, this harsh practice began to gradually give way to the principle that armed forces should attack only military objectives and spare civilian ones, including men, women, and children who did not fight, who were not combatants. This rule of discriminating between military objectives and civilians gradually expanded to include captured enemy soldiers, namely, soldiers *hors de combat* (soldiers out of combat). They could no longer be made an object of attack.

On the other hand, armed forces were allowed to attack military objectives, combatants, and combatant equipment and infrastructure that would advantage the military of the opposing side. This is the so-called doctrine of military necessity. Injury that went beyond military necessity was called superfluous injury, the intentional infliction of which could be considered unlawful. These practices finally culminated in The Hague Convention of 1907 and the attached Hague Regulations, one of which prohibits the military from attacking an "undefended city."[3] Before the advent of the airplane, an army would arrive at the enemy city and lay siege to it, if the city resisted; or enter and take it, if the city did not resist. If a city was "undefended," there was no need to attack it. Such attacks would cause "superfluous injury," and hence were unlawful.

The invention of the airplane (and later the intercontinental ballistic missile) permitted a military force, for the first time, to readily go far beyond the enemy's front line. An interior city could not easily surrender to an air invader.[4] In the First World War, and to a much greater extent in the Second World War, both the Allies and the Axis powers ignored the rule that undefended cities may not be subject to attack. Both sides bombed cities indiscriminately: Germany bombed London; the Allies fire-bombed Hamburg and Dresden. As many as 410,000 German civilians may have been killed in the bombing during the Second World War.[5] Immediately after that war, the victorious Allies understandably focused on the abuses of Nazi Germany and Imperial Japan and disregarded the abuses in which the Allies may have participated. For example, conspicuous by its absence from the Nuremberg trials was any indictment for indiscriminate bombing of civilians. Likewise, the four Geneva Conventions of 1949 deal primarily with the responsibility that an occupying power owes to civilians and prisoners of war that the power has within its control. The 1949 Geneva Conventions say little about the means and methods a country may employ in actual combat.

After the war in Vietnam and other conflicts, the world community at the instigation of the ICRC drafted a treaty that primarily aims to protect civilians, the 1977 Additional Protocol I to the Geneva Conventions of 1949 (AP I). AP I reaffirmed the principle of discrimination and underscored that civilians could not be made the object of an attack. There remained a problem. Agreed, combatants can only attack military objectives and must refrain from attacking civilians or civilian objects. But what are the obligations of an armed force when civilians are physically so close to military objectives that it is inevitable that some civilians will be killed or wounded in the event of an attack on the military objective?

Article 51 of AP I provides two examples of military force that fails to discriminate properly between military objectives and civilians.[6] The second example is most relevant here.[7] It refines the proportionality standard—the collateral damage rule—rather than presenting a concrete case. This example codifies the customary international law rule on proportionality, making indiscriminate: "an attack which may be expected to cause *incidental loss* of civilian life, injury to civilians, damage to civilian objects, or a combination thereof, which would be *excessive in relation to the concrete and direct military advantage anticipated.* . . ."[8] This provision was controversial and was contentiously debated by the members of the drafting conference.[9] The standard is vague and subject to abuse. How does one weigh the importance of a military objective as against anticipated "incidental" civilian casualties? As a practical matter, it can be expected only to apply to flagrant misconduct, misconduct where, in essence, reasonable minds cannot differ as to the disproportionate use of force.[10] The incendiary bombing of Tokyo during the Second World War might fit here, since though the bombing was purportedly designed to reach military targets, General Curtis LeMay ordered the attack knowing that thousands of civilians would be killed.[11] He defended the attack on the ground that the cottage industries in Japan, where work was done at home, justified targeting civilians in their dwellings.[12] The incendiary bombing of Tokyo cost the lives of well over 80,000 civilians.[13] (Consider for a moment that the horror of the 9/11 attacks cost, nonetheless, fewer than 3,000 lives.)

Note that even the ICRC Commentary interprets the proportionality clause loosely. The ICRC gives this example of disproportionate bombardment: "The presence of a solider on leave obviously cannot justify the destruction of a village."[14] Well, what if the soldier was not on leave? Would that justify an armed force in destroying the village? What if there had been two soldiers on leave in the village? Would an attack then be justified?

In *dicta*, the Israeli Supreme Court suggested a narrower interpretation of the proportionality rule. In *Public Committee against Torture v. Israel*,[15] the Supreme Court was dealing with the question of attacks by the Israeli Security Forces against suspected terrorists. The Court stated that of course the Security Forces could not destroy an entire apartment building because there was reasonable cause to believe that a single suspected terrorist was present inside.

To impose criminal liability on the military actors who carried out an attack that caused disproportionate civilian casualties is still harder. The high *mens rea* requirement for the War Crimes Article of the Protocol make prosecution of military actors for inflicting collateral damage extremely difficult. The relevant language of the war crimes Article is as follows:

[T]he following acts shall be regarded as grave breaches [war crimes] of this Protocol, when *committed willfully*, in violation of the relevant provisions of this Protocol, and causing death or serious injury to body or health:

(a) Making the civilian population or individual civilians the object of attack;

(b) launching an *indiscriminate attack affecting the civilian population* or civilian objects *in the knowledge* that such attack will cause *excessive* loss of life, injury to civilians or damage to civilian objects, as defined in Article 57, paragraph 2 (a)(iii).[16]

In the original draft, the ICRC made any violations of the Protocol a war crime.[17] The US and other states strenuously objected, insisting on including strict culpability requirements.[18] The express language of the war crimes Article requires that the actor "commit" the grave breach "willfully." Under Anglo-Saxon jurisprudence, "willfully" means at least intentionally and often is construed as also meaning "knowingly violating a legal duty."[19] The drafting history of this Article suggests that the drafters intended to make the culpability requirement high, so it is at least reasonable to believe that the stricter interpretation of willfully is the intended interpretation.

Not only must the actor willfully commit the grave breach, he or she must "launch an *indiscriminate attack affecting the civilian population* or civilian objects *in the knowledge* that such attack will cause *excessive* loss of life, injury to civilians or damage to civilian objects. . . ."[20] If, assuming a state of armed conflict existed, Russia were to bomb a Chechen village alleging that two Chechen terrorists were present therein, the Prosecutor would have serious difficulty in proving a "grave breach." To be held criminally liable, the actor—from the pilot all the way up the chain of command—(a) would have to know that bombing the village violated a legal duty, and (b) would have to deliver the bombs "in the *knowledge* that such attack will cause *excessive* loss of life, injury to civilians or damage to civilian objects." Aside from the fact that the latter standard is vague (what is excessive to you may not be excessive to me), a prosecutor would have to prove that the actor was subjectively aware of the excessiveness. Only in the most egregious cases would a prosecutor be able to make such a showing.

Although ignorance of the law is generally not an excuse, the strictest standard of willfulness does provide a defense for mistake of law. If that is the standard, frontline actors such as the pilot and crews would probably be able to successfully assert a defense. Even those higher up the chain of command may be able to successfully defend on this ground.

Aside from proving willfulness, showing that the actor knew the attack caused excessive loss of life and injury, as noted above, would be quite difficult. The discussion above demonstrated the ICRC's official commentary itself implies that such a bombing would not cause excessive civilian losses. If the ICRC is not sure, can the pilot willfully be acting in the knowledge that the bombing is causing excessive casualties? The "knowingly" standard requires that the actor be subjectively aware of, or at the very least, be consciously disregarding a high risk that a fact exists.[21] Reasonable minds can differ as to whether bombing a village to kill terrorists staying within it caused "*excessive* loss of life, injury to civilians or damage to civilian objects." To prove the actor knew that the bombing would cause such excessive civilian casualties would be thus that much harder.

The standard, thus, for war crimes, grave breaches, is strict:

> [P]aragraphs 3(b) and (c) are drawn so narrowly that they limit application of Article 85 to only a few situations in which the rule of proportionality would be breached. Specifically the attack must be launched in the knowledge that "it will cause excessive civilian casualties or damage to civilian objects." This makes most violations of obligations such as that found in Article 57, subparagraph 2(a)(iii) mere breaches of Protocol I. It also results in the conclusion that very few weapons violations will be grave breaches under Protocol I unless the weapon is used to violate some other proscription such as making civilians the object of attack.[22]

Under AP I, commanders can kill or wound a large number of innocent civilians without incurring either state responsibility or individual responsibility.

7.1 Prosecution under the Rome Statute establishing an International Criminal Court

In July 1998, the vast majority of countries of the world agreed to create an International Criminal Court (ICC).[23] The Statute of the ICC may ultimately constitute the primary judicial body for enforcing international humanitarian law. The ICC, however, focuses exclusively on criminal prosecution, not necessarily on protection of civilians. The *mens rea* and *actus reus* requirements are actually somewhat harder for a prosecutor to meet under the ICC than under the Protocol.

Under Article 8 of the ICC, an individual is guilty of a war crime when he or she:[24]

> *Intentionally launch{es} an attack in the knowledge* that such attack will cause incidental loss of life or injury to civilians or damage to civilian objects or widespread, long-term and severe damage to the natural environment which would be *clearly* excessive in relation to the concrete and direct *overall* military advantage anticipated . . .[25]

The language resembles that of Article 85 of AP I, which imposes criminal liability for grave breaches. ICC's Article uses the language "[i]ntentionally launches an attack," arguably similar to the Protocol's language,[26] requiring the defendant to have "willfully" committed the violation.[27] Both the ICC and the Protocol require that the defendant act "in the knowledge" of the key facts the attack will bring about, for example, under the ICC: "injury to civilians or damage to civilian objects or widespread, long-term and severe damage to the environment." AP I codifies the proportionality principle as a basis for criminal liability.[28] That article incorporates by reference language from another article, which prohibits: "launching any attack which may be expected to cause incidental loss of civilian life, injury to civilians, damage to civilian objects, or a combination thereof, *which would be excessive in relation to the concrete and direct military advantage anticipated. . . .*"[29]

The ICC waters down AP I's language in two ways. First, it adds the word "clearly" to "excessive." The prosecutor has to prove that the defendant knew that the attack would cause not merely "excessive" civilian casualties but rather "*clearly* excessive" civilian casualties. What this means in practice remains to be seen. As pointed out above, a prosecutor would probably be able to prove a violation of the Protocol's proportionality rule only in absolutely egregious cases. So even under AP I, the prosecution will, in fact, be able to meet that element of the offense only where, in fact, the attack caused "clearly" excessive civilian deaths and injuries. On the other hand, the tribunal could reasonably assume that the parties to the Conference intended "clearly" to convey some meaning, presumably to make the prosecutor's burden a heavier one: "The use of the word 'clearly' ensures that criminal responsibility would be entailed only in cases where the excessiveness of the incidental damage was obvious."[30]

Second, the ICC also qualifies "direct military advantage anticipated" by adding the one word "overall."[31] Under the ICC's version of the proportionality rule, the civilian casualty side of the scale is balanced against the weight of the "concrete and direct *overall* military advantage anticipated."[32] This proposal renewed a debate in the ICRC Conference establishing the First Additional Protocol. Instead of examining whether attacking a particular target caused excessive casualties, the "overall military advantage" language can be interpreted to mean whether, in examining the entire battle, if not the entire conflict, the tribunal determines whether the attack on this particular target caused excessive civilian casualties. Proponents of this view lost in the ICRC Conference, because the majority of the conference delegates believed this proposal would unreasonably weaken the already weak proportionality rule, leaving civilians largely unprotected.[33]

As previously observed, AP I provides relatively little protection for civilians. The Rome Statute of the ICC provides even less. Consequently labeling the struggle against terrorism a "war" seriously endangers the civilian population in which those suspected of terrorism live or are present.

7.2 The War in Afghanistan

The breadth of the collateral damage rule not only endangers civilians, but also may harm the cause of counterterrorist forces. The US and its coalition partners enjoyed what appeared to be a swift and brilliant victory over the Taliban, the ruling faction in Afghanistan. Where the Soviets and the British before them had failed, the US and its coalition partners had succeeded.

Despite the high, desolate mountains and the bitterly cold, snowy winters, the US had routed the Taliban and expelled al Qaeda from its Afghan haven. Unfortunately, the war in Iraq distracted the US from its mission in Afghanistan, drawing both military forces and development funds away from that country. In Afghanistan, the US and its NATO partners have relied on air power, among other things, to thwart the resurgence of the Taliban. Possibly flying at high altitudes, US pilots have had a difficult time telling the difference between a marriage feast where wedding guests shoot guns in the air to celebrate and Taliban fighters who shoot at a peasant village intending to terrorize or kill its inhabitants.[34]

The UN reported that in 2008, civilian casualties in Afghanistan exceeded 2,100, a 40 percent increase over the previous year.[35] Although the Taliban are responsible for 55 percent of these casualties, the US-led NATO coalition Afghan Government forces are responsible for 39 percent of these deaths and injuries.[36] The United Nations Assistance Mission in Afghanistan said, "Suicide attacks and the use of improvised explosive devices by insurgent groups inflicted heavy losses on civilians, as did aerial bombardments by international forces."[37] Some have suggested that the NATO forces have violated humanitarian law in inflicting so many civilian casualties. Close analysis of the various incidents where civilians have been killed belie that suggestion. The NATO forces appear to be operating within Article 51 of AP I, targeting only Taliban militants. Yet the proportionality rule is so broad that it allows for a large number of civilian deaths.

The number of civilian casualties in Afghanistan is causing an outcry. The Christian Science Monitor quotes Nasrulluh Stanikzai, a lecturer at Kabul University's Faculty of Law as saying, " 'Civilian casualties [are] becoming the main issue in the relationship between the West and Afghanistan.' If the trend of high levels of casualties continues, he says, it could drive a permanent wedge between Afghans and the US."[38] Some who initially supported the US's invasion of Afghanistan have changed their minds upon seeing how many civilians have been killed or wounded.[39]

7.3 A new approach to protecting civilians

Since the codification of the proportionality rule by AP I in 1977, there has been relatively little development of that rule. The Israeli Supreme Court in *dicta* suggests a modest tightening, restricting armed forces somewhat more than the drafters of the rule initially may have intended. The International Criminal Tribunal for the former Yugoslavia (ICTY) implicitly has suggested a modest tightening as well. But when violence is said to reach a level of "armed conflict," the proportionality rule is triggered, making a large number of innocent civilians vulnerable to attack.

There has, however, been an aggressive attack on the scope of the proportionality rule, an attack coming from an unexpected direction, an attack that does not even suggest an attack on the rule has been made. As Europe was rising from the ashes of the Second World War, some Western European nations founded the Council of Europe and agreed to a human rights treaty, the European Convention for the Protection of Fundamental Rights and Freedoms.[40] The Council through that Convention set up the world's first international human rights court, the European Court of Human Rights (ECtHR). Since its founding in 1953, the Court has become one of the most important international tribunals in the world, representing the world's most advanced international legal regime.

Starting initially with ten Member States in 1949, the Council of Europe has grown to 47 Member States as of this writing. It now includes former Eastern bloc nations such as Ukraine and Russia. The states over which it has jurisdiction contain over 800 million people.

The ECtHR has developed an extensive jurisprudence. Some of the states over which it has jurisdiction have experienced terrorist violence, and the Court has had to rule on the limits that the armed forces and police forces of Member States must follow in counterterrorism operations. In Ergi v. Turkey,[41] Turkish Security Force members set up an ambush of PKK members. An innocent civilian was inadvertently killed during the ambush; the fatal shot may have come from the PKK members, but more probably came from the Turkish Security Forces. The evidence never showed who the shooter was. Article 2 of the European Convention for the Protection of Human Rights and Fundamental Freedoms guarantees the right to life. The Convention, however, does make the following exceptions:

> Deprivation of life shall not be regarded as inflicted in contravention of this Article when it results from the use of force which is *no* more than *absolutely* necessary:
>
> (a) in defense of any person from unlawful violence;
> (b) in order to effect a lawful arrest or to prevent the escape of a person lawfully detained;
> (c) in action lawfully taken for the purpose of *quelling* a riot or insurrection.[42]

If one applied a plain meaning analysis to this Article, one might argue that subsection (c) expressly allows the use of deadly force to quell an insurrection, which arguably is exactly what the Turkish Security Forces were doing in *Ergi*. As has been mentioned earlier in these pages, the PKK is one of the most violent terrorist organizations on earth. One likewise might argue that an innocent civilian would be killed in an ambush against a terrorist organization is certainly regrettable, but not generally illegal in "quell[ing] an insurrection." Nothing in the record suggests that the innocent civilian was the object of the attack. The Court, however, rigorously interpreted Article 2:

> The use of the term 'absolutely necessary' suggests that a stricter and more compelling test of necessity must be employed than that normally

applicable when determining whether State action is 'necessary in a democratic society' under paragraph 2 of Articles 8 to 11 of the Convention. In
particular, the force used must be *strictly proportionate* to the achievement
of the aims set out in sub-paragraphs 2(a), (b) and (c) of Article 2. In
keeping with the importance of this provision in a democratic society,
the Court must, in making its assessment, subject deprivations of life
to the most careful scrutiny, particularly where deliberate lethal force
is used. . . .[43]

Even though the evidence never indicated who fired the fatal shot, the Court
concluded that Turkey had failed to plan the ambush so as to minimize
civilian casualties:

> [State responsibility] may also be engaged *where they* [state security per-
> sonnel] *fail to take all feasible precautions* in the choice of means and
> methods of a security operation mounted against an opposing group with
> a view to avoiding and, in any event, *to minimize incidental loss of civilian
> life*. Thus, even though it has not been established beyond reasonable
> doubt that the bullet which killed the applicant's sister was fired by the
> security forces, the Court must consider whether the security forces'
> operation had been planned and conducted in such a way as to avoid and
> minimize, to the greatest extent possible, any risk to the lives of the
> villagers, including from the fire-power of the PKK members caught in
> the ambush.[44]

As Christine Byron has observed, the Court never mentioned humanitarian
law (the law of war), yet the language the Court employed bears a close
resemblance to the proportionality rule set forth in Article 51 of AP I.[45] Recall
that that Article prohibits: "An attack which may be expected to cause *incidental loss of civilian life*, injury to civilians . . . which would be excessive in
relation to the concrete and direct military advantage anticipated." The
phrase "incidental loss of civilian life" appears to have been taken verbatim
from Article 51. Note, however, that the Court is applying a much stricter
form of the proportionality rule. Instead of permitting collateral damage, the
Court seems to suggest that the Security Forces have to essentially ensure
that there will be *no* collateral damage.

The Court has ruled similarly regarding claims that Chechens have
brought against Russia. In a series of cases, the Court has ruled against Russia
for failing to take precautions to safeguard civilian lives as the Russians
prosecuted their counterterrorism campaign against Chechen rebels. In
Isaveya, Yuropsa, and Bedayeva v. Russia,[46] Grozny was under attack and it was
not safe for civilians. On Russian television and radio stations, broadcasters
stated that there would be a safe exit route for the civilian population along
the KavKaz highway. Apparently, a large number of civilians fled with their
belongings in their cars and trucks on this highway. Clearly marked vehicles

of the local International Committee of the Red Cross were among those on the highway. An ICRC witness testified there was a line of cars and trucks waiting for a border checkpoint to open into neighboring Ingushetia. The line was over three kilometers (1.9 miles) long. One of the applicants was given the number 385. After waiting over three hours, a senior Russian military officer told those waiting that the checkpoint would not open and ordered them to return to Grozny.[47]

Here, there is a conflict in the evidence. The Russians claim that a truck carrying Chechen fighters on the highway fired at one or both of the Russian aircraft. The applicants claim that no one fired at the aircraft. The ICRC witness likewise testified that no one fired on the aircraft. In any event, after being told that the checkpoint would not open, people turned around to go back to Grozny. Then two Russian military aircraft launched missiles, killing and wounding a large number of people on the highway as well as destroying several vehicles.[48] Although clearly marked, Red Cross vehicles were hit; the evidence did not conclusively show that the Russian aircraft pilots knew they were killing innocent civilians rather than Chechen fighters. Apparently, no one communicated either to the pilot's controller or to the pilots that safe passage had been given to civilians to take the highway (or that the checkpoint had been kept closed).[49]

The Court noted that Article 2 applied both to intentional and unintentional state killing: "Article 2 covers not only intentional killing but also the situations where it is permitted to 'use force' which may result, as an *unintended outcome, in the deprivation of life*."[50] Noting the absolute protection that the Convention gives to preserving life, the Court declared that "[i]n particular, it is necessary to examine whether the operation was planned and controlled by the authorities so as to minimize, to the greatest extent possible, recourse to lethal force. The authorities must take appropriate care to *ensure that any risk to life is minimized*. The Court must also examine whether the authorities were not *negligent* in their choice of action."[51] Note again how much more strictly the Court is applying Article 2 of the European Convention as compared to the AP I proportionality rule. "Any risk to life" must be "minimized." Negligence in carrying out this obligation suffices for liability.

AP I contains similar language about taking precautions to safeguard civilians. Article 57 states that combatants must "[t]ake all feasible precautions in the choice of means and methods of attack with a view to avoiding, and in any event *to minimizing, incidental loss of civilian life, injury to civilians and damage to civilian objects*."[52] But what is missing from the Court's interpretation is any balancing of the "incidental loss of civilian life" against the "military advantage anticipated," which the very next subsection of Article 57 of AP I repeats.[53] The Court concluded that the Russian forces had violated Article 2 of the European Convention. The Court reasoned that "even assuming that the military were pursuing a legitimate aim . . . the Court does not accept that the operation . . . was planned and executed with the requisite care for the lives of the civilian population."[54]

The ECtHR dealt with another attack on a convoy under very similar circumstances. In *Isayeva v. Russia*, the Russians promised safe passage to Chechen fighters in Grozny, but the promise was a ruse to lure (or "incite") the Chechen fighters along a corridor that was mined and heavily fortified by Russian federal troops. At the end of the corridor was the village of Katyr-Yurt, with a population of 18,000 to 25,000. A large cohort of Chechen fighters made it through the corridor to the village. Russian forces attacked the town using heavy weapons:

> Between 8 and 9 a.m. on 4 February 2000 Major-General Nedobitko called in fighter jets, without specifying what load they should carry. The planes, apparently by default, carried heavy free-falling high-explosion aviation bombs FAB-250 and FAB-500 with a damage radius exceeding 1,000 metres.[55]

The civilians sought to escape. Around 3 p.m. that afternoon, Russian commanders apparently conveyed through loudspeakers from a helicopter and through word of mouth that the civilian population would have safe passage along a certain road. Had the civilian population been more cooperative with the Russians, they would have been given permission to escape along a second route as well, but they were only allowed to take the road toward Achkhoy-Martan. A number of cars were lining up to take the escape route. As the minibus in which an applicant, her 23-year-old son, and three nieces was about 500 meters (547 yards) from a Russian checkpoint, leaving the village toward Achkoy-Martin (on the authorized safe passage route), an aviation bomb exploded nearby, destroying the bus and killing many inside including the applicant's son and nieces.[56] Many others were wounded.

Although at the time of the incident the level of fighting in Chechnya probably reached the threshold for non-international armed conflict, the Russians never declared martial law or a state of emergency. They never submitted a derogation notice under Article 15 of the European Convention.[57] Surprisingly, the Court held them to their word, reasoning that failing to take these steps meant that "[t]he operation in question therefore has to be judged against a normal legal background."[58]

The Court did recognize, however, the exceptional circumstances under which the Russians were operating. Nonetheless, it found the Russian tactics violated the Convention:

> Even when faced with a situation where, as the Government submit (*sic*), the population of the village had been held hostage by a large group of well-equipped and well-trained fighters, the *primary* aim of the operation should be *to protect lives from unlawful violence*. The *massive use of indiscriminate weapons* stands in flagrant contrast with this aim and cannot be considered compatible with the standard of care prerequisite to an operation of this kind involving the use of lethal force by State agents.

The Court found that the operation had been planned days in advance, that the Russians had "incited" the rebels to enter the corridor and ultimately to enter the village, that the Russians never warned the village administration or the villagers, that it had opened a safe passage for the civilians not before but only hours after the indiscriminate bombing had begun. The Court, therefore, concluded that the Russian commanders had violated Article 2 by failing to take measures to protect the civilian population.

The cases in which the ECtHR has directly applied human rights law to counterterrorism operations have taken place within the member state itself. None of these cases had dealt in the strict sense with "international" terrorism. Since as one commentator has noted, the humanitarian law governing non-international armed conflict is far less developed than that of international armed conflict, it is appropriate for the Court to apply human rights law.[59] Nevertheless, many assert that when dealing with international armed conflict and international terrorism carried out by non-state actors, the law of international armed conflict, not human rights law, should control.[60] In that event, the broad interpretation of the proportionality rule presumably applies.

Yet, perhaps the ECtHR is providing a progressive development of rules governing not only non-international armed conflict, but also for international armed conflict. At least in the context of wars being fought in the name of counterterrorism, policies directed at sharply reducing civilian casualties may advance public world order. Given the experience of Russia in Chechnya and the United States and its NATO partners in Afghanistan, perhaps the time has come to recognize that permitting high civilian casualties only ignites rather than dampens the fires of anger, resentment, and humiliation that impel individuals to commit terrorist crimes or to help others who do.[61]

Notes

1   B.G. Williams, *The Russo-Chechen War: A Threat to Stability in the Middle East and Eurasia?*, 8(1) Middle East Policy 128 (2001), *available at* www.mepc.org/journal_vol8/williams.pdf (accessed 13 March 2009). Parts of this chapter are drawn from my article, *Cluster Bombs Over Kosovo*, 44 Ariz. L. Rev. 31 (2002), and are reprinted with permission of Arizona Law Review.

2   S. Efron, *Russia, Chechnya Trade Charges as Grozny Oil Refinery Blazes: Caucasus: Some Fear Ammonia Tanks Could Blow; No Evacuations Ordered. Moscow Denies Bombing*, L.A. Times, Dec. 31, 1994, at A10.

3   Regulations Respecting the Laws and Customs of War on Land, Annex to the 1907 Hague Convention Respecting the Laws and Customs of War on Land, formally named, Convention for the Pacific Settlement of International Disputes (Hague IV), art. 25, Oct. 18, 1907, 36 Stat. 2277 (entered into force Jan. 26, 1910), *reprinted in* 2 Am. J. Int'l L. 43 (2008), *and in* Documents on the Laws of War 48 (A. Roberts & R. Guelff eds., 1989) ("The attack or bombardment, by whatever means, of towns, villages, dwellings, or buildings which are undefended is prohibited.")

4   One commentator notes that "[t]he arrival of aircraft, however, totally undermined [The Hague rules], which were tied to the notion of advancing land-based armies through the field which could occupy without problem

undefended cities, but which needed to bombard defended cities in order to occupy them." Louise Doswald-Beck, *The Value of the 1977 Geneva Protocols for the Protection of Civilians*, *in* Armed Conflict and The New Law: Aspects of the 1977 Geneva Protocols and The 1981 Weapons Convention 137, 142 (M.A. Meyer ed., 1989).

5   H. Garretsen, M. Schramm & S. Brakman, *The Strategic Bombing of German Cities During World War II and its Impact for Germany* 5 (Utrecht School of Economics, Working Paper No. 03–09, 2003), *available at* www.uu.nl/uupublish /content/ 03-09i.pdf (accessed March 17, 2009).

6   1977 Protocol Additional to the Geneva Conventions of 12 August 1949, and Relating to the Protection of Victims of International Armed Conflict art. 51(5)(a), (b), June 8, 1977, 1125 U.N.T.S. 3–608, 16 I.L.M. 1391 (entered into force Dec. 7, 1978), *available at* www.icrc.org/IHL.nsf/FULL/470?Open Document [hereinafter AP I].

7   *Id.*, art. 51(5)(b).

8   *Id.* Including the rule of proportionality was an attempt to gain flexibility and also adherents to the Protocol to avoid the fate of the 1923 Rules of Aerial Warfare:

> Since the First World War there had been many vain attempts at codifying the immunity of the civilian population. The 1922/23 project [Draft Rules of Aerial Warfare] would have required combatants to abstain from bombing when it might affect the civilian population, but a good text was useless if it went unsigned, unratified and unimplemented. The Red Cross was conscious of the fact that the rule of proportionality contained a subjective element, and was thus liable to abuse. The aim was, however, to avoid or in any case restrict the incidental effects of attacks directed against military objectives.

Record of Proceedings of the 1974–1977 Geneva Diplomatic Conference on the Reaffirmation and Development of International Humanitarian Law Applicable in Armed Conflicts (statement of Mr. Mirimanoff-Chilikine of the ICRC), *reprinted in* Protection of War Victims: Protocol I to the 1949 Geneva Conventions, 126–27 (H.S. Levie ed., 1979) [hereinafter Levie].

9   *Id.* at 129–73. Note comment of Mr. Al-Adhami (Iraq), "[I]t would be impossible to prove that the military advantage expected was in fact disproportionate". *Id.* at 133; and comment of Mr. Samuels (Canada), "An absolute prohibition would result in a very difficult situation, for instance where there was a single civilian near a major military objective whose presence might deter attack". *Id.* at 134.

10   Comdr. C.A. Allen, *Panel Discussion, Implementing Limitations on the Use of Force: The Doctrine of Proportionality and Necessity*, 86 Am. Soc. Int'l L. Proc. 39, 43–46 (1992) (Frits Kalshoven, panelist, discussing the doctrine of proportionality, noting the "notoriously vague notion of 'military necessity'" and the difficulty of balancing it against humanitarian values); *see also* Michael Bothe, Karl Josef Partsch, & Waldemar A. Solf, New Rules for Victims of Armed Conflicts 310 (1982) (noting the difficulties of balancing the importance of the military target and foreseeable extent of civilian casualties and/or damage to civilian objects and concluding that "a plain and manifest breach of the rule will be recognizable"). In the Kupreskic Judgment, the ICTY Trial Chamber addressed the issue of proportionality as follows:

> In the case under discussion, [the Martens clause would mean] that the prescriptions of [AP I] Articles 57 and 58 (and of the corresponding customary rules) must be interpreted so as to construe as narrowly as possible the discretionary power to attack belligerents and, by the same token, so as to

expand the protection accorded to civilians. . . . 526. As an example of the way in which the Martens clause may be utilized, regard might be had to considerations such as the cumulative effect of attacks on military objectives causing incidental damage to civilians. In other words, it may happen that single attacks on military objectives causing incidental damage to civilians, although they may raise doubts as to their lawfulness, nevertheless do not appear on their face to fall foul per se of the loose prescriptions of Articles 57 and 58 (or of the corresponding customary rules). However, in case of repeated attacks, all or most of them falling within the grey area between indisputable legality and unlawfulness, it might be warranted to conclude that the cumulative effect of such acts entails that they may not be in keeping with international law. Indeed, this pattern of military conduct may turn out to jeopardize excessively the lives and assets of civilians, contrary to the demands of humanity.

International Criminal Tribunal for the Former Yugoslavia, Prosecutor v. Kupreskic, Case No. IT-95–16-T, Trial Judgment, paras 524–26 (Jan. 14, 2000) (citations omitted) (emphasis added), *available at* www.icty.org/x/cases/kupreskic/tjug/en/kuptj000114e.pdf> (accessed March 13, 2009).

The Report to the ICTY Prosecutor on the NATO bombing campaign criticized the tribunal reasoning:

This formulation in Kupreskic can be regarded as a progressive statement of the applicable law with regard to the obligation to protect civilians. Its practical import, however, is somewhat ambiguous and its application far from clear. It is the committee's view that where individual (and legitimate) attacks on military objectives are concerned, the mere cumulating of such instances, all of which are deemed to have been lawful cannot ipso facto be said to amount to a crime. The committee understands the above formulation, instead, to refer to an overall assessment of the totality of civilian victims as against the goals of the military campaign.

International Criminal Tribunal for the Former Yugoslavia (ICTY), Final Report to the Prosecutor by the Committee Established to Review the NATO Bombing Campaign Against the Federal Republic of Yugoslavia, June 13, 2000, 39 I.L.M. 1257, para. 52, *available at* www.icty.org/sid/10052.

11   C.C. Crane, Bombs, Cities, and Civilians: American Airpower Strategy in World War II, 1–3 (1993).
12   *Id.*

All you had to do was visit one of those targets after we'd roasted it, and see the ruins of a multitude of tiny houses, with a drill press sticking up through the wreckage of every home. The entire population got into the act and worked to make those airplanes or munitions of war . . . men, women, children. We knew we were going to kill a lot of women and kids when we burned that town. Had to be done.

Id. (quoting General Curtis LeMay). The ICRC gives this example of disproportionate bombardment: "The presence of a soldier on leave obviously cannot justify the destruction of a village." Int'l Committee of the Red Cross, Commentary on the Additional Protocols of 8 June 1977 to the Geneva Conventions of 12 August 1949, at 684 (Yves Sandoz et al. eds., 1987) [hereinafter ICRC, Commentary on the Additional Protocols].

13   The incendiary bombardment by American planes on the night of March 9, 1945 covered six important industrial targets and numerous smaller factories, railroad yards, home industries, and cable plants, "but it also included one of the

most densely populated areas of the world, Asakita Ku, with a population of more than 135,000 people per square mile." Crane, *supra* note 11, at 132. An estimated 90,000 to 100,000 people were killed in the raid. *Id.* Apparently, the incendiary bombs destroyed about one quarter of the buildings in Tokyo. Air Warfare, Microsoft Encarta Online Encyclopedia (2008), http://encarta.msn-.com/encyclopedia_761574056_2/Air_Warfare.html#s5 (accessed March 13, 2009).

14 ICRC, Commentary on the Additional Protocols, *supra* note 12, at 684.

15 H.C.J. 769/02 The Public Committee against Torture in Israel v. The Government of Israel [2005], *available at* http://elyon1.court.gov.il/Files_ENG/02/690/007/a34/02007690. a34.pdf (accessed March 13, 2009). The court outlined the parameters of a proportional response to a terrorist attack with the following hypothetical example:

> Take the usual case of a combatant, or of a terrorist sniper shooting at soldiers or civilians from his porch. Shooting at him is proportionate even if as a result, an innocent civilian neighbor or passerby is harmed. That is not the case if the building is bombed from the air and scores of its residents and passersby are harmed.

Id., para. 46.

16 AP I, *supra* note 6, art. 85(3) (emphasis added).

17 Levie, *supra* note 8, at 185, 194–95.

18 *Id.* at 194–95.

19 United States v. Cheek, 498 U.S. 192 (1991); *but see* Bryan v. United States, 524 U.S. 184 (1998) (over vigorous dissent of Justice Scalia, holding that "willfully" did not mean knowing of the legal duty).

20 The intent requirement is considerably higher than that necessary for a simple violation of the Protocol: "It is not sufficient that the will to launch an indiscriminate attack exists. In addition the person taking the action has to have the knowledge that certain consequences still follow. . . . The attack is already illegitimate if it may be expected to cause such losses [excessive loss of civilian life considering the 'concrete and direct military advantage anticipated']. A high degree of precaution is required. A grave breach on the other hand presupposes more: the knowledge (not only the presumption) that such an attack will cause excessive losses in kind." Bothe, *supra* note 10, at 516 (emphasis in original). *See also* ICRC, Commentary on the Additional Protocols, *supra* note 12, at 994 (defining *willfully* as follows: "the accused must have acted consciously and with intent, i.e., with his mind on the act and its consequences, and willing them ('criminal intent' or 'malice aforethought'); this encompasses the concepts of 'wrongful intent' or 'recklessness', viz., the attitude of an agent who, without being certain of a particular result, accepts the possibility of it happening; on the other hand, ordinary negligence or lack of foresight is not covered, i.e., when a man acts without having his mind on the act or its consequences (although failing to take necessary precautions, particularly failing to seek precise information constitutes culpable negligence punishable at least by disciplinary sanctions) . . .").

21 Article 30 of the Rome Statute for the International Court defines "knowingly" strictly:

> 2. For the purposes of this Article, a person has intent where:
>
> > (a) In relation to conduct, that person means to engage in the conduct;
> > (b) In relation to a consequence, that person means to cause that consequence or is aware that it will occur in the ordinary course of events.

3. For the purposes of this Article, "knowledge" means awareness that a circumstance exists or a consequence will occur in the ordinary course of events. "Know" and "knowingly" shall be construed accordingly."

Rome Statute of the International Criminal Court art. 30, July 17, 1998, 2187 U.N.T.S. 90. *See also* Yoram Dinstein, *Defences, in* 1 Substantive and Procedural Aspects of International Criminal Law: The Experience of International and National Courts 361, 371–8 (Gabrielle Kirk McDonald & Olivia Swaak-Goldman eds., 2000) for a discussion of the *mens rea* requirements established by the ICC for war crimes and crimes against humanity. The ICC statute apparently does not include a willful blindness provision, a lower standard for proving knowledge. *Compare* American Law Institute, Model Penal Code §. 2.02(7) (1985): "*Requirement of Knowledge Satisfied by Knowledge of High Probability*, When knowledge of the existence of a particular fact is an element of an offense, such knowledge is established if a person *is aware of a high probability of its existence*, unless he actually believes that it does not exist" (emphasis added). *See* United States v. Jewell, 532 F.2d 697 (1976) (In his dissenting opinion, the then Circuit Court of Appeals Judge Kennedy provides an informative gloss on this section, which codifies the "willful blindness doctrine.").

22 Maj. William G. Schmidt, *The Protection of Victims of International Armed Conflicts: Protocol I Additional to the Geneva Conventions*, 1984 A.F. L. Rev. 189, 242–43.

23 Rome Statute of the International Criminal Court, *supra* note 21. As of this writing, 114 countries had ratified the Rome Statute. United Nations, *Status of the Rome Statute of the International Criminal Court*, http://treaties.un.org/Pages/ViewDetails.aspx?src=TREATY&id=373&chapter= 18&lang= en (last visited March 17, 2009). Although President Clinton signed the ICC convention, President George W. Bush purported to "unsign" the Rome Statute. That administration signed so-called bilateral Article 98 agreements with over 100 countries to obtain a commitment that they would not extradite American nationals to the ICC. The Bush administration, however, abstained in the UN Security Council, allowing that body to refer Sudan and an investigation of Darfur to the ICC.

President Barack Obama has not thus far clearly indicated what position his administration will take toward the ICC.

24 Article 8 also criminalizes the following:

(b) Other serious violations of the laws and customs applicable in international armed conflict, within the established framework of international law, namely, any of the following acts:

(i) Intentionally directing attacks against the civilian population as such or against individual civilians not taking direct part in hostilities;

(ii) Intentionally directing attacks against civilian objects, that is, objects which are not military objectives;

(iii) Intentionally directing attacks against personnel, installations, material, units or vehicles involved in a humanitarian assistance or peacekeeping mission in accordance with the Charter of the United Nations, as long as they are entitled to the protection given to civilians or civilian objects under the international law of armed conflict. . . .

of the International Criminal Court, *supra* note 21, art. 8.

25 *Id.*, art. 7(4).

26 AP I states that:

> In addition to the grave breaches defined in Article 11, the following acts shall be regarded as grave breaches of this Protocol, when *committed willfully*, in violation of the relevant provisions of this Protocol, and causing death or serious injury to body or health:
>
> (a) Making the civilian population or individual civilians the object of attack;
> (b) Launching an *indiscriminate attack affecting the civilian population* or civilian objects *in the knowledge* that such attack will cause *excessive* loss of life, injury to civilians or damage to civilian objects, as defined in Article 57, paragraph 2 (a)(iii). . . .

AP I, *supra* note 6, art. 85(3).

27 The Prosecutor could argue that "willfully" may denote a mistake of law defense whereas "intentionally" does not. Consequently, in this respect the ICC's *mens rea* requirement is less strict than the Protocol's.

28 Thus, defendant is criminally liable when he or she "(b) launch[es] an *indiscriminate attack affecting the civilian population* or civilian objects *in the knowledge* that such attack will cause *excessive* loss of life, injury to civilians or damage to civilian objects, as defined in Article 57, paragraph 2(a)(iii)." AP I, *supra* note 6, art. 85(3)(b).

29 AP I, *supra* note 6, art. 57(2)(iii) (emphasis added).

30 Final Report to the Prosecutor, *supra* note 10, para. 21 (relying on the Rome Statute of the International Criminal Court, *supra* note 21, art. 7(a)(iv) as "evolving customary international law").

31 Rome Statute of the International Criminal Court, *supra* note 21, art. 7(a)(iv) (emphasis added).

32 *Id.* (emphasis added).

33 ICRC, Commentary on the Additional Protocols, *supra* note 12, at 683, para. 2207: "This Article [on proportionality] like Article 51 '(Protection of the civilian population)' is not concerned with strategic objectives but with the means used in a specific tactical operation." On the other hand, defendants before the ICC could argue that the word "overall" changes the test from examining a "specific tactical operation" to examining "strategic objectives" of at least the entire battle if not the entire conflict. It must be noted that some NATO members who are parties to Additional Protocol I attached reservations or declarations on this point. The Federal Republic of Germany's is typical: "In applying the rule of proportionality in Article 51 and Article 57, 'military advantage' is understood to refer to the advantage anticipated *from the attack considered as a whole* and not only from isolated or particular parts of the attack." Federal Republic of Germany, Declaration Made at Ratification of Additional Protocol 1, para. 5 (1991) (emphasis added), *available at* www.icrc.org/ihl.nsf/ 677558c021/3f4d8706b6b7ea40c1256402003fb3c7?Open (accessed March 13, 2009). The following NATO countries have made similar reservations or declarations: Belgium, Declaration at Time of Ratification, para. 5 (1986); Canada, Reservations Made at Time of Ratification, 1990; Italy, Declarations Made at Time of Ratification, 1986; Netherlands, Declaration Made at Time of Ratification, para. 5 (1987); Spain, Declarations Made at Time of Ratification, 1989; United Kingdom, *Reservations*, para. I (1998). These declarations are *available at* www.icrc.org/ihl.nsf/WebSign?ReadForm&id=470&ps=P.

34 An altitude of 15,000 feet was the lower limit for combat flights in Kosovo and Serbia, and was controversial because of pilots' inability to adequately distinguish military targets from civilians. However, the air force is making greater use of bombers now, as cheaper and better bomb guidance technology lets planes

fly above any threat – apparently B-52s have been used extensively in Afghanistan, and fly at 40,000 feet. Dave Moniz, *B-52 Still "BUFF" at 50*, USA Today, Apr. 23, 2002, *available at* www.usatoday.com/news/nation/2002/04/24/b-52.htm. '*Scores Killed' in US Afghan Raid*, BBC News, July 1, 2002, *available at* http://news.bbc.co.uk/2/hi/south_asia/2079565.stm.

And there have been other reports of civilians hit by B-52s: *See* Rory Carroll, *Bloody Evidence of US Blunder*, The Guardian, Jan. 7, 2002, *available at* www.guardian.co.uk/world/2002/jan/07/afghanistan. rorycarroll.

35   *Afghanistan: Civilian Deaths Up 40 Percent*, IRIN News, Feb. 25, 2009, *available at* www.irinnews.org/Report.aspx?ReportId=83131 [hereinafter *Afghanistan: Civilian Deaths Up 40 Percent*].

36   U.N. Assistance Mission in Afghanistan, Annual Report on Protection of Civilians in Armed Conflict 7 (2009), *available at* http://www.unchr.org/refworld/docid/499abd892.html.

37   *Afghanistan: Civilian Deaths Up 40 Percent, supra* note 35.

38   Anand Gopal, *Afghan Civilian Death Toll Undermines U.S. Support*, Christian Science Monitor, Sept. 18, 2008, *available at* http://www.csmonitor.com/World/Asia-South-Central/2008/0918/p01s02-wosc.html.

39   G. Mortenson & D. O. Relin, *Three Cups of Tea* 314–31 (2006). R. Synovitz, *Afghanistan: U.S., NATO Forces See Backlash Over Civilian Deaths*, Radio Free Europe/Radio Liberty, June 19, 2007; A. Baker, *Backlash from Afghan Civilian Deaths,* Time, June 23, 2007.

40   European Convention for the Protection of Fundamental Rights and Freedoms, Nov. 4, 1950, 213 U.N.T.S. 221 [hereinafter European Convention].

41   Ergi v. Turkey, App. No. 23818/94, Eur. Ct. Hum. Rts., paras 6–23, 77, July 28, 1998, *available at* www.qub.ac.uk/schools/SchoolofLaw/Research/HumanRightsCentre/Resources/EHRIS/EHRISHumanRightsMaterialsonTurkey/InternationalCaseLaw/icasefilestore/Filetoupload,72940,en.htm (accessed 15 March 2009).

42   European Convention, *supra* note 40, art. 2.

43   Ergi v. Turkey, *supra* note 41, para. 79.

44   *Id.*

45   C. Byron, *A Blurring of the Boundaries: The Application of International Humanitarian Law by Human Rights Bodies*, 47 Va. J. Int'l L. 839 (2007).

46   Isayeva, Yusupova & Bazayev v. Russia, 41 Eur. Ct. H.R. 847 (2005).

47   *Id.*, paras. 16–17. This was the uncontradicted testimony of the applicants, which apparently was credited by the court.

48   The ICRC witness estimated that 25 people were killed and 75 people were wounded. *Id.*, para. 31.

49   *Id.*, para. 79.

50   *Id.*, para. 169.

51   *Id.*, para. 171.

52   AP I, *supra* note 6, art. 57(2)(a)(ii) (emphasis added).

53   Article 57(2)(a)(iii) of AP I states as follows: "Refrain from deciding to launch any attack which may be expected to cause *incidental loss of civilian life*, injury to civilians, damage to civilian objects, or a combination thereof, which would *be excessive in relation to the concrete and direct military advantage anticipated*[.]" (Emphasis added.)

54   Isayeva, Yusupova & Bazayev v. Russia, 41 Eur. Ct. H.R. 847, para. 199 (2005).

55   Isayeva v. Russia, App. No. 57947/00, Eur. Ct. Hum. Rts., para. 190 (2005).

56   *Id.*, para 43.

57   Article 15 of the European Convention states, among other things, that "[a]ny High Contracting Party availing itself of this right [of derogation 'in time of war or other public emergency'] shall keep the Secretary General of the Council

of Europe fully informed of the measures which it has taken and the reasons therefor." European Convention, *supra* note 40, art. 15(3). By the way, subsection 2 of Article 15 prohibits a country from derogating from Article 2 "except in respect of deaths resulting from *lawful acts of war*. . . ." European Convention, *supra* note 40, art. 15(3) (emphasis added).

58   Isayeva v. Russia, App. No. 57947/00, Eur. Ct. Hum. Rts., para. 191 (2005).
59   W. Abresch, *A Human Rights Law of Internal Armed Conflict: The European Court of Human Rights in Chechnya*, 16 Eur. J. Int'l L. 741, 745–46 (2005).
60   Byron, *supra* note 45, at 854.
61   Robert Seely, Russo-Chechen Conflict, 1800–2000, A Deadly Embrace 269–70 (2001).

8 Assassinating suspected terrorists

The "dark side" of the war on terror?

Human rights advocates and the media have rightly paid a great deal of attention to the US disregarding the Geneva Conventions and international human rights in its treatment of detainees in Abu Ghraib, Bagram Air Base, Guantánamo Bay, and the CIA black sites. Yet, there is another area of concern that has been widely discussed in Europe and the Middle East, but has received less attention in the US, namely, state agents such as the CIA or Special Operation Forces deliberately targeting and killing a suspected terrorist rather than attempting to capture or arrest the targeted person.[1] Some have called these "assassinations," others "targeted killings." But, however denominated, the government identifies a specific individual and instructs its agents to kill that person. The question explored in this chapter is whether such premeditated and deliberate killing violates international law. Aside from morality, which also informs the debate, the legal question is a complex one, and as noted international humanitarian law scholar Michael Bothe put it, the short answer is "it depends."[2]

Absent armed conflict, a state-sponsored transnational assassination violates international law.[3] Article 2.4 of the UN Charter prohibits the use of force in the territory of another state.[4] Such assassinations also violate international human rights law. Customary international law[5] and such human rights treaties as the International Covenant on Civil and Political Rights[6] bar the extrajudicial taking of life.[7] So, for example, Chile's sending an assassin to Washington, D.C., to kill Orlando Letelier, Chile's former ambassador, violated both the Charter (as an impermissible use of armed force in the territory of another state (the US)) and international human rights law (as an arbitrary, extra-judicial killing).[8] Other examples include the US's bungled attempts to assassinate Fidel Castro—not in connection with armed conflict[9]—and Syria's alleged complicity, if proved, in the assassination of former Lebanon Prime Minister Rafik al-Hariri.[10]

If, however, an international armed conflict arises, a different set of rules may apply. When two states are at war, the law of war, generally referred to as "international humanitarian law" (IHL) permits the combatants on one side to attack without warning the combatants and other military targets of the other side. Generally, there is no obligation to request surrender before attack or an obligation to capture rather than kill unless the enemy has clearly thrown down their arms.[11] For example, during the Second World War, the US learned that Admiral Isoroku Yamamoto, the Japanese naval commander, was on a certain military plane; the US Command targeted that plane to kill him. Some have suggested that targeting Yamamoto was not chivalrous, but he was a combatant and therefore, presumably a lawful subject of attack.[12] Combatants may not, however, target civilians "unless and for such time as they *take a direct part* in hostilities."[13]

Does this paradigm translate to the struggle against non-state actors like al Qaeda? The Bush–Cheney administration had taken the position that it does. President Bush declared that the US had entered into a state of worldwide armed conflict with terror, covering al Qaeda and related terrorist groups,[14] thereby arguably permitting the US to kill/assassinate suspected terrorists anywhere in the world without attempting to capture or arrest them.[15] President Bush issued an order generally authorizing such operations.[16] During the argument of the case of Jose Padilla, an alleged "enemy combatant," Justice Kennedy asked Solicitor General Paul Clement, "Could you shoot him when he got off the plane [(rather than try to arrest him)]?"[17] The Solicitor General tried to avoid the question. But Geoff Corn, former International Law Advisor to the Army Judge Advocate General, stated that although the US should not do so (presumably as a matter of a discretion), IHL allows the US to carry out such a targeted killing.[18] Can this be the law?

From a legal perspective, as discussed in chapter 6, to trigger IHL and its combat privileges and immunities depends on finding that there is a "state of armed conflict." That term has not been clearly defined, but the available definitions particularly of "non-international armed conflict" impose geographic limits. The International Criminal Tribunal for the Former Yugoslavia concluded that an armed conflict "exists whenever there is a resort to armed forces between States or *protracted armed violence* between governmental authorities and *organized armed groups* or between such groups *within the State*."[19] According to this definition, armed conflicts between states trigger IHL, but in a conflict between a state and a non-state actor (such as al Qaeda) IHL applies only to actions of such groups "within the State." Non-international conflict is expressly covered by the 1977 Additional Protocol II (AP II) to the Geneva Conventions of 1949. Similarly, AP II first notes that it applies "in the territory of a high contracting party between its armed forces and dissident armed forces or *other organized groups* which, under responsible command, *exercise such control over a part of its territory as to enable them to carry out sustained and concerted military operations*."[20] One commentator underlines the geographic limitations: "While the area of war is extensive it is *not unlimited* and does not in general extend for example to the territory of other states not party to the conflict, unless those states allow their territory to be used by one of the belligerents."[21]

In addition, AP II notes that it does not apply to "situations of internal disturbances and tensions, such as riots, isolated and sporadic acts of violence. ... ."[22] In deciding whether the violence has risen to the level of an "armed conflict," the "nature, intensity, and duration of the violence and the nature and organization of the parties" should be considered.[23] Furthermore, the insurgent group must be able to be identified to trigger IHL: "Critically, the non-state (or 'insurgent') groups that may constitute parties must be capable of identification as a party to the conflict and have attained a certain degree of internal organization."[24]

Given the protracted nature of the hostilities in Afghanistan and Iraq, University of Geneva Professor Marco Sassoli asserts that IHL applies in those theaters, but not in the world as a whole.[25] Professor Sassoli further argues that the Geneva regime contains no black holes, that if an individual is considered an unprivileged combatant and ineligible for prisoner of war status under the Third Geneva Convention of 1949, then (as previously discussed in chapter 6) he or she defaults to civilian status, like that of saboteurs, who may be proceeded against criminally or held for security reasons under the Fourth Geneva Convention of 1949.[26] Unless there were evidence that a member of al Qaeda was involved in an imminent attack against the US or its allies, a law enforcement approach under the human rights law model should be pursued in those areas.[27] He notes that under human rights law, the government may not deliberately kill without trial "even the worst criminal [except] under the most extreme circumstances."[28] An overly broad definition of "armed conflict" can endanger the civilian population and potentially be a threat to peace, should the US act in a country without its consent.[29]

Those supporting the Bush–Cheney administration's position argue that al Qaeda's level and frequency of violence against the US and its allies do satisfy these criteria. In particular, the 1993 initial attack on the World Trade Center, the 1998 attack on two of the US's African embassies, the 2000 attack on the USS Cole, the 9/11 attack in 2001, the 2004 attack on Madrid (3/11), the 2002 and 2005 Bali bombings, and the 2005 7/7 attack in London (not to mention ongoing al Qaeda attacks in Iraq and Afghanistan), the 2007 assassination of Benazir Bhutto, and the 2008 Mumbai attacks fulfill the "protracted" element of armed conflict.[30] Even if one were to characterize these attacks as "sporadic," their intensity, particularly that of 9/11, satisfies the armed conflict requirement to invoke IHL.[31] Furthermore, how could one even suggest that the US could not target and kill Osama bin Laden under all circumstances?

Although on 9/11 al Qaeda members used America's own planes as weapons of mass destruction, al Qaeda is reportedly now seeking other WMD devices, including an atomic bomb.[32] This development and the transnational character of al Qaeda, said to operate in about 100 countries, some argue justifies President Bush's declaration that the US is in a global armed conflict, and thus entitled to extend geographic limits on non-international armed conflict, and apply IHL worldwide. As *lex specialis*, IHL supplants international human rights law, thereby permitting targeted killing globally.[33]

Professor David Kretzmer of Hebrew University of Jerusalem, however, argues that neither IHL nor human rights law precisely fit the challenge posed by highly organized, persistent non-state terrorist organizations and movements: "An armed conflict between a state and a transnational terrorist group is not an international armed conflict. However, as it transcends the borders of the state involved, it does not fully fit the mode of a non-international conflict either."[34]

Furthermore, he argues that IHL can no longer be considered in isolation from international human rights law. Since the end of the Second World War, international human rights law has undergone revolutionary development. For example, the world community has embraced the International Bill of Rights, including the Universal Declaration of Human Rights; the International Covenant on Civil and Political Rights; the International Covenant on Economic, Social and Cultural Rights[35] and several other multilateral treaties.[36] Aside from these treaties, new international institutions to safeguard human rights have been established. (See chapter 3 for a fuller discussion of the Human Rights Revolution.)

As demonstrated here and in chapter 6, international human rights law, particularly when it is more detailed than IHL, should at the very least inform the application of IHL. Professor Kretzmer illustrates the principle with *McCann v. the United Kingdom*,[37] the European Court of Human Rights case dealing with a British counterterrorism military unit (Special Air Service (SAS) soldiers) killing with a hail of bullets three unarmed Irish Republican Army operatives in Gibraltar, a British protectorate. The British possessed, beforehand, credible evidence that the IRA operatives were planning and in the process of carrying out a car bombing. The question for the Court was whether the British government had violated Article 2 of the European Convention, guaranteeing the right to life and prohibiting the use of deadly force unless "absolutely necessary." A sharply divided court (10 to 9) concluded that the British government did violate this Article, reasoning that failing to stop the IRA at the border and failing to tell the SAS unit that the evidence did not necessarily show that the IRA had a bomb or had detonators, demonstrated that the taking of life was not "absolutely necessary."[38] The Court, however, held unanimously that the SAS soldiers themselves—considering the information they were given [that the IRA operatives could and would detonate the bomb with a push button remote control device]—did not engage in conduct that violated Article 2. On this point the Court reasoned as follows:

> The Court accepts that the soldiers honestly believed, in the light of the information that they have been given . . ., that it was necessary to shoot the suspects in order to prevent them from detonating a bomb and causing serious loss of life. The actions which they took, in obedience to superior orders, were thus perceived by them as *necessary* in order *to safeguard innocent lives.*
>
> [T]he use of force by agents of the State in pursuit of one of the aims

delineated in Article 2(2) of the Convention may be justified under this provision where it is based on an honest belief which is perceived, for good reasons, to be valid at the time but which subsequently turns out to be mistaken. To hold otherwise would be to *impose an unrealistic burden* on the State and its law enforcement personnel in the execution of their duty, perhaps *to the detriment of their lives and those of others.*[39]

The Court noted that "in light of the advance warning . . . of an impending terrorist attack," that the UK "naturally" employed the SAS soldiers who had "received specialist training in combating terrorism."[40] Although a shoot to kill order would be illegal absent some kind of warning, the opinion suggests that when confronted with an impending attack, a state may use the military even if the intelligence was not completely accurate.[41]

McCann dealt with a terrorist organization with a long history of carrying out extremely violent attacks. Recognizing that law enforcement agents' lives and those of innocent third parties may hang in the balance, *McCann* envisions increased latitude for the police and implicitly authorizes the state to use the military when a significant threat is impending. In such circumstances, the Court expressly held that it should not place an "unrealistic burden" on the state or its law enforcement personnel. Absent such a threat, a strict regard for human life and the employment of police rather than military would be indicated. Such an approach should sufficiently safeguard United States' security and its pursuit of al Qaeda.[42] Absent intelligence of an impending operation, the US and its allies should primarily be able to use a law enforcement approach.[43,44] Only if the state in which suspected al Qaeda members is operating is either unwilling or unable to assist the US in arresting these individuals might a legitimate question of US security arise.[45,46]

The targeted killing question exposes the flaws in the Bush–Cheney administration's unprecedented extension of the concept of non-international conflict beyond any geographic boundaries and, simultaneously, dismissing a role for human rights law in this struggle. Professor Sassoli's approach differs from Professor Kretzmer's, the former saying that current IHL and international human rights law adequately address the challenge of terrorism; the latter arguing that a broader, new mixed model, combining IHL and international human rights law, needs to be adopted.[47] Balancing security interests with the rights of civilians and individuals, both professors, however, adhere far more closely both to the letter and to the spirit of IHL and international human rights law than did the Bush–Cheney administration's position.

Furthermore, expanding the notion of non-international conflict beyond any geographical limit, as the administration unilaterally declared, is likely to result in greater disruption to world order. If the US can claim it has the legal authority to carry out assassinations/targeted killings worldwide, then other countries facing "transnational terrorist threats" can do likewise. For example, Zelimkhan Yandarbiyev, the former president of Chechnya, was assassinated in 2004 in Doha, Qatar, by Russian Security Services.[48] Should

Russia be allowed to assassinate a suspected "terrorist" who is residing in the US or in the UK, or in any other country? Should India? Pakistan? China? North Korea?

Democratic countries that have successfully dealt with terrorism have used law enforcement to eliminate the threat. The UK, then West Germany, and Italy used law enforcement approaches against the IRA, against the Baader-Meinhof gang, and against the Red Brigades, respectively. As the *McCann* case demonstrates, international human rights law is sufficiently flexible when authorities are faced with an impending terrorist operation. Resort to targeted killings when law enforcement approaches would be effective may create martyrs, may be perceived literally as overkill, as immoral as well as illegal, and thus may undermine the US's reputation and tend to garner more support for the targeted terrorist group. Abu Ghraib, Bagram Air Base, and Guantánamo Bay teach that, even when confronted with extremely violent terrorist organizations, the US should not readily disregard the restraints imposed by international law in treating detained suspected terrorists. All the more reason, therefore, that the US should not readily disregard the restraints imposed by international law on the even more explosive stratagem of targeted killing. Given the outrage they engender and the suicide ethos that al Qaeda, its allies, and sympathizers embrace, such operations, even when otherwise legal, should be avoided.

It is disturbing that the Obama administration has expanded the use of predator drones in Afghanistan and in the tribal areas of Pakistan and is considering using them in the Pakistan province of Baluchistan.[49] The drones often are employed to carry out a targeted killing: "Top national security leaders have approved lists of people who can be attacked, officials say."[50] That the targeting of such individuals is largely entrusted to the Central Intelligence Agency is particularly troubling, given the agency's role in the detainee abuse scandal and in its inaccurate intelligence reporting in the run-up to the war in Iraq.

The use of such drones may be legal in areas of armed conflict, such as Afghanistan and possibly the tribal areas of Pakistan, against individuals who are directly taking part in hostilities. Yet, the tactical advantage they may deliver is likely outweighed by their potential to inflame not only the extremists (one Taliban leader threatened two suicide attacks for each drone attack) but also a significant portion of the Muslim world. Targeting from afar will inevitably result in mistakes and the killing of innocent civilians. Their use violates the principle of chivalry even if otherwise legal. Over-reliance on such a device is thus likely to be counter-productive.[51]

Notes

1   According to Seymour Hersh's Article in The New Yorker in 2005, President Bush signed executive orders, authorizing Secretary of State Donald Rumsfeld to use "secret commando groups and other Special Forces units to conduct

covert operations against suspected terrorist targets in as many as ten nations in the Middle East and South Asia." Seymour M. Hersh, *The Coming Wars; What the Pentagon Can Now Do in Secret*, The New Yorker, Jan. 25, 2005, at 40 (noting that these authorizations completely escape normal congressional oversight of CIA covert operations). The Bush–Cheney administration instituted a secret assassination program which apparently was never fully put into effect. Mark Mazzetti & Scott Shane, *CIA had plan to assassinate Qaeda leaders*, N.Y. Times, July 13, 2009, *available at* http//www.nytimes.com/2009/07/14/us/14intel.html. This chapter is largely taken from my article, *Assassination/Targeted Killing of Suspected Terrorists—A Violation of International Law?*, posted on *Jus in Bello* Blog, Dec. 1, 2005.

2   Statement to author, Conference on ICRC Restatement of the Customary Humanitarian Law, Montreal, September 2005.

3   Some have argued that assassinating/targeted killing of a country's leader or high military command may be justified in anticipatory self-defense. *See, e.g.*, Michael N. Schmitt, *State-Sponsored Assassination in International and Domestic Law*, 17 Yale J. Int'l L. 609, 646 (1992). Such a position, however, must meet the standards of Article 51 of the UN Charter, which, on its face, requires an "armed attack" to invoke the use of armed force. Arguing that the customary law of self-defense permitted preemptive attack in narrowly defined circumstances, many scholars assert that Article 51 must be read broadly to include this pre-existing custom. *See* chapter 11 on the Invasion of Iraq for a more detailed discussion of this issue. (This chapter on targeted killing focuses on *jus in bello* rather than *jus ad bellum*, because the 9/11 attacks and the invasion of Afghanistan and Iraq have moved the debate to the former rather than to the latter.)

Others argue that there is an inherent natural law right of the oppressed to assassinate a tyrant. *See, e.g.*, Jordan Paust et al., International Criminal Law Cases and Materials 501 (2000) (citing Kutner, *A Philosophical Perspective on Rebellion, in* International Terrorism and Political Crimes 51, 52–63 (M. C. Bassiouni ed., 1975)).

Lastly, the Convention on Preventing Crimes Against Internationally Protected Persons, had it been in force at the time of the Castro assassination attempts, might have been violated. *See* Convention on the Prevention and Punishment of Crimes Against Internationally Protected Persons, Dec. 14, 1973, 1035 U.N.T.S. 167, *reprinted in* 13 I.L.M. 41 (entered into force Feb. 20, 1977). This Convention prohibits the murder or attempted murder of, among others, the "Head of State." *Id.*, arts. 1(a) and 2(a), (d). The Convention, however, is generally interpreted as applying only when the protected person travels abroad.

4   Of course, a state [the "receiving state"] could give another state [the "sending state"] permission to carry out a targeted killing on the receiving state's soil, thus absolving the sending state from any Article 2.4 violation. Unless another exception applies, such a killing would still violate human rights law. *See infra* note 29 for a discussion of the drone attack in Yemen.

5   Unless permitted by IHL, an extrajudicial killing violates a peremptory norm of international law. *See* Restatement (Third) of Foreign Relations § 702 (1987).

6   International Covenant on Civil and Political Rights art. 6, Dec. 6, 1966, 993 U.N.T.S. 171, *reprinted in* 6 I.L.M. 368 (1967) [hereinafter ICCPR].

7   Applying the Covenant and other human rights treaties requires interpreting the treaties to impose obligations on states when they are acting outside their own territory. *See* chapter 6 for a more detailed discussion of the issue. Although some *travaux préparatoires* suggest that the drafters did not intend the ICCPR to apply extraterritorially, the trend in decision in international tribunals and bodies is toward imposing obligations under human treaties wherever a state's

military or law enforcement agents are operating: "[Article 2.1] does not imply that the State party concerned cannot be held accountable for violations of rights under the Covenant which its agents commit upon the territory of another State." Antonio Cassese, International Law 385 (2d edition, 2005) (quoting Delia Saldias de Lopez v. Uruguay, U.N. Human Rights Committee, Comm. No. 52/ 1979 (29 July 1981), U.N. Doc. CCPR/C/OP/1 at 88 (1984). *But see* Michael J. Dennis, *Agora: ICJ Advisory Opinion on Construction of a Wall in the Occupied Palestinian Territory, Application of Human Rights Treaties in Times of Armed Conflict and Military Occupation*, 99 Am. J. Int'l L. 119 (2005) (arguing that the original intent of the drafters limited human right treaties to the territory of the party).

8 Although the US had not ratified the ICCPR at the time of Letelier's assassination, Chile had done so. *See* ICCPR, Ratifications · and Reservations, www.ohchr.org/english/countries/ratification/4.htm (noting that Chile ratified the ICCPR in 1972). *See also supra* note 7 (discussing extraterritorial application of human rights treaties). In any event, such an extrajudicial execution at that time can be said to have violated customary international law as well as human rights treaties.

9 The ICCPR was not open for signature until 1966, so that the human rights convention could not have applied at that time. Furthermore, the US did not ratify the ICCPR until 1992. Customary international law, even in the early 1960s, probably would have barred assassination in peacetime. Today, assuming the extraterritorial application of human rights treaties, there would have been such a treaty violation. In addition, there would be a customary international law violation.

10 *See* S.C. Res. 1636, U.N. Doc. S/RES/1636 (Oct. 31, 2005) (adopted under chapter VII) (requiring Syria to cooperate with UN investigators concerning Prime Minister's al Hariri's murder). Such an assassination would also violate Syria's obligations as an occupying power. Geneva Convention (IV) Relative to the Protection of Civilian Persons in Time of War arts. 27, 47, Aug. 12, 1949, 6 U.S.T.S. 3516, 75 U.N.T.S. 287.

11 Helen Duffy, The 'War on Terror' and the Framework of International Law 311 n.177 (2005) (acknowledging this proposition, but noting that a preference for arrest rather than killing is "implicit . . . at least as far as [it] causes no military disadvantage"); *cf.* Schmitt, *supra* note 3, at 644 ("targeting someone meeting the criteria of a combatant in armed conflict, but whose death is not 'necessary' would be illegal."). *But see* Vincent-Joel Proulx, *If the Hat Fits, Wear it, If the Turban Fits, Run for your Life: Reflections on the Indefinite Detention and Targeted Killing of Suspected Terrorist*, 56 Hastings L.J. 801, 84–85 (2005) (arguing that the right to quarter bars targeted killing). *See also* Louise-Doswald Beck, *Background – Development of the San Remo Manual and its intended purpose – Content of the San Remo Manual on International Law Applicable to Armed Conflict at Sea*, 309 Int'l Rev. Red Cross 583 (1995) *available at* www.icrc.org/Web/Eng/siteeng0.nsf/ html/57JMST (noting that the San Remo Manual makes clear "the prohibition of the denial of quarter").

12 The targeted killing of Yamamoto does not appear to have violated the Hague Convention, which prohibits treacherous killing of the enemy. *See* Hague Convention (IV) Respecting the Laws and Customs of War on Land and Its Annex: Regulations Concerning the Laws and Customs of War on Land, Reg. 23, Oct. 18, 1907, 36 Stat. 2277, T.S. No. 539 (noting that "is especially forbidden: . . . (b) to kill or wound *treacherously* individuals belonging to the hostile nation or army" (emphasis added)). Compare the assassination of S.S. General Reinhardt Heydrick, military governor of German occupied Bohemia and Moravia in 1942. The British RAF flew in two Free Czechoslovak soldiers who were not wearing uniforms. After parachuting down, they were threw a bomb into

Heydrick's car, killing him. Patricia Zengel, *Assassination and the Law of Armed Conflict*, 43 Mercer L. Rev. 615, 628 (1992). In retaliation, the Germans killed 120 people in a church, executed 1,331 Czechs, and transported 3,000 Jews, who had been detained in Theresienstadt, to death camps. *Id*. Since the two carried out the assassination were out of uniform, arguably they committed an act of perfidy, falsely trading on their apparent civilian status, thereby endangering the civilian population, and violating Regulation 23, attached to the Hague Convention. *Id*. at 629–30, *but see id*. at 629 (noting Heydrick's assailant made "no affirmative misrepresentation" nor betrayed any "personal trust or confidence"). *See also* Schmitt, *supra* note 3, at 639 (killing an enemy during armed conflict constitutes an illegal killing if the actor feigns civilian status or wears a uniform of the enemy and notes that "irregular combatants commit treachery if they use their apparent noncombatant status to get closer to the target than they otherwise would."). On the other hand, the war crimes and crimes against humanity perpetrated by the Nazi regime mitigate the violation of the laws of war by those opposing them.

13   1977 Geneva Protocol I Additional to the Geneva Conventions of 12 August 1949, and Relating to the Protection of Victims of International Armed Conflicts art. 51(3), June 8, 1977, 1125 U.N.T.S. 3–608, 16 I.L.M. 1391 [hereinafter AP I]. *See also* Documents on the Laws of War 443 (Adam Roberts & Richard Guelff eds., 1989). The ICRC Commentary on this Article notes that " 'hostile acts' should be understood to be acts which by their nature and purpose are intended to cause actual harm to the personnel and equipment of armed forces." Int'l Committee of the Red Cross, Commentary on the Additional Protocols of 8 June 1977 to the Geneva Conventions of 12 August 1949, at para. 1942 (Yves Sandoz et al. eds., 1987) [hereinafter ICRC, Commentary on the Additional Protocols]. "Thus a civilian who takes part in armed combat, either individually or as part of a group, thereby becomes a legitimate target, though only for as long as he takes part in hostilities." *Id*. The Commentary notes that "the word 'hostilities' covers not only the time that the civilian actually makes use of a weapon, but also, for example, the time that he is carrying it, as well as situations in which he undertakes hostile acts without using a weapon." *Id*. at 618–19, para. 1943. Although the US has not ratified AP I, it considers Article 51 as reflecting customary international law. The ICRC has published an interpretive guide on direct participation, Int'l Committee of the Red Cross, Direct Participation in Hostilities (June 2, 2009), http://www.icrc.org/web/eng/siteeng0.nsf/htmlall/direct-participation-ihl-faq-020609#al.

14   Military Order, Detention, Treatment, and Trial of Certain Non-Citizens in the War Against Terrorism, 66 Fed. Reg. 57833 at sec. 1(a) (Nov. 13, 2001) (noting that there exists "a state of armed conflict" between the United States and terrorist groups, including al Qaeda).

15   A Canadian judge advocate supports this position, but argues that some who provide merely financial support for a terrorist organization should be immune from attack: "Mere financial donors or those providing moral support would not be targeted (although they may be arrested), but members of the organization employed in supplying weapons and/or carrying out intelligence activities could be attacked." Col. Kenneth Watkins, *Canada/United States Military Interoperability and Humanitarian Law Issues: Land Mines, Terrorism, Military Objectives, and Targeted Killings*, 15 Duke J. Comp. & Int'l L. 281, 313 (2005).

16   David Johnston & David E. Sanger, *Yemen Killing Based on Rules Set Out by Bush* N.Y. Times, Nov. 6, 2002 *available at* www.nytimes.com/2002/11/06/international/middleeast/06YEME.html?pagewanted=2 (noting that "[t]he lethal

missile strike [fired from a drone] that killed a suspected leader of Al Qaeda in Yemen [in 2002] was carried out under broad authority that President Bush had given the C.I.A. over the past year to pursue the terror network well beyond the borders of Afghanistan, senior government officials said today.").

17   Tony Mauro, *Justices Appear Split, Troubled by Terror Cases*, N.Y.L.J. Apr. 29, 2004, at 1.

18   Statement made on October 1, 2005, at ICRC Conference on Customary International Humanitarian Law, Montreal, Canada. Geoff Corn is a professor of national security law at South Texas College of law and is a retired Army lieutenant colonel. The actual question posed was whether Khalid Sheikh Mohammed, alleged mastermind behind 9/11, could be deliberately killed by US military forces while Khalid was swimming in a swimming pool in Islamabad, Pakistan.

19   Duffy, *supra* note 11, at 218 (quoting Prosecutor v. Dusco Tadic, Case No. IT-94-1-AR72, Appeals Chamber Decision on the Defense Motion for Interlocutory Appeal on Jurisdiction para. 70 (Oct. 2, 1995) (emphasis added)).

20   1977 Geneva Protocol II Additional to the Geneva Conventions of 12 August 1949, and Relating to the Protection of Victims of International Armed Conflicts art. 1(1), June 8, 1977, 1125 U.N.T.S. 609 (emphasis added) [hereinafter AP II]. Although the US has not ratified AP II, this Article can be said to reflect customary international law.

21   Professor Mary Ellen O'Connell, Presentation at the American Branch of International Law Association's International Law Weekend Conference in New York, NY (Oct. 21, 2005).

22   AP II, *supra* note 20, art. 1.2.

23   Duffy, *supra* note 11, at 221 (citations omitted) (emphasis added). *See also* Kriangak Kittchaisaree, International Criminal Law 137 (2001) (noting that "situations of internal disturbances and tensions, unorganized and short lived insurrections, banditry, or *terrorist activities* are not subject to international humanitarian law") (emphasis added).

24   Duffy, *supra* note 11, at 221–22 (citing Int'l Committee of the Red Cross, International Humanitarian Law and the Challenges of Contemporary Armed Conflicts 19 (Feb. 19, 2008)). Professor Duffy also notes that control of territory is not necessary for armed conflict despite the language of AP II quoted above. *Id.* at 22. *See also* Gabor Rona, *Interesting Times for International Humanitarian Law: Challenges from the "War on Terror,"* Fletcher F. of World Aff., Summer/Fall 2003, at 55, 60 (noting that "there can be no humanitarian law conflict without identifiable parties" and criticizing the formulation "war on terror," because "terror" cannot be a party). Given the decentralized nature of al Qaeda, with some adherents receiving little more than inspiration from Osama bin Laden, identification of parties to the alleged non-international armed conflict is problematic. Thomas M. McDonnell, *The Death Penalty—An Obstacle to the "War against Terrorism"?*, 37 Vand. J. Transnat'l L. 353, 397 n.205 (2004) (discussing so-called "leaderless resistance").

25   Marco Sassoli, *Use and Abuse of the Laws of War in the "War on Terrorism,"* 22 Law & Ineq. 195, 197–98 (2004).

26   *Id.* at 208. The authoritative ICRC commentary to Article 5 of Geneva IV supports Sassoli's position. The relevant part of the Commentary is discussed in chapter 6 in note 43 and accompanying text.

On the other hand, one commentator criticizes one aspect of Professor Sassoli's view, noting that "[t]he assumption that terrorists are merely civilians taking a direct part in hostilities might make sense if the hostilities of an international nature were also taking place." David Kretzmer, *Targeted Killing of Suspected Terrorists: Extra-Judicial Executions or Legitimate Means of Defence?*, 16(2)

Eur. J. Int'l L. 171, 209 (2005). Such apparently is the case in Afghanistan where al Qaeda members have "taken a direct part" with the Taliban against the US and the new regime there. That analysis might also apply to Iraq, where al Qaeda members have apparently "taken a direct part" in the Iraqi insurgents' efforts against the United States and against the new government. The Iraqi situation is hard to categorize neatly. For a good description and analysis of the confusing legal nature of the conflict, *see* Geoffrey S. Corn, *"Snipers in the Minaret—What is the Rule?" The Law of War and the Protection of Cultural Property: A Complex Equation,* 2005–July Army Law. 28, 31. This point has been discussed principally in chapter 6, but it also resurfaces in other parts of the book.

27   *Id.* at 212–13.

28   *Id.* at 213.

29   Apparently, the US predator drone attack in Yemen, a targeted killing of an al Qaeda member, was carried out with the permission of the Yemeni government. Had the US lacked such permission, only a state that committed an act triggering self-defense under Article 51 of the UN Charter would authorize the US invoking its rights therein to act in individual or collective self-defense. Compare the majority and dissenting opinion in Case Concerning Military and Paramilitary Activities in and Against Nicaragua (Nicaragua v. United States), 1986 I.C.J. 14, para. 195 (June 27); *id.* at paras. 166–77 (Schwebel. J., dissenting) (discussing when a state's support of an armed group rises to the level of armed attack upon the state the group targets). For a good discussion of this issue, *see* Kittchaisaree, *supra* note 23, at 135–36. Assuming the target of the drone attack was not taking a "direct part" in the hostilities in Afghanistan or Iraq, some commentators have argued that the targeted killing violated international law. *But see* Norman G. Printer, *The Use of Force Against Non-State Actors Under International Law: An Analysis of the U.S. Predator Strike in Yemen,* 8 U.C.L.A. J. Int'l L. & Foreign Aff. 331 (2003) (arguing that as an "enemy combatant," the al Qaeda member originally thought to have been killed in the attack had no greater rights than a privileged combatant and therefore was a proper military target under IHL).

30   Professor Jane G. Dalton of the Naval War College, Presentation at the American Branch of International Law Association's International Law Weekend Conference in New York, NY (Oct. 21, 2005) [hereinafter Dalton, American Branch Presentation]. One might add to this list, among others, the 2002 truck bombing of a Tunisian synagogue, apparently aimed at French and German vacationers; an attack on a French oil tanker off Yemen that same year; the 2003 suicide bombing on civilian targets in Morocco, targeting not only Moroccan nationals but possibly Spanish nationals; the 2003 bombing of the Marriott hotel in Jakarta, *see* McDonnell, *supra* note 24, at 414–15; and the bombing of Jordanian hotels. Sabrina Tavernise, *Suicide Bombing Leaves 29 Dead in Baghdad Café,* N.Y. Times, Nov. 11, 2005, at 1. (A group claiming to be Al Qaeda has taken "credit" for bombing three Jordanian hotels and killing over 55 people.)

31   Dalton, American Branch Presentation, *supra* note 30. *See also* Sassoli, *supra* note 25, at 202. He notes that the Bush–Cheney administration adopted a "very wide" concept of armed conflict:

> Its instructions to Military Commissions explain that it does not require "ongoing mutual hostilities, or a confrontation involving a regular national armed force. A single hostile act or attempted act may provide sufficient basis . . . so long as its magnitude or severity rises to the level of an 'armed attack' or an 'act of war,' or the number, power, stated intent or organization of the force with which the actor is associated is such that the act or attempted act is tantamount to an attack by an armed force. Similarly, conduct under-

taken or organized with knowledge or intent that it initiate or contribute to such hostile act or hostilities would satisfy the nexus requirement." *Id.* (quoting Department of Defense, Crimes and Elements for Trials by Military Commission, Military Commission Instruction No. 2, Section 5(C) (Apr. 30, 2003), available at: www.dtic.mil/whs/directives/corres/mco/mci2.pdf). In other words, if I attack a single Montreal police officer with the intent to initiate an armed conflict between French-speaking and English-speaking Canadians, there is, according to the U.S. administration, an armed conflict (and the police may detain me as an enemy combatant without any judicial guarantees).

Sassoli, *supra* note 25, at 202.

32   Proponents would also argue that, with modern technology and advanced communications, a transnational non-state terrorist group threatens democratic societies as much, if not more than, hostile states because such a terrorist group may wreak great damage and at the same be undeterrable. See, e.g., *Legal Aspects To the Control of Transnational Terrorism: An Overview,"* 13 Ohio N.U. L. Rev. 117, 117 (1986) ("With the development of small, highly portable and technologically sophisticated weapons, a terrorist group consisting of a very few members can hold a city anywhere in the world hostage—or destroy it.").

33   *See, e.g.*, Legality of the Threat or Use of Nuclear Weapons, Advisory Opinion, 1996 I.C.J. 226, (July 8), *available at* 1996 WL 939337.

34   Kretzmer, *supra* note 26, at 201.

35   *See, e.g.*, Universal Declaration of Human Rights, G.A. Res. 217A, U.N. GAOR, 3d Sess. 1st plen. mtg., U.N. Doc. A/810 (Dec. 12, 1948); ICCPR, *supra* note 6; International Covenant on Economic, Social and Cultural Rights, Dec. 16, 1966, 993 U.N.T.S. 3, *reprinted in* 6 I.L.M. 360 (1967). Convention on the Prevention and Punishment of the Crime of Genocide, Dec. 9, 1948, 102 Stat. 3045, 78 U.N.T.S. 277.

36   Just to name a few: the Convention on the Elimination of All Forms of Discrimination Against Women, Dec. 18, 1979, 1249 U.N.T.S. 13; the Convention Against Torture and Other Cruel Inhuman or Degrading Treatment or Punishment, Dec. 10, 1984, 1465 U.N.T.S. 85; and the Convention on the Rights of the Child, Nov. 20, 1989, 1577 U.N.T.S. 3, *reprinted in* 28 I.L.M. 1456 (1989)

37   McCann and Others v. United Kingdom, App. No. 18984/91, 21 Eur. H.R. Rep. 97 (ser. A) (1996), *available at* 1995 WL 1082324.

38   *Id.*, paras. 202–14. The Court, however, refused to award any compensation, reasoning that the decedents were planning to carry out a terrorist attack in Gibraltar at some point. *Id.*

39   *Id.*, para. 200 (emphasis added).

40   *Id.*, para. 183.

41   On the other hand, the British police's killing Brazilian Jean Charles Menezes, an innocent man suspected of carrying out an imminent terrorist attack, demonstrates the need to limit the use of lethal force until it is in fact "absolutely necessary." *See No Warning Needed Before Brazilian Was Shot*, The Australian, Aug. 8, 2005, at 15, *available at* 2005 WLNR 12044942.

42   The international human rights approach rests on applying human rights treaties extraterritorially. See chapter 6 for a more detailed discussion of this issue. Even were one to include that such treaties do not have extraterritorial application, customary international law would suffice. *See* Restatement (Third) of Foreign Relations § 702 (1987).

43   David Johnston & David E. Sanger, *Yemen Killing Based on Rules Set Out by Bush*, N.Y. Times, Nov. 6, 2002 *available at* www.nytimes.com/2002/11/06/

international/middleeast/06YEME.html?pagewanted=2 (noting "F.B.I. agents overseas and foreign military and security services worked in concert, detaining several thousand suspects since the last year's attacks at the World Trade Center and the Pentagon.").

44   *See* David Sanger, *The Struggle for Iraq: President's Address; 10 plots Foiled Since Sept. 11, Bush Declares*, N.Y. Times, Oct. 7, 2005, at A1; *Threats and Responses, Excerpts from the Statement by Sept. 11 Commission Staff*, N.Y. Times, June 17, 2004, at A16. The arrests of Khalid Sheikh Mohammed and Ramzi Bin al Shibh were carried out by Pakistani Security Forces, with the assistance of the CIA. *See also The Search for Al Qaeda*, Frontline, www.pbs.org/wgbh/pages/frontline/shows/search/behind/28.html.

45   Chapter 12 on the invasion of Afghanistan covers this issue. Any such action must comport with Article 51 of the UN Charter. *See also* Kretzmer, *supra* note 26, at 201.

46   For example, in January 2006, the CIA launched a predator drone attack against a village in Northern Pakistan, targeting Ayman al Zawahiri, bin Laden's chief of staff. The CIA had intelligence that Zawahiri was in the village. The drone's missiles destroyed the village, killing 18 civilians, including five children, according to Pakistani authorities. Eben Kaplan, *Q&A: Targeted Killings*, N.Y. Times, Jan. 25, 2006, *available at* http://www.nytimes.com/cfr/international/slot3_012506.html. Zawahiri was not in the village. The strikes caused outrage and protests in Pakistan against the United States. *Id.*

47   Consequently, "[a]s opposed to the general rule in armed conflicts, under which a party may target combatants of the other side even when they pose no immediate danger, under the necessity requirement the targeting of suspected terrorists must be restricted to cases in which there is credible evidence that the targeted persons are actively involved in planning or preparing further terrorist attacks against the victim state and no other operational means of stopping those attacks are available." Kretzmer, *supra* note 26, at 203. Professor Kretzmer notes the use of lethal force "must always conform to the proportionality test." Kretzmer, *supra* note 26, at 203. He constructs a three-part balancing test: "(1) the danger to life posed by the continued activities of the terrorists; (2) the chance of the danger to human life being realized if the activities of the suspected terrorist are not halted immediately; and (3) the danger that civilians will be killed or wounded in the attack on the suspected terrorist." *Id.* The proportionality test, he constructs, is much stricter than required by IHL for so called collateral (civilian) damage. In his view, the state bears a particularly "heavy burden" to justify any civilian casualties caused by a targeted killing. *Id.* at 203–04. See chapter 7 for a detailed discussion of the collateral damage and proportionality rule. *See also* Schmitt, *supra* note 3, at 676 ("[E]very operation must be tested against the overarching principles of necessity and proportionality, for even non-treacherous killing of combatants using acceptable methods may be deemed impermissible.").

48   Steven Lee Myers, *Qatar Court Convicts 2 Russians in Top Chechen's Death*, N.Y. Times, July 1, 2004 *available at* www.nytimes.com/2004/07/01/world/qatar-court-convicts-2-russians-in-top-chechen-s-death.html ("'The Russian leadership issued an order to assassinate the former Chechen leader Yandarbiyev,' the judge said, according to news reports.").

49   Eric Schmidt & Christopher Drew, *More Drone Attacks Planned for Pakistan*, N.Y. Times, Apr. 7, 2009, *available at* http://www.nytimes.com/2009/04/07/world/asia/07drone.html?_r=1&pa.

50   US and Pakistani officials claim that "half of an initial list of 20 high value targets have been either killed or captured over the past six months." Jay

Solomon, Siobhan Gorman & Matthew Rosenberg, *U.S. Plans New Drone Attacks in Pakistan*, Wall St. J., Mar. 26, 2009.

51 The New York Times reported that the Obama administration's Pentagon has placed on its "kill or capture" list "fifty Afghans believed to be drug traffickers with[financial] ties to the Taliban." *U.S. to Hunt Down Afghan Drugs Lords Tied to the Taliban*, N.Y. Times, Aug. 10, 2009, at A01, *available at* http://www.nytimes.com/2009/08/10/world/asia/10afghan.html?th&eme=th.
However apparently tactically advantageous, using predator drones to kill suspected drug kingpins who finance the Taliban violates international law. For it is hard to claim that providing financial support to insurgents amounts to "taking active part in hostilities" under common Article 3 of the Geneva Conventions or to "taking a direct part in hostilities" under Article 51(3) of AP I. True there has been some debate whether "taking a direct part in hostilities" extends beyond civilians who carry their arms openly to those who gather intelligence, plan terrorist attacks, or drive a truck with ammunition for terrorists's use. *See, e.g.*, Watkins, *supra* note 15, at 313; H.C.J. 769/02 The Public Committee against Torture v. Government of Israel [2005], para 35, *available at* http://elyon1.court.gov.il/Files_ENG/02/690/007/A34/02007690.A34.pdf.
The Israel Supreme Court, for example, answered the above question in the affirmative. *Id.*

That Court, hardly a tribunal biased in favour of suspected terrorists, has agreed with the International Committee on the Red Cross that the above quoted AP I Article 51(3) language is binding international custom. *Id.*, para. 30. The Israel Supreme Court held, however, that the class of individuals "taking a direct part in hostilities" does not extend to financial supporters of terrorists. *Id.*, para. 35. The Court implicitly concluded that the State may arrest, charge, convict, and imprison such individuals (presumably including drug kingpins), but may not target and kill them. *Id.* Targeting such an individual would constitute an extrajudicial killing. *See* ICCPR, *supra* note 6, arts, 4.2, 9.1 ("No one shall be arbitrarily deprived of his life.").

Like Israel, the US is not a party to AP I, but is a party to the four universally accepted Geneva Conventions. It should also be considered bound, as the Israeli Supreme Court held, to AP I, Article 51(3), as a matter of customary international law. In addition, widening the target list risks greater civilian deaths, further undercutting the moral authority of the United States, particularly because an unchivalrous method of warfare, drone-attack-targeted killing, is often employed.

9 Carrying out the death penalty in the "war on terrorism"

Getting just desert or creating martyrs?

September 11 burned into America's collective memory perhaps even more vividly than December 7, 1941, and has evoked a natural demand both for security and for retribution. Al Qaeda, its allies, and its adherents have continued to carry out terrorist crimes, killing innocent civilians, not only in the US, but elsewhere around the globe. Such widespread and systematic murder of innocent civilians constitutes not only a domestic crime but also an international one. Given the existing statutory and judicial authority for capital punishment, the US has had to confront the issue whether to seek the death penalty against the perpetrators of these attacks. Meting out the death penalty to international terrorists involves difficult moral, legal, and policy questions. The magnitude of these crimes, including the killing of nearly 3,000 innocent people on 9/11, cries out for redress.

Yet, most countries in the world, including nearly all the US's closest allies, have abolished capital punishment. None of the five currently operating international criminal tribunals are authorized to give a death sentence. In addition, the advent of the suicide bomber turns the deterrence justification for the death penalty inside out. Might the death penalty help create martyrs rather than discourage similar attacks? Could the US imposing the death penalty increase support in the Islamic world for al Qaeda and other extremist groups? Furthermore, to what extent as a matter of constitutional law and policy, should a secondary actor, one who did not kill, but who was a member of a terrorist conspiracy, be subject to the death penalty? This chapter examines these questions.

Even if the US Supreme Court were to conclude that executing secondary actors (those who helped or who conspired, but who did not directly kill innocent civilians) is constitutional, sound policy considerations argue against such executions. This chapter will first summarize the arguments in favor of imposing the death penalty on terrorists. After proposing a definition of terrorism, this chapter will discuss arguments against imposing the death penalty on politically motivated terrorists in general and on the al Qaeda terrorists in particular. Included here are a constellation of policy questions, namely, how the death penalty interferes with an alternative strategy against terrorism; how the death penalty might create martyrs; how it might hinder cooperation with US allies in the war against terror; and how executing al Qaeda members might affect US civilians and military in the field.

9.1 Summary of arguments in favor of the death penalty

Some of the arguments generally advanced in favor of the death penalty apply to international terrorists. Chief among these would be retribution, both the just desert strand[1] as well as the revenge strand[2] of retribution theory. Killing nearly 3,000 innocent people, not to mention the other grave crimes that the hijackers committed, demands retribution.[3] Even under the just desert strand as opposed to the wild justice strand, the penalty of death is justified. Intentionally taking the life of so many innocents recalls the horrors of the Nazi regime.[4] The culpability level, at least of the active conspirators, is as high as can be imagined.[5] Even if suicide bombers may not be generally deterred,[6] those responsible for the September 11 attacks warrant the death penalty: "The truth is that some crimes are so outrageous that society insists on adequate punishment, because the wrongdoer deserves it, irrespective of whether it is a deterrent or not."[7]

Furthermore, the theories of incapacitation and specific deterrence would appear to be furthered by the death penalty.[8] Reformation of these offenders is unthinkable. Imposing the death penalty would also be justified under the denunciation theory, the theory espoused by the French sociologist, Emile Durkheim, that the death penalty serves to "express society's condemnation and the relative seriousness of the crime,"[9] in this case, the September 11 attacks[10] and other heinous terrorist offenses.

9.2 Terrorism and counterterrorism

Despite the strength and appeal of many of the arguments for imposing the death penalty on terrorist killers in general and those responsible for the outrage of September 11 in particular, there are other arguments that should be considered. Although the arguments that follow appear grounded in utilitarian theory,[11] I suspect they ultimately reflect Professor Charles Black's observation that the death penalty is an evil, because, among other things, "it extinguishes, after untellable suffering, the most mysterious and wonderful thing we know, *human life*; this reason has *many harmonics*. . . ."[12]

9.2.1 Defining terrorism

The term "terrorism" has defied attempts at definition.[13] Some define it as acts of violence by a private organization against the state or civilians.[14] Others say terrorism largely embraces attacks animated by racism or colonialism and excludes acts of "struggle" and "resistance" carried out by so-called "national liberation movements" even if those acts are aimed at innocent civilians.[15] For purposes of this chapter, I consider crimes of terrorism to mean "war crimes" and "crimes against humanity" as defined by the Rome Statute of the International Criminal Court (ICC).[16] The Rome Statute defines a crime against humanity as "a widespread or systematic attack directed against any civilian population."[17] Such attacks are defined as "a course of conduct involving the multiple commission of [such] acts . . . pursuant to or in further-ance of a state or *organizational* policy to commit such attack."[18] As of this writing, the Rome Statute of the ICC has been signed by 139 countries and has been ratified by 110 countries.[19] Using the ICC definitions accomplishes a twofold objective: it draws from a source of law now recognized by the vast majority of states as authoritative, and it addresses critics' major objection to policies treating state terror and private terror disparately.[20]

The attacks of September 11 easily satisfy the elements of crimes against humanity. By hijacking the four civilian airliners, deliberately crashing two of the planes into huge civilian office buildings, thus murdering all the civilians on the aircrafts and murdering thousands of civilians within the buildings, the 19 hijackers and their accomplices committed "multiple" acts "directed at any civilian population." The coordination of the attacks demonstrates that the attacks were committed "pursuant to or in furtherance of a State or organizational policy." The language "organizational policy"[21] was expressly intended to include non-state actors such as private terror groups.[22] If al Qaeda acted on its own in carrying out the September 11 attacks, those responsible in al Qaeda should be found guilty of crimes against humanity.

If a state, such as Taliban Afghanistan, sponsored these attacks, then those responsible in the Taliban government as well as any other accomplices or conspirators are almost certainly guilty of war crimes for carrying out the outrages of September 11.[23] Restating long-established treaty and customary international law, the ICC codifies as a war crime "intentionally directing attacks against the civilian population as such or against individual civilians not taking direct part in the hostilities; [and] (ii) intentionally directing attacks against civilian objects, that is, objects which are not military object-ives."[24] Except for the attack on the Pentagon, all the attacks were on civilians and civilian objects.[25]

9.2.2 Alternative strategies against terrorism

In the struggle against terrorism, the US must consider with whom it is dealing and the most effective approach for reducing, if not eliminating, the threat to American cities and suburbs, facilities, aircraft, communications, and, above all, its people. There are more than one billion Muslims in the world.[26] In the Arab world, there are more than 200 million people.[27] Few democracies exist in the Islamic world;[28] the vast majority of the Arab countries are run by dictators or kings, some more despotic than others.[29] The Arab countries rank last in the world in ratings on freedom of the press and other freedoms.[30] Aside from the lack of individual rights, the standard of living has declined in that part of the world for the last 30 years.[31] Nearly 50 percent of the population in the Arab world is under the age of 25,[32] with one-third under the age of 15.[33] In the oil-rich countries—the Gulf States, for example—"economic wealth has benefited a relatively limited few, and has not been distributed to poorer Islamic countries or to their very large migrant communities."[34] The young face little chance of climbing out of devastating and demoralizing poverty and repression.[35] "Throughout [the Middle East] [Arab] people have become evermore disillusioned with the deeply-entrenched dictatorships in their own countries, with the collapse of democratic institutions, hollow nationalistic rhetoric, and with their failing economies."[36]

Given the failure of economic and political institutions in the Arab world, it is not surprising that religion emerged as a major force.[37] In the Muslim culture, religion and politics are intertwined in a way reminiscent of Western Europe before the Reformation.[38] The struggle against terrorism thus needs to embrace the social and political reality of the Arab world and the nature of the terrorist organizations that are threatening the West.

The available evidence suggests that al Qaeda is a network rather than a single, unified military organization.[39] As one commentator has written, "[H]aving suffered the destruction of its sanctuary in Afghanistan two years ago, al Qaeda's decentralized organization has become more decentralized still."[40] Another commentator has analogized al Qaeda to "a holding company run by a council (shura) including representatives of terrorist movements."[41] It has also been described as the terrorist equivalent of the Ford Foundation, providing money and other resources for individual terrorists or movements that propose terrorist projects.[42]

The nature of the organization suggests a different approach than the Bush–Cheney administration employed. Tactically, the US and its allies must bring to justice those responsible for carrying out the outrages of September 11 and to arrest those who continue to attempt to terrorize the US.[43] Strategically, the US and its allies must take steps to end support in the Arab and greater Muslim world for al Qaeda and others who would resort to terrorism.[44] The decentralized nature of al Qaeda underlines the importance of the US gaining the cooperation and good will not only of governments, but also of their law enforcement personnel and of individual citizens in Arab and other Muslim states.[45] In other words, to root out those responsible for the attacks and those who pose a continuing threat, the US needs to adopt a firm, but measured response, simultaneously demonstrating that the US is not attacking all Muslims or Arabs or applying a double standard to Muslims or Arabs.[46]

Putting it another way, "[T]he first principle of responding to unlimited warfare against civilians is ... not to respond with similar behavior."[47] Otherwise, the US risks inflaming the Islamic world. Unfortunately, the invasion of Iraq, a Muslim country (albeit with a secular regime) has created such a response.[48] Likewise, executing members of a terrorist group like al Qaeda invites retaliation in kind. As one commentator has noted, "[R]eprisal begets reprisal."[49] The US has seen, in other theaters, retaliatory strike followed by retaliatory attack from the other side, devolving into a vicious cycle of seemingly ever-increasing violence.[50] Experience suggests that executing al Qaeda members would help create such a cycle.[51] The US should adopt, not only with use of its military, but also with the use of the death penalty, an approach that is most likely to gain the cooperation of Western allies and most likely to isolate al Qaeda.[52]

Achieving this strategic objective requires that the US gives both the fact and appearance of treating any accused Muslim fairly. If the US ultimately uses the vague doctrines of conspiracy and of willful blindness to impose the death penalty on actors who did not directly participate in the September 11 or other terrorist crimes, such executions will be perceived by Muslims as anything but fair. Even if the evidence ultimately shows that the individual not only directly participated in the planning of the September 11 attacks but also played a major role, resorting to the death penalty will likely be deemed by Muslims as unjust.[53]

9.3 Using the death penalty to punish politically motivated terrorists

9.3.1 Creating martyrs

Making individuals martyrs by killing or executing them has, throughout history, often advanced the cause of repressed political groups. For example, Britain's execution in 1916 of all 15 leaders and others involved with the Easter rebellion led to the formation of the Irish Free State five years later.[54] As mentioned in chapter 1, Osama bin Laden was greatly influenced by Sayyid Qutb, a religious leader who espoused Salafiyya, the central doctrine of Wahhabism, a "highly regressive monolithic interpretation of Islam."[55] Qutb has been described as "the real founder of Islamic fundamentalism in the Sunni world."[56] He called for martyrs to the cause of Islamic revolution: "Those who risk their lives and go out to fight, and who are prepared to lay down their lives for the cause of God are honorable people, pure of heart and blessed of soul."[57] Although he had opportunities to flee the country right before his arrest, Qutb refused and was executed in 1966 by Egyptian president, Gamal Abdel Nasser.[58]

The United Kingdom, Israel, and Germany, all democratic countries threatened by terrorist groups, have rejected pleas for reinstatement of the death penalty. In the early 1980s when the British Parliament was considering a death penalty bill, James Prior, former Secretary to Northern Ireland, wrote to conservative supporters in Parliament, "I believe that the execution of terrorists in Northern Ireland would act as a new inspiration for the IRA and other extremists."[59] Conservative British Prime Minister John Major opposed efforts to bring back the death penalty in 1990 and 1994. Israeli Prime Minister Yitzhak Rabin noted that Israel had not judicially executed "a single terrorist."[60] German Chancellor Helmut Schmidt likewise fought against those who attempted to reinstate the death penalty "during the reign of terror brought by the Red Army faction."[61]

Because 19 hijackers were willing to kill themselves to carry out these crimes, the threat of the death penalty, if limited to actual perpetrators, is not likely to deter similar actors in the future.[62] In fact, in a perverse way, the death penalty might actually encourage such actors, standing deterrence theory "on its head."[63] If caught, they can still be martyrs after being executed by the government of the US.[64] In fact, executing them may elevate such persons to the status of true martyrs, at least in Muslim eyes.[65] Furthermore, as one commentator observed, "Terrorism is theatre."[66] Trial followed by execution in the US may put the potential terrorist and his or her movement on a world stage. Witness, for example, the Bali bomber's reaction to his conviction and death sentence in Indonesia in August 2003: "Amrozi," as he is known, was beaming with his both hands giving the thumbs-up as if he had just won an academy award.[67] His picture appeared in the *New York Times*.[68] Following Amrozi's execution, nearly 1,000 radical Indonesian Muslims took to the streets in anger, and officials raised security in response to threats to the American and Australian embassies and hotels frequented by foreign tourists.[69]

The 19 individuals who carried out the September 11 attacks intentionally killed not only themselves, but also nearly 3,000 innocents. Although we may accurately describe the 19 as suicidal mass killers, many in the Arab and Islamic worlds probably believe that the 19 combine martyrdom with rebellion and revolution.[70] Thus, executing individuals who aided and abetted or conspired with the 19 may very well run against a strategic objective—eliminating support in the Muslim world for acts of terrorism.[71]

9.3.2 The Kasi Case—Muslim reaction to a US execution

The case of Aimal Khan Kasi suggests how executing politically motivated terrorists may influence the Arab and Muslim worlds. Apparently "upset" with US air attacks on Iraq and with the CIA's involvement in Muslim countries,[72] Aimal Kasi, in 1993, opened fire with an AK-47 assault rifle at CIA headquarters in Langley, Virginia, intentionally killing two unarmed CIA employees as they were driving to work and wounding three others.[73] Kasi fled to his native Pakistan on the day following the shooting and remained at large for four and a half years, traveling in Afghanistan and occasionally returning to Pakistan.[74] In 1997, FBI agents abducted Kasi from his hotel in Pakistan and arranged for him to be flown by military aircraft to the US.[75] Presumably because Congress had not reinstated the death penalty under federal law as of the time of the killings,[76] the FBI handed Kasi over to the State of Virginia. He was subsequently tried for murder in a Virginia state court, convicted, and sentenced to death.[77]

Religious and tribal leaders in Baluchistan called on Washington to commute the sentence.[78] In the days before Kasi's scheduled execution by lethal injection, Quetta, a Pakistani city with over a million inhabitants and Kasi's hometown, was "rocked by protests."[79] In the day following the execution, Quetta was "complete[ly] shut down" by Pakistani authorities.[80] The protests were echoed in other parts of Pakistan.[81] Hundreds of men, wearing black armbands, walked behind the ambulance carrying Kasi's body upon its arrival in Pakistan.[82] The Quetta Trade Association called for a half-day strike on the day of his funeral because, a spokesperson for the Association declared, "A son of Baluchistan has embraced martyrdom."[83] Apparently, more than 10,000 people attended his funeral, which was held in a stadium.[84] The US Department of State issued a worldwide warning that Kasi's execution "could trigger retaliatory attacks on the US or on other foreign interests overseas."[85] On the Friday after Kasi's execution, a bomb exploded in the southern Pakistani city of Hyderabad, killing two people at a bus stop.[86] The bomb was reportedly retaliation for Kasi's execution.[87]

Some point out that refusing to execute terrorists may still lead to retaliatory strikes or violent efforts to free them from prison.[88] I do not claim that violence would never come from imposing long prison terms rather the death penalty,[89] but I suspect that the risk of violence is likely greater from imposing death, particularly in the context of religiously motivated suicide bombers.[90] Aside from the possibility of retaliatory strikes, as the Kasi case shows, death sentences almost certainly provoke a much greater resentment and anger in the community and country, if not, in this case, in the Islamic world from which the executed individual comes.[91]

9.3.3 *The* Robbins *Case—early US reaction to a British execution*

Demonstrating empirically that imposing the death penalty will inflame the Islamic world cannot be done. Aside from the *Kasi* case, an example from US history does, however, suggest that imposing the death penalty on politically motivated terrorists is likely to have such an effect. The outrage that much of the Muslim world may feel if the US executes members of al Qaeda probably resembles the outrage much of the US felt when a US court acceded to President John Adams' request to extradite a sailor, Jonathan Robbins (also known as Thomas Nash), to the British in 1799.[92] After the US surrendered him, the British took Robbins to Jamaica for trial. The day Robbins reached Jamaica, a Thursday, the British started his trial for murder and mutiny. On the following Monday, they hanged him and left him hanging in chains for all to see.[93] The extradition and execution led to a public outcry and to attempts to censure and impeach President Adams. It also contributed to his defeat by Thomas Jefferson the following year.[94]

Robbins was alleged to be the bosun's mate of the ship *Hermione*, a British ship of war.[95] *Hermione*'s captain was a Captain Bligh, infamous for the harsh measures he adopted in treating his crew. After the captain threatened to flog the last topman to reach the deck, causing two crewmen in the rush to fall to their deaths, the crew mutinied.[96] However, the mutineers not only killed the despised captain, they killed three lieutenants, the purser, the ship's doctor, a midshipman, the boatswain, and a lieutenant of the marines.[97] Robbins apparently played a leading role not only in the mutiny but also in the homicides.[98] The mutineers later sailed the ship to what is now Venezuela and surrendered the ship to the Spanish authorities, then the enemy of Britain.[99]

Robbins claimed to be a US citizen and claimed to have been impressed into the British Navy.[100] With the memory of the war of independence fresh, many Americans felt that Robbins was a victim of British tyranny. Americans apparently never seriously questioned his direct complicity in the killing of the captain and his officers. Nevertheless, many Americans were apparently appalled by the President's role in turning Robbins over to then hated superpower, England, to carry out Robbins' prompt execution.

Robbins was not a mass murderer, but he was a leader in a conspiracy that took nine lives. His apparent guilt did not quell the anger that many Americans felt towards Adams and England. The apparent guilt of al Qaeda is not likely to quell the anger that many Muslims would feel if the current superpower executes al Qaeda members. The Robbins affair resembles the political offense exception to extradition, "reflecting [in part] a concern that individuals—particularly unsuccessful rebels—should not be returned to countries where they may be subjected to unfair trials and punishments [usually the death penalty]."[101]

Given the magnitude of the September 11 attacks, one could credibly argue that the death penalty is a "fair punishment." Yet one could make a similar argument about Robbins, particularly in 1799 when the death penalty was carried out in a far greater percentage of homicide cases. Although the reports suggest that Robbins directly participated in the killing of innocents, the political undertones and US's notions about the right to rebellion help explain Americans' outrage. It is hard to deny that similar political undertones exist throughout the Islamic world in the context of the current struggle between al Qaeda and its allies, and the US.

At the time of the Robbins incident, the US had a democratic process Americans could resort to, to channel their outrage. Not only was Adams defeated, but no one was extradited by the federal government for more than 40 years afterwards.[102] The countries making up the Islamic world, however, generally have not possessed such a democratic process. There is still reason to believe, therefore, that Muslim outrage and resentment about such executions might be channeled towards extralegal means and groups.

9.3.4 *Venue decision and its possible impact in the Muslim world*

The Bush–Cheney Justice Department chose the most pro-prosecution venue in indicting not only Zacarias Moussaoui, but also John Walker Lindh, the

"American Taliban."[103] The Justice Department had laid venue in the Eastern District Court of Virginia, with generally pro-prosecution judges and a conservative jury pool.[104] That district lies within the Fourth Circuit Court of Appeals, which has been the most conservative and pro-prosecution of all the federal circuit courts of appeals.[105] This decision was not an accident. The government could have laid venue in New York, where the overwhelming number of people were killed, but reportedly chose the Eastern District of Virginia, because of its "strong record of imposing the death penalty."[106] New York federal juries, on the other hand, had been reluctant to give the death penalty in other terrorist cases.[107]

The *New York Times* reported that the venue decision helped Michael Chertoff, then Chief of the Criminal Division of the Justice Department, to persuade the Bush administration to try Moussaoui in the federal court rather than by military tribunal.[108] So one could plausibly argue that the venue decision was the lesser of two evils.[109] Ironically, however, the Justice Department's choosing this venue argues against imposing the death penalty. Selecting the most pro-prosecution venue for all the defendants was probably viewed in the Arab and Islamic worlds as a cynical ploy to deny the accused a fair trial. If that district court had meted out any death sentences, Muslims would likely have viewed the Department's choice of such a venue as a veiled attempt to use the justice system to kill the Muslims involved.[110] In short, the procedural advantages accorded to the government in a conspiracy[111] may be considered unjust in the Arab and Islamic worlds, at least when the death penalty is sought.[112]

9.4 Might imposing the death penalty thwart cooperation from US allies?

9.4.1 *International cooperation as essential in defeating terrorism?*

September 11 changed the political and strategic landscape in countless ways, but one of the most significant is the recognition that the US needs the help of other countries in the struggle against terrorism. Al Qaeda reportedly has cells in over 100 countries.[113] To gather intelligence on such a diffused enemy requires cooperation from many countries.[114] To apprehend those individuals requires states that are willing to arrest and either prosecute or, in some cases, extradite members of the al Qaeda conspiracy to the US. Furthermore, the decentralized nature of al Qaeda requires that individual citizens of these states come forward with information about suspected members and activities of al Qaeda: "The more useful anti-insurgency [and anti-terror] tactic is to compete, literally door to door, for people's loyalty (with the coinage of loyalty being willingness to inform on one side or the other)."[115]

The Bush–Cheney administration at least initially recognized the necessity of international cooperation by immediately ordering the payment of back dues owed to the United Nations.[116] Forming a coalition rather than unilaterally attacking Afghanistan likewise was consistent with the need to cooperate with other nations of the world to stop the menace of terrorism.[117] With the invasion of Iraq, the Bush–Cheney administration seemed intent, however, on reverting to the pre-September 11 unilateralist approach to foreign affairs. "In the international realm, we seem to believe that our claim to national sovereignty allows us to operate unilaterally—America first and foremost, not together or in conformity with a global contract [comparable to the domestic social contract]."[118] Such an approach could prove, at the very least, counterproductive in the struggle against al Qaeda.[119]

At a time when the US needs help from other countries the most, retaining the death penalty alienates a growing number of countries that have abolished the death penalty or are taking steps to abolish or limit it. Most countries have abolished the death penalty in law or in practice, while only fifty-nine countries retain the death penalty.[120] Virtually all of Europe, including many of the Soviet Union's former satellite states, have abolished the death penalty.[121] All the US's NATO allies have done so.[122] Neither Canada nor Mexico has the death penalty. Excluding the small Caribbean Island states, the only countries in the Americas that permit capital punishment are the US, Guyana, Guatemala, and Belize.[123] European countries strongly oppose the death penalty.[124] As leading proponents of the five currently operating international criminal tribunals, the Europeans and Latin Americans, among others, successfully argued for banning capital punishment from the sentencing authority of the International Criminal Court, the International Criminal Tribunals for the former Yugoslavia and Rwanda, the Special Court for Sierra Leone, the Special Tribunal for Lebanon, and the Extraordinary Chambers in the Courts of Cambodia.[125] Many abolitionist countries refuse to extradite fugitives to death penalty states absent an absolute assurance that the death penalty will not be carried out.[126] For example, the Home Secretary of staunch ally UK, has told US officials that he "would approve extradition [of suspected terrorists] only if the US waived the right to impose the death penalty."[127] The Supreme Court of Canada has taken the unusual step of requiring the Minister of Justice of Canada to demand assurances from the US that it will not impose capital punishment on Canadian citizens whose extradition is sought.[128] Insisting on executing members of al Qaeda could thus deprive the US of necessary evidence and, in some cases, of the fugitives themselves.[129] In short, US's closest allies are abolitionist states. To the extent that the US uses the death penalty in the "war on terror," the US may find those allies reluctant to cooperate fully:[130]

> The possibility of the United States imposing the death penalty on convicted terrorists makes it difficult for any European country to determine how far to cooperate with the American investigation. Outlawing the death penalty is a condition of membership to the 15-nation European Union, and the Council of Europe, which embraces more than

47 countries, not only forbids the death penalty but also recently decided that it should not apply even in wartime.[131]

Al Qaeda, however, appears to be attacking not just the US, but also other Western countries. Since September 11, the following attacks (among others) linked to al Qaeda have taken place: (1) In April 2002, a suicide truck bomb exploded at a Tunisian synagogue, killing 21 people, mostly French and German vacationers;[132] (2) On October 6, 2002, a speedboat packed with explosives crashed into a French oil tanker moored off the Yemen coast, piercing both hulls and causing the tanker to dump 90,000 barrels of oil into the sea;[133] (3) Six days later, bombs detonated at a resort in the Indonesian island of Bali, killing more than 200 civilians, including 88 Australians;[134] (4) On November 28, 2002, militants attacked an Israeli-owned hotel in Kenya as well as making an attempted missile attack, which "narrowly missed an airliner carrying home Israeli vacationers";[135] (5) On May 12, 2003, al Qaeda attacked the living quarters of Western workers in Riyadh, Saudi Arabia;[136] (6) On May 16, 2003, suicide bombers simultaneously carried out several attacks on civilian targets in Morocco, targeting not only Moroccans, but, possibly, Spanish nationals as well;[137] (7) On August 5, 2003, a bomb blew up the Marriott Hotel in Jakarta, capital of Indonesia;[138] and (8) on March 11, 2004, 10 bombs were detonated on four commuter trains in Madrid, killing over 200 people and wounding over 1,400, constituting the worst terrorist attack on European soil since the Second World War.[139] Although the Spanish government initially blamed ETA, the Basque separatist group, the government has arrested, among others, three Moroccans, one of whom apparently "dealt closely with an [al] Qaeda cell based in Spain. . . .";[140] (9) In 2005, individuals linked to al Qaeda allegedly conspired to take liquid explosives disguised in soft drinks on nine passenger airliners bound from London to the US;[141] (10) On December 27, 2008, Benazir Bhutto, former Prime Minister of Pakistan, was assassinated, probably by pro-al Qaeda, pro-Taliban "elements,"[142] since they had openly threatened to kill her upon her return to Pakistan months earlier;[143] (11) On November 26–29, 2008, Lashkar-e-Toiba carried out murderous attacks in Mumbai.[144]

On November 12, 2002, an audiotape containing the voice of Osama bin Laden was broadcast. On the tape, bin Laden expressly named as targets Australia, Canada, France, Germany, Israel, Italy, and the UK.[145] Responding to the threat, European governments "departed from their relatively circumspect low-key approach to terrorism alerts and issued stark warnings about planned attacks in Europe."[146]

If the US's allies are also under attack, they might, arguably, not be so concerned about the US position on the death penalty for accused al Qaeda killers. For example, France and Germany initially refused to turn over evidence against Moussaoui to the US, because the Justice Department sought the death penalty in his case. France and Germany, however, later softened their stance and agreed to turn over the requested evidence provided it was only used in the "guilt phase" of the trial.[147] The change in position, however, might have been primarily due not to the urge to fight a common enemy, but to US pressure on those two countries, because their governments were so outspoken in opposing the US and UK plan to invade Iraq.[148]

To help fight the terrorist threat, the US and the EU entered into an agreement to speed extradition of suspected terrorists to and from the US.[149] That agreement, however, contains an anti-death penalty article that the European states can expect to invoke before extraditing any individuals to the US.[150] Despite a possible growing perception of a threat from a common enemy, the US resort to the death penalty resonates deeply within the European community and almost certainly affects the degree of cooperation the US can expect from abolitionist countries in general, from Canada and Mexico, and from the citizens and governments of Europe.[151]

9.4.2 *US violations of the Vienna Convention on Consular Relations*

The US has also angered its allies by refusing to enforce article 36 of the Vienna Convention on Consular Relations, particularly in death cases.[152] That article requires a state-party to inform "without delay" any foreign nationals whom it arrests of their right to consult with their consular official.[153] In a string of cases, US federal and state courts, including the US Supreme Court, have rejected challenges to the imposition of the death penalty when local law enforcement authorities failed to notify foreign nationals of their right under the Convention to consult their consul.[154] The International Court of Justice (ICJ) has ruled that the US violated international law in refusing to notify the defendants of their rights under the Vienna Convention and in refusing to stay the order of execution pending the outcome of challenges filed by complaining states in the ICJ.[155] Apparent US disregard of the Convention and the ICJ could make US allies not only less concerned about the rights of US citizens traveling abroad,[156] but also could make them somewhat less eager[157] to help America in the war on terror.[158]

9.5 Other troubling issues involving the death penalty and terrorism

9.5.1 *The death penalty, a necessary tool to obtain information from the "ticking bomb terrorist"?*

Some might argue that US should still wield the threat of death to force suspected terrorists to reveal information about plots of mass destruction. After all, private terror groups might be able to obtain chemical weapons, biological weapons, and even nuclear arms. The devastation that these weapons could wreak would justify US taking extreme measures—including the threat of the death penalty—against individual suspects who would be thus compelled to tell us how to thwart such an attack.[159] One governmental official gave such a justification for seeking the death penalty in the Moussaoui case.[160] Thus, the issue is not one of retributive justice or of general or specific deterrence, but of instrumentalism,[161] an issue indistinguishable from whether torture may be used to extract information from suspected terrorists.[162] Since the issue of torture has been covered in chapter 3 and chapter 4, here we will just note that for all the reasons set forth in the torture chapters, using the death penalty for this reason is at best questionable on both moral and practical grounds.

9.5.2   *Placing US military personnel and civilians at risk*

If individuals associated with al Qaeda learn that the US is executing imprisoned al Qaeda members, then US civilians, military personnel, and federal agents may be at greater risk. First, if al Qaeda captures any Americans, there may be a greater chance that they will be killed.[163] Second, if al Qaeda members know they will face death by execution, they have a strong incentive to fight to the death when US military or special agents are trying to subdue or arrest them in the field.[164]

These policies rest on the same foundation as some basic rules of international humanitarian law. The Geneva Conventions that protect prisoners of war are based not only on humanitarian concerns, but also on pragmatic ones. If state *A* mistreats the captured soldiers of state *B*, then state *B* may be inclined to mistreat the captured soldiers of *A*.[165] Granted, reciprocity does not always happen. During its war with the US, North Korea and China routinely mistreated US soldiers and airmen, violating the third Geneva Convention, while the US generally abided by it.[166] One could readily argue that a terrorist organization like al Qaeda is certain to treat captives harshly no matter how well the US treats arrested al Qaeda members. On the other hand, al Qaeda is a loosely structured organization. Who is to say that some people associated with that organization might be motivated to treat captured Americans humanely but for the fact that captured al Qaeda members have been mistreated by the US and may be subject to execution.[167]

In addition, humanitarian law prohibits an armed force from killing soldiers who are attempting to surrender, who have given up, or who are wounded and otherwise "hors de combat." Thus, a "take no prisoners" order is per se illegal. Specifically, the 1977 Additional Protocol I to the Geneva Convention of 1949 provides as follows: "It is prohibited to order that there shall be no survivors, to threaten an adversary therewith or to conduct hostilities on this basis."[168] This requirement "to give quarter" also appears in the Hague Regulations of 1907.[169] The US has never ratified Protocol I, but is a party to the Hague Convention of 1907, including the Annex containing the Hague Regulations. The requirement "to give quarter" is considered binding customary international law.[170]

If the US embarks on a policy of executing al Qaeda members, it may be viewed by al Qaeda members, their allies and adherents, in the field, essentially as refusing to give quarter. This is not to suggest that carrying out the death penalty would violate international law or would in fact violate the provisions referred to above. (The Geneva Conventions expressly authorize criminal prosecution for war crimes and crimes against humanity.[171] These Conventions, including the 1977 Protocols, permit capital punishment, except for juveniles and women with dependent infants.[172]) Nonetheless, one of the benefits gained by the attacking force in giving quarter, aside from potential reciprocity, is that the besieged force has greater incentive to lay down their arms. If they know they are going to be killed in any event, why not fight to the last? If the besieged force, in this case, members of al Qaeda, their allies and their adherents, believe that they will face execution anyway (or indefinite detention without trial or both),[173] they may be more motivated to die a glorious warrior's death in battle rather than to go quietly.[174]

The thundering weight of the crimes of September 11 inevitably demands the maximum punishment that the US judicial system allows. If anyone deserves the death penalty, then those who planned and actively participated in the September 11 conspiracy do. Assuming that Khalid Sheikh Mohammed, Ramzi bin al-Shibh, and Abu Turab al-Urduni[175] are found at trial to be directly responsible for the attacks, they can certainly be considered death eligible. Yet as the "war against terrorism" wears on, year after year, the US, and particularly the Obama administration, has recognized that the US needs the UN, the help of allies, and respect for the rule of law.

Similarly, the natural demand for retribution after a terrorist organization has committed mass murder and other heinous crimes needs to be tempered by the fact that carrying out the death penalty may strengthen the terrorists. Given the perceived and actual grievances that the Arab and the greater Islamic worlds have towards the West in general and the US in particular, carrying out such executions will probably tend to inflame the Arab and Islamic worlds, increase their support of terrorist movements, and thwart cooperation with western allies, almost all of whom have abolished the death penalty. Even if the evidence shows that the above-named individuals directly participated in the September 11 conspiracy, executing them will, as the Kasi case so well illustrates, almost certainly make them martyrs for Muslims.

Although many states within the US have continued to embrace the death penalty,[176] the US should learn from the mistakes and the successes of the British in fighting the IRA, that executing politically motivated agents of terror is likely to spawn greater terrorism.[177] Such restraint is a surer path towards isolating al Qaeda and its allies in the lands of the aggrieved and the repressed. The death penalty is a luxury that the US can ill afford in this international struggle.

Notes

1   This strand attempts to arrive at *"just* outcomes; the emphasis is on what the offender fairly merits for his crime." Andrew Von Hirsch, *Penal Theories, in* The Handbook of Crime and Punishment 659, 666 (Michael Tonry ed., 1998) (emphasis added). *See also* Joshua Dressler, Understanding Criminal Law 17 (3d edition 2001) (describing this notion of retributive justice as "punishment [being] . . . a means of securing a moral balance in the society"). Most of this chapter has been taken from my Article, *The Death Penalty—An Obstacle to the "War against Terrorism"?*, 37 Vand. J. Transnat'l. L. 353 (2004), and is reprinted here with the permission of the Vanderbilt Journal of Transnational Law.

2   *See* Robert Nozick, *Retributive Punishment, in* Readings in the Philosophy of Law 196–98 (John Arthur & William Shaw eds., 1984) (distinguishing in detail retribution from revenge).

3   Furthermore, the Islamic countries themselves are strong advocates of the death penalty. *See, e.g.*, William A. Schabas, *International Law and Abolition of the Death Penalty: Recent Developments*, 4 ILSA J. Int'l & Comp. L. 535, 545 (1998) (quoting Sudan delegate to Rome Conference to establish International Criminal Court, who "described capital punishment as 'a divine right according to some religions, in particular Islam' "); Jennifer Cunningham, *Frontier Justice is Put on the Dock*, The Glasgow Herald, June 25, 1997, at 17 (noting Saudi Arabia's practice of beheading convicted rapists, drug smugglers, and murderers); *see* Susan Dominus, *Their Day in Court*, N.Y. Times Mag., Mar. 30, 2003, at 30 and *passim*.

4   After the Second World War, the Nuremberg International Military Tribunal sentenced to death 12 high-ranking members of the Nazi German regime for war crimes and crimes against humanity. A number of doctors and SS leaders were likewise given the death penalty. See *War Crimes Trials*, 27 Funk & Wagnalls New Encyclopedia 146–47 (1986).

5   Retribution looks only backward at what the actor has done: "Even if a civil society resolved to dissolve itself . . . the last murderer lying in the prison ought to be executed. . . ." Dressler, *supra* note 1, at 18 (quoting Immanuel Kant, The Philosophy of Law 197–98 (W. Hastie trans., 1887)). The utilitarians, on the other hand, look forward to determine whether the punishment will provide "an overall social benefit." Dressler, *supra* note 1, at 16. The arguments that are set forth below draw greatly from utilitarian theory.

6   One could also argue that, although suicide bombers may not be deterred by the death penalty, their handlers might be. *Cf.* Norman L. Green et al., *Capital Punishment in the Age of Terrorism*, 41 Cath. Law. 187, 225 (2002) (comments of Kenneth Roth) (noting that some of the leaders of al Qaeda, including Osama bin Laden himself, seemed less than keen on serving as suicide bombers).

7   *See* Furman v. Georgia, 408 U.S. 238, 453 (1972) (Powell, J., dissenting) (quoting Lord Justice Denning, Minutes of Evidence, *Royal Commission on Capital Punishment*, 207 (1949–1953)).

> Because the only genuinely humane, immediate response to atrocities like the Washington sniper attacks and Mohamed Atta's airline hijackings—and the necessary formal response of an organized civil society—is collective fury. Along with a controlled but ferocious determination to incapacitate and crush the perpetrators as quickly as possible. Deep-think analysis can and must wait.

David Tell, Editorial, *Yes, The Sniper Was a Terrorist*, 8 Wkly. Standard, Nov. 4, 2002 at 7, 8; *cf.* Note, *Responding to Terrorism, Crime, Punishment, and War*, 115 Harv. L. Rev. 1217, 1233 (2002) (noting that "the resurgence of the death penalty in the thirty years since the Supreme Court's ruling in Furman v. Georgia reflects the ascendancy of retributive theories of punishment").

8 *See, e.g.,* William F. Buckley, Jr., *String Them Up,* Nat'l Rev., June 6, 2003, at Vol. LV, No. 13, *available at* www.nationalreview.com/buckley/ buckley060603.asp. *See also* Hirsch, *supra* note 1, at 660–61 (describing incapacitation as "penal consequentialism"). But given the apparently overwhelming number of individuals who are willing to engage in so-called "martyrdom operations," incapacitating one offender may do little to stop others. *Cf.* Nasra Hassan, *An Arsenal of Believers, Talking to the Human Bombs,* The New Yorker, Nov. 19, 2001, at 36. In discussing Palestinian suicide bombers, Hassan writes as follows:

> Generally, each cell consists of a leader and two or three young men. . . . Each cell is tightly compartmentalized and secret. Cell members do not discuss their affiliation with their friends or family, and even if two of them know each other in normal life, they are not aware of the other's membership in the same cell. Only the leader is known to both. Each cell, which is dissolved after the [suicide] operation has been completed, is given a name from the Koran or from Islamic history.

Id.; see also Yosri Fouda & Nick Fielding, Masterminds of Terror 12, 70 (2003) (quoting Ramzi bin al Shibh, apparent coordinator of the September 11 attacks, who described how the attacks were organized: "[I]t is in short, a process of lining the cells to one another. . . .").

9 Dressler, *supra* note 1, at 18; Denning, *supra* note 7, at 207 ("Punishment is the way in which society expresses its denunciation of wrong doing; and, in order to maintain respect for law, it is essential that the punishment inflicted for grave crimes should adequately reflect the revulsion felt by the great majority of citizens for them.").

10 Sanford H. Kadish & Stephen J. Schulhofer, Criminal Law and its Processes, Cases and Materials 106 (7th edition, 2001) (reprinting an excerpt from Emile Durkheim, The Division of Law in Society 62–63 (W.D. Halls trans., 1984)).

11 *See* Jeremy Bentham, *Cases Unmeet for Punishment, in* The Portable Enlightenment Reader 541 (Issaack Kramnick ed., 1995) (reasoning that punishment should not be meted out "3. Where it is unprofitable, or too expensive: where the mischief it would produce would be greater than what is prevented. 4. Where it is needless: where the mischief may be prevented, or cease of itself without it . . ."); *see also* Dressler, *supra* note 1 and accompanying text.

12 Charles L. Black, Jr., *The Crisis in Capital Punishment,* 31 Md. L. Rev. 289, 291 (1971); *see also* Anthony G. Amsterdam, *Capital Punishment, in* The Death Penalty in America 346, 352–53 (Hugo Adam Bedau ed., 1982) ("The plain message of capital punishment . . . is that life ceases to be sacred whenever someone with the power to take it away decides that there is a sufficiently compelling pragmatic reason to do so.") (emphasis added). *But see* Walter Berns, *The Morality of Anger, in* The Death Penalty in America, *supra,* at 333–34 ("[Simon] Wiesenthal allows us to see that it is right, morally right, to be angry with criminals and to express that anger publicly, officially, and in an appropriate manner, which may require the worst of them to be executed."); Ernest Van den Haag, *In Defense of the Death Penalty: A Practical and Moral Analysis, in* The Death Penalty in America, *supra,* at 332 ("If it were shown that no punishment is more deterrent than a trivial fine, capital punishment for murder would remain just, even if not useful.").

13 The Convention for the Suppression of Terrorist Financing has created a work-

able definition, which is as follows: "Any other act *intended* to cause death or serious bodily injury to a *civilian, or to any other person not taking an active part in the hostilities* in a situation of armed conflict, when the purpose of such act, by its nature or context, is to intimidate a population, or to compel a government or an international organization to do or to abstain from doing any act." International Convention for the Suppression of the Financing of Terrorism art. 2.1(b), *adopted* Dec. 9, 1999, 39 I.L.M. 270 (2000), *available at* http:// untreaty.un.org/english/Terrorism/Conv12.pdf (emphasis added). We will have to see if the world community follows the definition. One hundred fifty states have joined the Convention.

14   *See* Jordan J. Paust et al., International Criminal Law Cases and Materials 995, 997 (2000) (quoting U.S. Dept. of State, *Patterns of Global Terrorism*, Mar. 1989) ("'[T]errorism' is premeditated, politically motivated violence perpetrated against noncombatant targets by subnational groups or clandestine state agents, usually intended to influence an audience. 'International terrorism' is terrorism involving the citizens or territory of more than one country."). For a good discussion of this issue, *see* Bruce Hoffman, Inside Terrorism 13–44 (1998).

15   *See, e.g.*, Noam Chomsky & Edward S. Herman, The Washington Connection and Third World Fascism 6 (1979) (criticizing the terms "terrorism" and "terrorist" as being applied to "the use of violence by individuals and marginal groups" while characterizing much more favorably "[o]fficial violence [by states] which is far more extensive in both scale and destructiveness," that is, "wholesale as opposed to retail terror"); Charles Krauthammer, *The Ball's Still in Arafat's Court*, Wash. Post, Nov. 19, 1988, at A23 (criticizing U.N. Resolutions defining terrorism).

16   Rome Statute of the International Criminal Court art. 7.1, July 17, 1998, 2187 U.N.T.S. 90, *available at* www.un.org/law/icc /statute/romefra.htm [hereinafter ICC Statute].

17   *Id.* Article 7.1(a) provides as follows: "For the purpose of this Statute, 'crime against humanity' means any of the following acts when committed as part of a widespread or systematic attack directed against any civilian population, with knowledge of the attack: (a) Murder; . . ." *Id.*; *see also* Jordan Paust, *Threats to Accountability after Nuremberg: Crimes against Humanity, Leader Responsibility and National Fora*, 12 N.Y.L Sch. J. Hum. Rts. 547, 553–54 (1995) (criticizing Article 5 of International Criminal Tribunal for former Yugoslavia statute on the ground that its definition of crimes against humanity needlessly restricted its scope as compared to customary law definition of crimes against humanity).

18   ICC Statute, *supra* note 16, art. 7.2(a). The subsection in full states as follows: "Attack directed against any civilian population means a course of conduct involving the *multiple commission of acts* referred to in paragraph 1 against any civilian population, pursuant to or in furtherance of a State or *organizational policy* to commit such attack." *Id.* (emphasis added). Compare the definition of terrorism provided by Caleb Carr, a definition that includes state terrorism as well as terrorism carried out by non-state actors: "Terrorism . . . is simply the contemporary name given to, and the modern permutation of, warfare deliberately waged against civilians with the purpose of destroying their will to support either leaders or policies that the agents of such violence find objectionable." Caleb Carr, The Lessons of Terror 6 (2002). Note, however, that Jordan Paust argues that the ICC formulation of crimes against humanity is too narrow, ignoring customary law approaches. *See* Jordan Paust, Linda Jon M. van Dyke & Linda Malone, International Law and Litigation in the United States (3d edition 2008).

19   Coalition for the International Criminal Court, World Signatures and Ratification, http://www.iccnow.org/?mod=romesignatures.

20   *See* Chomsky, *supra* note 15, at 6; *see also* Alan Dershowitz, Why Terrorism
     Works 4–9 (2002). *But see* Grenville Byford, *The Wrong War*, Foreign Aff.,
     July 2002, at 34–36 (arguing that a simple definition of "terrorism" is
     impossible to make, that both ends and means employed to those ends must be
     examined to determine whether individuals have engaged in "terrorism").

21   *See* International Criminal Court, *Report of the Preparatory Comm'n on the Int'l
     Criminal Court. Addendum. Part II, Finalized draft text of the Elements of Crimes,* art.
     7, U.N. Doc. PCNICC/2000/1/ADD.2 (Nov. 2, 2000), *available at*
     www1.umn.edu/humanrts/instree/iccelementsofcrimes.html#_ftn36   (last
     visited Mar. 13, 2003). The Final Draft Elements of Crimes of the ICC further
     supports this interpretation:

   > "Attack directed against a civilian population" in these context elements is
   > understood to mean a course of conduct involving the multiple commission
   > of acts referred to in Article 7, paragraph 1, of the Statute against any civilian
   > population, pursuant to or in furtherance of a State or organizational policy to
   > commit such attack. The acts need not constitute a military attack. It is
   > understood that "policy to commit such an attack" requires that the State or
   > *organization* actively promote or encourage such attack against a civilian
   > population.

   Id., art. 7, Intro. (emphasis added); *see also* James D. Fry, *Terrorism as a Crime
   Against Humanity and Genocide: The Backdoor to Universal Jurisdiction*, 7 UCLA J.
   Int'l L. & Foreign Aff. 169, 191 (2002); Jordan J. Paust, *Antiterrorism Military
   Commissions: Courting Illegality*, 23 Mich. J. Int'l L. 1, 27 (2001). *But see*
   William A. Schabas, *Punishment of Non-state Actors in Non-International Armed
   Conflict*, 26 Fordham Int'l L. J. 907, 924–25 (2003) (arguing that the September
   11 attacks do not constitute "crimes against humanity" within the definition of
   either the ICC or custom).

22   Lucy Martinez, *Prosecuting Terrorists at the International Criminal Court: Possi-
     bilities and Problems*, 32 Rutgers L.J. 1, 36 (2002) (citing Mahnoush H.
     Arsanjani, *The Rome Statute of the International Criminal Court*, 93 Am. J. Int'l L.
     22, 31 (1999)); *see also In Re* Doherty, 599 F. Supp. 270, 274 (S.D.N.Y. 1984)
     (rejecting the UK's request to extradite a Provisional Irish Republican Army
     (PIRA) member charged with attacking a convoy of British soldiers in Northern
     Ireland, but stating in *dicta* that the political offense exception would not pro-
     tect individuals who placed bombs in public places, an act that violates inter-
     national law or acts that would violate the Geneva Conventions); *cf. In Re*
     McMullen, No-3–78–1899 M.G. (N.D. Cal. 1979) *reprinted in* Cong. Rec.
     16,585 (1986) (denying the UK's request to extradite PIRA member and
     noting that PIRA member's allegedly attacking British military barracks did
     not constitute war crime or crime against humanity).

23   *See* Paust, *supra* note 21, at 8 n.16.

24   ICC Statute, *supra* note 16, art. 8.2(b) (emphasis added). This full subsection,
     with its prefatory language is as follows:

   > For purposes of this statute, "war crimes" means: . . . (b) Other serious viola-
   > tions of the laws and customs applicable in international armed conflict,
   > within the established framework of international law, namely, any of the
   > following acts: (i) Intentionally directing attacks against the civilian popula-
   > tion as such or against individual civilians not taking direct part in hos-
   > tilities; (ii) intentionally directing attacks against civilian objects, that is,
   > objects which are not military objectives.

   Id., art. 8.2.

25   To keep the focus on attacks on unequivocally noncombatant civilians, this

discussion of crimes against humanity does not include the attack on the Pentagon, even though civilian employees of the Defense Department died in that attack. Furthermore, this is not to suggest that the attack against the Pentagon, aside from the manner of making the attack, was not a crime. It certainly was a domestic crime (actually numerous domestic crimes), and, to the extent that al Qaeda was not the alter ego of the Taliban and thereby acting as a state, those who conspired to carry out or who aided and abetted the attack are criminally responsible. If the Taliban were the alter ego of al Qaeda and entered into a state of armed conflict with the US on September 11, 2001, that component of the attack would probably not constitute a war crime but seizing and crashing the civilian airliner into the Pentagon would be.

26 *Islam* (2003), Funk & Wagnalls New Encyclopedia, *available in* LEXIS Reference File.

27 *Arabs* (2003), Funk & Wagnalls New Encyclopedia, *available in* LEXIS Reference File.

28 Among the leading ones is Turkey, which, unfortunately, possesses one of the worst, if not the worst, human rights records in Europe. *See* Amnesty International, *Endemic Torture in Turkey Must End Immediately*, Nov. 8, 2001, *available at* http://www.amnesty.org.uk/news_details.asp?NewsID=14025. Turkey's parliament has, however, abolished the death penalty in peacetime, a step that Amnesty International had been urging for decades and which the EU has required as a condition of Turkey's membership. *See* Amnesty International, *Turkey: Abolition of the Death Penalty Welcomed*, Aug. 2, 2002, *available at* http://web.amnesty.org/ai.nsf/Index/EUR440362002?OpenDocument&of=Abolition COUNTRIES/TURKEY (last visited Mar. 13, 2003). Whether this also signals that Turkey will end its practice of torture and other human rights abuses remains to be seen. Indonesia and Mali (at 2.5) are ranked a half point lower than Turkey (at 3.0) on Freedom House's seven point democracy index, the lowest being the most free. Overall Muslim countries do not fare well under the index falling into the "partly free" and "not free" categories. Freedom House, Combined Average Ratings—Independent Countries 2002, http://www.freedomhouse.org/ template.cfm?page=475&year=2009.

29 *See* Bernard Lewis, The Crisis of Islam 117–18 (2003); *see also* Fareed Zakaria, *The Politics of Rage: Why Do They Hate Us?*, Newsweek, Oct. 15, 2001, at 22.

30 *See* Zakaria, *supra* note 29, at 24.

31 *Id.* at 25; *see also* Lewis, *supra* note 29, at 114–17. Concerning economic failure Lewis notes that "Israel's per capita GDP was three and half times that of Lebanon and Syria, twelve times that of Jordan, and thirteen and a half times that of Egypt." *Id.* at 117 (citing Arab Human Development Report 2002; Creating Opportunities for Future Generations, sponsored by the Regional Bureau for Arab States/UNDP, Arab Fund for Economic and Social Development). He discussed the intellectual life of the Arab world again quoting the Arab Human Development Report: "The Arab world translates about 330 books annually, one-fifth of the number that Greece translates. The accumulative total of translated books since the Caliph Maa'moun's [*sic*] time [the ninth century] is about 100,000, almost the average Spain translates in one year." *Id.* at 115–16. Even in Saudi Arabia, per capita income plummeted from $28,600 in 1981 to $6,800 in 2001. Eric Rouleau, *Trouble in the Kingdom*, Foreign Aff., July–Aug. 2002, at 75, 85.

32 Zakaria, *supra* note 29, at 22, 32.

33 *Id.* "Today, two in five Saudis are under 16 years old. [Saudi Arabia's] population has exploded while its economy has stagnated with the result that its per capita income has dropped." Michael Scott Doran, *Palestine, Iraq, and American*

Strategy, Foreign Aff., Jan.–Feb. 2003, at 19, 28; *see also* Editorial, *The Anger of Arab Youth*, N.Y. Times, Aug. 15, 2002, at A22.

34 Max Taylor & John Horgan, *The Psychological and Behavioural Bases of Islamic Fundamentalism*, 13 Terrorism & Pol. Violence 37, 41 (2001). These commentators add that "to many devout Muslims the effects of increased oil wealth have been to increase the influence of the West and challenge the social basis of Islam, rather than to complement and enhance it." *Id.*

35 "Even if many terrorists are not directly driven by poverty, the inequities of globalization feed a general anti-Westernism that is a seedbed for Islamism." Michael Hirsh, *Bush and the World*, Foreign Aff., Sept.–Oct. 2002, at 18, 28. *But see* Dershowitz, *supra* note 20, at 25 (noting that "the vast majority of groups with equivalent or more compelling causes—and with far greater poverty and disadvantage—have never resorted to terrorism"); Fareed Zakaria, The Future of Freedom Illiberal Democracy at Home and Abroad 138 (2003) (arguing that "[t]he problem is wealth not poverty" and that unearned income from oil revenues, or, for example in the case of Egypt from the Suez Canal and the US, "relieves the government of the need to tax its people—and in return provide something to them, in the form of accountability, transparency, and even representation").

36 *See* Abbas Amanat, *Empowered through Violence: The Re-inventing of Islamic Extremism*, *in* The Age of Terror 29 (Strobe Talbott & Nayan Chanda eds., 2001); *see also* Lewis, *supra* note 29, at 117–19. Given the failure of the economic and political institutions in Islamic countries, their people are outraged: "The resulting anger is naturally directed first against their rulers, and then against those whom they see as keeping those rulers in power for selfish reasons." *Id.* at 119. This chapter does not discuss economic and political measures necessary to enhance human, civil and economic rights in the Arab and Islamic worlds. *See* Peter G. Peterson, *Public Diplomacy and the War on Terrorism*, Foreign Aff., Sept.–Oct. 2002, at 74, 75.

37 A noted scholar of religion, Karen Armstrong, has observed that the resounding defeat of the Arab States by Israel in the 1967 war led to a religious revival in the Arab States: "After the humiliating defeat of the Arab armies during the 1967 Six-Day War against Israel in 1967, there was a swing toward religion throughout the Middle East." Karen Armstrong, Islam: A Short History 171 (2000). *See* chapter 1 for a fuller discussion.

38 *Id.* at 169–73; *see also* Lewis, *supra* note 29, at 6–8 (noting that "[d]uring Muhammad's lifetime, the Muslims became at once a political and a religious community with the Prophet as head of state" and contending that Islam remains deeply involved with politics and state power); Taylor & Horgan, *supra* note 34, at 42 (noting that one of the central positions of Islamic fundamentalism is "the general equation of the state with the implementation of Islam").

39 *See* Diaa Rashwan, *Impossible to Fight*, Al-Ahram Wkly., Aug. 8–14, 2002, *available at* www.weekly.ahram.org.eg/2002/598/op11.htm (observing that Americans had now accepted the European view that "Al Qa'eda is actually nothing more than a network and that the violent Islamacist groups have no unified command, but communicate and cooperate when it suits their different purposes"). Al Qaeda was created in the 1980s from three terrorist organizations: "bin Laden's circle of 'Afghan' Arabs, together with two factions from Egypt, the Islamic Group and Egyptian Islamic Jihad, the latter led by Dr. Ayman al-Zawahiri, al Qaeda's top theoretician." *See* Paul Berman, *The Philosopher of Islamic Terror*, N.Y. Times Mag., Mar. 23, 2003, at 24.

40 Jessica Stern, *The Protean Enemy*, Foreign Aff., Jul.–Aug. 2003, at 27, *available at* 2003 WL 57276699. Stern adds that al Qaeda apparently has put into practice so-called " 'leaderless resistance,' " a tactic popularized by Louis Beam

of the Aryan Nations, an American Neo-Nazi group. With the advent of the Internet, leaders do not necessarily have to secretly issue orders or to "pay operatives," rather, "they inspire small cells or individuals to take action on their own initiative." *Id.*; *see also* Jonathan Stevenson, *How Europe and America Defend Themselves*, Foreign Aff., Mar–Apr. 2003, at 85; Eric Bonabeau, *Scale Free Networks*, Science, May 2003, abstract *available at* www.sciam.com/Article.cfm ?colID=1&ArticleID= 000312F5-B86B-1E90-8EA5809EC5880000.

41   *See* Pierre Conesa, *Background to Washington's War on Terror: Al Qaida, The Sect*, Le Monde Diplomatique, Jan. 2002, *available at* http://mondediplo.com/2002/ 01/07sect?var_s+zacarias+moussaoui.

42   Scott Peterson, *Islamacists Escalate Fight in N. Iraq*, Christian Sci. Monitor, Nov. 22, 2002, at 1 (quoting James Lindsay of the Brookings Institution); *see also* Jason Burke, Al Qaeda, Casting Shadow of Terror 208 (2003) (noting that the "al Qaeda hardcore" rejected volunteers who requested martyrdom operations unless they "came up with their own ideas for attacks"). Al Qaeda can also be analogized to joint venture capitalists, ("individuals would approach the chief executive and board (bin Laden, Atef et al.) with ideas they believed were worthy of support") or a publishing house ("Freelancers would approach them with ideas that would sometimes be funded and resourced but often rejected"). *Id.* at 208–09.

43   *See* Nicholas Lemann, *Letter from Washington, What Terrorists Want; Is There a Better Way to Defeat al Qaeda?*, New Yorker, Oct. 29, 2001, at 36.

44   *See* Harold H. Koh, *On American Exceptionalism*, 55 Stan. L. Rev. 1479, 1497– 1500 (2003) (criticizing, as counterproductive, Bush–Cheney administration's largely unilateralist approach to combating terrorism and its violating international law in process); Thomas Carothers, *Promoting Democracy and Fighting Terror*, Foreign Aff., Jan.–Feb. 2003, at 84, 97 (criticizing the Bush administration's strategy in handling the war on terror as not paying enough attention to evenhandedly promoting democracy around world). *See also* Hirsh, *supra* note 35, noting as follows:

> But at the same time, the nature of the terrorist threat demonstrated the necessity of bolstering the international community, which is built on non-proliferation agreements, intelligence cooperation, and legitimizing institutions such as the UN, as well as a broad consensus on democracy, free markets, and human rights. It also demonstrates the necessity of a values-driven foreign policy—and of nation building under multilateral auspices in places such as Afghanistan.

Id. at 18; Michael P. O'Connor & Celia M. Rumann, *Into the Fire: How to Avoid Getting Burned by the Same Mistakes Made Fighting Terrorism in Northern Ireland*, 24 Cardozo L. Rev. 1657, 1750–51 (2003) (noting that the US is resorting to draconian emergency measures similar to those employed by the UK in Northern Ireland against the IRA, measures that both failed to enhance security or to defeat the IRA. The authors advocate "[d]ialogue, cooperation, and attention to civil liberties as necessary and effective elements in the strategy to eliminate terrorism"); Robert I. Rotberg, *Failed States in a World of Terror*, Foreign Aff., July–Aug. 2002, at 127, 140 (concluding that "[s]tate building trumps terror," requires the cooperation of many states, and cannot be done "on the cheap"); *cf.* Philip A. Thomas, *Emergency and Anti-Terrorist Powers, 9/11: USA and UK*, 26 Fordham Int'l L.J. 1193, 1228 (2003) (quoting Christopher Hewitt's extensive study of British counterterrorism measures, The Effectiveness of Anti-Terrorist Policies (1984) ("heavy handed repression is counterproductive")).

As one commentator has observed concerning how the then impending war in Iraq was being viewed by U.S. Muslims and others:

> If 1 percent of that one billion [the world population of Muslims] felt that they had sympathy for extremist views, then we are dealing with 10 million people. And if 10 percent of those 10 million were a little more active in pursuing those extreme beliefs and views, then we are dealing with a potential pool of one million people from which extremist groups and terrorists can recruit.

Michele Norris & Melissa Block, *All Things Considered: How a Potential War with Iraq Is Being Viewed by American Muslims and Others* (Nat'l Public Radio broadcast Mar. 14, 2003) (quoting Hussein Hakani of Carnegie Endowment for International Peace), *available in* LEXIS, National Public Radio Newsfile.

45   *But see* Anthony Cordesman, *How Should the United States Respond to Terrorism*, Cato Institute Policy Forum, Nov. 27, 2000, at 16, *available at* www. artitranscripts.com (arguing that "law enforcement partnerships are extremely political, extremely limited, often inherently corrupt . . ."). Religious terrorists may also be less subject to societal constraints than secular terrorists:

> Whereas secular terrorists attempt to appeal to a constituency variously composed of actual and potential sympathizers, members of the communities they purport 'to defend' or the aggrieved people for whom they claim to speak, religious terrorists are at once activists and constituents engaged in what they regard as a total war. They seek to appeal to no other constituency than themselves. Thus the restraints on violence that are imposed on secular terrorists by the desire to appeal to a tacitly supportive or uncommitted constituency are not relevant to the religious terrorist.

Hoffman, *supra* note 14, at 94–95

46   *See* Ocalan v. Turkey, App. No. 46221/99, Eur. Ct. Hum. Rts., Mar. 12, 2003, *available at* http://www.unhcr.org/refworld/docid/3e71a9d84.html; Koh, *supra* note 44, at 1509 (noting that the US joined with the EU in demanding that Turkey not execute notorious Kurdish Terrorist Abdullah Ocalan); Richard Falk, *A Roadmap for War: A Flawed Debate*, Treasures, Sept. 27, 2002, *available at*   http://www.transnational.org/SAJT/forum/meet/2002/Falk_WarFlawed Debate.html (last visited Mar. 13, 2003). *Cf.* Lewis, *supra* note 29, at 103–12 (noting that many in the Islamic world have criticized the West and particularly the US for applying double standards to Muslims and Muslim states).

47   The 2007 National Intelligence Estimate, prepared by US intelligence agencies, indicated that the war in Iraq helped al Qaeda: "[W]e assess that its [al Qaeda's] association with AQI [al Qaeda in Iraq] helps al Qa'ida to energize the broader Sunni extremist community, raise resources, and to recruit and indoctrinate operatives, including for homeland attacks." The National Intelligence Estimate, *The Terrorist Threat to the US Homeland* (2007), http://www.dni.gov/press_ releases/20070717_release.pdf. *See also* Carr, *supra* note 18, at 231 (emphasis added). Some experts now believe, however, that by attacking other Muslims, al Qaeda and its related Muslim violent terror groups are beginning to decline. *See* Scott Shane, *Rethinking What to Fear*, N.Y. Times, Sept. 29, 2009, *available at* 2009 WLNR 19039532.

48   *See also Iraq War Helped Boost Al Qaeda*, Toronto Star, May 20, 2003, at A1 (quoting Paul Wilkinson, head of the Centre for the Study of Terrorism and Political Violence at St. Andrew's University in Scotland: "The political masters in U.S. and Europe underestimated the extent to which bin Laden would use the war in Iraq as a propaganda weapon to rejuvenate the movement and attract more funds."); Steven R. Weisman, *U.S. Must Counteract Image in Muslim World,*

Panel Says, N.Y. Times, Oct. 1, 2003, at A1 (quoting a Bush–Cheney administration panel, "[h]ostility toward America has reached shocking levels" as a
result of the Iraq war and increased tension in the Middle East). Many had
predicted this outcome:

> A U.S. invasion of Iraq would likely trigger a surge in the already prevalent
> anti-Americanism in the Middle East, strengthening the hand of hard-line
> Islamist groups and provoking many Arab government to tighten their grip,
> rather than experiment more boldly with political liberalization.

Carothers, *supra* note 44, at 93. Don Van Natta Jr. & Desmond Butler, *Threats
and Responses: Terror Network: Anger on Iraq Seen as New Qaeda Recruiting Tool*,
N.Y. Times, Mar. 16, 2003, at A1 (noting that officials in the US, Europe, and
Africa observed that the then imminent invasion of Iraq caused a sharp increase
in efforts "to identify and groom a new generation of terrorist operatives" and
the officials worry that the invasion of Iraq "is almost certain to produce a
groundswell of recruitment for groups committed to attacks in the United
States, Europe and Israel"). *But see* Fouad Ajami, *Iraq and the Arabs' Future*,
Foreign Aff., Jan.–Feb. 2003, at 2 (arguing that the US need not apologize for
its unilateralism and that the focus of the invasion "should be modernizing the
Arab world").

49   R.C. Hingorani, Prisoners of War 65 (1982).
50   "[M]eeting the tactics of terror in kind will only perpetuate the cycle of terrorist
     violence. . . ." Carr, *supra* note 18, at 23.
51   *See infra* notes 72–89 and accompanying text. Note that in obvious retaliation
     for imposing a death sentence on Omar Sheikh, for killing Daniel Pearl, nine
     Pakistani police officers were wounded from four letter bombs sent to the station;
     one police officer lost his hand. Fouda & Fielding, *supra* note 8, at 12, 70.
     After receiving a series of death threats, Sheikh's Pakistani prosecutor resigned
     and is "under constant police guard." *Id.* at 70.
52   This approach would require:

> [O]btaining as much specific local information as possible and then, perhaps
> through the use of native 'subcontractors,' convincing people that linking
> their future to bin Laden is a bad idea. It would have to be a slow, careful,
> patient process that combined punishment of specific violent people with the
> offer of rewards for potential allies of the West. None of this would alter the
> strategy of attempting to disrupt bin Laden's access to money and electronic
> communications and forestall further attacks. But, for the present, quiet is
> America's friend, *killing, of Americans by bin Laden, and of Arab civilians by
> Americans, is bin Laden's friend*, because it draws ordinary people as well as
> combat troops to his side.

Lemann, *supra* note 43, at 36 (emphasis added).
53   *See infra* notes 72–89 and accompanying text.
54   The effect of the executions on Irish people was electric:

> [T]housands of people who ten days ago were bitterly opposed to the whole
> Sinn Fein movement, and to rebellion, were now becoming infuriated against
> the Government on account of these executions. . . . It is not murderers
> who are being executed; it is insurgents who have fought a clean fight, a
> brave fight, however misguided, and it would be a damned good thing
> if your soldiers were able to put up as good a fight as did these men in
> Dublin—three thousand men against twenty thousand with machine guns
> and artillery.

Tim Pat Coogan, The IRA 88 (2002) (quoting John Dillon of Irish Parliamentary Party and noting that there were in fact far fewer than 3000 rebels). Coogan also observed that the "indiscriminate roundup of suspects after the rising, had . . . involved so many innocent along with the guilty that alienation from Westminster was given a further powerful impetus." *Id.*

55 *See* Amanat, *supra* note 36, at 36–37. The doctrine of Salafiyya "and its articulation by Sayyid Qutb gained an overwhelming currency among Islamic radicals in the early 1980s." *Id.* at 37. An eminent legal scholar has discussed martyrdom in a legal context:

> Martyrdom is an extreme form of resistance to domination. As such it reminds us that the normative world building which constitutes Law is never just a mental or spiritual act. A legal world is built only to the extent that there are commitments that place bodies on the line. The torture of the martyr is an extreme and repulsive form of the organized violence of institutions. It reminds us that the interpretive commitments of officials are realized, indeed, in the flesh. As long as that is so, the interpretive commitments of a community which resists official law must also be realized in the flesh, even if it be the flesh of its own adherents.

Robert Cover, *Violence and the Word*, 95 Yale L.J. 1601, 1604–05 (1986) (citations omitted).

56 Armstrong, *supra* note 37, at 169; *see also* Berman, *supra* note 39, at 24.

57 Berman, *supra* note 39, at 33.

58 *Id.; see also* Armstrong, *supra* note 37, at 170. Anwar al Sadat had presided at his trial before Sadat became Egyptian president. Sadat was apparently assassinated by Muslims linked to the present al Qaeda for, among other things, his role against Qutb. For a more detailed discussion of Sadat, see chapter 1, notes 79 to 84 and accompanying text.

59 *See* Thomas M. McDonnell, *A Potentially Explosive Execution*, Nat'l Law J., July 7, 1997, at A17. Portions of this section are drawn from this op-ed piece that I wrote in connection with the Timothy McVeigh execution.

60 *Id.* Although neither the UK nor Israel has used capital punishment against convicted terrorists, some allege that their armed services have carried out extrajudicial executions. *See* Coogan, *supra* note 54, at 575–82; *For the Sake of Democracy, Britain's 'Dirty War' Must be Investigated*, Irish Times, May 21, 2003, at 14; Amnesty International, *Israel and the Occupied Territories: Israel Must Put an Immediate End to the Policy and Practice of Assassinations*, July 3, 2003, *available at* http://web.amnesty.org/library/Index/ ENGMDE150562003 (last visited Aug. 6, 2003); Ardi Imseis, *On the Fourth Geneva Convention and the Occupied Palestinian Territory*, 44 Harv. Int'l L.J. 65, 107–11 (2003). *But see* J. Nicholas Kendall, *Israeli Counter-Terrorism, 'Targeted Killings' Under International Law*, 80 N.C. L. Rev. 1069, 1070 (2002) (arguing that terrorists are legitimate military targets, that "targeted killings" are justified by self-defense, and that such killings do not amount to prohibited killing by "perfidy"); Louis Rene-Beres, *On Assassination as Anticipatory Self-Defense: The Case of Israel*, 20 Hofstra L. Rev. 321 (1991) (reaching a similar conclusion). Israel has imposed the death penalty only once, on Adolf Eichman, the author of the "Final Solution." Attorney General of Israel v. Eichmann, 36 I.L.R. 277 (S. Ct. Israel 1962), *reprinted in* Paust et al., *supra* note 14, at 868.

61 McDonnell, *supra* note 59.

62 *But see* Green et al., *supra* note 6, at 225 (comments of Kenneth Roth) (noting the lack of enthusiasm that al Qaeda leaders have for serving as suicide bombers themselves).

63 *Id.* at 194 (comment of David Bruck).

64 As one noted capital defense attorney stated:

> Having been involved directly, as defense counsel, in one of the al Qaeda prosecutions, I can tell you that in the world of martyrdom it doesn't get any better than to be captured by the United States, brought to New York, or to Alexandria, Virginia, tried on a world stage, and then ritually put to death by the United States. That's the gold standard of martyrdom. For someone who considers blowing himself up on a plane to be a good thing, getting executed by the United States is as good as it gets.

Id. at 194 (comments of David Bruck).

65   *See* Lewis, *supra* note 29:

> Those who are killed in the jihad are called martyrs, in Arabic and other Muslim languages *shahid*. . . . The Arabic term shahid also means 'witness' and is usually translated 'martyr'. . . . In Islamic usage the term *martyrdom* is normally interpreted to mean death in a jihad and its reward is eternal bliss. . . . Suicide, by contrast, is a mortal sin and earns eternal damnation, even for those who would otherwise have earned a place in paradise.

Id. at 38.

66   Hoffman, *supra* note 14, at 132 (quoting Brian Michael Jenkins, *International Terrorism: A New Mode of Conflict*, *in* Int'l Terrorism and World Security 16 (1975)).

67   Jane Perlez, *Court Decides to Sentence Bali Bomber to Death*, N.Y. Times, Aug. 8, 2003, at A8.

68   *Id.*

69   Peter Gelling, *Anger Erupts After Executions in Bali Blasts*, N.Y. Times, Nov. 9, 2008, *available at* www.nytimes.com/2008/11/10/world/asia/ 10bali.html?_r=1&scp=47&sq=amrozi&st=cse.

70   Professor Cover noted as follows:

> Martyrdom is not the only possible response of a group that has failed to adjust to or accept domination while sharing a physical space. Rebellion and revolution are alternative responses when conditions make such acts feasible and when there is a willingness not only to die but also to kill for an understanding of the normative future that differs from that of the dominating power.

Cover, *supra* note 55, at 1605 (citations omitted).

71   *See infra* notes 72–89 and accompanying text for a discussion of the Aimal Kasi execution and an analogous British execution of a supposed American.

72   Kasi characterized his actions as " 'between jihad and tribal revenge,' jihad against America for its support of Israel and revenge against the CIA, which he apparently felt had mistreated his father during Afghanistan's war against the Soviets." Stern, *supra* note 40, at 27.

73   Kasi v. Angelone, 300 F.3d 487, 490–91 (4th Cir. 2002).

74   *Id.* at 491.

75   *Id.* Kasi's motives have been described as typical of those bent on engaging in terrorist activities against the US:

> [T]he reasons that drove Kasi to kill are very similar to those commonly used to justify anti-American acts of terrorism. Kasi said he was angry about the United States' policies abroad, believing that it was bent on destroying Muslims. He deliberately targeted the CIA because, in his eyes, it was one of the prime instruments of that destruction.

Iffat Malik, *An Uncertain Start*, Al-Ahram Wkly., Nov. 21, 2002, *available at* http://weekly.ahram.org.eg/print/2002/613/in1.htm. *But see Kasi*, 300 F.3d at 491 (noting that in his confession Kasi stated he targeted the CIA not only because of his anti-American views, but also because he knew CIA workers were unarmed).

76   Although Congress had enacted a limited death penalty statute in 1988 dealing with so-called "drug king-pins," it did not enact a broad death penalty statute until 1994. *See* The Federal Death Penalty Act of 1994, 18 U.S.C. § 3591 *et seq.*; *see also* The Anti-Drug Abuse Act of 1988, 21 U.S.C. § 848(e)–(r) (providing penalty of death for drug king-pins under certain circumstances).

77   *Kasi*, 300 F.3d at 490.

78   *Id.*

79   *Pakistan on Alert After US Execution* (BBC News television broadcast Nov. 15, 2002), *available at* http://news.bbc.co.uk/2/low/south_asia/2480009.stm.

80   *Pakistan City Mourns Execution* (BBC News television broadcast Nov. 15, 2002), *available at* http://news.bbc.co.uk/2/low/south_asia/2480327.stm.

81   *See Pakistanis in Death Row Protest* (BBC News television broadcast Nov. 11, 2002), *available at* http://news.bbc.co.uk/ 2/low/south_asia/2445307.stm; *see also Pakistanis in Karachi protest the execution of Mir Aimal Kasi in the US*, Al-Ahram Wkly., Nov. 21, 2003, *available at* http://weekly.ahram.org.eg/2002/61 3/in1.htm.

82   Carlotta Gall, *World Briefing – Asia: Pakistan: Body of Man Executed in U.S. Is Back*, N.Y. Times, Nov. 19, 2002, at A18; *Thousands Receive Aimal Kasi's Body as a Hero and a Martyr*, Daily Times (Pakistan), Nov. 18, 2002, *available at* www.ummahnews.com/print.php?sid=272.

83   *Id.*

84   Mazhar Abbas, *Thousands Mourn Executed Pakistani*, Iafrica.com, *available at* www.iafrica.com/news/worldnews/187519.htm.

85   *See Pakistanis in Death Row Protest, supra* note 81; State Department, U.S. Mission to Pakistan, U.S. Embassy Islamabad, *Warden Notice 3/4/2002, available at* http://usembassy.state.gov/posts/pk1/wwwhwarden11212002.html (last visited July 23, 2003); *see also State Department Press Releases and Document*, Fed. Information and News Dispatch, Nov. 19, 2002, *available at* 2002 WL 25973321 (press briefing with Philip T. Reeker, Deputy Spokesperson for State Department).

86   Malik, *supra* note 75.

87   *Id.*; *see also Thousands Receive Aimal Kasi's Body as a Hero and Martyr, supra* note 82. In addition, four US oil company employees were assassinated in Karachi on November 11, 1997, two days after Kasi's conviction, apparently in retaliation. Bill Baskervill, *Pakistani who Killed CIA Agents in '93 is Executed, Appeal Rejected; Reprisals Feared*, Boston Globe, Nov. 15, 2002, at A2, *available at* 2002 WL 101983863; *see also* Oliver Roy, *Hazy Outlines of an Islamist International: Fundamentalists without a Common Cause*, Le Monde, Oct. 1998 (Barry Smerin trans.), *available at* http://mondediplo.com/1998/10/04afghan?var_recherche=%22hazy +outlines%22. Harakat al Ansar, a group with connections to the "Afghan camps," claimed credit for the assassinations. *Id.*

88   *See, e.g.*, Buckley, *supra* note 8, *available at* www.nationalreview.com/buckley/buckley060603.asp.

89   For example, al Qaeda members have kidnapped western tourists and hijacked at least one airliner for the sole purpose of freeing other extremist fundamentalists from prison. *See* Fouda & Fielding, *supra* note 8, at 60–63 (noting, among other things, that six Western tourists were kidnapped by Kashmiri rebels with links to al Qaeda in southern Kashmir and were almost certainly killed when Indian authorities refused to release 15 jailed Islamists).

90   *Cf.* Woodson v. North Carolina, 428 U.S. 280, 305 (1976) (noting that a plurality of the US Supreme Court has recognized that "death is different," specifically

stating, "Death, in its finality, differs more from life imprisonment than a 100-year prison term differs from one of only a year or two").

91 *See supra* notes 72–89 and accompanying text.

92 United States v. Robbins, 27 F. Cas. 825 (D.S.C. 1799) (No. 16,175).

93 Christopher H. Pyle, Extradition, Politics, and Human Rights 36 (2001); Ruth Wedgwood, *The Revolutionary Martyrdom of Jonathan Robbins*, 100 Yale L.J. 229, 233–35 (1990).

94 Pyle, *supra* note 93, at 37–47; *see also* Michael Edmund O'Neill, *Article III and the Process Due a Connecticut Yankee before King Arthur's Court*, 76 Marq. L. Rev. 1, 43–44 (1992).

95 Jean Edward Smith, John Marshall 258–259 (1998); Wedgwood, *supra* note 93, at 224.

96 Wedgwood, *supra* note 93, at 236 n.9 (citing Instruction of Lord Grenville to British Minister Robert Liston (Oct. 7, 1796), *in Instructions to the British Ministers to the United States 1791–1812*, 3 Ann. Rep. Am. Hist. Ass'n 122 and n.56 (B. Mayo ed. 1936), *reprinted as* H.R. Doc. No. 13, 75th Cong., 1st Sess. (1941)).

97 *Id.*

98 *Id.* at 305–306.

99 *Id.*

100 The evidence the British put forward suggests that he was probably Irish and that he probably enlisted. *Id.*

101 Quinn v. Robinson, 783 F.2d 776, 793 (9th Cir. 1986) (citing M. Bassiouni, International Extradition and World Public Order 425 (1974)). Note, however, that the political offense exception generally may not be successfully invoked by individuals who have committed war crimes or crimes against humanity. *See Quinn*, 783 F.2d at 799; Eain v. Wilkes, 641 F.2d 504, 523 (7th Cir. 1981)), *cert. denied*, 454 U.S. 894 (1981). As demonstrated above, those involved with the September 11 attacks have committed crimes against humanity, war crimes, or both. Some of Robbins' acts resemble war crimes, if one analogizes his and his conspirators' treatment of the captives to treatment of prisoners of war. Yet the heinousness of his crimes did not apparently assuage the US reaction. *Quinn*, 783 F.3d at 793.

102 Wedgwood, *supra* note 93, at 361. Professor Wedgwood argues that President Adams did not deserve the reaction he received given a full study of the actual facts of the case. *Id.* at 362.

103 *See* Indictment, United States v. Lindh, No. 02–37a (E.D. Va. Feb. 5, 2002), *available at* http://news.findlaw.com/hdocs/docs/lindh/uswlindh020502cmp. pdf.

104 *See* Don Van Natta, *A Nation Challenged: The Legal Venue: Compromise Settles Debate Over Tribunal*, N.Y. Times, Dec. 12, 2001, at B1.

105 Philip Shenon, *After the War: the Courts; Hearing to Affect Government's Ability to Try Terror Suspects in Civilian Courts*, N.Y. Times, June 2, 2003, at A12 (noting the conservative reputation of the Fourth Circuit); John Gibeaut, *Prosecuting Moussaoui*, 88 A.B.A.J. 36 (2002) (noting the "traditionally conservative" jury pool in Virginia). The ideological cast of the Fourth Circuit may be on the point of changing. *See* Neil A. Lewis, *Obama's Court Nominees Are Focus of Speculation*, N.Y. Times, Mar. 10, 2009, *available at* www.nytimes.com/2009/03/11/us/politics/11judges.html. As of this writing, there is a 6–5 majority of Republican-appointed judges in the 15-member United States Court of Appeals for the Fourth Circuit—a composition that can be drastically altered by the four vacancies to be filled by President Obama.

106 Shenon, *supra* note 105, at A12. The Pentagon is located in Virginia. In the East African embassy bombings case, it was later reported that one juror apparently

misled the district court and refused to consider imposing the death penalty, and another juror as the sole Jew on the jury feared retaliation from al Qaeda and thus refused to vote for the death penalty. Benjamin Weiser, *A Jury Torn and Fearful in 2001 Terrorism Trial*, N.Y. Times, Jan. 5, 2003, at A1.

107 *Id.* New York was also reportedly not chosen, because Justice Department prosecutors believed that the district court there would probably have granted defendant's motion to change venue. *Id.*

108 Van Natta, *supra* note 104. Moussaoui ultimately received life imprisonment because one juror refused to vote for the death penalty.

109 *See* Paust, *supra* note 21, at 1. The Bush–Cheney administration reportedly has indicated that they considered transferring Moussaoui to a military tribunal to avoid the defendants' carrying on in court. *See* Philip Shenon & Eric Schmitt, *Threats and Responses: the 9/11 Suspect; White House Weighs Letting Military Tribunal Try Moussaoui, Officials Say*, N.Y. Times, Nov. 10, 2002, at A17.

110 The Justice Department could defend its decision by arguing that using civilian courts against terrorists is difficult enough, so the Department must use every procedural advantage at its disposal. Otherwise, the government may be forced to engage in self-help or in refusing to use the civilian courts at all and transferring all these cases to military tribunals.

111 Professor Johnson concisely explained the weighted advantages that the prosecutor obtains when seeking a conspiracy charge:

> Where there is evidence of conspiracy, the defendant may be tried jointly with his criminal partners and possibly with many other persons whom he has never met or seen, the joint trial may be held in a place he may never have visited, and hearsay statements of other alleged members of the conspiracy may be used to prove his guilt. Furthermore, a defendant who is found guilty of conspiracy is subject to enhanced punishment and may also be found guilty of any crime committed in furtherance of the conspiracy, whether or not he knew about the crime or aided in its commission.

Phillip E. Johnson, *The Unnecessary Crime of Conspiracy*, 61 Cal. L. Rev. 1137, 1140 (1973).

112 *See supra* notes 72–89 and accompanying text.

113 *See* Dan Balz & Bob Woodward, *America's Chaotic Road to War; Bush's Global Strategy Began to Take Shape in First Frantic Hours after Attack*, Wash. Post. Jan. 27, 2002, at A1. Note, by the way, that the "surge in recruitment efforts" for al Qaeda has been observed most prominently in Britain, Spain, Italy, and the US. *See* Van Natta & Butler, *supra* note 48, at 1. "The destruction of the Afghan camps had one perverse and unintended effect[:] Terrorists and their supporters who had formerly been concentrated in one known place were dispersed to home regions and new hideouts like Chechnya, Yemen, East Africa and Georgia's Pankisi Gorge. Regional commanders of al Qaeda, says Rohan Gunaratna, author of a leading book on the network, are now 'operating independently of centralized control' ... and no longer depend on anything from bin Laden and his top brass except for ideological inspiration." *World*, Time, May 26, 2003, at 26.

114 "In the fight on terrorism, the United States needs cooperation from European and Asian countries in intelligence, law enforcement, and logistics." G. John Ikenberry, *America's Imperial Ambition*, Foreign Aff., Sept.-Oct. 2002, at 44, 58; *see also supra* note 44 (collecting authorities noting need for international cooperation); Sebastian Rotella, *THE WORLD 5 Suspects Helped Fund Al Qaeda, Spain Says*, L.A. Times, Mar. 9, 2003, at A3 (noting that in arresting five alleged al Qaeda money launderers, the "Spanish investigation involved close cooperation with authorities in France, where the Djerba bomber lived, and in Germany.

Spanish investigators also received assistance from U.S., Tunisian, Swiss and Portuguese law enforcement"). *But see* Cordesman, *supra* note 45, at 16 (minimizing the practical worth of such cooperation).

115   *See also* Lemann, *supra* note 43, at 36.

116   Mike Allen & Glenn Kessler, *Bush's Tax Cut Proposal Renews Party Differences; Democrats Object to President's Call for Billions in Tax Relief as Major Part of Stimulus Package*, Wash. Post, Oct. 7, 2001, at A16.

117   The US forces and planes, however, have carried out the vast majority of the attacks. *See* Pamela Hess, *Afghan Terrorist Camps in Cross Hairs*, United Press Int'l, Oct. 9, 2001, *available in* LEXIS, News Group File.

118   Benjamin R. Barber, *A Failure of Democracy, Not Capitalism*, N.Y. Times, July 29, 2002, at A19. For an excellent article detailing the pitfalls of US unilateralism, see Koh, *supra* note 44, at 1526–27. Professor Koh asks which fork in the international road the US will take. Professor Koh was named as Legal Adviser to the Secretary of State by the Obama administration.

> Will it be power-based internationalism, in which the United States gets its way, because of its willingness to exercise power whatever the rules? Or will it be norm-based internationalism, in which American power derives not just from hard power, but from perceived fidelity to universal values of democracy, human rights, and the rule of law?

Id.

119   *See also* Koh, *supra* note 44, at 1501.

120   Amnesty International USA, List of Abolitionist and Retentionist Countries (Dec. 31, 2008), *available at* www.amnestyusa.org/abolish/annual_report/AbolitionistRetentionist.pdf (last visited Apr. 4, 2008).

121   The 47-member Council of Europe has required states applying for admission to abolish the death penalty. Russia, Georgia, the Ukraine, Estonia and other eastern states are or have already taken steps to do so to gain admission to the Council. *See Montenegro Abolishes Death Penalty*, Agence France Presse, June 19, 2002 (noting that Montenegro abolished the death penalty to fulfill condition of admission to Council of Europe), *available in* LEXIS, News Group File. Furthermore, the Council of Europe voted to extend the abolition of the death penalty to wartime offenses. *See European States Drop Wartime Exception to Death Penalty Ban*, Agence France Presse, May 3, 2002, *available in* LEXIS, News Group File. Protocol No. 13 to the European Convention on Human Rights and Fundamental Freedoms, Concerning the Abolition of the Death Penalty in All Circumstances, *opened for signature* May 3, 2002, ETS 187, *available at* www.statewatch.org/news/2003/jul/prot13.pdf (*entered into force* July 1, 2003) [hereinafter European Convention on Human Rights] (abolishing death penalty in wartime as well as peacetime). In Europe and Central Asia, Belarus is the only state that has not abolished the death penalty: Amnesty International USA, *Death Penalty Statistics 2008*, *available at* www.amnestyusa.org/death-penalty/international-death-penalty/death-penalty-statistics/page.do?id=1011348 (last visited Oct. 26, 2010).

122   The Turkish parliament has, however, abolished the death penalty for offenses committed in peacetime. *See* Amnesty International, *Turkey: Abolition of the Death Penalty Welcomed*, *available at* http://web.amnesty.org/ai.nsf/Index/EUR440362002? Open Document of Abolition COUNTRIES/TURKEY (last visited Mar. 13, 2003); *see also* Ocalan v. Turkey, App. No. 46221/99, Eur. Ct. Hum. Rts., Mar. 12, 2003, *available at* http://www.unhcr.org/refworld/docid/3e71a9d84.html (concluding that imposing death penalty on notorious Kurdish terror group leader, Abdullah Ocalan, would violate Article 3 of the European Convention on Fundamental Rights and Freedoms, because of unfair trial

procedures to which Turkey subjected him), available at: http://legal.aptich/Mechanisms/Europe/European_Court/Death%20Penalty/ec_ocalan_12-03-2003.htm.

123 Alan Clarke, *Terrorism, Extradition, and the Death Penalty*, 29 Wm. Mitchell L. Rev. 783, 806 (2003).

124 Ethan Bronner, *Power vs. Peace: a Clash of Worldviews; Trans-Atlantic Tension*, Int'l Herald Trib., Feb. 1, 2003, at 4.

125 Somini Sengupta, *African Held for War Crimes Dies in Custody of a Tribunal*, N.Y. Times, July 31, 2003, at A6.

126 The Spanish government has indicated it will not extradite suspected al Qaeda members to the US absent assurances that the death penalty will not be sought. *See* Rotella, *supra* note 114, at A3; *Europe's Doubts*, Fin. Times, Dec. 14, 2001, at 20. In 2001, the Canadian Supreme Court ruled against extraditing two Canadian nationals to the US absent assurances that they will not be subject to the death penalty. United States v. Burns, [2001] S.C.R. 283, para. 143 (Can.). *See* Bruce Zagaris, A. *Canadian Supreme Court Rules Suspects Can Be Extradited to US Only With Assurances, Extradition Part IV*, 17 Int'l L. Enforcement Rep. 145 (Apr. 2001), *available in* LEXIS, Int'l Law Newsletters file; *see also* Bruce Zagaris, *Uruguay Supreme Court Approves Extradition of Suspected Terrorist to Egypt, Counter-terrorism Enforcement Cooperation*, 19 Int'l L. Enforcement Rep. 303 (Aug. 2003), *available in* LEXIS, Int'l Law Newsletters file, at *1 (noting that the Uruguayan Supreme Court upheld the extradition of the terrorist suspect "after Egypt agreed not to apply the death penalty or life imprisonment").

127 *U.S. Death Penalty Could Prove Hurdle to Extradition of Terror Suspects from Britain*, Assoc. Press, Oct. 8, 2001 (statement of David Blunkett, Home Secretary); *cf.* Bruce Zagaris, *British Court Denies U.S. Extradition Request on Algerian Pilot in Alleged Terrorism Conspiracy*, 18 Int'l L. Enforcement Rep. 6 (June 2002) (noting that the British judge refused to extradite Lotfi Raissi, an Algerian national, to the US on the ground that the US failed to provide sufficient evidence that Raissi participated in the September 11 conspiracy by training one of the pilots).

128 Minister of Justice v. Burns, [2001] 1 S.C.R. 283, 2001 SCC 7 (Can.), *available at* www.canlii.org/ca/cas/scc/2001/2001scc7.hmtl; *see also* Soering v. United Kingdom, 161 Eur. Ct. H.R. (ser. A) at 217 (1989) (refusing to extradite a German national, accused of double murder, to Virginia on the ground that the "death row phenomenon" there violated Article 3 of the European Convention on Fundamental Rights and Freedoms).

129 *See* Mohamed Dalvie v. President of the Republic of South Africa 2001 (7) SA 685 (CC) (S. Afr.) (concluding that an al Qaeda suspect in embassy bombings was wrongfully deported to the US absent receiving assurances that the US would not impose the death penalty and ordering that judgment be sent to the US District Court of Southern District of New York where the suspect was being tried). *See* Toni Locy, *Moussaoui Prosecutors Wary of Tribunal*, USA Today, May 14, 2003, at A4.

130 In dealing with other crises, the US has given assurances that the death penalty will not be sought in order to obtain certain fugitives. *Israel Agrees to Extradite Man Sought in Letter-Bomb Killing*, L.A. Times, July 13, 1993, at B10; Keith B. Richburg, *Court in France Approves Extradition of U.S. Fugitive*, Wash. Post, June 29, 2001, at A31 (two instances in which extradition was approved after the death penalty was taken off the table). Whether pursuing the death penalty would hinder the interchange of intelligence and of other matters remains to be seen.

131 Steven Erlanger, *Traces of Terror: The Intelligence Reports; Germany Disputes Visit of Qaeda Figure*, N.Y. Times, June 11, 2002, at A19.

132 Josh Meyer, *Attack in Saudi Arabia*, L.A. Times, May 14, 2003, at A1.

133 Bill Coffin, *Rough Water*, 50 Risk Mgmt. Mag., Mar. 3, 2003, at 10 (noting that on October 6, 2002, al Qaeda terrorists "slammed an explosive laded [sic]

speedboat" into a French oil tanker moored off the coast of Yemen, causing it to spill oil into the sea); *see also* Meyer, *supra* note 132.

134 Amrozi, the alleged mastermind behind the Bali attacks, said at a news conference after his arrest that he regretted the bombings killed so many Australians when he intended to target Americans. *Death Penalty Sought for Main Suspect in Bali Bombings*, Kyodo News Int'l, July 8, 2003, *available in* LEXIS, International Newsletters file. Aside from blowing up the discotheque, bombs went off inside Patty's Irish Pub also in Kuta, Indonesia as well as close to the US consulate in Denpasar, Indonesia. *Alleged Field Coordinator for Bali Bombing Goes on Trial*, Kyodo News Int'l, July 22, 2003, *available in* LEXIS, International Newsletter file.

135 Meyer, *supra* note 132.

136 Americans suffered the most casualties in these attacks carried out by al Qaeda, but other foreigners also died. *Saudis More Open About Recent Attacks Than They Were About September 11*, *available in* Westlaw, Allnews Plus Wires Database. Along with eight Americans killed in these attacks, seven Saudis, three Filipinos, two Jordanians, and one each from Australia, the UK, Ireland, Lebanon, and Switzerland also died. Donna Abu-Nasr, Assoc. Press, May 15, 2003.

137 The Asian Wall Street Journal reported, however, that the low-level Jordanian al Qaeda coordinator of the Moroccan attacks came up with the targets. Peter Finn, *Story of Moroccan Bombers Is Rooted in Casablanca Slum*, Asian Wall St. J., June 4, 2003, *available at* 2003 WL-WSJA 55992014. The al Qaeda leadership had apparently informed him that they wanted attacks in Morocco without specifying any targets. *Id.* He chose targets that had Jewish links or were associated with "debauchery"—namely, a Spanish restaurant, a Jewish-owned Italian restaurant, a Jewish social club, and the Jewish cemetery. *Id.* The Farah Hotel was also on the list. *Id.* Al Qaeda apparently gave the local coordinator $50,000 to $70,000 to fund the attacks. *Id.*

138 Jane Perlez, *The Attack: Group Linked to Al Qaeda Seen Behind Jakarta Blast*, N.Y. Times, Aug. 7, 2003, at A12 (noting that 33-story Marriott Hotel was "the most visibly American building in the city").

139 Elaine Sciolino, *10 Bombs Shatter Trains in Madrid, Killing 192*, N.Y. Times, Mar. 12, 2004, at A1; Tim Golden & Craig S. Smith, *Spain Arrests 5 More Suspects in Madrid Bomb Attacks*, N.Y. Times, Mar. 19, 2004 (noting that the death toll had risen to 202).

140 Golden & Smith, *supra* note 139, at A12. There is other evidence that is pointing towards individuals who may be linked to al Qaeda as responsible for the bombings. *See id.* Furthermore, an audiotape was broadcast in October 2003, "reportedly" in the voice of Osama bin Laden, in which he directly threatens Spain. Sciolino, *supra* note 139, at A1. Spain initially had been a staunch ally of the Bush administration and had sent 1,300 troops to Iraq. *Id.* Richard Norton-Taylor & Rosie Cowan, *Madrid Bomb Suspect Linked to UK Extremists*, The Guardian, Mar. 17, 2004, *available at* 2004 WL 56438604 (reporting that a suspect in the Madrid bombings met an extremist Islamist who may have shared a flat with Zacarias Moussaoui in London).

141 Brian Bennett & Douglas Waller-Washington, *Thwarting the Airline Plot: Inside the Investigation*, Time, Aug. 10, 2006, *available at* www.time.com/time/nation/Article/0,8599,1225453,00.html.

142 Carlotta Gall, *Pakistan Asserts Link to Al Qaeda in Bhutto Death*, N.Y. Times Dec. 29, 2007, *available at* www.nytimes.com/2007/12/29/world/asia/29pakistan.html; Salman Masood & Carlotta Gall, *Bhutto Assassination Ignites Dissaray*, N.Y. Times, Dec. 28, 2007, *available at* www.nytimes.com/2007/12/28/world/asia/28pakistan.html?pagewanted=1&sq=benazir%20bhutto&st=cse&scp=3.

143 *Benazir Bhutto Assassination: Questions and Answers*, BBC World News, http://news.bbc.co.uk/2/hi/south_asia/6653475.stm; *see also* David Loyn, *Pakistan's Past Haunts India*, BBC America World News, Nov. 29, 2008, http://news.bbc.co.uk/2/hi/south_asia/7756583.stm.

144 *Timeline: Mumbai under Attack*, BBC America World News, Dec. 1, 2008, http://news.bbc.co.uk/2/hi/south_asia/7754438.stm *See also* Profile: Lashkar-e-Taiba, BBC America World News, Dec. 4,2008, http://news.bbc.co.uk/2/hi/south_asia/3181925.stm.

145 *See* Rajiv Chandrasekaran, *Purported Bin Laden Tape Lauds Bali, Moscow Attacks*, Wash. Post, Nov. 13, 2002, at A1; *see also* Stevenson, *supra* note 40.

146 *Id*. at 75.

147 Germany and France announced their change in position approximately two weeks after the Osama bin Laden audiotape was broadcast. Germany had initially refused to provide the evidence needed by the US Justice Department for the Moussaoui case, because of German law and practice of not doing so in capital cases. *See* Steven Erlanger, *Traces of Terror: The Terror Trial; German Chancellor Hopes to Release Evidence Soon*, N.Y. Times, June 11, 2002, at A26. Apparently, Germany's constitutional ban on the death penalty prohibits handing over any evidence that "could lead to a conviction that results in execution." *Id*. Germany had apparently refused to hand over bank transfers that show that *Moussaoui* was wired money from Ramzi Muhammad Abdullah bin al-Shibh. *Id*. The transfers apparently had al-Shibh's fingerprints on them. *Id*. Germany requested assurances that the death penalty not be sought for Moussaoui, but the US rejected that request. *Id*. France had also initially indicated that it would not turn over any evidence on Moussaoui, because the US is seeking the death penalty. *Id*. Germany and France, however, ultimately agreed to hand over the requested evidence after receiving assurances that the evidence would only be used during the guilt phase of the capital trial and not in the penalty phase. Dan Eggen, *U.S. to Get Moussaoui Data from Europe*, Wash. Post, Nov. 28, 2002, at A19; *see also* Larry Margasak, *U.S. Seeks to Block Moussaoui Documents*, Assoc. Press, Mar. 27, 2003, *available at* 2003 WL 17302860.

   As Moussaoui's standby attorney pointed out, however, the jury in the guilt phase sits for the penalty phase if a guilty verdict is reached. *Id*. Evidence heard in the guilt phase cannot help but influence the jury in the penalty phase of the trial. *See* Bruce Zagaris, *Germans and French Agree to Give Evidence in Moussaoui Case Evidence Gathering and International Human Rights*, 19 Int'l L. Enforcement Rep. 21, 22 (2003), *available in* LEXIS, Int'l Law Newsletter file. The evidence was important to the Government's case:

> [The documents] arguably establish important connections between Moussaoui and al Qaeda operatives. In particular, documents in the possession of German authorities show money transfers from a member of the Hamburg group that carried out the September 11, 2001 terrorist attacks in the U.S. In particular, they include details of two money transfers that totaled $14,000 from Ramzi Binalshibh, an alleged member of the al Qaeda cell in Hamburg, to Moussaoui. Mr. Binalshibh, who is in U.S. custody, has told U.S. authorities that Moussaoui was only a backup in the September 11 plans, because the al Qaeda cells did not view him as trustworthy. The French documents include the original version of a dossier showing Moussaoui's childhood and early adult life in southern France, including his links with Islamic radicals both there and in London.

   Id. at 21 (citations omitted).

148 *See also* Stevenson, *supra* note 40, at 75; *cf*. Richard Bernstein, *Germany Offers to Expand Afghan Force if the U.N. Approves*, N.Y. Times, Aug. 28, 2003, at A5 (the

German offer to send 250 troops to Kabul "seems likely to help warm relations with the United States after Germany's opposition to the American military action in Iraq").

149   Agreement on Extradition, U.S.–E.U., June 25, 2003, 2003 O.J. (L 181) 27, Celex No. 203A0719 (01) [hereinafter EU-US Extradition Agreement]. *But see* European Convention on Human Rights, *supra* note 121 (abolishing the death penalty in wartime as well as peacetime).

150   The capital punishment Article provides as follows:

> Where the offence for which extradition is sought is punishable by death under the laws in the requesting State and not punishable by death under the laws in the requested State, the requested State may grant extradition on the condition that the death penalty shall not be imposed on the person sought, or if for procedural reasons such condition cannot be complied with by the requesting State, on condition that the death penalty if imposed shall not be carried out. If the requesting State accepts extradition subject to conditions pursuant to this Article, it shall comply with the conditions. If the requesting State does not accept the conditions, the request for extradition may be denied.

EU-US Extradition Agreement, *supra* note 149, art. 13.

151   Clarke, *supra* note 123, at 807; *see* Harold Hongju Koh, *Paying "Decent Respect" to World Opinion on the Death Penalty*, 35 U.C. Davis L. Rev. 1085, 1130 (2002). *But see* Michael Novak, *North Atlantic Community, European Community*, Nat'l Rev., July 24, 2003, *available at* www.nationalreview.com/novak072403.asp (noting that people of Europe may be in line with people of the United States on the death penalty, but that elites in Europe strongly oppose it).

> What distinguishes the United States from the United Kingdom, France and Canada is not the percentage of the population that expresses support for the death penalty but the intensity of some elements of that support and the distinctive political structure that exists to translate sentiment into political action at the state level.

Franklin E. Zimring, The Contradictions of American Capital Punishment 136 (2003).

152   Ginger Thompson, *Texas Executes Mexican for Murder Despite President Fox's Plea*, N.Y. Times, Aug. 15, 2002, at A5. Noting the failure of the Texas police to advise the executed Mexican national of his right to consult with the Mexican consul, President Vicente Fox complained that "[n]ot only was Mr. Suarez Medina deprived of his right to the benefit of his country's assistance when he most needed it, but the Mexican government was also prevented from providing priority assistance that might have influenced the outcome of his trial." *Id.* As of July 2009, there were 30 foreign nationals on US death rows. Death Penalty Information Center, *Foreign Nationals and the Death Penalty in the United States*, June 19, 2009, *available at* http://deathpenaltyinfo.org/foreign-nationals-and-death-penalty-US#background. At least 24 foreign nationals have been executed, none of whom apparently received notice of their right to consult with a consular official from their country. *Id.*

153   Article 36 provides as follows:

> 1. With a view to facilitating the exercise of consular functions relating to nationals of the sending State: . . . (b) if he so requests, the competent authorities of the receiving State shall, *without delay*, inform the consular post of the sending State if, within its consular district, a national of that State is arrested or committed to prison or to custody pending trial or is detained in any other manner . . . *The said authorities shall inform the person concerned without delay of his rights under this sub-paragraph.*

Vienna Convention on Consular Relations art. 36.1(b), Apr. 24, 1963, 596 U.N.T.S. 262 (emphasis added); *see also* U.N. Body of Principles for the Protection of All Persons Under Any Form of Detention or Imprisonment, G.A. Res. 43/173, at prin. 16(2), U.N. GAOR, 43d Sess., Supp. No. 49, U.N. Doc. A/43/49 (1988); U.N. Standard Minimum Rules for the Treatment of Prisoners, E.S.C. Res. 663(c), art. 38(1), U.N. ESCOR 24th Sess., Supp. No. 1, U.N. Doc. E/3048 (1957) (providing essentially the same right of consular notification and assistance as Article 36 of the Vienna Convention).

154 *See* Medellin v. Texas, 128 S. Ct. 1346 (2007) (ruling that neither the Vienna Convention on Consular Relations nor the ICJ's statute relating to compulsory jurisdiction were self-executing treaties; consequently, the ICJ's judgment against the US, requiring review of death penalty sentences where the defendant was not given required consular notification was unenforceable); Breard v. Greene, 523 U.S. 371, 375–76 (1998) (ruling that since Vienna Consular Convention claim was not raised at trial in state court, that claim was procedurally defaulted); United States v. Li, 206 F.3d 56, 71 (1st Cir. 2000) (rejecting challenge under Vienna Consular Convention); United States v. Chaparro-Alcantara, 226 F.3d 616, 621 (7th Cir. 2000); United States v. Santos, 235 F.3d 1105, 1107 (8th Cir. 2000); United States v. Cordoba-Mosquera, 212 F.3d 1194, 1196 (11th Cir. 2000); United States v. Carrillo, 70 F.2d 854, 859 (N.D. Ill. 1999); United States v. Hongla-Yamche, 55 F. Supp. 2d 74, 77 (D. Mass. 1999).

A few state and federal courts have given foreign defendants some limited relief. *See, e.g.*, United States v. Calderon-Medina, 591 F.2d 529, 531–32 (9th Cir. 1979) (suppressing the foreign defendant's statement because police failed to tell the defendant of his right to speak with a consular official from his country); *See also* United States v. Rangel-Gonzalez, 617 F.2d 529, 532 (9th Cir. 1980) (stating that rights established by the Vienna Convention on Consular Relations are personal to the defendant); United States v. Lombrera-Camorlinga, 170 F.3d 1241 (9th Cir. 1999); United States v. Standt, 153 F. Supp. 2d 417 (S.D.N.Y. 2001) (concluding that a foreign national who is arrested but not informed of his rights under the Vienna Convention has private cause of action under Section 1983); Valdez v. State, 46 P.3d 703 (Okla. Crim. App. 2003) (granting a Mexican national's petition for post-conviction relief, reasoning that while the ICJ's judgment in LaGrand did not mandate abandonment of procedural default rules, failure to provide consular notice, along with other evidence indicating lack of diligence on the part of assigned counsel justified the relief requested). An Ohio Supreme Court justice noted the policy ramifications of violating the Convention on Consular Relations:

> Our best way to ensure that other nations honor the treaty by providing consular access to our nationals is to demand strict adherence to the right to consular access for foreigners in our country . . . If the United States fails in its responsibilities under the convention, then other member countries may choose to do unto us as we have done unto them.

State v. Issa, 93 Ohio St. 3d 49, 80–81 (2001) (Lundberg Stratton, J., dissenting). *See also* William J. Aceves & Bernard H. Oxman (ed.), *International Decision*, LaGrand (Germany v. United States), 96 Am. J. Int'l L. 210, 218 n.48 (2002) (noting that "[i]n September 2001, the Oklahoma Court of Criminal Appeals stayed the execution of a Mexican national, in part because of the purported Consular Relations Convention violation and the broader implications of the ICJ's ruling) (citing *Okla. Court Postpones Execution of Mexican; International Law Cited in Ruling*, Wash. Post, Sept. 11, 2001, at A16). William

J. Aceves, LaGrand (Germany v. United States), 96 Am. J. Int'l L. 210, 218 n.48 (2002) (citing *Okla. Court Postpones Execution of Mexican; International Law Cited in Ruling*, Wash. Post, Sept. 11, 2001, at A16).

155 Case Concerning Avena and Other Mexican Nationals (Mexico v. United States), 2004 I.C.J. 12. *See also* Press Release, Request for Interpretation of the Judgment of 31 March 2004 in the Case concerning Avena and Other Mexican Nationals (Mexico v. United States of America, Jan. 19, 2009, *available at* www.icj-cij.org/docket/files/139/14937.pdf?PHPSESSID=a35daaeaab35b 653b05acc57c35791bc LaGrand Case (Federal Republic of Germany v. United States), 2001 I.C.J. 1 (June 27), *available at* www. icj-cij.org/icjwww/idocket/ igus/igusframe.htm (last visited Aug. 1, 2002). Note that on February 5, 2003, the Court granted Mexico's request for provisional measures against the United States to stop the pending executions of three Mexican nationals who likewise were not provided consular advice. Case Concerning Avena and Other Mexican Nationals (Mexico v. United States), Request for the Indication of Provisional Measures, Order, I.C.J. Feb. 5, 2003), *available at* http://212.153.43.18/ icjwww/idocket/imus/imusframe.htm; Bruce Zagaris, *ICJ Grants Provisional Remedies for Mexicans on U.S. Death Row*, 19 Int'l L. Enforcement Rep. 148 (Apr. 2003), *available in* LEXIS, Int'l Law Newsletters file, at *1, *3. "Coming only 18 months after the ICJ decision in LaGrand, the decision indicates that opponents of the death penalty are gaining momentum in international courts." *The Right to Information on Consular Assistance in the Framework of the Guarantees of the Due Process of Law*, Inter-Am. C.H.R. 16, Advisory Op. OC-16/99, Ser. A (1999) (reaching the same result as the ICJ in LaGrand). The U.N. General Assembly passed a resolution by a vote of 121–1 endorsing the Advisory Opinion. See Protection of Migrants, G.A. Res. A/Res/54, Agenda Item 4, U.N. GAOR, 55th Sess., U.N. Doc. 16624 (2000) ("[t]aking note of the decisions of the relevant international juridical bodies on questions relating to migrants, in particular the Advisory Opinion OC-16/99 issued by the Inter-American Court of Human Rights . . . regarding the right to information about consular assistance within the framework of due process guarantees"). *See generally* Declaration on the Human Rights of Individuals Who Are Not Nationals of the Country in Which They Live, G.A. Res. 144, U.N. GAOR, 40th Sess., Supp. No. 53, U.N. Doc. A/Res/40/144 (1985) (linking consular assistance to due process). The US was the *only* country to vote against the resolution. Under the purpose and plain meaning of "the Supremacy Clause," the LaGrand case is binding on state and federal courts. *See* U.S. Const. art. VI, § 2. *But see* Medellin, 128 S. Ct. 1346 (holding that the Vienna Convention on Consular Relations and article 94 of the UN Charter are non-self-executing).

156 The US's moral standing to argue for the protection of its nationals when they are arrested abroad is compromised by the judicial rejection of the Vienna Convention. *Note: Too Sovereign but not Sovereign Enough: Are U.S. States Beyond the Reach of the Law of Nations?*, 116 Harv. L. Rev. 2654, 2677 (2003). That standing has further been weakened by the US's initial unqualified resort to military tribunals in virtually all cases involving the Taliban and al Qaeda. Charles V. Pena, *Blowback: The Unintended Consequences of Military Tribunals*, 16 N.D.J.L. Ethics & Pub. Pol'y 119, 122–23 (2002). Appeals of the sort that the US has made on behalf of Laurie Berenson, tried by military tribunal in Peru, would have little credibility today. *Id.* at 125.

157 But note that al Qaeda has broadened its targets.

158 The President of the EU opposed the execution of Stanley Faulder, a Canadian national denied his consular rights in Texas. The Death Penalty Information Center, *1998 Year End Report: New Voices Raise Dissent, Executions, Decline*, Dec. 1998, *available at* www.deathpenalty info.org.

159 Even terrorists' resort to conventional weapons could prove devastating, as September 11 so tragically illustrates.

160 Dan Eggen & Brooke A. Masters, *U.S. Indicts Suspect in Sept. 11 Attacks; Action Formally Links Man to Al Qaeda, States Evidence Against Bin Laden*, Wash. Post, Dec. 12, 2001, at A01 (quoting one law enforcement official as declaring that "[i]f the death penalty doesn't make him talk, nothing will").

161 Immanuel Kant, for example, who advocated the death penalty under a theory of just desert or retribution, opposed punishing an individual "merely as a means of promoting another good either to himself or to civil society. . . ." Kadish & Schulhofer, *supra* note 10, at 102 (quoting Immanuel Kant, The Philosophy of Law (W. Hastie trans., 1887)); *see also* Chanterelle Sung, *Torturing the Ticking Bomb Terrorist: An Analysis of Judicially Sanctioned Torture in the Context of Terrorism*, (Book Review), 23 B.C. Third World L.J. 193, 200 (2003). *See also* Dershowitz, *supra* note 20, at 142–43 (quoting Jeremy Bentham as justifying torture in certain extraordinary situations) (quoted in W.L. Twining & P.E. Twining, "Bentham on Torture," N. Ir. Legal Q., Autumn 1987, at 347). Kant strongly opposed the idea of mistreating those who are condemned to death. Kadish & Schulhofer, *supra* note 10, at 103.

162 This issue has arisen with the capture of leading figures of al Qaeda, such as Ramzi Bin al-Shibh and Khalid Sheikh Mohammed. The Bush–Cheney administration insisted that Khalid Sheikh Mohammed would be treated humanely. Eric Lichtblau & Adam Liptak, *Questioning to be Legal, Humane and Aggressive, the White House Says*, N.Y. Times, Mar. 4, 2003, at A13. (A Justice Department memorandum indicates, however, that the CIA waterboarded Khalid Shaikh Mohammed 183 times.) "There are a lot of ways short of torturing someone to get information from a subject," said one US official. *Id.* In dealing with other al Qaeda suspects, "[t]he United States has deprived suspects of sleep and light, kept them in awkward positions for hours and used psychological intimidation or deception to confuse and disorient them." *Id.* The European Court of Human Rights, however, declared a similar practice engaged in by the British against IRA prisoners to be "inhuman and degrading treatment," but not "torture" within the meaning of Article 3 of the European Convention on Human Rights. *See* Ireland v. United Kingdom, 25 Eur. Ct. H.R. (ser. A), para. 167 (1978). See chapters 3 and 4 for a more detailed discussion of this issue.

163 Green, et al., *supra* note 6, at 219 (comments of Kenneth Roth, Director of Human Rights Watch). Note the statement allegedly made by Daniel Pearl's kidnappers:

> The National Movement for the Restoration of Pakistani Sovereignty had kidnapped him [Pearl] and was holding him in 'very inhuman [*sic*] circum-stances', similar to the way that 'Pakistanis and nationals of other sovereign countries were kept in Cuba by the American Army . . . If the Americans keep our countryman in better conditions we will better the conditions of Mr. Pearl and all the other Americans we capture.

Fouda & Fielding, *supra* note 8, at 65 (quoting an email message sent report-edly by the kidnappers of Daniel Pearl, the Wall Street Journal reporter). A second email was sent threatening the execution of Pearl within 24 hours. *Id.* Apparently, authorities believe that Pearl was already dead by the time that the second email was sent. *Id.* That executing al Qaeda terrorists puts Americans and the US military at greater risk cannot be proved empirically. Furthermore, we cannot accept at face value the statements made by such individuals. But these and other experiences suggest that executing or otherwise mistreating al Qaeda captives *may* increase this risk.

164 *Id.* at 224.

165 *See* George H. Aldrich, *Some Reflections on the Origins of the 1977 Geneva Protocols*, *in* Studies and Essays on International Humanitarian Law and Red Cross Principles in Honor of Jean Pictet 129, 131 (Christophe Swinarski ed., 1984) (noting that "it was apparent that mistreatment of North Vietnamese prisoners by the South Vietnamese undermined our efforts to obtain better treatment for our men captured by North Vietnam"). However, there is an opposing view:

> The Geneva Conventions are coming to be regarded less and less as contracts concluded on a basis of reciprocity in the national interests of the parties . . . A state does not proclaim the principle of protection due to prisoners of war merely in the hope of improving the lot of a certain number of its own nationals. It does so out of respect for the human person.

3 Commentary, The Geneva Conventions of 12 August 1949, Geneva Convention III Relative to the Treatment of Prisoners of War 20 (Jean S. Pictet ed. 1960). In a colloquy between Professor Ruth Wedgwood of the Johns Hopkins University and Professor Jordan Paust of the University of Denver on January 3, 2004, Professor Wedgwood argued that humanitarian law is based, to a great extent, on reciprocity. In answer to a question from the audience, Professor Paust argued that certain aspects of humanitarian law, the prohibition against torture being the prominent example, are fundamental rights, not founded on the notion of reciprocity. The Constitutional and Enemy Combatants, Panel Discussion of the American Association of Law Schools' Annual Meeting, Atlanta, Georgia (Jan. 3, 2003) (attended by the author).

166 Ralph Michael Stein, *"Artillery Lends Dignity to What Otherwise Would be a Common Brawl"; An Essay on Post-Modern Warfare and the Classification of Captured Adversaries*, 14 Pace Int'l L. Rev. 133, 146 (2002). North Vietnam mistreated US captives, but South Vietnam, to whom the US turned over a large percentage of captured Viet Cong and North Vietnamese fighters generally mistreated them in turn. *See id.* By the way, the American Continental Army in the War of Independence generally treated British captives well, but the British did not return the favor, viewing the Americans as lawless rebels, not so different from how the US views al Qaeda today. *See id.* at 142.

167 This is not to suggest that all al Qaeda and Taliban are necessarily entitled to the protection of Geneva Conventions as prisoners of war. For a discussion of that issue, see Paust, *supra* note 21, at 8 n.16; Laura A. Dickinson, *Using Legal Process to Fight Terrorism, Detentions, Military Commissions, International Tribunals and the Rule of Law*, 75 S. Cal. L. Rev. 1407, 1472–77 (2003). *See also*, Jonathan D. Glater, *A.B.A. Urges Wider Rights in Cases Tried by Tribunals*, N.Y. Times, Aug. 13, 2003, at A18 (noting that the American Bar Association called upon Congress and the White House to ensure that all defendants before military tribunals have "adequate access" to civilian lawyers). *But see* Ruth Wedgewood, *al Qaeda, Terrorism and Military Commissions*, 96 Am. J. Int'l L. 328, 330 (2002) (defending detentions in Guantánamo Bay and use of military commissions as necessary security measures, and noting that "the fabric of American liberalism and democracy would be irreparably coarsened if government proves unable to provide a reasonable guarantee of life and safety to its citizens"); Lee A. Casey, David B. Rivkin, Jr., & Darin R. Bartram, *An Assessment of the Recommendations of the American Bar Association Regarding the Use of Military Commissions in the War on Terror*, The Federalist Society White Papers on Terrorism, *available at* www. fed-soc.org/Publications/Terrorism/ABAResponse.pdf (last visited Aug. 1, 2003) (criticizing some ABA recommendations on military commissions).

168 1977 Geneva Protocol I Additional to the Geneva Conventions of 12 August 1949, and Relating to the Protection of Victims of International Armed Con-

flicts art. 40, June 8, 1977, 1125 U.N.T.S. 3–608, 16 I.L.M. 1391 [hereinafter 1977 AP I]; *see also* Documents on the Laws of War 443 (Adam Roberts & Richard Guelff eds., 1989).

169 Regulations Respecting the Laws and Customs of War on Land, Annex to the International Disputes (Hague IV) art. 23(2), Oct. 18, 1907, 36 Stat. 2277 ("In addition to the prohibitions provided by special Conventions, it is especially forbidden . . . (d) To declare that no quarter will be given. . . .").

170 L.R. Penna, *Customary International Law and Protocol I: an Analysis of Some Provisions, in* Studies and Essays on International Humanitarian Law and Red Cross Principles in Honor of Jean Pictet, *supra* note 165, at 212.

171 *See, e.g.*, 1977 AP I, *supra* note 168, art. 75.7, at 465–66 (implicitly authorizing trial of individuals, including prisoners of war, for war crimes or crimes against humanity or both). *See also* Ronald J. Sievert, *War on Terrorism or Global Law Enforcement Operation*, 78 Notre Dame L. Rev. 307, 357 (2003).

172 1977 AP I, *supra* note 168, art. 77.5, at 467 (prohibiting imposition of death penalty upon minors, but implicitly authorizing death penalty for adults); *id.*, art. 7, at 466 (prohibiting execution of death penalty on mothers with "dependent infants").

173 One could add to this list the possibility of captured al Qaeda members being subject to degrading treatment and torture. As noted in chapter 4, Abu Zubaydah was originally thought by authorities to have a leadership position in al Qaeda, but they have largely reversed themselves on that position. According to the 2008 Washington Post article *available at* www.washingtonpost.com/wp-dyn/content/Article/2009/03/28/AR2009032802066_2.html, "Abu Zubaydah was not even an official member of al-Qaeda, according to a portrait of the man that emerges from court documents and interviews with current and former intelligence, law enforcement and military sources. Rather, he was a 'fixer' for radical Muslim ideologues, and he ended up working directly with al Qaeda only after Sept. 11—and that was because the United States stood ready to invade Afghanistan" and Abu Zubaydah "had strained and limited relations with bin Laden and only vague knowledge before the Sept. 11 attacks that something was brewing."

174 Furthermore, the failure to give quarter may ultimately strengthen the terrorist organization. Coogan, *supra* note 54, at 578. In 1987, the UK's Special Air Services Unit (SAS) lay in wait for IRA members who had planned to blow up a police barracks in Northern Ireland. *Id.* at 575–78. Allegedly carrying out a "shoot to kill" order, the SAS killed nine men, eight IRA members and one innocent bystander who happened to be Protestant. *Id.* at 578. Allegedly, the SAS ordered three IRA men to lie on the road and then proceeded to kill each of them. One commentator noted that each of the eight men's funerals drew enormous crowds and each probably recruited more than "fifty replacements for the IRA" while greatly increasing support for Sinn Fein. *Id.*

175 Juan Sanchez, Terrorism & Its (*sic*) Effects (2007).

176 *See* David Royse, *Abortion Clinics Safe So Far, Police Say; No Credible Threats Since Execution*, Miami Herald, Sept. 5, 2003, at B1, *available at* 2003 WL 62530293.

177 *See* Coogan, *supra* note 54. The crude execution of Saddam Hussein and his seemingly dignified response to his executioners may have had the effect of transforming one of the most brutal tyrants to walk the world's stage in the last century into a kind of martyr: "Suddenly we forgot that he was a dictator and that he killed thousands of people," said Roula Haddad, 33, a Lebanese Christian. "All our hatred for him suddenly turned into sympathy, sympathy with someone who was treated unjustly by an occupation force and its collaborators." Hassan M. Fattah, *Hanging Images Make Hussein a Martyr to Many in the Arab World*, N.Y. Times, Jan. 6, 2007, at A1, *available at* 2007 WLNR 234659.

10 Ethnic and racial profiling

A misguided counter-terror tactic?

Increased security measures naturally followed directly from 9/11, but they unfortunately included the authorities' ethnic and racial profiling of mostly foreign-born South Asians and Middle Eastern-appearing individuals. US governmental officials responded frenetically to September 11. Among other things, federal authorities immediately questioned and detained hundreds of immigrants from Islamic countries,[1] and Congress rushed to pass the Patriot Act[2] in such a short time that not only did US representatives little debate the bill, but few had time to read the "complex, far reaching anti-terrorism [and anti-immigrant] legislation" in its entirety.[3] Following the aftermath of September 11, policies and practices against the foreign-born have continued. Aside from former President George W. Bush's authorizing military tribunals to try only foreigners, not American citizens,[4,5] both the state and federal governments, often with the help of private citizens,[6] have engaged in unprecedented racial profiling of innocent South Asians, Arabs, and Muslims living in the US.[7]

Times of emergency may justify certain restrictions on liberties, but the nature of the terrorist challenge calls for a much more measured and nuanced response. Al Qaeda is said to have cells operating in as many as 100 countries.[8] As mentioned in the previous chapter, al Qaeda is best described as a decentralized network of extremist Islamic groups and individuals rather than a unified military organization.[9] To reduce or eliminate the threat they pose requires the cooperation of the governments, police officers, and individual citizens in the countries where al Qaeda-linked individuals and groups operate. Such help is necessary to obtain intelligence, arrests, capture, prosecution, and extradition of alleged terrorists, not to mention to cut off their funds and to confiscate their arms and other assets. Thus, to the extent that the US discriminates against or otherwise unfairly treats Arabs and Muslims living in America or wishing to visit, the more difficult it will be for the US to get the help it so desperately needs not only in the US, but also in Arab and Muslim countries and communities throughout the world.[10]

10.1 Ethnic and racial profiling in the wake of September 11

Despite strong words from high-ranking government officials that the Executive Branch had not engaged in ethnic profiling of Arabs and Muslims,[11] the policies and practices of Bush–Cheney administration departments negated that claim. Specifically, those departments carried out the following: (1) arresting, in mass, Arab and Muslim immigrants,[12] and carrying out preventive detention;[13] (2) conducting secret (closed) immigration hearings for these detainees;[14] (3) (a) requiring all male Arab and Muslim immigrants 16 and older who had been residing in the US with student visas, visitors' visas, and other temporary visas to register personally with the US Immigration and Customs Enforcement (ICE)[15] and (b) requiring that visitors from Arab and other selected countries be fingerprinted, photographed, and subjected to an interrogation under oath at ports of entry;[16] (4) changing priority for deporting "aliens," namely, the Immigration and Naturalization Service and legacy agencies seeking to deport 6,000 from Arab countries first, ahead of the 314,000 foreign nationals who had absconded;[17] (5) the Justice Department's interviewing 5,000–8,000 young immigrant men "based solely on their age, date of arrival, and country from which they [had come]," all being either Arabs or Muslims;[18] and (6) enlisting state and local police to enforce immigration laws, thereby implicitly encouraging those police forces to engage in more traditional racial profiling of Arabs, Muslims, Sikhs, and South Asians, namely, by stopping for questioning and investigation Arab-appearing drivers and pedestrians.[19] All these policies and practices will be examined in turn.

10.2 Mass arrests and preventive detention of Arab and Muslim immigrants

Within a matter of weeks after September 11, the federal government began to arrest a large number of primarily Arab and Muslim immigrants.[20] The federal government stopped reporting the number when it reached 1,147,[21] but at least 1,200 persons were arrested and later charged with immigration violations.[22] One scholar estimates that 2,000 had been arrested by April 2002.[23] A significant additional number of individuals were held as "material witnesses."[24] Only a handful of the detentions ultimately resulted in arrests for terrorist offenses.[25] Many of the detainees were held "for weeks or months" without charge.[26] Few were permitted initial access to counsel.[27] Some against whom orders of deportation or voluntary departure had already been served and entered were still held by the Immigration and Naturalization Service (now called Immigration and Customs Enforcement) under the Department of Homeland Security, even though they had been scheduled to leave the country.[28] Preventive detention generally is not permitted in the US,[29] but it was essentially carried out against some of these detainees:

[Of all those arrested, 752] were charged with immigration violations. These so-called "special interest" immigration detainees were presumed guilty of links to terrorism and incarcerated for months until the government "cleared" them of such connections. By February 2002, the Department of Justice acknowledged that most of the original "special interest" detainees were no longer of interest to its anti-terrorist efforts, and none were indicted for crimes related to the September 11 attacks. Most were deported for visa violations.[30]

One study of the detentions revealed that more than one-third of the detainees for whom information was available came from either Egypt or Pakistan.[31] The researchers were unable to find any rational basis for targeting nationals from these two countries.[32] Perhaps more troubling, the researchers found that the arrest of foreign nationals from Muslim countries did not appear to be based on an official policy of racial profiling but upon private citizens, engaging in racial profiling themselves, who phoned in tips to law enforcement agents about Muslims or Muslim-looking individuals living in their communities or places of work.[33] Apparently, law enforcement personnel acquiesced in the practice of racial profiling by picking up those whom citizens had identified.[34]

10.3 Conducting secret (closed) immigration hearings for the Arab and Muslim immigrants who were arrested and detained

The public, the press, and family members had been excluded from virtually all immigration hearings conducted for these immigrants.[35] Before September 11, immigration judges had the discretion to close immigration hearings on a case-by-case basis. Generally, immigration hearings are not closed.[36] The Attorney General, however, changed the rule, requiring immigration judges to close the proceedings at the request of the prosecutor.[37] Apparently, the Justice Department ordered all the prosecutors to make such a request in these post September 11 cases.[38] Attorneys representing the immigrants during the closed hearings reported that no classified information had been introduced in the hearings.[39] Although due process is more limited in immigration hearings than in a criminal trial, the principle of public trials and hearings is fundamental.[40] It should only be deviated from in cases of extreme necessity. The blanket approach here, where virtually every one of these immigrants had a closed proceeding, on its face violates that principle, particularly absent any apparent demonstrated need for the closures in all these cases.[41]

Aside from closing the immigration hearings, the Justice Department had conducted the proceedings against these immigrants in virtually unparalleled secrecy.[42] "Chief Immigration Judge Michael Creppy instructed immigration judges not to list the cases on the public docket, and to refuse to confirm or deny that they even exist."[43] The Justice Department refused to disclose the names of those it detained.[44] The US Supreme Court refused to grant *certiorari* in a case that upheld the Justice Department's decision.[45]

10.4 Requiring Arab and Muslim immigrants who had been residing in the US with student visas, visitors visas, and other temporary visas to personally register with the Immigration and Naturalization Service

During the 1979 Iran hostage crisis, all Iranian students studying in the US were required to report to the Immigration and Naturalization Service (INS).[46] As a result, the INS deported a significant number of Iranians.[47] In 2002, the Justice Department issued a similar order, under its "Special Registration" Program, establishing the National Security Entry-Exit Registration System (NSEERS)[48] and requiring that the following personally appear at INS offices: foreign-born males, 16 years of age or older, from almost exclusively Arab and Muslim countries, who hold student visas, visitors' visas, and other temporary visas.[49] Apparently, the Congressional mandate driving the implementation of NSEERS intended that the program cover all foreign visitors, but it started with Iran, Iraq, Syria, Sudan, Libya, and North Korea, all Arab and Muslim countries except for the last mentioned.[50] The Department established four groups from the following countries that were required to come in and register at designated dates: "[I] Iraq, Iran, Libya, Sudan, and Syria; [II] Afghanistan, Algeria, Bahrain, Eritrea, Lebanon, Morocco, North Korea, Oman, Qatar, Somalia, Tunisia, United Arab Emirates, and Yemen; [III] Bangladesh, Egypt, Indonesia, Jordan, and Kuwait; and [IV] Saudi Arabia and Pakistan."[51] The first registration deadline was in December 2002;[52] the registration deadline for the first two groups ended February 7, 2002.[53] The third group's deadline was March 21, 2002,[54] and the fourth group's deadline was April 25, 2003.[55]

Although the Justice Department initially assured those subject to the call-in registration program that the purpose of the registration was to track foreigners and to obtain leads on terrorists, the Department also used the registration process to determine if those registering had violated immigration regulations. Apparently, 500 to 1,000 individuals "were detained" after registering on December 10, 2003 "in the Los Angeles/Orange County area alone. . . ."[56] The program, however, apparently yielded little in the way of arrests for terrorist crimes.

10.5 Requiring that visitors from Arab and other selected countries be fingerprinted, photographed, and subjected to an interrogation under oath at ports of entry

A second aspect of the NSEERS required selected individuals at various points of entry to be fingerprinted, photographed, and subjected to interrogation under oath.[57] Again, this program targeted foreigners from the same 24 Arab and Muslim countries, with the addition of North Korea.[58] These controls applied to students, tourists, business visitors, and other temporary visa holders.[59]

After considerable protest on the part of the Arab-American community and others,[60] the Department of Homeland Security decided to abolish the mandatory annual reregistration requirement, under the Special Registration Program or under the Port of Entry (POE) program, effective December 2, 2003.[61] Then Department of Homeland Security Deputy Secretary, Asa Hutchinson, said that the DHS "will utilize a more tailored system that is individual-specific rather than the broad categories [of people] by geography."[62] By September 30, 2003, 177,260 people had registered with the NSEERS program as a whole. They will not have to reregister annually as had been required under the original program.[63] Exit controls, however, for these individuals remain in effect.[64]

10.6 Changing priority for deporting "aliens," namely, the Immigration and Naturalization Service's seeking to deport 6,000 from Arab countries first, ahead of the 314,000 foreign nationals who absconded

At first glance, the so-called "Absconder Apprehension Initiative" appears to be a sound enforcement tactic. Of the estimated 314,000 foreign-born from nations around the world who had removal orders against them, the US government targeted approximately 6,000 from Arab and Muslim countries first.[65] The 9/11 hijackers and al Qaeda were Arab and Muslim. The argument runs that it stands to reason that other members of that organization might be among the 6,000 from these selected "al Qaeda harboring" countries.[66]

The difficulty is that the targeted persons are being singled out solely because of their nationality. This kind of racial/nationality profiling has apparently yielded little, if any intelligence or arrests for terrorism offenses, when employed in the call-in registration program or in the "voluntary" interview program.[67] The Absconder Initiative has apparently been equally fruitless. A report of the Presidential Commission investigating the 9/11 attacks expressly found as follows: "[W]e have not learned that any of the absconders were deported under a terrorism statute, prosecuted for terrorist-related crimes, or linked in any way to terrorism."[68] As some commentators have noted, including the former Commissioner of the Immigration and Naturalization Service, "[t]his [absconder initiative] has marginal security benefits, while further equating national origin with dangerousness."[69] Furthermore, there is every reason to believe that Arabs and Muslims living here or abroad will see this as yet another example of the American government blatantly discriminating against individuals with Arab and Islamic backgrounds.[70]

10.7 The Justice Department Task Force's interviewing 5,000–8,000 young immigrant men based solely on their age, date of arrival, and country from which they had come, all being either Arabs or Muslims

The Justice Department also initiated a Task Force program to "voluntarily" interview 5,000 immigrant men, between the ages of 18 and 33, who came almost exclusively from Arab or Muslim countries and who entered the US after January 1, 2000.[71] The program was expanded to include an additional 3,000. The Task Force was composed not only of Justice Department personnel, but also of local and state police officers.[72] Nominally to obtain leads on terrorism both here and abroad, a Justice Department memo suggests that the voluntary interviews also had the purpose of potentially arresting suspicious interviewees and those who had violated immigration laws.[73] Apparently, approximately 20 were arrested as a result of the interviews.[74] Before the interviews, the authorities apparently lacked either probable cause or reasonable suspicion that any of these immigrants had committed immigration violations, let alone that they were engaged in terrorist crimes or knew about terrorist activities. The basis of the interviews was the nationality of the targeted persons, plus their gender, age, and time of entry.

10.8 Enlisting state and local police in immigration enforcement, implicitly encouraging those police forces to engage in more traditional racial profiling of Arabs, Muslims, Sikhs, and South Asians, namely, by stopping for questioning and for investigation Arab-appearing drivers and pedestrians[75]

Before September 11, state and local police were generally precluded from enforcing the civil provisions of the immigration laws.[76] Reasons for discouraging local policing in this area included the complexity of immigration law, an area that is generally outside a police officer's training and knowledge, and the risk of discriminatory enforcement of the law against people of color and other "foreign looking" individuals.[77] The Bush–Cheney Justice Department, however, changed that policy, enlisting the aid of state and local police in enforcing the immigration laws.[78] For example, the Justice Department added to the FBI's National Crime Information (NCIC) Database, the names of the approximately 314,000 "aliens" who remained in the country despite deportation or removal orders.[79] Local law enforcement personnel can access the NCIC.[80] The INS Commissioner explained that this policy change would enable local and state police to help with "removal efforts."[81] Furthermore, the Justice Department asked local police forces to help interview 8,000 Muslim males, as noted in the previous section.[82]

Although using the local police to enforce immigration regulations in the wake of September 11 may appear superficially reasonable, such a policy raises serious questions.[83] "Co-opting state and local police to make immigration arrests undermines public safety and encourages racial profiling."[84] It discourages undocumented immigrants from coming forward to help the police solve crimes[85] and fosters resort to vigilante justice. Numerous police departments, the National Association of Counties, and the National League of Cities have taken stands against using state and local police to make immigration arrests.[86]

Unfortunately, immediately after 9/11 there was substantial evidence that state and local police engaged in racial profiling of Arabs, Muslims, Sikhs, and South Asians.[87] As in the case of profiling African–Americans and Latinos, many local police were apparently stopping Arab-looking drivers and pedestrians pretextually, solely or in part because of their appearance.[88] Arab-looking individuals were also being stopped or questioned in other places at least in part because of their ethnicity.[89] Local police have apparently gone back to profiling African–Americans and Latinos, particularly the latter.

10.9 Racial profiling: a history and an analysis— September 11 as justifying racial profiling

Given the nationality of the authors of the September 11 attacks, why should the US not target immigrants and visitors from Arab and Muslim countries for investigation, prosecution, and deportation? After all, there may be other sleeper al Qaeda cells here in the US.[90] Furthermore, Arab, Muslims, and their organizations may be financing terror groups against us.

For example, Stuart Taylor had opposed racial profiling black drivers for drugs, "driving while black" (DWB). He argues, however, that racial profiling of Arabs and Muslims is justified in airports, because *inter alia* "preventing mass murder . . . is [an] infinitely more important rationale than the rationale behind DWB profiling (finding illegal drugs or guns)[, and a] virulent perversion of Islam is, so far, the only mass movement in the world so committed to mass-murdering Americans that its fanatics are willing to kill themselves in the process [and that some of these people] have lived legally in America for years. . . ."[91] Taylor adds that "DWB is singularly race-based, which contravenes both the letter and the spirit of the Constitution. Airport profiling takes multiple factors into account, such as when the ticket was purchased, how the subject responds to questions, etc."[92]

This argument, however, fails to recognize how crude the device of racial profiling is, the ease with which al Qaeda and other terrorist groups can circumvent it,[93] the corrosive effect it can have on Arabs and Muslims and Middle Eastern-appearing men living in the US and elsewhere, and how much it creates the perception of an American anti-Arab and anti-Muslim animus[94] both at home and in other parts of the world.

History may help explain why both this intuitive and reasoned justification of ethnic profiling is wrong. In the Second World War, the US interned 110,000 to 120,000 people of Japanese descent, including 70,000 American citizens.[95] Far fewer German nationals were interned in the US during the Second World War.[96] The US never interned German Americans or Italian Americans during that conflict.[97] Italian nationals living in the US at the time, however, did suffer hardship.[98]

Americans generally regard the internments as a blot on US history. Nearly every member then serving on the US Supreme Court had by September 11, 2001, condemned *Korematsu v. United States*,[99] the decision that upheld the Japanese internments against constitutional attack. Congress has condemned the program and enacted legislation, authorizing reparations to surviving victims.[100]

But perhaps most significant for this analysis, few Japanese-Americans or Japanese immigrants ever engaged in espionage, sabotage, or acts against the US during the Second World War.[101] Unlike the present "war against terrorism," the US had declared war against the enemy, Japan, and, at least the non-American-citizen Japanese immigrants then residing in the US theoretically owed their allegiance to that country.[102] Despite that presumption,[103] nationality and ethnicity actually provided little basis for demonstrating that the individuals involved posed a threat to the US.

10.10 US practice of racial profiling before September 11

Well before September 11, the US had an unfortunate history with race relations generally and, more specifically, with allowing the police to pick out, stop, question, and investigate individuals based wholly or in part on their race.[104] Many police throughout the country often routinely stopped black and Latino drivers, suspecting (or hoping) to find evidence of drugs or other crimes.[105] In the last ten years, however, racial profiling has been increasingly attacked. DWB has been roundly condemned.[106] Picking individuals out because they belong to a minority group and then subjecting them to criminal investigation encourages lazy police practices,[107] humiliates the individuals who are so selected,[108] and causes resentment in the minority community against the police.[109] Lastly, such "racial profiling," which is bound to produce a large number of false positives, is an inefficient use of scarce police resources.[110]

10.11 The fallacy of racial profiling

In a country as racially diverse as the US, with millions of people representing each identifiable ethnic or racial group, the racial or ethnic background of an individual has virtually no probative value except to exclude that person from the "circle of suspicion."[111] Thus, for example, let us assume that reliable witnesses told the police that they saw a white male leave a van (which turned out to be filled with explosives) outside of the federal building in Oklahoma City. The explosives are subsequently detonated, causing massive loss of life and property. In investigating this crime, the police could properly exclude all non-white persons from the "circle of suspects."[112] That the alleged perpetrator is apparently white and male hardly justifies questioning every white male in Oklahoma or in surrounding states. Not only would it require enormous police resources to do so, the odds of finding the actual perpetrator by this method would be exceedingly remote.

One might argue that there are fewer members in a minority group than there are whites in the US.[113] Mathematical analysis, however, supports the notion that race or ethnicity alone provide scant basis for suspecting an individual of terrorist crimes. Most population surveys estimate that there are 2.8 million to 6 million Arabs and Muslims living in the US.[114] In purely mathematical terms, the odds that race or ethnicity alone will yield suspects is in the order of one in several thousands, odds so remote as to make race or nationality of relatively little help in identifying terrorists.[115]

Professor Sharon Davies explains these phenomena through the following hypotheticals. Assume a reliable witness identifies the perpetrator of a robbery as being a "white male." One could set forth the following syllogism:

> Major Premise: "The person who committed this robbery was a white
>   male.",
> Minor Premise: "Defendant is a non-white male."
> Conclusion: "Defendant did not commit this robbery."[116]

The result of this syllogism appears almost self-evident,[117] but Professor Davies correctly points out that the converse is not true:

> Major Premise: "The person who committed this robbery was a white
>   male."
> Minor Premise: "Defendant is a white male."
> Conclusion: "Defendant committed the robbery."[118]

Unless there is only one white male, the syllogism is false. She notes:

> [T]he addition of just one other white male to the cohort would reduce
> the chances of Defendant's responsibility for the crime by a full half. The
> addition of two white males to the group would lower the odds to one
> third, and so on. This should make it clear how the possession of a
> characteristic shared by a group very quickly loses its usefulness as means
> of including a particular individual within a circle of suspicion. The
> significance of group characteristics, such as race or ethnicity, drops
> precipitously as more and more persons are known to share that same
> characteristic. In a diverse population, which espouses a commitment to
> the principle of unfettered freedom of movement, its utility quickly
> approaches (even if it never quite reaches) zero.[119]

The mathematical result appears counterintuitive, but it demonstrates that racial or ethnic profiling is among the shallowest bases for suspecting a particular individual of criminal activity in a society like the US, with millions representing each ethnic group.[120]

10.12 Racial profiling encourages sloppy and inefficient police practices

Relying on racial profiles rather than evidence that a particular person or persons have engaged in criminal or other terrorist activities stifles sound policing and investigating practices. By focusing on individuals who fit a racial profile, the police are inevitably going to come up with a large number of false positives.[121] This may have the effect of lulling officers and causing them to overlook those who do not fit the profile.[122] For example, Richard Reid, the al Qaeda shoe bomber, is a British citizen, originally from Jamaica, and is not Arab or "Middle-Eastern looking."[123] Zacarias Moussaoui, convicted of conspiring to carry out the September 11 attacks, is a French citizen. Jose Padilla, the alleged dirty bomber, is a Puerto Rican-American.[124] None of these individuals would have been subject to the "Special Registration" program after having arrived in the US.

During the Second World War, the Japanese relied primarily upon Caucasian spies, not those of Japanese ancestry.[125] Al Qaeda is said to have over one billion dollars in assets.[126] With such resources, al Qaeda could easily hire white Americans or non-Arab or non-Muslim nationals to carry out operations in the US. Senior law enforcement officials stated in a memo of October 2002, which "circulated to American law enforcement agents worldwide," that "[f]undamentally, believing that you can achieve safety by looking at characteristics [racial profiling] is silly, If your goal is preventing attacks . . . you want your eyes and ears looking for pre-attack behaviors, not characteristics."[127]

Some police officials have argued that members of minority groups commit certain crimes in greater numbers than other racial groups, justifying the use of race as grounds for "reasonable suspicion."[128] Researchers and scholars have questioned this assumption, particularly in the context of drug offenses.[129] Some scholars argue that racial profiling of minorities has created a self-fulfilling prophecy: because more members of minority groups are investigated, more are found criminally responsible for the target offenses.[130] Had white persons been investigated as thoroughly, according to these scholars, more white persons would be found criminally responsible for the target offenses.[131]

To the extent that some minorities are believed to commit certain crimes more than other groups, query whether the difference may be attributable to economic class rather than to race or ethnic group identification.[132] If one controls for economic class, might even the perceived difference in crime rates among racial groups disappear or become significantly less? Even assuming *arguendo* that some racial groups commit more of a certain offense than others do, statistics demonstrate that the overwhelming number of members of a given race or ethnic group are law-abiding. Since race or national origin is generally an improbable indicator of criminality, racial profiling is unjustified even if one accepts for argument sake the above-mentioned assumption.[133]

Regarding Arab and Muslim immigrants, not to mention Sikhs and South Asians, there is little data to support the conclusion that members of those populations are more likely to engage in terrorist activities against the US than members of other groups.[134] After all, before September 11, the author of the most serious terrorist crime on US soil was a white, Roman Catholic male who was raised in upstate New York.[135] Perhaps the most telling evidence of the ineffectiveness of racial profiling is the apparent failure of the US government's policies profiling Arabs, Muslims, Sikhs, and South Asians to uncover terrorist criminal activity against the US.[136]

10.13 Racial profiling offends Arabs, Muslims, Sikhs, and South Asians and their communities, discouraging them from being willing allies in the fight against terrorism

Some have argued that although Arabs and Muslims living in the US have been subjected to racial profiling, such a measure is reasonable given the enormity of September 11 (and subsequent terrorist attacks) and the ethnic identity of the perpetrators, their membership in al Qaeda, and the ethnicity of other Islamic fundamentalist terrorist actors.[137] Furthermore, the government has detained some Arabs and Muslims and has scrutinized the activities of many Arabs and Muslims, but it has not forcibly detained all Arabs and Muslims regardless of their citizenship as the US did to the Japanese during the Second World War. Many Americans are likely to agree with Kathleen Parker, who stated, "Being threatened or otherwise harmed because of your ethnic origin is persecution. Being subjected to a little extra scrutiny because, as it happens, your ethnic origin is the same as that of terrorists who just killed more than 6,000 innocent civilians, is inconvenience."[138]

The targets of racial profiling, however, appear to have a different perception. "Even the suggestion that people should tolerate modest impositions is galling . . . [w]hat looks like a light touch to observers can feel like an awfully heavy hand to those that feel it."[139] There is some evidence that racial profiling might inflict both humiliation and "psychic harm."[140] For example, in June 1993, a black bank executive was pulled over by Toledo, Ohio police allegedly for not having a front license plate. He had just attended a conference. Instead of issuing a ticket, the officer required him to assume a spread eagle position while the officer subjected him to a body search. At that precise moment, a bus of conference participants passed by. He is reported to have stated, "I never felt so degraded, humiliated and belittled in all my life."[141] Likewise, Texas state judge Gilberto Hinojosa is often pulled over by immigration authorities because of his Latino appearance. He stated that "Southern

Texas 'feels like occupied territory . . . [i]t does not feel like we're in the United States of America.' "[142]

Alternatively, consider Ejaz Haider, an editor of an English-language news magazine in Pakistan, who was visiting the US as a Fellow of the Brookings Institution in Washington, D.C. Complying with immigration regulations upon arriving here, Mr. Haider registered with the INS (now ICE) who told him to report for an interview within 40 days.[143] After speaking with officials in the State Department and INS, he was told he did not have to report. INS agents subsequently arrested him and told him he would be spending a night in jail.[144] Through the intercession of the Brookings Institution, he was released, but others lacking such connections might have faced harsher treatment.[145]

Racial profiling is humiliating because it amounts to discriminatory treatment based on race.[146] In the antiterrorism context, the population as a whole does not share the burden of heightened security measures. Rather, those who bear the burden are a discrete and insular minority, the foreign-born from a select group of countries and others who look like them.[147] Racial profiling amounts to presuming someone is a criminal solely because of his or her race or nationality. Even when race is "but a factor" among other factors considered, it helps serve as a substitute for real evidence that a person may be involved in criminal activity.[148]

What authorities seem to ignore is the effect that such race-based policies have on the innocent individuals and the communities that the policies inevitably touch.[149] The overwhelming number of Arabs, Muslims, Sikhs, and South Asians that live or temporarily reside in the US are law-abiding. They are or could be natural allies of the US in the so-called "war against terrorism." They are in the best position to know if members of their communities are plotting against us.[150] They could give us intelligence, leads, tips, and serve as witnesses to any planned "terrorist activity." Good law enforcement requires developing close ties to community leaders and gaining the trust of individual members of the community.[151] Racially profiling Arabs and Muslims and others weakens ties to community leaders and undermines the trust of the community in the fairness and impartiality of law enforcement officials. Instead of enhancing security racial profiling thus may be threatening US security by weakening the best source of evidence the US would probably be able to obtain, evidence from others in the Arab, Muslim, Sikh, and South Asian communities. The next section discusses the international implications of mistreating Arabs and Muslims in the US and elsewhere.

10.14 Combating a terrorist organization like al Qaeda

Examining the policies of the US towards Iraq and al Qaeda, one gets the impression that, to paraphrase Einstein's comment about the advent of the nuclear bomb,[152] September 11 has changed everything but our thinking.

The Bush–Cheney administration certainly attempted to change our ideas about fundamental legal principles such as access to legal counsel, confidentiality of communications with counsel, the condemnation of indefinite detention, of torture and degrading treatment, and of so-called preventive wars against countries that do not immediately threaten the US. But such reflexive ideas and policies seem based on the notion this nation lives in a vacuum, that any violations of basic principles of domestic or international law that the US commits in the name of security are not only justified, but will necessarily advance US security. The growing evidence, however, suggests that the Bush–Cheney administration's international and domestic policies directed against Arabs and Muslims may actually have been counterproductive in the "war on terror."

A classic terrorist tactic is to provoke an overreaction:

> One [terrorist] recruiting tactic is to stage spectacular acts of aggression that make the insurgency appear to be powerful and exciting. What the [terrorist] entrepreneur wants to have happen next is a big indiscriminate counterattack, which, in effect, means that his enemy has been put to work as his chief recruiter.[153]

Unfortunately, the invasion of Iraq, a Muslim country (albeit with a secular and repressive regime), has been perceived as "a big indiscriminate counterattack" in the Arab and Muslim worlds.[154] Likewise, mistreating Arabs and Muslims, both in the US and abroad, is likely to strengthen the extremist elements in Muslim communities in the US and overseas.[155] Moderate, more democratic leading elements in those societies have had difficulty defending against the argument that the US is anti-Arab and anti-Muslim.[156] Consequently, the US should adopt, not only with use of its military but also with its policies at home, an approach that is most likely to gain the cooperation of US allies and of the moderates within the Muslim world and that will most likely isolate al Qaeda.[157] President Barack Obama has directly engaged Muslims to help improve relations with the Islamic World, but healing such a rift will require challenging deeds that match inspiring words.

This chapter does not discuss economic and political measures necessary to enhance human, civil, and economic rights in the Arab and Islamic worlds.[158] To achieve its strategic objectives, the US must give both the fact and appearance of treating any accused Muslim fairly. For example, after the UK established internment without trial in Northern Ireland in 1971 to combat the Irish Republican Army, a policy that was largely directed only at the Northern Irish Catholic community, support for the IRA increased: "The use of internment effectively alienated a sizeable minority of the population of Northern Ireland and made impossible any cooperation with authorities."[159]

That experience is particularly relevant for the struggle against al Qaeda. As previously discussed, one would expect that members of the Arab and Muslim communities in the US would know most about the activities of other Muslims and Arabs in the US.[160] Instead of attacking the communities, law enforcement should embrace them.[161] In that way, the US law enforcement is more likely to be able to identify and apprehend those likely to be plotting against the US.[162] This scattershot method of racial and ethnic profiling is likely to discourage community members from coming forward with the information American law enforcement needs to stop this threat.[163]

Furthermore, racial profiling of Muslims has another fatal flaw: Most Muslims, like most Catholics, for example, do not fit into any particular racial profile. Additionally, racial criteria are disturbing because they harken back to the era of world colonization, slavery, and Jim Crow. The baggage of race and racial discrimination distorts clear thinking and logical analysis, so necessary in the investigation of criminal activity, including terrorist offenses. Developing more effective counterterrorism policies and practices demands jettisoning faulty and prejudicial approaches, however intuitively reasonable they may seem.

Although understandable given the authors of September 11 and the awesome magnitude of the attacks, the US government's policy of racial profiling Arabs and Muslims generally is likely to contribute to anti-American attitudes, both within the US and elsewhere, to discourage Arabs and Muslims from cooperating with the US police and military officials, and to weaken moderate elements of Arab and Muslim societies while strengthening the extremist elements both domestically and overseas.

Additionally, racial profiling is morally wrong. During the Iran hostage crisis, the author represented two Iranian students. Then, as after 9/11, Iranians (like Iraqis) were required to report to and register with the Immigration and Naturalization Service. Accompanying the Iranian students into the federal building in Los Angeles, one saw in the institutional corridors of INS a sea of Iranian faces. It was chilling. America is more true to itself and can better protect its people by adopting more measured investigative approaches to fully garner the aid of its allies and the cooperation of the Muslim and Arab communities throughout the world.

Notes

1 *See* Ctr. for Nat'l Sec. Studies v. Dep't of Justice, 331 F.3d 918 (D.C. Cir. 2003). Furthermore, the New York FBI office, which had carried out more arrests than any other FBI office, took an "aggressive" approach to the 9/11 detainees. Without making an individual assessment of a detainee's ties to terrorism, the New York office "broadly" interpreted the "[person] of interest" designation to apply to virtually all Arab Muslims who were arrested on immigration violations. Office of Inspector General, Department of Justice, *The 9/11 Detainees: A Review of the Treatment of Aliens Held on Immigration Charges in Connection with the Investigation of the 9/11 Attacks*, Apr. 2003, at 16, *available at* http://www.fas.org/irp/agency/doj/detainees.pdf [hereinafter IG Justice Dep't Report]. This designation had "enormous impact" on the detainees, causing them to be sent to maximum security prisons and drastically decreasing the chance that they would be released on bond. *Id.*

    This chapter is largely adapted from my article *Targeting the Foreign Born by Race and Nationality: Counter-Productive in the "War on Terrorism"?*, 16 Pace Int'l L. Rev. 19 (2004), and is reprinted here with permission of the Pace International Law Review.

2   Uniting and Strengthening America by Providing Appropriate Tools Required to Intercept and Obstruct Terrorism Act of 2001, Pub. L. No. 107–56, 115 Stat. 272 (2002).

3   Robin Toner & Neil L. Lewis, *A Nation Challenged, House Passes Terrorism Bill Much Like Senate's, but With 5-Year Limit*, N.Y. Times, Oct. 13, 2001, at B6. The Patriot Act contains several provisions that may in application, if not on their face, be unfair to immigrants. Section 411, for example, makes an immigrant deportable for contributing "material support" to an organization designated by the Secretary of State as a terrorist organization. The Act does not require that the immigrant know the organization has been so designated or that the support provided will necessarily contribute to a terrorist operation. *See New Antiterrorism Legislation Summarized*, 78 Interpreter Releases 1703, 1704 (Nov. 5, 2001). Section 412 permits the Attorney General to detain any alien he certifies that he "reasonably believes to be a terrorist or to have engaged in any other activity that endangers the national security of the United States." *Id.*

4   *See* President George W. Bush's Military Order, Detention, Treatment, and Trial of Certain Non-Citizens in the War Against Terrorism, 66 Fed. Reg. 57833 at sec. 1(a) (Nov. 13, 2001).

5   The US also initially targeted only visitors from predominantly Arab and Muslim countries, requiring them to be fingerprinted, photographed, and subjected to an interrogation under oath. *See* David Cole, *Enemy Aliens*, 54 Stan. L. Rev. 953 (2002); excerpts from which are reprinted with the permission of Stanford Law Review.

       . To those who pit Americans against immigrants and citizens against non-citizens, to those who scare peace-loving people with phantoms of lost liberty, my message is this: Your tactics only aid terrorists, for they erode our national unity and diminish our resolve. They give ammunition to America's enemies, and pause to America's friends.

    Id. at 593 (quoting Attorney General John Ashcroft's Dec. 6, 2001 address). I am indebted to Professor Cole for his leadership and inspiration in this area.

    Leadership Conference on Civil Rights and Education Fund, *Wrong Then, Wrong Now, Racial Profiling before and after September 11, 2001*, at 23, *available at* www.civilrights.org/publications/reports/racial_profiling_report.pdf [hereinafter Civil Rights and Education Fund] (noting that after September 11, the government "detained hundreds – perhaps thousands – of Arabs, South Asians and Muslims on suspicion of terrorist activity" (citing Ctr. for Nat'l Sec. Studies v. Dep't of Justice, 215 F. Supp. 2d 94 (D.D.C. 2002))).

6   Since September 11, Arabs and Muslims living in the US have reported increased incidence of discrimination in housing and employment. *See* Muzaffar A. Chishti, et al., *America's Challenge: Domestic Security, Civil Liberties, and National Unity after September 11*, 80 Interpreter Releases 1193, 1195–96 (Aug. 25, 2003) (noting that the Equal Employment Opportunity Commission ("EEOC") "received over 700 complaints concerning September 11-related employment discrimination in the first 15 months after the attacks"). In addition, hate crimes against Muslims "soared after September 11, rising more than 1,500 percent [but] [t]he number of violent hate crimes has since tapered off." *Id.* at 1195. The study also showed that the "majority of noncitizens detained since September 11 . . . had spouses, children, or other family relationships in the U.S." *Id.* at 1194. *See* Cole, *supra* note 5, at 961. Memorandum from Michael

Creppy, Chief Immigration Law Judge, *Memorandum to All Immigration Judges* (Sept. 21, 2001), *in* 78 Interpreter Releases 1386 (Dec. 3, 2001).

See North Jersey Media Group, Inc. v. Ashcroft, 205 F. Supp. 2d 288, 299–300 (D.N.J. 2002) (citing 8 C.F.R. § 242.16(a) and 8 C.F.R. § 3.27), (noting that the immigration regulations promulgated since 1964 created a presumption that deportation hearings would be open) *rev'd*, 308 F.3d 198 (3d Cir. 2002), *cert. denied* 123 S. Ct. 2215 (2003) (holding that the INS may close so-called "special interest" immigration deportation hearings).

See also United States, Hate Crimes Against Arabs and Muslims and Persons Perceived to be Arab or Muslim After September 11, 14 Human Rights Watch Annual Report, No. 6(g) (Nov. 2002) (noting that Arab and Muslim organizations reported over 2,000 hate crimes and the FBI received a 17-fold increase in complaints of hate crimes in 2001 after September 11).

7   *See infra* note 49 and *see* Sharon L. Davies, *Profiling Terror*, 1 Ohio St. J. Crim. L. 45, 51 n.27 (2003). *See also* State Department Press Release on New Exit-Entry System, *infra* note 49, at 2. Registration of Certain Nonimmigrant Aliens From Designated Countries, 67 Fed. Reg. 67,766, 67,767 (Nov. 6, 2002). Registration of Certain Nonimmigrant Aliens From Designated Countries, 67 Fed. Reg. 77,136, 77,137 (Dec. 16, 2002). *See also* Permission for Certain Nonimmigrant Aliens From Designated Countries to Register in a Timely Fashion, 68 Fed. Reg. 2,366 (Jan. 16, 2003) (reopening the registration period for the first two groups, extending the time for them to register to February 7, 2003).

Registration of Certain Nonimmigrant Aliens from Designated Counties, 68 Fed. Reg. 2,363-03, 2,364 (Jan. 16, 2003) (requiring the specified nationals from Bangladesh, Egypt, Indonesia, Jordan, and Kuwait to register by March 28, 2003). Registration of Certain Nonimmigrant Aliens from Designated Countries, 68 Fed. Reg. 8,046, 8,047 (Feb. 19, 2003) (extending the previous deadline). *See also* State Department Press Release on New Exit-Entry System, *infra* note 49, at 2.

Such a policy may be counterproductive for other reasons. Individuals who have information about terrorist activity, but who have minor immigration infractions may decide not to register or to cooperate with authorities. Civil Rights and Education Fund, *supra* note 5. As of December 2, 2003 when the Department of State announced that the Special Registration Program was to end, 83,519 individuals had been registered. State Department Press Release on New Entry-Exit System, *infra* note 49, at 2.

Data from Asian American Legal Defense Fund, citing to the Bureau of Citizenship and Immigration Services (formerly part of the Immigration and Naturalization Service), current as of May 11, 2003. It is not known what intelligence leads, if any, have come from these various programs.

8   Jayshree Bajoria, *al-Qaeda (aka al-Qaida, al-Qa'ida)*, The Couns. on Foreign Rel., Apr. 18, 2008, *available at* www.cfr.org/publication/9126/#5. *See* Dan Balz & Bob Woodward, *America's Chaotic Road to War; Bush's Global Strategy Began to Take Shape in First Frantic Hours After Attack*, Wash. Post, Jan. 27, 2002, at A1. *See* chapter 9, note 113, for a discussion of how the invasion of Afghanistan had the presumably unintended consequence of further decentralizing al Qaeda and its allies.

9   *See* Bajoria, *supra* note 8; *see also* chapter 9, notes 40–43, discussing so-called leaderless resistance, the nature of al Qaeda, and the importance of gaining the support of the Muslim communities throughout the world to counterterrorism.

10 The UN Committee on the Elimination of Racial Discrimination, which monitors compliance with the Race Convention, has condemned racial profiling and has urged states to end the practice. *Concluding observations of the Committee on the*

Elimination of Racial Discrimination: United States of America, paras. 380–407, 14/08/2001, A/56/18. *See* International Convention on the Elimination of All Forms of Racial Discrimination arts. 8–15, Dec. 21, 1965, 600 U.N.T.S. 195, 212, *available at* http://www2.ohchr.org/english/law/cerd.htm (authorizing the establishment of the Committee and defining its competence).

11   Cole, *supra* note 5, at 593 (quoting Attorney General John Ashcroft's December 6, 2001 address).

12   *Id.* at 961. *See also* Civil Rights and Education Fund, *supra* note 5, at 23.

13   Professor Cole estimated that 2,000 Arab and Muslim immigrants had been held for months without charge by April 2002. *See* Cole, *supra* note 5, at 960. *See also* Center for National Security Studies v. Dep't. of Justice, 331 F.3d 918, 921 (D.C. Cir. 2003) (noting that in the course of the post September 11 investigation, the government interviewed over 1,000 persons, detained 700 of them for violation of immigration laws, 134 on federal criminal charges, and an undisclosed number as material witnesses); Lawyers Committee for Human Rights, *Treatment of Immigrants, Refugees, and Minorities*, *in* A Year of Loss, *available at* www.lchr.org/us_law/loss/loss_ch3a.htm (June 20, 2003).

14   *See* Civil Rights and Education Fund, *supra* note 5, at 23–25. *See also* Cole, *supra* note 5, at 962.

15   Immigration and Naturalization Service Dep't of Justice, [AG Order No. 2626-2002] Registration of Certain Nonimmigrant Aliens From Designated Countries, 67 Fed. Reg. 67766-01 (Nov. 6, 2002), *available at* 2002 WL 31464912. This order, issued by Attorney General John Ashcroft, required that males from certain Muslim countries register in person at an INS office by December 16, 2002. The order covered those males who were over the age of 16 and who held tourist visas, business visitor visas, student visas, and other temporary visas. The order applied to "nationals or citizens of Iran, Iraq, Libya, Sudan or Syria. . . ." *Id.* An "alien" who does not comply with this order commits an immigration law violation and is subject to deportation. *Id.* ("A willful failure to comply with the requirements of this Notice constitutes a failure to maintain nonimmigrant status under section 237(a)(1)(C)(i) of the Act, 8 U.S.C. 1227(a)(1)(C)(i). *See* 8 C.F.R. 214.1(f)"). *See* Davies, *supra* note 7, at 51 n.27. Attorney General Ashcroft issued similar orders covering nationals from other Arab and Muslim countries as well as from North Korea. *See* Immigration and Naturalization Service, AG Order No. 2631-2002, Registration of Certain Nonimmigrant Aliens from Designated Countries, 67 Fed. Reg. 70526 (Nov. 22, 2002) (requiring males, 16 and older, from Afghanistan, Algeria, Bahrain, Eritrea, Lebanon, Morocco, North Korea, Oman, Qatar, Somalia, Tunisia, United Arab Emirates, and Yemen to register by January 10, 2003). *See also* INS, Dep't of Justice, Registration of Certain Nonimmigrant Aliens from Designated Countries, (AG Order No. 2636-2002), 67 Fed. Reg. 77136 (Dec. 16, 2002); *see also* INS, Dep't of Justice, Registration of Certain Nonimmigrant Aliens from Designated Countries (AG Order No. 2638-2002), 67 Fed. Reg. 77642 (Dec. 18, 2002) (ordering male nationals 16 and above, from Pakistan and Saudi Arabia, to register between January 13, 2003 and February 21, 2003). ICE is an agency within the Department of Homeland Security (DHS) and was formed in March 2003 as a result of the reorganization of the Immigration and Naturalization Service. *About US Immigration and Customs Enforcement (ICE)*, US ICE, *available at* www.ice.gov/about/index.htm.

16   Civil Rights and Education Fund, *supra* note 5, at 25–26.

17   *DOJ Focusing on Removal of 6,000 Men for Al Qaeda Haven Countries*, 79 Interpreter Releases, 115–16 (Jan. 21, 2002); Cole, *supra* note 5, at 975 (citing Dan Eggen & Cheryl W. Thompson, *U.S. Seeks Thousands of Fugitive Deportees; Middle Eastern Men Are Focus of Search*, Wash. Post, Jan. 8, 2002, at A1).

18 *See* Cole, *supra* note 5, at 975; Civil Rights and Education Fund, *supra* note 5, at 24–25. The mandatory interrogation program required Arab men who had entered the US on nonimmigrant visas before January 1, 2000 to report to DHS for questioning. (Nonimmigrant visas include student visas, tourist visas, business visas, and other temporary visas). *Id.* Although Attorney General John Ashcroft apparently stated that the interviews were to be "voluntary and friendly," a Department of Justice Memorandum authorized holding "interested" individuals on bond. *Id.* at 25, n.104 (citing *Memo Adds to Suspicions of Immigrants on Interviews*, N.Y. Times, Nov. 29, 2001). Press Release, Am. Civil Liberties Union, TSA Officials and JetBlue Pay $240,000 to Settle Discrimination Charges (Jan. 5, 2009), *available at* www.aclu.org/free-speech-racial-justice/tsa-officials-and-jetblue-pay-240000-settle-discrimination-charges.

19 *See* Civil Rights and Education Fund, *supra* note 5, at 22–23. *See also DOJ Focusing on Removal of 6,000 Men for Al Qaeda Haven Countries, supra* note 17 ("The ADC stressed that [the government] has the right to remove persons who are not in the country legally but said that it is 'unconscionable' to proceed 'based on a hierarchy that is ethnically defined.' " (quoting the Arab American Anti-Discrimination Committee (ADC))). *See* American Civil Liberties Union, *TSA Officials And JetBlue Pay $240,000 To Settle Discrimination Charges,* Jan. 5, 2009, *available at* http://www.aclu.org/free-speech-racial-justice/tsa-officials-and-jetblue-pay-240000-settle-discrimination-charges. "New York – In a victory for constitutional rights, two Transportation Security Authority (TSA) officials and JetBlue Airways have paid Raed Jarrar $240,000 to settle charges that they illegally discriminated against the US resident based on his ethnicity and the Arabic writing on his t-shirt. TSA and JetBlue officials prevented Jarrar from boarding his August 2006 flight at New York's John F. Kennedy Airport until he agreed to cover his shirt, which read 'We Will Not Be Silent' in English and Arabic, and then forced him to sit at the back of the plane. The American Civil Liberties Union and the New York Civil Liberties Union filed a federal civil rights lawsuit on Jarrar's behalf in August 2007." *See* Complaint and Jury Demand, Jarrar v. Harris, No. 07-CV-3299 (CBA)(JO) (E.D.N.Y. Aug. 9, 2007), *available at* www.aclu.org/freespeech/gen/31272lgl20070809. html.

20 Susan M. Akram & Kevin R. Johnson, *Migration Regulation Goes Local: The Role of States in US Immigration Policy: Race, Civil Rights, and Immigration Law after September 11, 2001: The Targeting of Arabs and Muslims,* 58 N.Y.U. Ann. Surv. Am. L. 295, 331 (2002) (citing, *inter alia,* David E. Rovella, *Clock Ticks on 9/11 Detentions,* Nat'l L. J., Nov. 5, 2001, at A1).

21 *See* Cole, *supra* note 5, at 960.

22 *See* Chishti & Meissner, *supra* note 6, at 1194.

23 Cole, *supra* note 5, at 960. A Justice Department official claimed that the Department stopped providing the number of 9/11 after it reached 1,200 "because the statistics became confusing." IG Justice Dep't Report, *supra* note 1, at 1, n.2. Despite the above statement, the IG Report asserted that only 762 immigrants were arrested (at least by the federal authorities). *Id.* at 2. In 2006, ICE formed a subagency/taskforce called the National Fugitive Operations Program (NFOP), which is responsible for reducing the fugitive alien population in the US. "'Fugitive aliens' are defined as those who have failed to leave the US after a final order of removal, deportation or exclusion OR who has (*sic*) failed to report to ICE after receiving a notice to do so." ICE, NFOP Factsheet, *available at* www.ice.gov/doclib/news/library/factsheets/pdf/fugops.pdf. This taskforce arrested 34,155 people in FY08. ICE has two web pages dedicated to examples of how their work has protected the US from further terrorist threat, but does not set forth specific numbers of individuals arrested who actually threatened

the US. *See* www.ice.gov/pi/news/factsheets/terrorismthreats.htm; www.ice.gov/doclib/news/library/factsheets/pdf/fugops/pdf.

24   *See* Akram & Johnson, *supra* note 20, at 327 (noting that a large number of Arab and Muslim citizens were put into custody as "material witnesses" in the aftermath of 9/11). One study found that "nearly 50 people" had been detained as material witnesses since September 11. *See also* Chishti & Meissner, *supra* note 6, at 1195.

25   *See* Chishti & Meissner, *supra* note 6, at 1194–95.

26   Cole, *supra* note 5, at 962 (citing Amnesty International, *Amnesty International's Concerns Regarding Post September 11 Detentions in the USA*, Mar. 14, 2002, *available at* http://web.amnesty.org/library/Index/ENGAMR510442002; Dan Eggen, *Delays Cited in Charging Detainees; With Legal Latitude, INS Sometimes Took Weeks*, Wash. Post, Jan. 15, 2002, at A1; Dan Eggen, *Long Wait for Filing of Charges Common for Sept. 11 Detainees; Delays Reasonable, INS Officials Say*, Wash. Post, Jan. 19, 2002, at A12). *See also* Chishti & Meissner, *supra* note 6, at 1194 (noting that of the 406 detainees from whom information was available, over half were held "for more than five weeks. Almost nine per cent were detained for more than nine months before being released or repatriated").

27   *See* Chishti & Meissner, *supra* note 6, at 1194 ("Many of these detainees had severe problems notifying or communicating with their family members and lawyers or arranging for representation at all.").

28   Cole, *supra* note 5, at 964. *See also* Chishti & Meissner, *supra* note 6, at 1194 ("Of the detainees for whom such information was available, approximately 52 per cent were believed to be subject to a Federal Bureau of Investigation (FBI) hold, preventing their repatriation for weeks or months even after they were ordered removed from the US and did not appeal.").

29   The manner in which courts handle bail, however, often operates as a form of preventive detention. Where there is evidence that a defendant has committed a particularly dangerous crime regardless of whether he or she has strong community ties and is unlikely to abscond, courts generally impose high bail to keep the individual incarcerated. *See* chapter 6 on indefinite detention for a more detailed discussion of this issue.

30   Alison Parker & Jamie Fellner, *Above the Law: Executive Power after September 11 in the United States*, *in* Human Rights Watch World Report 2004 (2004) *available at* http://hrw.org/wr2k4/8.htm#_Toc4458744957.

31   Chishti & Meissner, *supra* note 6, at 1194.

32   *Id.*

33   *Id.*

34   *Id.* The study also showed that the "majority of noncitizens detained since September 11 . . . had spouses, children, or other family relationships in the US." *Id.* The Inspector General of the Justice Department issued a report on the arrests of immigrants after 9/11, and noted that the FBI followed up, among others, "anonymous tips called in by members of the public suspicious of Arab and Muslim neighbors who kept odd schedules." IG Justice Dep't Report, *supra* note 1, at 15–16.

35   *See* Cole, *supra* note 5, at 961. *See also* Memorandum from the Chief Immigration Judge, *supra* note 6 and accompanying Instructions to Immigration Judges.

36   *See* North Jersey Media Group, Inc. v. Ashcroft, 205 F. Supp. 2d 288, 299, 300 (D.N.J. 2002) (citing 8 C.F.R. § 242.16(a) and 8 C.F.R. § 3.27), (holding that the INS may close so-called "special interest" immigration deportation hearings), *rev'd*, 308 F.3d 198 (3d Cir. 2002) *cert. denied*, 123 S. Ct. 2215 (2004), (noting that the immigration regulations promulgated since 1964 created a presumption that a deportation hearing would be open).

37 Michael Creppy, *supra* note 6. The memorandum states as follows: "[T]he Attorney General has implemented additional security procedures for certain cases in the Immigration Court. Those procedures require us to hold the hearings individually, *to close the hearing[s] to the public*, and to avoid discussing the case or otherwise disclosing any information about the case to anyone outside the Immigration Court." *Id.* (emphasis added). The instructions that were subsequently issued state in part as follows: "The courtroom must be closed for these cases . . . no visitors, no family, no press." *Instructions for Cases Requiring Additional Security*, 78 Interpreter Releases 1837 (Dec. 3, 2001).

38 *See Instructions for Cases Requiring Additional Security, supra* note 37, at 1837; *but see* Akram & Johnson, *supra* note 20, at 321 (noting that by 1999, the government used secret evidence in 25 removal proceedings brought against Arab and Muslim immigrants).

39 *See* Cole, *supra* note 5, at 961.

40 *See id. See also* Richmond Newspapers Inc., v. Virginia, 448 U.S. 555 (1980).

41 The Sixth Circuit noted as follows:

> Nothing in the Creppy directive counsels that it is limited to "a small segment of particularly dangerous individuals." In fact, the Government so much as argues that certain non-citizens known to have no links to terrorism will be designated "special interest" cases. Supposedly, closing a more targeted class would allow terrorists to draw inferences from which hearings are open and which are closed.

Detroit Free Press v. Ashcroft, 303 F.3d 681, 692 (6th Cir. 2002) (holding that INS may not close "special interest" immigration deportation cases).

42 *See Instructions for Cases Requiring Additional Security, supra* note 37, at 1837 ("This restriction on information includes confirming or denying whether such a case is on the docket or scheduled for a hearing. . . . You should instruct all courtroom personnel, including both court employees and contract interpreters, that they are not to discuss the case with anyone.")

43 *Id. See also* Cole, *supra* note 5, at 961 (citing Michael Creppy, *supra* note 6).

44 *See id.* at 960.

45 North Jersey Media Group, Inc. v. Ashcroft, 308 F.3d 198 (3d Cir. 2002), *cert. denied*, 123 S.Ct. 2215 (2003).

46 8 C.F.R. §214.5 (1981). *See also* Narenji v. Civiletti, 617 F.2d 745 (D.C. Cir. 1979) (upholding INS regulations requiring Iranian students to report to the INS).

47 *See* Shoaee v. INS, 704 F.2d 1079 (9th Cir. 1983) (upholding an Iranian student's deportation).

48 Dep't of Justice, INS, AG Order No. 2626–2002, 67 Fed. Reg. 67766-01 (Nov. 6, 2002). This was in an attempt to comply with a Congressional mandate issued in 1996 to INS, requiring the agency to implement a comprehensive entry–exit program by 2005. *Changes to National Security Entry/Exit Registration Program (NSEERS)*, ICE Website, Press Release, DHS, Factsheet: Changes to National Security Entry/Exit Registration System (NSEERS) (Dec. 1, 2003). *available at* www.ice.gov/pi/news/factsheets/nseersFS120103.htm. However, the NSEERS program was touted as "promot[ing] several important national security objectives," such as "run[ning] the fingerprints of aliens who may present elevated national security concerns against a database of wanted criminals and known terrorists," and allowing instant identification of people who have overstayed their visas, "which was the case with three of the 9/11 hijackers." *Id.* Moreover, the countries selected for special registration were selected because "all of these countries are places where al Qaeda or other terrorists organizations have been active." *Id.* These justifications imply that more was at work than

compliance with a 1996 Congressional mandate. In 2003 the program was replaced by US-VISIT. Press Release, DHS, Fact Sheet: US-VISIT Program (May 19, 2003).

49 *See* State Department Press Releases and Documents, *New Entry-Exit System to Focus on Individuals, not "Broad Categories,"* Fed. News & Info. Dispatch, Dec. 2, 2003, *available at* 2003 WL 64739209. There are three components to the National Security Entry-Exit Registration System: the "Special Registration" program described above, the "Point of Entry Registration," for immigrants who are at the point of entering the country, and "Exit-Departure" controls for immigrants who are leaving the country. *Id.* at 1. The POE program is described *infra* note 59 and accompanying text. *See also* Davies, *supra* note 7, at 51 n.27 (2003) (noting that Attorney General John Ashcroft "instituted special registration requirements known as the National Security Entry-Exit Registration System (NSEERS) that require select individuals to be fingerprinted, photographed, and interviewed under oath at US ports-of-entry. These registration requirements were subsequently extended to nationals of certain designated countries who had already been permitted to enter the US. . . . These Registration requirements affect non-immigrant aliens from four groups of countries: Iraq, Iran, Libya, Sudan, and Syria; Afghanistan, Algeria, Bahrain, Eritrea, Lebanon, Morocco, North Korea, Oman, Qatar, Somalia, Tunisia, United Arab Emirates, and Yemen; Bangladesh, Egypt, Indonesia, Jordan, and Kuwait; and Saudi Arabia and Pakistan.") Professor Davies also notes that the FBI appeared to be openly investigating Arab and Muslims in the US. *See id.* (citing Eric Lichtblau, *FBI Tells Offices to Count Local Muslims and Mosques*, N.Y. Times, Jan. 28, 2003, at A13).

50 Davies, *supra* note 49. There is a new system now, called "US-VISIT," and it applies to certain non-US Citizens (USC) traveling on nonimmigrant visas or without a visa as part of the Visa Waiver Program (VWP). As of December 19, 2008, all non-USC (except Canadians applying for admission on B-1 or B-2 visas or those specifically exempted) are subject to US-VISIT procedures. See the website below for a specific list of categories of people who will be required to provide biometrics when entering the US: www.dhs.gov/xtrvlsec/programs/gc_1231972592442.shtm (Jan. 14, 2009).

51 Davies, *supra* note 7, at 51 n.27. *See also* State Department Press Release on New Exit-Entry System, *supra* note 49, at 2.

52 Registration of Certain Nonimmigrant Aliens From Designated Countries, 67 Fed. Reg. 67,766, 67,7667 (Nov. 6, 2002).

53 Registration of Certain Nonimmigrant Aliens From Designated Countries, 67 Fed. Reg. 77,136, 77,137 (Dec. 16, 2002). *See also* Permission for Certain Nonimmigrant Aliens From Designated Countries to Register in a Timely Fashion, 68 Fed. Reg. 2,366 (Jan. 16, 2003) (reopening the registration period for the first two groups, extending the time for them to register to February 7, 2003).

54 Registration of Certain Nonimmigrant Aliens from Designated Countries, 68 Fed. Reg. 2,363-03, 2,364 (Jan. 16, 2003) (requiring the specified nationals from Bangladesh, Egypt, Indonesia, Jordan, and Kuwait to register by March 28, 2003).

55 Registration of Certain Nonimmigrant Aliens from Designated Countries, 68 Fed. Reg. 8,046, 8,047 (Feb. 19, 2003) (extending the previous deadline). *See also* State Department Press Release on New Exit-Entry System, *supra* note 49, at 2.

56 New Exit-Entry System, *supra* note 54 (citing James Nash, *INS Frees Some Detainees; No Apology for Middle Easterners' Arrests*, L.A. Daily News, Dec. 20, 2002). Such a policy may be counterproductive for other reasons. Individuals

who have information about terrorist activity, but who have minor immigration infractions, may decide not to register or to cooperate with authorities. *Id.*

57 *See* Davies, *supra* note 7, at 51, n.27.

58 *See id. See also supra* note 54 and accompanying text.

59 These measures were subsequently expanded to include other countries under the US-VISIT program, Brazil being among the countries on the list. Irate at these security measures, a Brazilian judge ordered that all visitors from the US to Brazil be subject to the same treatment. *See* Audrey Hudson, *U.S. Requires Fingerprints, Photos From Visitors,* Wash. Times, Jan. 6, 2004, at A01. The US-Visit program requires biometric identification of all visitors and nonimmigrants, including foreigners entering the US to study here. *Implementation of the United States Visitor and Immigration Status Indicator Technology Program ("US-Visit"); Biometric Requirements,* 69 Fed. Reg. 2468, (Jan. 5, 2004). The program excepts visitors from waiver countries, which generally include the Western European countries. *Id.* The DHS plans to expand this program to include visitors from all countries. It appears that it essentially will supplant NSEERS. *Id.* at 476.

60 ICE, however, denied that this had occurred. Press Release, DHS, Factsheet: Changes to National Security Entry/Exit Registration System (NSEERS) (Dec. 1, 2003).

61 State Department Press Release on New Exit-Entry Procedures, *supra* note 49, at 1; 8 C.F.R. Part 264 (Dec. 2, 2003) ("Supplementary Information" section for this interim rule states that DHS "will use a more tailored system in which it will notify individual aliens of future registration requirements"). By the way, the DHS absorbed the INS on 1 March 2003. The "more tailored" program is US-VISIT.

62 State Department Press Release, *supra* note 61.

63 State Department Press Release, *supra* note 61.

64 8 C.F.R. part 264 (Dec. 2, 2003). *See also* Kathleen Taylor, *Editorial,* Seattle Post Intelligencer, Dec. 18, 2003 (noting that temporary immigrants from the named 25 countries have to leave the US from designated points of entry and must register upon leaving the country).

65 *Middle Eastern "Absconders" to be Rounded Up,* 7 Bender's Immigr. Bull. No. 5, Mar. 1, 2002, at 264. It is estimated that approximately 1,000 of the 6,000 absconders have felony convictions. They will be targeted first; then the rest will follow. *Id.*

66 American Immigration Lawyers Association, *Boiling the Frog Slowly: Executive Branch Actions Since September 11,* 7 Bender's Immigr. Bull. No. 20, Oct. 15, 2002, at 1237: INS Commissioner Ziglar announced the initiative in December 2001. *Id.*

67 *See supra* notes 46–64 and accompanying text and *infra* notes 83–89.

68 Michael Janofsky, *9/11 Panel Calls Policies On Immigration Ineffective,* N.Y. Times, Apr. 17, 2004, at A8. The Commission reported that "as of early 2003, 1,139 had been apprehended, a group that included 803 who had been deported, 224 who were awaiting deportation and 45 waiting prosecution. . . ." *Id.*

69 Chishti & Meissner, *supra* note 6.

70 Cam Simpson, Flynn McRoberts & Liz Sly, *Immigration Crackdown Shatters Muslims' Lives,* Chic. Tribune, Nov. 16, 2003, at C1. *Cf.* Geneive Abdo & E.A. Torriero, *Spy Charges Dropped, but Fear Remains, Chaplain's Kin Feel "Like the Enemy,'* Chic. Tribune, May 3, 2004, at 1 (although espionage charges were dropped against Army Capt. James Yee, a chaplain, for allegedly mishandling classified documents in Guantánamo Bay, Muslims feel targeted by the government).

71 Akram & Johnson, *supra* note 20, at 334 (citing *DOJ Orders Incentives, "Voluntary"*

Interviews of Aliens to Obtain Info on Terrorists, 78 Interpreter Releases 1816, 1817-18 (2001)).

72   *DOJ Orders Incentives, "Voluntary" Interviews of Aliens to Obtain Info on Terrorists; Foreign Students, Visa Processing Under State Dept. Scrutiny*, 78 Interpreter Releases 1816, 1817–18 (Dec. 3, 2001).

73   Akram & Johnson, *supra* note 20, at 334 (citing Memorandum from the Deputy Attorney General, to all US Attorneys and all Members of the Anti-terrorism Task Forces (Nov. 9, 2001), *reprinted in DOJ Orders Incentives, "Voluntary" Interviews of Aliens to Obtain Info on Terrorists, Foreign Students, Visa Processing Under State Dept. Scrutiny*, 78 Interpreter Releases 1816 app. (Dec. 3, 2001). The memorandum states in relevant part as follows: "While the primary purpose of these interviews is not to ascertain the legality of the individuals' immigration status, the federal responsibility to enforce the immigration laws, as exercised by the Immigration and Naturalization Service is an important one. Therefore, if you suspect that a particular individual may be in violation of the federal immigration laws, you should call the INS representative on your Anti-Terrorism Task Force or the INS officials at the closest Law Enforcement Support Center. Those officials will advise you whether the individual is in violation of the immigration laws and whether he should be detained." 78 Interpreter Releases at 1829, 1830.

74   Civil Rights and Education Fund, *supra* note 5, at 24–25. The approximately 20 who were detained were held for immigration violations, not for terrorist linked offenses. *Id.* (The Department planned on interviewing approximately 5,000 in 2001 and 3,000 in 2002; approximately 90 percent appeared.) *Id.* Although it is not known whether any useful leads concerning terrorist activity were obtained from those who reported, there is little reported evidence to suggest that the questioning of Arab men provided substantial intelligence on terrorists. *Id.* Some police departments refused to participate in the interrogations, because of concerns about racial profiling. *See id.* at 25 n.106 (citing Fox Butterfield, *Police are Split on Questioning of Mideast Men*, N.Y. Times, Nov. 22, 2001).

75   *See* Civil Rights and Education Fund, *supra* note 5, at 22–23.

76   *See* Kevin Johnson, *September 11 and Mexican Immigrants: Collateral Damage Comes Home*, 52 DePaul L. Rev. 849, 863 n. 90 (2003) (citing DeCanas v. Bica, 424 U.S. 351, 354 (1976) ("Power to regulate immigration is unquestionably exclusively a federal power.") (citations omitted); *see, e.g.*, League of United Latin Am. Citizens v. Wilson, 908 F. Supp. 755 (C.D. Cal. 1995) (holding that most of Proposition 187, a California law seeking to effectively regulate undocumented immigration, was preempted by federal law). *But see* Peter J. Spiro, *The States and Immigration in an Era of Demi-Sovereignties*, 35 Va. J. Int'l L. 121 (1994) (contending that states should have an increased role in immigration regulation). *See also* Ignatius Bau, *Cities of Refuge: No Federal Preemption of Ordinances Restricting Local Government Cooperation with the INS*, 7 La Raza L.J. 50, 66 (1994) (citing a 1989 Memorandum of Understanding between the INS and the City of San Francisco, agreeing that the San Francisco police will not enforce the federal immigration law). *But see* Paul Smith, *An Argument against Mandatory Reporting of Undocumented Immigrants*, 29 Colum. J.L. & Soc. Probs. 147 (1995) (noting that although generally prohibited from enforcing the civil provisions of the Immigration and Naturalization Act (INA), but finding no constitutional preemption for state and local police from enforcing the criminal provisions of the INA) (citing Gonzales v. City of Peoria, 722 F.2d 469, 475 (9th Cir. 1983); Gates v. Superior Court, 193 Cal. App. 3d 205, 214–15 (1987). *See also* D. L. Hawley, *The Powers of Local Law Enforcement to Enforce Immigration Laws*, 99-6 Immigr. Briefings (June 1999).

77 *See* Mithre J. Sandrasagra, *U.S.: Rights Groups Fight Use in Immigration Cases*, Inter. Press Service, Dec. 18, 2003, *available at* 2003 WL 66986827; *see also* Linda Reyna Yanez & Alfonso Soto, *Local Police Involvement in the Enforcement of Immigration Law*, 1 Hisp. L.J. 9, 12 (1994) (noting that local police enforcement risks violating the rights of US citizens, legal residents, and aliens); *see also* Johnson, *infra* note 132, at 252 n.228 (noting patterns of the police abuse of undocumented immigrants).

78 *DOJ Legal Opinion Would Broaden Use of State, Local Personnel in Immigration Enforcement*, 79 Interpreter Releases 519 (Apr. 8, 2002) (noting that the DOJ Office of Legal Counsel is issuing an opinion permitting local police to enforce the civil provisions of the Immigration laws, reversing its 1996 opinion). *See also* Marie Taylor, *Immigration Enforcement Post September 11, Safeguarding the Civil Rights of Middle Eastern American and Immigrant Communities*, 17 Geo. L.J. 63, 91 (2002) (citing Eric Schmidt, *Ruling Clears Way to Use State Police in Immigration Duty*, N.Y. Times, Apr. 4, 2002, at A15). The House is debating a bill that would expressly authorize state and local police to enforce immigration laws. *See House Subcommittee Debates Local Enforcement of Immigration Laws under Proposed CLEAR Act*, 80 Interpreter Releases 1407 (Oct. 13, 2003); H.R. Res. 2671, 108th Cong., 149 Cong. Rec. H6463 (daily edition July 9, 2003). The bill was reintroduced by Rep. Marsha Blackburn on May 14, 2009, and it was referred to the judiciary committee; on June 12, 2009, it was referred to the Subcommittee on Immigration, Citizenship, Refugees, Border Security and International Law.

79 *See INS Commissioner Announces Data Sharing Arrangement with the FBI, Other Security Measures*, 78 Interpreter Releases 1899, 1899 (Dec. 17, 2001) (citing Chris Adams, *INS to Put in Federal Criminal Databases the Names of People Ordered Deported*, Wall St. J., Dec. 6, 2001, at A22). *See also supra* notes 65–67 and accompanying text for a discussion of the Absconder Apprehension Initiative.

80 *Id.* ("Sharing this information with the FBI will allow local law enforcement personnel to assist with removal efforts.").

81 *Id.*

82 *See* Chishti & Meissner, *supra* note 6, at 1195 ("Problems occurred [in the 'voluntary interview' program] when poorly trained police officials were tasked to implement the program.").

83 In testifying before Congress, Members of the Mexican Legal Defense Fund noted:

> Immigrants, generally, prefer not to draw attention to themselves from the government or the private sector even if they are here legally. This explains, in part, why Latino immigrants under-report when they are the victims of crime or when they are the victim of illegal civil practices, such as employment discrimination, unsafe working environments, or housing discrimination even though they experience these practices in significant numbers. Current trends post-9/11 to involve local law enforcement in enforcing immigration laws, particularly civil laws, will only drive Latino immigrant communities further underground and make them less willing to provide information to law enforcement that would be helpful in solving crimes and resolving legal violations that affect not just Latinos but others with whom they work and live. *It will also lead to less cooperation from immigrant communities with law enforcement searching for leads to fight terrorism.*
>
> *INS Interior Enforcement Strategy: Hearing Before the Subcomm. on Immigration and Claims Interior Enforcement Strategy of the H. Comm. on the Judiciary,* 107th Cong.

(June 19, 2002) (statement of Marisa J. Demeo, Regional Counsel, and Aisha Qaasim, Legislative Staff Attorney, Mexican American Legal Defense and Educational Fund (MALDEF)), *available at* 2002 WL 20318304 (emphasis added).

84   Sandrasagra, *supra* note 77 (quoting Raul Yzaguirre, president and CEO of the National Council of La Raza).

85   *See* Johnson, *supra* note 76, at 864.

86   Sandrasagra, *supra* note 77.

87   See Teresa Watanabe, *Anti-Muslim Incidents Rise, Study Finds; Group says hate crimes and harassment in California tripled in 2003 from previous year*, L.A. Times, May 3, 2003, at B1; Mary Beth Sheridan, *Bias Against Muslims Up 70%, Radio Talk Shows, Iraq War Among Reasons, Study Finds*, Wash. Post, May 3, 2004, at A12.

88   *See* Civil Rights and Education Fund, *supra* note 5, at 22–23 (discussing cases of "Driving while Arab (or Arab looking)").

89   *See id.* at 23. Aside from this local profiling, "flying while Arab," the profiling of Arab and Muslim airline passengers by private screeners and now governmental officials has reached unprecedented heights. *Id.* at 27–28. *See also* Charu A. Chandrasekhar, *Note & Comment: Flying While Brown: Federal Civil Rights Remedies to Post-9/11 Airline Racial Profiling of South Asians*, 10 Asian L.J. 215, 218 (2003).

90   "[I]f the people that are flying your airplanes into buildings are from the Middle East, you don't look for New Zealanders." *Id.* at 223, n.48 (quoting Nurith C. Aizenman, *Middle Eastern Travelers Face Scrutiny; Arab American Activist Attacks Lengthy Interrogations as Profiling, Doubts Usefulness*, Wash. Post, Sept. 23, 2001, at A11 (quoting a former security head of the FAA)).

91   R. Spencer Macdonald, *Notes & Comments: Rational Profiling in America's Airports*, 17 BYU J. Pub. L. 113, 126 (2002) (citing Stuart Taylor, Jr., *The Case for Using Racial Profiling at Airports*, Atlantic, Sept. 25, 2001, *available at* www.theatlantic.com/politics/nj/taylor2001-09-25.htm).

92   *Id.*

93   *Cf.* Ruth Wedgwood, *The Enemy Within*, Wall St. J., June 14, 2002, at A12, *available at* 2002 WL-WSJ 3397712 (noting that al Qaeda can circumvent watch-lists (and presumably profiles) by recruiting American citizens).

94   The Department of Transportation issued a policy statement less than a month after September 11 prohibiting racial profiling by airlines: "Do not subject persons or their property to inspection, search and/or detention solely because they appear to be Arab, Middle Eastern, Asian, and/or Muslim; or solely because they speak Arabic, Farsi, or another foreign language; or solely because they speak with an accent that may lead you to believe they are Arab, Middle Eastern, Asian, and/or Muslim." Charu A. Chandrasekhar, *supra* note 89, at 218 (quoting Policy Statement, US Dep't of Transp. Office of Aviation Enforcement and Proceedings, Carrying Out Transportation Inspection and Safety Responsibilities in a Nondiscriminatory Manner (Oct. 12, 2001) (emailed to airline trade associations and major US airlines on October 17, 2001), *available at* http://airconsumer.ost.dot.gov/rules/20011012.htm.

95   Frank H. Wu, *Profiling in the Wake of September 11: The Precedent of Japanese American Internment*, 17 Crim. Just. 52, 52–53 (2002).

96   At least 1,600 Germans were interned in America during the First World War (they were sent home on October 26, 1919). The Encyclopedia Americana: A Library of Universal Knowledge 655 (1920), *available at* http://books.google.com/books?id=wCIVAAAAYAAJ&printsec=toc#PPA655,M1. As heinous a crime as September 11 was, it pales in comparison with the Second World War. In that conflict Americans alone lost 292,131 to battle deaths and 115,187 to deaths from other causes. *World War II*, 27 Funk & Wagnalls Encyclopedia 448 (1986). Total allied civilian and military losses were 44 million; those of the Axis were 11 million. *Id.*

97 *See* Wu, *supra* note 95, at 55–56.

98 On December 8, 1941, President Roosevelt signed Public Proclamation 2527. This Proclamation declared all the Italian resident aliens in the country over the age of 13 "alien enemies" and directed the Attorney General to investigate and arrest those who threatened the public peace and safety of the US. Presidential Proclamation No. 2527, 6 Fed. Reg. 6324 (Dec. 8, 1941), *available at* www.foitimes.com/internment/Proc2527.html. After the US declared war against Mussolini, each Italian-born "alien enemy" was required to file a passport-sized photograph with the federal government, be fingerprinted, and always carry their photo-identity card. Additionally, a curfew was instituted, travel of more than five miles from home was regulated for these people; their possession of guns, ammunition, short-wave radios, cameras, and signaling devices was forbidden; and they were required to report any change of residence or employment to local police. Maddalena Tirabassi & Piero Gastaldo, *Italics in Time of Crisis in Italic Identity in Pluralistic Contexts* (Piero Bassetti & Paolo Janni eds., 2004), *in* IV.6 Cultural Heritage and Contemporary Change (George F. McLean ed.), *available at* www.crvp.org/book/Series04/IV-6/chap-5.htm, (citing Guido Tinton, *New Discoveries, Old Prejudices: The Internment of Italian Americans during World War II, in* Una Storia Segreta: The Secret History of Italian American Evacuation and Internment during World War II 236–54 (Lawrence D. Stasi ed., 2001)).

The internment of "enemy aliens" began on the night of December 7, 1941. A total of 1,566 Japanese were detained, along with 1,301 Germans and 243 Italians, most of whom were permanent residents, not US citizens. Records later showed that most of the detained Italians were members of the Federation of Italian War Veterans, Italian-language journalists, or instructors in Italian-language schools sponsored by an Italian consulate. *Id.*

99 Korematsu v. United States, 323 U.S. 214 (1944); *see also* Cole, *supra* note 5, at 993 n.165.

100 Civil Liberties Act of 1988, Pub. L. No. 100–383, 102 Stat 903.

101 *See* Wu, *supra* note 95, at 55.

102 *See* The Nottebohm Case (Liech. v. Guat.), 1955 I.C.J. 4 (Apr. 4), *available at* 1955 WL 1 (noting that nationality denotes a "bond of allegiance" by the national to his or her country).

103 National and international law permit the detention of "enemy aliens" during wartime. *See* Cole, *supra* note 5, at 959 (citing the Enemy Alien Act of 1798).

104 The Supreme Court has upheld the use of pretextual traffic stops in an effort to catch those the police suspect to be individuals who have engaged in criminal activity. *See* Whren v. United States, 517 U.S. 806 (1996). "Racial profiling is *any* use of race, religion, ethnicity, or national origin by law enforcement agents as a means of deciding who should be investigated, *except* where these character-istics are part of a specific suspect description." Civil Rights and Education Fund, *supra* note 5, at 11 (emphasis in original). Note that the Civil Rights and Education Fund also observed that profiling includes "law enforcement activity that relies *in part*, as well as solely, on race (in the absence of a specific suspect description). . . ." Such a definition of racial profiling was included in consent decrees between the Department of Justice and the State of New Jersey. *Id.* at 37, n. 17 (citing Consent Decree in United States v. State of New Jersey, Civil No. 99–5970 (MLC) (Dec. 30, 1999), *available at* www.usdoj.gov/crt/split/documents/jerseysa.htm, at 2. "Selective enforcement based in part on race is no less pernicious or offensive to the principle of equal justice than is enforcement based solely on race." Civil Rights and Education Fund, *supra* note 5, at 11.

105 Civil Rights and Education Fund, *supra* note 5, at 12 (citing studies showing

that blacks were stopped in significantly higher numbers than whites, including a study that between 1988 and 1991, "[b]lacks were 35 per cent of those stopped" on the New Jersey Turnpike "though only 13.5 per cent of the cars on the Turnpike had a [b]lack occupant and [b]lacks were only 15 per cent of all traffic violators").

106 Before September 11, President George W. Bush not only condemned racial profiling, but was committed to stopping it in America: racial profiling "is wrong and we will end it in America." Mike Allen, *Bush Issues Ban On Racial Profiling; Policy Makes Exceptions For Security*, Wash. Post, June 18, 2003, at A14, *available at* 2003 WL 56498502. Attorney General John Ashcroft also condemned racial profiling. Eric Ferkehnhoff & Noah Isakson, *Ashcroft Calls on Police to End Racial Profiling*, Chic. Trib., Apr. 7, 2001, at 17. The House introduced a bill not only to ban racial profiling, but also to permit profiling victims to sue the police. *See* H.R. 2074/S, 107th Cong. (2001). After September 11, neither the House nor the Senate moved on the bill.

107 *See* Davies, *supra* note 7, at 63 (noting the unreliability of determining whom the US Customs Service decided to strip search using a racial profile).

108 For example, US District Court Judge Filemon Vela has apparently been frequently stopped around Brownsville, Texas by Border Patrol agents and questioned, because of his Latino appearance. *See* Civil Rights and Education Fund, *supra* note 5, at 16–17 (citing David Harris, Profiles in Injustice 3–6 (2002)).

109 *See* Davies, *supra* note 7, at 74.

110 *See* Cole, *supra* note 5, at 976–77, 985.

111 *See* Davies, *supra* note 7, at 65–66.

112 For purposes of this hypothetical, assume that the perpetrator acted completely alone. *See id.* at 54–63 (setting forth a series of hypotheticals to explain racial and ethnic profiling and how it violates basic principles of fundamental fairness).

113 Whites, however, are an increasingly smaller part of the overall population of the US.

114 *See also* Bill Broadway, *Number of US Muslims Depends on Who's Counting*, Wash. Post, Nov. 24, 2001, at A1 (noting that a study commissioned by four Muslim organizations estimated the number of Muslims living in the US to be six to seven million, that a study commissioned by the American Jewish Committee estimated the number to be from 1.5 to 3.5 million, that the 2001 Britannica Book of the Year estimated 4.1 million, and that a CUNY telephone survey estimated 2.8 million). *See also* Davies, *supra* note 7, at 52 (estimating 3.5 million).

Since by law an individual's religious affiliation may not be inquired of by the census takers, the exact numbers of Muslims living in the US is not definitively known. Some estimate the number to be as high as six million, others in between two million and three million. *See* Joyce Howard Price, *1.2 million Arabs in US, Census States*, Wash. Times, Dec. 3, 2003, *available at* http://washingtontimes.com/national/20031203-113839-9531r.htm (noting that the 2000 census reported 1.2 million Arabs, but that many Arabs do not practice the Muslim faith and that many Muslims are not Arab).

115 *See* Davies, *supra* note 7, at 73–74.

116 *See id.* at 66.

117 This assumes that one can always distinguish white persons from black persons, a questionable assumption at best, and another reason for discarding racial profiling as a law enforcement approach.

118 *Id.*

119 *Id.*

120 *But see* R. Spencer Macdonald, *supra* note 91, at 126 (arguing that racial profiling is justified in airports as compared to racial profiling black drivers for drugs (DWB), because "preventing mass murder . . . is infinitely more important than . . . DWB profiling (finding illegal drugs or guns)"; Daniel Pipes, *A Call for Intelligent Profiling*, N.Y. Sun, Dec. 30, 2003, at 7.

121 Cole, *supra* note 5, at 976–77.

122 Apparently some US governmental officials have recognized this problem and are fearful that al Qaeda will use some individuals who do not appear Arab or Middle-Eastern to carry out an attack on the US. Frank Millar, *Police quiz al-Qaeda suspects as US warns of attacks*, Irish Times, Jan. 19, 2002, at 13, *available at* 2002 WL 4782744.

123 Cole, *supra* note 5, at 976.

124 *See* Human Rights Watch Report on the US Detainees, *available at* www.hrw.org.

125 *See* Thomas P. Ludwig, *The Erosion Of Online Privacy Rights in the Recent Tide of Terrorism*, 8 Comp. L. Rev. & Tech. J. 131, 139 (2003) (noting that "during the entire course of the war, ten people were convicted of spying for Japan, all of whom were Caucasian" (citing Debra LaFountaine & Pei P. Wang, Historical Background (1995) [and] . . . Curtis B. Munson, The Munson Report, *available in part at* http://www.curriculumunits.com/crucible/whunts/munsonreport.htm (last visited Oct. 25, 2003) (noting in this special report to President Roosevelt that all evidence pointed to the fact that Japanese Americans were perfectly loyal to the United States)). No case of espionage has been documented against any Japanese immigrants or Japanese-Americans for activities during World War II. *See also* Robert Pear, *$1.5 Billion Urged For Japanese Held in War*, N.Y. Times, June 17, 1983, at A1.

126 Zachary Abuza, *Funding Terrorism in Southeast Asia: The Financial Network of Al Qaeda and Jemaah Islamiya*, 14(5) THE NATIONAL BUREAU OF ASIAN RESEARCH 5, Dec. 2005 *available at* 2003 WL 58378389. As of 2002, over $100 million of al Qaeda's assets were frozen, but they were allegedly still able to operate off Bin Laden's personal wealth. U.N.: *Al Qaeda still has 'considerable . . . resources'*, CNN.com, Aug. 29, 2002, *available at* http://archives.cnn.com/2002/US/08/29/al.qaeda. funds/index.html.

According to the Council for Foreign Relations, "Magnus Ranstorp, an expert on Islamist terrorism, told Radio Free Europe in September 2007 that al-Qaeda is now "exponentially much stronger" than before. . . . The international crackdown that followed the 9/11 attacks greatly cut into al-Qaeda's resources and many of al-Qaeda's former leaders were captured or killed, leading experts to question the relevance of al-Qaeda's central leadership. This Backgrounder points out how in these years al-Qaeda *transformed* from what was once a *hierarchical organization* with a large operating budget *into an ideological movement.* Whereas al-Qaeda once trained its own operatives and deployed them to carry out attacks, it is just as likely to *inspire* individuals or small groups to carry out attacks, often with *no* operational support from the larger organization. Experts say al-Qaeda is able to spread its ideology effectively through the internet and al-Sahab, its media wing." Jayshree-Bajoria, *al-Qaeda (a.k.a. al-Qaida, al-Qa'ida)*, Counsel on Foreign Relations, last updated Dec. 30, 2009: www.cfr.org/publication/9126/ (emphasis added).

See also U.S. Dep't of State, Country Reports on Terrorism (2007): www.state.gov/s/ct/rls/crt/2006/82738.htm. They describe al Qaeda's strength as follows:

Al-Qaida's organizational strength is difficult to determine in the aftermath of extensive counterterrorist efforts since 9/11. The arrests and deaths of mid-level and senior al-Qaida operatives have disrupted some communication, financial, and facilitation nodes and disrupted some terrorist plots. Additionally, supporters and associates worldwide who are inspired by the group's ideology may be operating without direction from al-Qaida's central leadership; it is impossible to estimate their numbers. Al-Qaida also serves as a focal point of inspiration for a worldwide network that is comprised of many Sunni Islamic extremist groups, including some members of the Gama'at al-Islamiyya, the Islamic Movement of Uzbekistan, the Islamic Jihad Group, Lashkar i Jhangvi, Harakat ul-Mujahedin, Ansar al-Sunnah, the Taliban, Jemaah Islamiya, and the Libyan Islamic Fighting Group.

127 Civil Rights and Education Fund, *supra* note 5, at 29 (quoting Bill Dedman, *Words of Caution Airport Security: Memo Warns Against Use of Profiling as Defense,* Boston Globe, Oct. 12, 2001).

128 *See* Civil Rights and Education Fund, *supra* note 5, at 17. *See also* R. Richard Banks, *Beyond Profiling: Race, Policing, and the Drug War,* 56 Stan. L. Rev. 571, 578 n.29 (2003) (quoting Jeffrey Goldberg, *The Color of Suspicion,* N.Y. Times Mag., June 20, 2001) (quoting a Los Angeles police chief, Bernard Parks: "It's not the fault of the police when they stop minority males. . . . It's the fault of the minority males for committing the crime").

129 *See* Civil Rights and Education Fund, *supra* note 5, at 17–19 (collecting studies of racial profiling).

130 *Development in the Law—Race and the Criminal Process, Racial Discrimination on the Beat Extending the Racial Critique to Police Conduct,* 101 Harv. L. Rev. 1494, 1496 (1988) (arguing that targeting African-Americans leads to higher arrests and convictions for African-Americans which the police then use to justify continuing to target African-Americans). *See also* Banks, *supra* note 128, at 578 n.31 (citing Marc Mauer, Race to Incarcerate 143 (1999); Scott L. Johnson, *The Self-fulfilling Nature of Police Profiles, in* The System in Black and White 93 (Michael W. Markowitz & Delores D. Jones-Brown eds., 2000)).

131 *See* Civil Rights and Education Fund, *supra* note 5, at 17–19.

132 Sheri Lynn Johnson, *Race and the Decision to Detain a Suspect,* 93 Yale L.J. 214, 238 (1983) (citing Roger McNeely & Carl Pope, *Race and Involvement in Common Law Personal Crime: A Response to Hindelang,* 8 Rev. of Black Pol. Econ. 405, 405–06 (1978)).

133 State and federal courts have been slow to condemn racial profiling by governmental officials. Although authority exists for the proposition that police may not stop an individual based *solely* on that individual's race, United States v. Brignoni-Ponce, 422 U.S. 873, 885 (1977), the Supreme Court has specifically upheld pretextual traffic stops where the officer has used race in whole or in part as the real reason for the stop. Whren v. United States, 517 U.S. 806 (1996); *cf.* United States v. Armstrong, 517 U.S. 456, 465 (1996) (reinstating the district court's order denying discovery to the claimant in a selective prosecution claim and ruling that "claimant must demonstrate that the federal prosecutorial policy 'had a discriminatory effect and that it was motivated by a discriminatory purpose' ").

The Supreme Court recently rejected a Fifth Amendment claim, alleging racial, religious, and national origin discrimination in the FBI's post 9/11 mass arrests of Arab and Muslims and for the federal government's alleged mistreatment of the individual plaintiff while incarcerated. Ashcroft v. Iqbal, 129 S. Ct. 1937, 1951 (2009). The Court stated: "[After the 9/11 attacks perpetrated by 19 Arabic Muslims acting for al Qaeda, an Arab Muslim organization,] [i]t should come as no surprise that a legitimate policy directing law enforcement to arrest and detain individuals because of their suspected link to the attacks would produce a disparate, incidental impact on Arab Muslims, even though the purpose of the policy was to target neither Arabs nor Muslims." *Id.*

Lower courts have followed the Supreme Court's lead in endorsing racial profiling. *See, e.g.*, United States v. Harrington, 636 F.2d 1182, 1184 (9th Cir. 1980) (finding significance in the fact that a "Mexican" male visited the defendant's hotel room); United States v. Collins, 532 F.2d 79, 82 (8th Cir. 1976) (rejecting the defendant's claim that his skin color is irrelevant because "the color of a person's skin, be it black or white, is an identifying factor which, while insufficient by itself, assists the police in narrowing the scope of their identification procedure"); State v. Dean, 543 P.2d 425, 427 (Ariz. 1975) ("[T]he fact that a person is obviously out of place in a particular neighborhood is one of several factors that may be considered by an officer and the court in determining whether an investigation and detention is reasonable and therefore lawful."); *see also* United States v. Richard, 535 F.2d 246, 248–49 (3d Cir. 1976) (holding that, even though an informant may be using race as the only basis for suspicion, if police couple this with other factors, a reasonable articulable suspicion to initiate a Terry stop may be justified); State v. Barber, 823 P.2d 1068, 1075 (Wash. 1992) (noting that race may sometimes be a factor in a stop). Even a fairly recent case seems to have looked the other way regarding charges of racial profiling. *See* United States v. Stone, 73 F. Supp. 2d 441, 447 (S.D.N.Y. 1999) ("Nevertheless, even assuming that the defendant was singled out for closer inspection on the basis of his race in concert with the time and the location in which he walked, I am satisfied that the officers' subsequent actions fully comply with the Fourth Amendment[]. . . .").

Sean P. Trende, Note, *Why Modest Proposals Offer the Best Solution for Combating Racial Profiling*, 50 Duke L.J. 331, 356 n.151 (2000).

A few courts have begun to provide redress to those who have been victims of racial profiling. For example, the Ninth Circuit has expressly repudiated the language in Brignoni-Ponce, suggesting that race may be a factor to be considered in stopping individuals suspected of committing immigration violations. United States v. Montero-Camargo, 208 F.3d 1122 (9th Cir. 2000). The court stated that "[t]he likelihood that in an area in which the majority or even a substantial part of the population is Hispanic, any given person of Hispanic ancestry is in fact an alien, let alone an illegal alien, is not high enough to make Hispanic appearance a relevant factor in the reasonable suspicion calculus." *Id.* at 1122. Given the widely reported racial profiling of African-Americans by the New Jersey State police, the New Jersey courts appear to have applied Armstrong far more liberally, permitting discovery of police records on stops and profiling only upon a showing of colorable discrimination. *See, e.g.*, State v. Ballard, 752 A.2d 735, 752 (N.J. Super. Ct. App. Div. 2000); *see also* State v. Kennedy, 588 A.2d 834 (N.J. Super. Ct. App. Div. 1991).

A few other courts have likewise ruled that racial profiling is unlawful. *See, e.g.*, City of St. Paul v. Uber, 450 N.W.2d 623, 628 (Minn. Ct. App. 1990) (reversing a conviction where part of the officers' suspicion stemmed from the defendant's being a white person in a black neighborhood); Lowery v. Commonwealth, 388 S.E.2d 265, 267 (Va. Ct. App. 1990) ("While we agree that the State has a substantial interest in apprehending drug traffickers, we do not agree with the Commonwealth's argument that this type of racial classification is necessary to accomplish that objective. A person's race or national origin does not indicate a propensity to traffic in drugs."); *see also* State v. Barber, 823 P.2d 1068, 1075 (Wash. 1992) ("Distinctions between citizens solely because of their ancestry are odious to a free people whose institutions are founded upon the doctrine of equality."). *See also* Montero-Camargo, 208 F.3d at 1131–36 (9th Cir.

2000) (holding that language justifying the use of race at border stops in Brignoni-Ponce was "dictum," that circumstances and subsequent Supreme Court decisions had changed to justify abrogation of that "dictum," and abrogating that "dictum"); cf. Washington v. Lambert, 98 F.3d 1181 (9th Cir. 1996) (condemning repeatedly the indignities suffered by African-Americans at the hands of law enforcement officials); Martinez v. Village of Mount Prospect, 92 F. Supp. 2d 780, 782–85 (N.D. Ill. 2000) (approving a settlement agreement, while offering three pages of policy reasons for allowing more racial profiling cases to proceed). *See* Trende, *supra* at 357 n.153.

It is, however, generally not considered racial profiling for the police, after they have received a specific description of a perpetrator, including the perpetrator's race, to stop individuals of the same race as the perpetrator. *See* Minn. Stat. Ann. § 626.8471(2) ("Racial profiling does not include law enforcement's use of race or ethnicity to determine whether a person matches a specific description of a particular subject"). Even in such a case, however, the police should not be empowered to stop and investigate every member of a minority community sharing the same racial characteristic as the perpetrator. *See* Brown v. Oneonta, 253 F.3d 769 (2d Cir. 2000) (denying hearing *en banc*) (Calabresi, J., dissenting) ("Is the state creating an express racial classification that can only be approved if it survives strict scrutiny when state officers (like the police) ignore essentially everything but the racial part of a victim's description, and, acting solely on that racial element, stop and question all members of that race they can get hold of, even those who grossly fail to fit the victim's description? The answer to that question, all but ignored by the panel, seems to me—both on the precedents and on plain logic—to be a resounding yes.").

Aside from the courts, Congress and some state legislatures have taken some beginning steps to stop racial profiling. A bill was reintroduced in Congress that would require that police create a record of the race of all persons who are stopped along with other relevant criteria to help prevent racial profiling. *See Sens. Corzine, Feingold Introduce New Racial Profiling Bill Act of 2004,* State News Service, Feb. 26, 2004, *available at* 2004 WL 62442723. The bill would also give victims of racial profiling a private cause of action. *Id.* Some states have enacted legislation aimed at reducing or eliminating racial profiling. *See, e.g.,* N.J. Stat. Ann. § 2C: 30–5(d); Minn. Stat. Ann. § 26.8471. For a list of states with some form of anti-racial profiling legislation and a brief description thereof, *see* David A. Harris, *The New Data: Over-Representation of Minorities in The Criminal Justice System The Reality of Racial Disparity In Criminal Justice: The Significance of Data Collection,* 66 Law & Contemp. Probs. 71, 82 n.57 (2003). In some other states, legislators are proposing similar measures. *See, e.g.,* Bruce Landis, *Proposal Focuses on Racial Profiling,* Provid J-Bull (RI), Feb. 24, 2004, at B01 (noting that two Rhode Island legislators are proposing a bill to eliminate racial profiling).

134   "[T]errorism is not a Muslim monopoly." Donald A. Dripps, *Terror and Tolerance: Criminal Justice for the New Age of Anxiety,* 1 Ohio St. J. Crim. L. 9, 26 (2003). There are terrorists on both the left and the right, from American Nazis and some in the so-called Patriot movement, to environmental terrorists, not to mention lone acting individuals like the Unabomber.

135   For a good discussion of Timothy McVeigh, *see* Peter G. Chronis, *Prejudiced Profilers Had Sniper Figured All Wrong,* Denv. Post, Oct. 29, 2002, at B07, *available at* 2002 WL 6579220.

136   *See supra* notes 68–70 and accompanying text.

137   *Cf.* Eric L. Muller, *Inference or Impact? Racial Profiling and the Internment's True Legacy,* 1 Ohio St. J. Crim. L. 103 (2003) (arguing that racial profiling may be appropriate in some circumstances and that the major failure of interning the

Japanese during the Second World War was the enormity of the deprivation, not racial profiling itself).

138 Davies, *supra* note 7, at 46 (quoting Kathleen Parker, *All is Fair in War Except Insensitivity*, The Record, Sept. 26, 2001, at A1).

139 Wu, *supra* note 95, at 57.

140 *See, e.g.*, Banks, *supra* note 128, at 591 n.112 (citing Paul Brest, *The Supreme Court, 1975—In Defense of the Antidiscrimination Principle*, 90 Harv. L. Rev. 1, 9–10 (1976)).

141 Civil Rights and Education Fund, *supra* note 5, at 20.

142 *Id.* at 20 (quoting Jim Yardley, *Some Texans Say Border Patrol Singles Out Too Many Blameless Hispanics*, N.Y. Times, Jan. 26, 2000).

143 Civil Rights and Education Fund, *supra* note 5, at 26 (citing George Lardner, Jr., *Brookings Scholar is Detained by INS; Registration Rule Snags Pakistani Editor*, Wash. Post, Feb. 5, 2003. *See also* Ejaz Haider, *Wrong Message to the Muslim World*, Wash. Post, Feb. 5, 2003).

144 *Id.*

145 *Id.* The controversy concerning the arrest of African-American Harvard professor Henry Louis Gates and President Obama's involvement in the controversy speaks loudly about racial profiling, race relations, and differing perceptions of people of different racial backgrounds in America. *See* Helene Cooper, *Obama criticizes arrest of Harvard Professor*, N.Y. Times, July 22, 2009, *available at* http://www.nytimes.com/2009/07/23/us/politics/23gates.html?scp=30&sq=obama%20racial%20profiling%20Louis%20gates&st=cse.

146 Justice Brennan noted the effects of racial profiling persons of Mexican ancestry:

> To be singled out for referral and to be detained and interrogated must be upsetting to any motorist. One wonders what actual experience supports my Brethren's conclusion that referrals "should not be frightening or offensive because of their public and relatively routine nature." Ante, at 3084. In point of fact, referrals, viewed in context, are not relatively routine; thousands are otherwise permitted to pass. But for the arbitrarily selected motorists who must suffer the delay and humiliation of detention and interrogation, the experience can obviously be upsetting. And that experience is particularly vexing for the motorist of Mexican ancestry who is selectively referred, knowing that the officers' target is the Mexican alien. That deep resentment will be stirred by a sense of unfair discrimination is not difficult to foresee.

United States v. Martinez-Fuerte, 428 U.S. 543, 572–73 (1976) (Brennan, J., dissenting).

147 *See* Cole, *supra* note 5, at 977, 981 (quoting John Hart Ely for the proposition that "aliens" were an "easy case" for a "discrete and insular minority").

148 Note that the bill entitled "End Racial Profiling Act of 2004" makes any use of race illegal in deciding whether to stop a motorist absent a specific description of the perpetrator. *See supra* notes 106 and 133.

149 In the domestic context, racial profiling undermines the credibility of the police and, "[a]s a result, it is a natural reaction of distrustful law abiding citizens to think of officers as enemies and fail to cooperate with them in community policing programs and general investigations." Jenna K. Perrin, *Towards Eradicating the Pervasive Problem of Racial Profiling in Minnesota: State v. Fort 660 N.W.2d 415 (Minn. 2003)*, 27 Hamline L. Rev. 63 (2004).

150 *See* Dripps, *supra* note 134, at 27. Professor Dripps notes as follows: "[A]ny division of suspects along racial, ethnic or religious lines runs the standing risk of invidious discrimination. Many entirely innocent persons will be targeted simply because of national origin or religion. This not only compromises an important principle; it also runs the risk of alienating the very people who are in

the best position to observe suspicious activity among persons of Middle Eastern extraction or Islamic faith." *Id.*

151 Maintaining trust and close ties to the community enhances police effectiveness: "Establishing and maintaining mutual trust is the central goal of community partnership. Trust will give the police greater access to valuable information that can lead to the prevention of and solution of crimes. It will also engender support for police activities and provide a basis for a productive working relationship with the community that will find solutions to local problems." *About Community Policing*, The Community Policing Consortium, *available at* www.communitypolicing.org/about2.html.

152 "The unleashed power of the atom has changed everything save our modes of thinking, and we thus drift toward unparalleled catastrophes." John Bartlett, Familiar Quotations (15th edition 1980) (quoting Albert Einstein).

153 *See* Lemann, *supra* note 43 in ch. 9 (citing Dr. Feron).

154 *See* ch. 9, note 48, for a discussion of how the US invasion of Iraq strengthened al Qaeda in the Muslim World.

155 *See* Chishti & Meissner, *supra* note 6, at 1196 ("By targeting Muslim and Arab immigrants, the US government has deepened the perception abroad that the US is anti-Muslim and that its democratic values and principles are hypocritical . . . undermining US relationships with exactly the moderate, pro-Western nations and social groups that we need to fight against terrorism.").

156 *Id.* at 1200 ("Immigration policy should not rely on enforcement programs that give propaganda advantages to terrorist foes and contribute to their ability to influence and recruit alienated younger generations.").

157 When dealing with private terror organizations operating clandestinely in several countries, getting help from the authorities and populace of many countries is essential. *See* ch. 9, notes 43–44, 52 and accompanying text for a grass roots approach to counterterrorism, depending upon gaining the trust and help of the Muslims.

158 Peter G. Peterson, *Public Diplomacy and the War on Terrorism*, Foreign Aff., Sept–Oct 2002, at 74, 75.

159 Michael P. O'Connor & Celia M. Rumann, *Into the Fire: How to Avoid Getting Burned by the Same Mistakes Made Fighting Terrorism in Northern Ireland*, 24 Cardozo L. Rev. 1657, 1680 (2003). *See also British Actions {in Northern Ireland}*, Frontline, Public Broadcasting Service, Oct. 21, 1997, *available at* www.pbs.org/wgbh/pages/frontline/shows/ira/conflict/brits.html.

160 For a discussion of the need for citizen and community cooperation for effective law enforcement, *see supra* notes 149–52 and accompanying text.

161 For example, law enforcement officials could establish a program like that of Dearborn, Michigan's that guaranteed that "no immigration consequences would flow from [immigrants] coming forward to be interviewed." Chishti & Meissner, *supra* note 6, at 1198.

162 Peter M. German, *Panel III. Criminal law, Rule of Law, Post-September 11th Counterterrorism Measures, Money Laundering and Corporate Governance from a Canadian Perspective*, 16 Fla. J. Int'l L. 107, 110 (2003) ("Simply put, a collaborative approach is the only way to detect, deter, and destabilize global criminal entities.") For a discussion of collaboration and cooperation on the community level, *see supra* notes 149–52 and accompanying text. For a discussion of such collaboration on the international level *see* Tom Ridge, Secretary of the Department of Homeland Security, [Address] on Fighting Global Terrorism: Security and Cooperation in the 21st Century before Singapore Institute of Defence and Strategic Studies, Mar. 4, 2004, *available at* http://www.dhs.gov/dhspublic/display?content=3318. Secretary Ridge stated as follows:

So to fight back [against terrorists], we too must exploit our assets. We must investigate and prosecute and confiscate. We must utilize diplomacy, intelligence, law enforcement and asset seizure—a multilateral approach to a multinational problem. *We must enlist stronger collaboration and cooperation*, and improved information-sharing, both within nations and between them. We must use every available tool to repel these shadow soldiers.

Id. (emphasis added).

163 For a discussion on the retail approach to combating terrorism, see ch. 9, note 115 and accompanying text.

Part III

Invading and occupying Muslim countries

11 The invasion and occupation of Iraq

Aggression or a justified resort to force?

September 11 seared the US and its people. In the end, that momentous event provided the justification for the invasion and occupation of Iraq. But was invading Iraq permissible under international law? The answer is complex. This chapter will focus on the invasion but will briefly discuss the occupation as well.[1]

International law rests mainly on treaty and international custom. The Charter of the United Nations, the most important world treaty, prohibits any nation-state from using or threatening to use force against another state.[2] The Charter provides only two exceptions: (1) individual or collective self-defense,[3] and (2) UN Security Council approved military actions, such as occurred in Korea and in Desert Storm.[4]

11.1 Self-Defense

The first step in the analysis is to determine whether the invasion was justified under either of these exceptions. Article 51 of the UN Charter on self-defense expressly states in relevant part as follows: "Nothing in the present Charter shall impair *the inherent right* of individual or collective self-defense *if an armed attack occurs against a Member of the United Nations*, until the Security Council has taken measures necessary to maintain international peace and security."[5] If state sponsored, the use of civilian passenger jets as missiles on 9/11 easily satisfies the requirement of "armed attack." If Iraq had sponsored the 9/11 attacks, the US would, therefore, have the right under this Article to act in self-defense to prevent a continuing threat. Although some initially suspected Iraq, little evidence suggests that Saddam Hussein's Iraq supported or was allied with al Qaeda. No credible evidence has emerged to suggest that Iraq sponsored 9/11.

While Article 51 appears to require an "armed attack" before triggering the right of self-defense, a great many scholars[6] agree that the language "inherent right" of self-defense includes the international customary law of self-defense predating the Charter. That pre-Charter custom permits anticipatory or preemptive self-defense. As noted in chapter 1, the classic statement on the customary international law of self-defense comes from then Secretary of State

Daniel Webster in the *Caroline* case, which allows anticipatory self-defense only when "the necessity of that self-defense is instant, overwhelming, and leaving no choice of means and no moment for deliberation."[7] For example, there is general agreement that, because several Arab countries had mobilized their troops in preparing to invade Israel in 1967, because Egypt's President Ben Abdel Nasser made oral threats against Israel, and because the Arab states refused to negotiate, Israel was initially justified under Article 51 in striking first in the Six Day War.[8]

It is difficult to claim, however, that the invasion of Iraq fits within the Israeli example. There was no evidence that Iraq was mobilizing to attack the US or that a potential attack by Iraq was imminent ("instant, overwhelming, and leaving no choice of means and no moment for deliberation.") True, Iraq had plotted to assassinate former President George Henry Walker Bush in 1993 while he was visiting Kuwait. Under the pre-Charter customary international law of self-defense, a state may use force to protect its nationals, especially a former head of state. The use of force must be proportionate, however, to the threat.[9] The Clinton administration launched a nighttime cruise missile attack against the Iraqi Intelligence Ministry in response to the assassination attempt.[10] The George W. Bush administration did not expressly assert that the conspiracy to assassinate his father was a basis for the invasion, but rather that Iraq had weapons of mass destruction and was developing nuclear weapons. Even if these assertions were true, however, the requirement of imminency was not met. Iraq had not threatened either the US or its NATO allies with weapons of mass destruction or with conventional weapons[11] and there is little evidence to suggest that Iraq was planning such an attack.

Defenders of the invasion could point to the 1962 Cuban Missile Crisis as precedent for the use of force against the deployment of nuclear weapons in the absence of an imminent threat. There, the Soviet Union put middle range ballistic missiles with nuclear warheads in Cuba, its client state, just 90 miles from the US. The Joint Chiefs of Staff and many leaders in the House and the Senate urged President John F. Kennedy to invade Cuba. Rejecting that advice, President Kennedy imposed a naval blockade, a limited but unquestionable "use of force," around Cuba.[12]

Note that the USSR never actually "threat[ened] the use of force." Presumably, the US and the USSR's sailing their nuclear armed submarines 90 miles or less from each other's coasts but in international waters would be as threatening—and perfectly legal. The missile deployment, nevertheless, was highly provocative. The US and the Soviet Union were arch-enemies engaged in an increasingly dangerous nuclear arms race. Furthermore, the USSR secretly deployed these missiles during the height of the Cold War.

Reviewing the Cuban Missile Crisis, the UN Security Council implicitly approved America's use of force and the ultimate successful and peaceful resolution of the standoff.[13] The US, however, had acted with restraint. Had the US actually invaded Cuba to destroy the missiles and missile silos, query whether the Security Council and the international community would have viewed such a use of force as lawful.

Comparing the Israeli first use of force in 1967 with the US's in 1962, one could argue that the Security Council has made a practical application of Article 51, namely, that the imminency requirement may be eased somewhat when dealing with the awesome threat of nuclear weapons. However, the degree of force must be kept at a minimum, and tightly proportioned so as not to further threaten peace or encourage aggression.[14]

In the Cuban Missile Crisis, the USSR installed nuclear weapons with delivery systems that could reach the US in minutes. At the time of the invasion, Iraq had not even developed a single atomic warhead, let alone a delivery system that could reach the US. The evidence now suggests that Iraq had not been developing nuclear weapons, although it had attempted to do so in the 1980s. At best, one could characterize the nuclear threat Iraq posed before the invasion as remote; UN Security Council sanctions on Iraq had apparently forestalled Saddam Hussein's regime from building nuclear weapons and from rebuilding its chemical weapons arsenal. Furthermore, the US did not respond with restraint as it had in the Cuban Missile crisis. The US refused to wait until the UN weapons inspectors had finished their work. While Saddam Hussein was a mass killer and a brutal tyrant, the US invasion fails to meet even a loose definition of imminency and the US's response—a full-scale invasion—was not tightly proportioned to the threat as in the Cuban Missile Crisis.

11.2 The UN Security Council

11.2.1 Resolution 1441

To the surprise of many, the Bush–Cheney administration initially took their case to the UN Security Council, successfully arguing for a strict resolution, adopted in November 2002, that would insure that Iraq destroyed whatever weapons of mass destruction it possessed. When apparently a majority of the 15-member Security Council refused to pass a second resolution expressly authorizing the use of force against Iraq, the Bush–Cheney administration argued that the 2002 resolution coupled with Security Council Resolutions issued 12 and 13 years earlier gave the US the authority to invade. Such an argument, however, does not withstand scrutiny.

The relevant language of the Security Council Resolution 1441 adopted a year after 9/11 is as follows:

> The Security Council acting under chapter VII of the United Nations Charter recalls that in that context that the Council has repeatedly warned Iraq *that it will face serious consequences* as a result of its continued violations of its obligations.

Note, the Council is warning Iraq. To say that this language, "Iraq . . . will face serious consequences," authorizes unilateral *military* action by a minority of the Security Council strains the meaning of the Resolution. "Facing serious consequences" may mean force, but not necessarily a full-scale invasion; it could mean enhanced sanctions or a limited use of force. Furthermore, the context of the language implies that a second resolution would be necessary to determine whether Iraq has "continued [to] violat[e]" its obligations and, if so, what those "serious consequences" would be. Because Article 2.4 of the Charter generally prohibits the use of force and because the central purpose of the Charter is to promote peace and to resolve disputes peacefully, a state should not be entitled to take such general language as a license to launch an invasion, particularly when it has attempted and apparently failed to obtain express Security Council authorization to do so.[15]

11.2.2 *The Supposed Revival of the 1990 and 1991 Security Council Resolutions*

The US never contended that Article 51 of the UN Charter justified its invasion of Iraq. The US claimed that the two UN Security Council Resolutions of 1990 and 1991, adopted under UN Charter chapter VII, not only authorized Desert Storm and set the terms of peace at the end of the conflict, but also authorized the US's invasion in 2003. US Ambassador to the UN, John D. Negroponte, wrote to the Security Council on 20 March 2003, justifying the invasion:

> The government of Iraq decided not to avail itself of its final opportunity under Resolution 1441 and has clearly committed additional violations. . . . It has long been recognized and understood that a material breach of these obligations [under the cease-fire set by Resolution 687 adopted in 1991] removes the basis of the cease-fire and revives the authority to use force under Resolution 678, . . . In view of Iraq's material breaches, the basis for the cease-fire has been removed, and use of force is authorized.[16]

The British Attorney General, Peter Goldsmith, set forth that argument publicly and somewhat more fully than Amabassador Negroponte:

> Authority to use force against Iraq exists from the combined effect of [UN Security Council] Resolutions 678, 687 and 1441.
> 3. A material breach of Resolution 687 [adopted in 1991 to set forth ceasefire conditions ending that conflict (Desert Storm) with Iraq] revives the authority to use force under Resolution 678 [adopted in 1990 to oust Iraq from Kuwait].
> 4. In Resolution 1441 [adopted in November 2002], the Security Council determined that Iraq has been and remains in material breach of

Resolution 687, because it has not fully complied with its obligations to disarm under that resolution.

5. The Security Council in Resolution 1441 gave Iraq "a final opportunity to comply with its disarmament obligations" and warned Iraq of the "serious consequences" if it did not.

6. The Security Council also decided in Resolution 1441 that, if Iraq failed at any time to comply with and co-operate fully in the implementation of Resolution 1441, that would constitute a further material breach.

7. It is plain that Iraq has failed so to comply and therefore Iraq was at the time of Resolution 1441 and continues to be in material breach.

8. Thus, the authority to use force under Resolution 678 has revived and so continues today.

9. Resolution 1441 would in terms have provided that a further decision of the Security Council to sanction force was required if that had been intended. Thus, all that Resolution 1441 requires is reporting to and discussion by the Security Council of Iraq's failures, but not an express further decision to authorize force.[17]

There are, however, fatal flaws in Attorney General Goldsmith's argument. He himself admitted in a secret, confidential opinion given to Prime Minister Tony Blair about 10 days before issuing the public opinion that invading Iraq would probably violate international law.[18] In this secret, confidential opinion issued on March 7, 2003, Attorney General Goldsmith stated that a "reasonable case can be made" that the 2002 Security Council Resolution 1441 was sufficient by itself to authorize the use of force. Yet he affirmatively states that obtaining a second Security Council Resolution authorizing the invasion would be "the safest legal course." He further notes in his secret opinion that there would have to be "hard evidence" of Iraq's willful non-compliance and points out that "in light of the recent reporting of UN Monitoring, Verification and Inspection Commission (UNMOVIC), you will have to consider extremely carefully whether the evidence of non-compliance and non-cooperation is so compelling as to justify the conclusion that Iraq has failed to take its final opportunity."[19]

Aside from questioning the legal basis for using armed force against Iraq, Attorney General Goldsmith stressed in his secret, confidential opinion that any use of force must be proportionate. Thus, any use of force against Iraq, assuming for argument sake that Security Council 1441 did authorize the use of force, would have to be proportionate to achieving the requirements of the 1991 Security Council Resolution 687, Iraq's disarmament obligations. Thus, any use of force must be "limited to what is necessary to achieve that objective."[20] Regime change would generally not be permissible absent a showing that it was the only way to ensure that Iraq's disarmament obligations were carried out.[21]

Attorney General Goldsmith's secret opinion applies with equal force to

Ambassador Negroponte's arguments. The plain meaning of Security Council Resolution 1441 suggests that a second resolution would have been necessary to authorize the invasion under chapter VII of the UN Charter. Furthermore, the scope of the US invasion and occupation went far beyond the objective of insuring that Iraq complied with its disarmament obligations. UNMOVIC had not completed its mission when the US demanded that they leave because of its plan to invade Iraq. Hans Blix, head of UNMOVIC, observed that the US apparently had intended to invade Iraq regardless of the outcome of UNMOVIC's inspections.[22] Regime change emerged as a major US objective. Ironically, no weapons of mass destruction were found in Iraq, undermining one of the Bush–Cheney Administration's primary justifications for the war.

11.2.3 *Resolution 1483*

After the US and the UK had invaded and occupied Iraq, they sought a UN Security Council Resolution that would recognize their occupation and end UN sanctions. Apparently, US officials discovered that they would be unable to sell Iraqi oil unless the Security Council lifted the sanctions. On 22 May 2003, the Security Council voted unanimously to recognize the occupation by the US and the UK, to lift the economic sanctions on Iraq, and to grant the UN a minor, advisory role in the reconstruction.[23] One could argue that this Resolution ratified the invasion and thus purged the apparent illegality of using force absent Security Council approval. Nothing in the Resolution expressly so states, but nothing in the Resolution expressly states that it should not be taken as such a ratification either. Another interpretation is that the occupation of Iraq by the UK and the US was a *fait accompli*. In the words of the French ambassador, that while not perfect, the Resolution provides "a credible framework within which the international community will be able to lend support for the Iraqi people," words almost identical to that of US ambassador John Negroponte. Hans Corell, the Chief Legal Advisor to the UN Security Council, who played an active role in negotiating this Resolution 1483, stated that the resolution was never intended to ratify the US's invasion.[24]

11.3 Humanitarian intervention and the right to protect

A better argument under international law for the invasion of Iraq rests on the controversial doctrine of humanitarian intervention or, as it is more modernly fashioned, the Responsibility to Protect. Saddam Hussien emulated Stalin and adopted Stalinist policies, murdering and maiming political opponents, creating a reign of terror, and ruling as absolute dictator. In addition, he was the author of two aggressive wars and used banned poisonous weapons against Iran and against the Kurds.

A government's gross abuse of the human rights of its own citizens (its own nationals) challenges the existing international legal order. The doctrines of humanitarian intervention and the Responsibility to Protect authorize military intervention to stop a state from continuing to engage in such gross human rights violations.[25] Since the Second World War, these doctrines have been further supported by the wide ratification of human rights treaties and the emergence of international tribunals and other bodies mandated to protect human rights. The plain text of the UN Charter, however, permits countries to use force, absent Security Council consent, only for self-defense.[26] Neither the US nor any of its NATO allies had been attacked by Iraq nor were any under an imminent threat of such an attack. Permanent Security Council Members France, China, and Russia presumably would have vetoed any Security Council Resolution calling upon a UN military intervention, but apparently the US could not even muster a majority of the 15-member Security Council to approve such a resolution.

On the other hand, the world community can no longer idly stand by while a government grossly abuses its citizens' human rights. The Charter itself suggests that the human rights of all persons within a government's borders must be respected and that a government does not have absolute sovereign power to deprive its citizens of these rights.[27] A few noted scholars and jurists have recognized the doctrine of humanitarian intervention under sharply defined conditions: first, that "widespread and grave international crimes as [defined in the Rome Statute of the International Criminal Court] are being committed in the state [and] that the state supports them, acquiesces in them or cannot control them;"[28] second, that all alternative means to ending such abuses have been exhausted; third, that the Security Council has refused to act; and fourth, that the intervenors use only that degree of force necessary to stop the human rights abuses from recurring.[29]

The first condition presumably was met, although most of crimes that Saddam Hussein's regime committed had occurred years earlier. Nothing short of overthrowing Saddam Hussein would probably have been enough to stop the gross human rights abuses. Some, however, might argue whether all alternative means to ending such abuses had been exhausted. The focus of the national and international debate was not on Iraqi human rights violations, but on Iraq's alleged weapons of mass destruction. If human rights were the issue, one would expect substantial debate in the Security Council on this point. Another alternative means might have been establishing an ad hoc criminal tribunal for Iraq, like the ad hoc tribunals for Yugoslavia, Rwanda, Sierra Leone, Cambodia, and Lebanon. Indicting Slobodan Milosevic and key Serbian military leaders, for example, changed the dynamic in a positive direction in Yugoslavia. Opponents may argue, that since these alternatives were not explored, we cannot say for sure that the invasion was narrowly tailored to eliminating the human rights abuses. Despite these arguments, Saddam Hussein had built a powerful police state that could swiftly demolish any local resistance movement. Military force from the outside was almost certainly the only way to topple that regime.

Aside from these criteria, respected jurist and scholar Antonio Cassese, who supported NATO's intervention in Kosovo under this doctrine, included the following requirements for humanitarian intervention:

- [A] group of states (*not a single hegemonic Power*, however strong its military, political and economic authority, nor such a Power *with the support of a client state or an ally*) decides to try to halt the atrocities, with the support or at least the non-opposition of the majority of Member States of the UN;
- [A]rmed force is exclusively used for the limited purpose of stopping the atrocities and restoring respect for human rights, not for any goal going beyond this limited purpose.[30]

Although the US and its ally, the UK, cobbled together a coalition of states, the operation was essentially carried out only by the US and the UK. Many of the other states that went along could fit under the term "client states," many of whom seemed to be more interested in currying favor with the US than in insuring that human rights were restored in Iraq. Consequently, here the intervention would appear to have been carried out "by a single hegemonic power," aided by a close ally.[31]

Lastly, it is difficult to maintain that the invasion was carried out "exclusively for the purpose of stopping atrocities and restoring human rights." The main reason the Bush–Cheney administration offered was US security, not the human rights of the Iraqi people. In his letter to the Security Council justifying the invasion, US Ambassador to the UN, John Negoponte, never mentioned protecting the human rights of the Iraqi people as a ground for the invasion. As previously noted, the UN Security Council debate centered on Iraq's weapons of mass destruction.

The US is not well-positioned to make the human rights argument. The US helped install the Baath party in Iraq, having sponsored a bloody coup to overthrow the then Soviet leaning military government in 1963. The US ignored Saddam Hussein's grossly violating his citizens' human rights during the 1970s and 1980s and actively supported him, even though the US government knew he violated the ban on chemical weapons use in the war against Iran. After Desert Storm in 1991, US troops stood idly by while Saddam Hussein massacred the Shiites in Southern Iraq, Shiites whom the George H. W. Bush administration had encouraged to rise up against Saddam Hussein.[32]

On the other hand, the US's past indifference to the Iraqi people caught in the clutches of the Saddam Hussein regime might argue for humanitarian intervention, as a way for the US to atone for past sins. Research has uncovered little evidence to suggest that the invasion of 2003 was carried out for this purpose.[33]

US occupation of Iraq provides little evidence to suggest that its primary objective was to restore human rights to that country. US troops did secure the oil fields, but the administration failed to plan adequately to prevent looting of civilian infrastructure, including museums, electrical facilities, and government offices. As of this writing, the US has made progress but has not succeeded in providing adequate security to permit a return to ordinary life and the concomitant development of a civil society. Under the Geneva Conventions and the Hague Regulations, the US has the obligation to do so.

In summary, a broad interpretation of the doctrines of humanitarian intervention and Responsibility to Protect and of Security Council Resolution 1483 can be advanced to justify the invasion of Iraq under international law. A close examination of the facts, treaties, custom, the doctrines and Resolution 1483, however, suggests otherwise, that the invasion was essentially unilateral and in violation of international law.

The invasion and occupation have been strongly opposed by the Organization of the Islamic Conference and most of the US's Western allies.[34] The invasion enraged the Islamic world, increased recruitment for al Qaeda, and sparked an Iraqi civil war. Despite a considerable drop in violence, the chances that a truly democratic, stable Iraq will emerge appear remote. Although no international tribunal is likely to decide whether the invasion violated international law, the consensus of international scholars is that it did.[35] The price that the US will ultimately have to pay for this violation will probably not be fully assessed for a long time. The deeper questions are to what extent the invasion of Iraq has damaged the moral authority of the US and to what extent the invasion and occupation has strengthened al Qaeda, its allies, and sympathizers.[36]

Appendix A

Ambassador John D. Negroponte's Letter to the President of the UN Security Council Justifying the Invasion of Iraq by the United States

The Representative of the United States of America to the United Nations

March 20, 2003

To: Mr Mamady Traore

President – Security Council
United Nations
New York, New York

Excellency:

Coalition forces have commenced military operations in Iraq. These operations are necessary in view of Iraq's continued material breaches of its disarmament obligations under relevant Security Council resolutions including 1441 (2002). The operations are substantial and will secure compliance with these obligations. In carrying out these operations, our forces will take all reasonable precautions to avoid civilian casualties.

The actions being taken are authorized under existing Council resolutions: including resolution 678 (1990) and resolution 687 (1991). Resolution 687 imposed a series of obligations on Iraq, including most importantly, extensive disarmament obligations, that were the conditions of the cease-fire established under it. It has been long recognized and understood that a material breach of these obligations removes the basis of the cease-fire and revives the authority to use force under resolution 678. This has been the basis for coalition use of force in the past and has been accepted by the Council, as evidenced, for example, by the Secretary General's public announcement in January 1993 following Iraq's material breach of resolution 687 that coalition forces had received a mandate from the Council to use force according to resolution 678.

Iraq continues to be in material breach of its disarmament obligations under resolution 687, as the Council affirmed in resolution 1441. Acting under the authority of chapter VII of the UN Charter, the Council unanimously decided that Iraq has been and remained in material breach of its obligations and recalled its repeated warnings to Iraq that it will face serious consequences as a result of its continued violations of its obligations. The resolution then provided Iraq a "final opportunity" to comply, but stated specifically that violations by Iraq of its obligations under resolution 1441 to present a currently accurate, full and complete declaration of all aspects of its weapons of mass destruction programs and to comply with and cooperate fully in the resolution's implementation would constitute a further material breach.

The Government of Iraq decided not to avail itself of its final opportunity under resolution 1441 and has clearly committed additional violations. In view of Iraq's material beaches, the basis for the cease-fire has been removed, and the use of force is authorized under resolution 678.

Iraq repeatedly has refused, over a protracted period of time, to respond to diplomatic overtures, economic sanctions, and other peaceful means designed to help bring about Iraqi compliance with its obligations to disarm and to permit full inspection of its WMD and related programs. The actions that coalition forces are undertaking are an appropriate response. They are necessary to defend the United States and the international community from the threat posed by Iraq and to restore international peace and security in the area. Further delay would simply allow Iraq to continue its unlawful and threatening conduct.

It is the Government of Iraq that bears full responsibility for the serious consequences of its defiance of the Council's decisions. I would be grateful if you could circulate the text of this letter as a document of the Security Council.

Sincerely,

(signed) John D. Negroponte

Notes

1 Much of this chapter is drawn from my article *The Invasion and Occupation of Iraq: A Violation of International Law?*, Pace Alumni Mag., Spring 2004, at 16, and is reprinted with permission of the Pace Alumni Magazine.

2 UN Charter, art. 2.4

3 *Id.*, art. 51.

4 *Id.*, art. 41.

5 *Id.*, art. 51 (emphasis added).

6 The sources of international law include, treaties, custom, general principles of civilized countries, and scholarly treatises and Articles. *See* Statute of the International Court of Justice, art. 38, June 26, 1945, 59 Stat. 1031, 33 U.N.T.S. 993. Despite the growing number of international bodies and tribunals, the number of court cases is relatively small as compared with domestic law. Consequently, the writing of international law scholars generally plays a greater role in international as opposed to domestic law.

7 Mark W. Janis & John Noyes, International Law Cases and Commentary 424–25 (1997) (quoting the Caroline decision).

8 Conversely, Israel's bombing Iraq's allegedly civilian nuclear reactor in 1981 was condemned by the Security Council as an impermissible use of force because there was no threat of an imminent attack on Israel by Iraq. Given what the world now fully appreciates about Saddam Hussein that precedent may not necessarily be as weighty today. *But see* Mary Ellen O'Connell, *Lawful Self-Defense to Terrorism*, 63 U. Pitt. L. Rev. 889 (2002) ("Subsequent evidence suggests that Israel knew Egypt did not plan to attack Israel. If so, Israel's attack was unlawful.").

9 *See* Burns H. Weston, Richard A. Falk & Hilary Charlesworth, International Law and World Order 441 (1997) (quoting Myres S. McDougal & Florentino Panlilio Feliciano, Law and Minimum Public World Order—The Legal Regulation of International World Order 217 (1961)).

10 There were, however, some reports indicating that the Bush family believed that the Clinton administration's response to the plot was inadequate.

11 Granted, Iraq did fire at US and British warplanes patrolling the "no-fly" zone over Iraqi airspace, a zone that the UK and the US put into place absent direct authorization from the Security Council. The rule of proportionality, however, would limit any response by either the US or the UK. News reports indicate that the American military used a pretext defense of US warplanes in the zone as a basis for destroying command and control communications in Iraq in preparation for the US invasion.

12 Apparently, the Kennedy administration purposely rejected the term "embargo" and used the less threatening term "quarantine" to characterize the blockade. It still constituted a "use of force" within the meaning of the UN Charter.

13 *See* Roger K. Smith, *The Legality of Coercive Arms Control*, Yale J. Int'l L. 455, 488–90 (1994).

14 The Vienna Convention on the Law of Treaties states that the parties' actual practice under a treaty may be considered in interpreting a particular treaty term's meaning. *See* Vienna Convention on the Law of Treaties, art. 31(3)(b), May 23, 1969, 1155 U.N.T.S. 331, *reprinted in* 8 I.L.M. 679.

15 The Attorney General of the UK claimed that the invasion would be justified under a 1991 Security Council Resolution, authorizing initial use of force against Iraq. *See* Christopher Greenwood, *International law and the Pre-emptive Use of Force: Afghanistan, Al Qaida, and Iraq*, 4 San Diego Int'l L.J. 7, 36 (2003). The context of Resolution 1441, the express language that the Council would consider any alleged breach, the statements of several members saying the

Resolution did not carry with it automaticity (the right to engage in military action absent a second Resolution), and the changed conditions 12 years later, all undermine such an argument.

16   *US Cites Cease Fire Resolution as the Basis for the Invasion*, L.A. Times, Mar. 21, 2003, at 18.

17   *A case for war Lord Goldsmith's published advice on the legal basis for the use of force against Iraq*, The Guardian, Mar. 17, 2003, *available at* www.guardian.co.uk/world/2003/mar/17/iraq2.

18   Att'y Gen. Peter H. Goldsmith, Opinion [On Legality of Invading Iraq] For the Prime Minister (Mar. 7, 2003), *available at* http://image.guardian.co.uk/sys-files/Guardian/documents/2005/04/28/26legal.pdf (last visited Feb. 23, 2009).

19   *Id.*, para. 29.

20   *Id.*, para. 36.

21   *Id.*

22   Caitlin May, *Hans Blix, Disarming Iraq, Pantheon Books, 2004*, 12 J. Conflict & Security L. 332 (2007) (book review).

23   SC. Res. 1483, U.N. Doc. S/RES/1483 (May 22, 2003). There have been a series of resolutions extending 1483's deadline, S.C. Resolution 1859 being the most recent extending to Dec. 31 2009. The other resolutions were S.C. Res. 1790, S.C. Res. 1723, S.C. Res. 1637, & S.C. Res. 1546.

24   Hans Corell, Remarks at the Annual Conference of the American Society of International Law (Mar. 15, 2008) (attended by author).

25   *See, e.g.*, International Commission on Intervention and State Sovereignty, The Responsibility to Protect 17–18 (2001); Thomas G. Weiss, Humanitarian Intervention: Ideas in Action 11 (2007). Note, however, R2P was not expressly intended to revive the right to humanitarian intervention at least not in its old form. *See, e.g.*, Gareth Evans, The Responsibility to Protect (2008); Brian Barboure & Brian Gorlick, *Embracing the Responsibility to Protect: A Repertoire of Measures Including Asylum for Potential Victims*, 20 Int'l J. of Refugee L. 532 (2008).

26   Article 2 of the UN Charter requires members to "refrain in their international relations from the threat or use of force against the territorial integrity or political independence of any state." *See* UN Charter, art. 2.4. The Article requires states to settle their international disputes "by peaceful means," *Id.*, art. 2.3, only permitting intervention in another state by the Security Council under its chapter VII authority. *Id.*, art. 2.7. States may otherwise only use force in individual or collective self-defense. *Id.*, art. 51. The Charter also prohibits regional agents from using force without Security Council permission, "[N]o enforcement action shall be taken under regional arrangements or by regional agencies without the authorization of the Security Council." *Id.*, art. 53, para. 1. *See* Antonio Cassese, *Ex Inuria Ius Oritur: Are We Moving Towards International Legitimation of Forcible Humanitarian Countermeasures in the World Community?*, 10 Eur. J. Int'l L. 23, 24 (1999) (citing Oscar Schachter, International Law in Theory and Practice 128 (1991) for the proposition that humanitarian intervention absent Security Council authorization violates international law).

27   "Nothing contained in the present Charter shall authorize the United Nations to intervene in matters which are *essentially* within the domestic jurisdiction of any state or shall require the Members to submit such matters to settlement under the present Charter; but this principle shall not prejudice the application of enforcement measures under chapter VII." U.N Charter, art. 2.7 (emphasis added). *See also id.*, arts. 55(c) and 56 (member states pledging to promote universal respect for human rights).

28   *See, e.g.*, Jonathan I. Charney, *Anticipatory Humanitarian Intervention in Kosovo*, 32 Vand. J. Transnat'l L. 1231, 1244 (1999).

29 *Id.*; *see also* Richard A. Falk, *Kosovo, World Order and the Future of International Law*, 93 Am. J. Int'l L. 847, 853 (1999) (suggesting a five-prong test authorizing humanitarian intervention: "[1]-there is a strong burden of persuasion associated with the rejection of the United Nations framework of legal restraint on the use of force; [2]-this burden can be initially met if there is a credible prospect that a humanitarian catastrophe will otherwise occur; [3] such a burden cannot be discharged fully if diplomatic alternatives to war have not been fully explored in a sincere and convincing manner; [4] the humanitarian rationale is also sustained or undermined by the extent to which the tactics of warfare exhibit sensitivity to civilian harm, and the degree to which the intervenors avoid unduly shifting the risks of war to the supposed beneficiaries of the action so as to avoid harm to themselves; and [5] the humanitarian rationale is also weakened if there were less destructive means to protect the threatened population than those relied upon.").

30 *See* Cassese, *supra* note 26, at 27 (emphasis added). *See also* International Commission on Intervention and State Sovereignty, The Responsibility to Protect: Research, Bibliography, Background 140–41 (2001) (noting that many scholars have argued that for the use of force to be legitimate, "the overarching purpose of [intervention] should be to protect victimized populations . . . intervention should be exclusively apolitical and disinterested." Furthermore, "[i]n order to limit abuse and foster more disinterested calculations, many commentators have called for all humanitarian interventions to be multilateral").

31 Although the US failed to obtain a Security Council resolution (or apparently a majority of the Security Council) to approve the use of force against Iraq, the UN General Assembly failed to put up strong opposition to the war.

32 *See* George E. Bisharat, *Facing Tyranny with Justice: Alternatives to War in the Confrontation with Iraq*, 7 J. Gender Race & Just. 1, 28 (2003) (noting that although the US wanted Saddam Hussein removed, it did not want his regime ousted to be replaced by a Shiite regime representing the majority of the country but with potentially strong ties to fundamentalists Muslims in Iran).

33 *See, e.g.*, Kenneth Roth, *War in Iraq: Not a Humanitarian Intervention*, *in* Human Rights in the 'War on Terror' 144 (Richard A. Wilson ed., 2005). Roth notes that before the invasion "[a] humanitarian rationale was occasionally offered for the war [in Iraq], but it was so plainly subsidiary to other reasons." *Id*. However, arguments for a humanitarian motive for the Iraq war appeared frequently *after* the invasion, when it became clear that Saddam had not possessed weapons of mass destruction or a WMD program. *Id*.

34 At a summit shortly before the invasion the Organization of the Islamic Conference categorically rejected "any strike against Iraq." Communiqué on Iraq, adopted at the Second Emergency Session of the Islamic Summit Conference (Mar. 5, 2003). Just five days before the invasion France, Germany, and Russia issued a joint statement urging "*all* [Security] Council members to do everything possible for a peaceful course to prevail." Joint Statement by Russia, France and Germany, Mar. 15, 2003, *available at* www.ln.mid.ru/brp_4.nsf/english.

35 *See, e.g.*, John W. Head, *Responding to 9/11: Lurching Toward a Rule of Scofflaw*, 15 Kan. J.L. & Pub. Pol'y 1 (2005) ("Virtually all international lawyers . . . agree that the actions of the Bush administration in attacking and invading Iraq in March 2003 were inconsistent with legal rules that have been in place for over half a century"); Richard A. Falk, *What Future for the UN Charter System of War Prevention?*, 97 Am. J. Int'l L. 590 (2003) ("[T]here are strong legal, moral and political reasons to deny both legality and legitimacy to such a use of force [in Iraq]."). For links to numerous other articles discussing the illegality of the

Iraq War *see Links to Opinions on Legality of War Against Iraq, available at* www.robincmiller.com/ir-legal.htm.

36   *See, e.g.*, Thomas J. Biersteker, Sue E. Eckert & Nikos Passas, Countering the Financing of Terrorism 57 (2007) (commenting that "[the Iraq war has provided a substantial impetus to al Qaeda . . . providing it with a base to recruit, train, and fight"); Mohammed M. Hafez, Suicide Bombers in Iraq: the Strategy and Ideology of Martyrdom 232 (2007) (stating that "[t]he insurgency in Iraq . . . might generate the necessary opportunities, networks, and ideological frame-work for the revival of al Qaeda"); James J. F. Frost, Countering Terrorism and Insurgency in the 21st Century 64 (2007) (noting that "the U.S. invasion of Iraq has become a ready symbol tailor-made for al Qaeda recruitment").

12 The invasion and occupation of Afghanistan

The legal challenge posed by the haven state

12.1 Pre-9/11 legal regime

In 1996, Osama bin Laden had made himself unwelcome in Sudan where he had arrived five years before with high hopes for himself and his terrorist organization.[1] He had spent a good deal of his inherited fortune in Sudan with little to show for it. The only country accepting him in 1996 was Afghanistan, or, more accurately, the Taliban government that controlled about 90 percent of Afghanistan. Bin Laden's organization is reputed to have paid the Taliban government a considerable amount of money to set up bases in that country. From 1996 to 2001, some 20,000 individuals reportedly received terrorist training in al Qaeda's bases there.[2] The September 11, 2001 attacks, sponsored by al Qaeda, prompted the US to invade Afghanistan a month later. This chapter seeks to answer the question of whether the invasion of Afghanistan violated international law.

The question posed here is not unique to the US and Afghanistan. Rebel groups have often used neighboring countries as safe havens for training, for obtaining and storing military equipment and supplies, for sheltering themselves, and for launching attacks on the victim state. Analytically, non-state-actor terrorist organizations closely resemble rebel groups attempting to overthrow their native governments. The UN General Assembly Declaration on Aggression concludes that states which aid such organizations are responsible for their acts under the following circumstances: "The sending by or on behalf of a State of *armed bands, groups, irregulars or mercenaries*, which carry out acts of armed force against another State of such gravity as to amount to . . . [armed attack] or its [the haven state's] *substantial involvement* therein." Private non-state actors such as al Qaeda fit within "armed bands, groups [or] irregulars." The US has attacked the tribal areas of Pakistan apparently because the Taliban are using the areas to launch attacks on Afghanistan. Similarly the US has attacked Syria near its border with Iraq allegedly because Syria has not done enough to prevent foreign fighters from passing through Syria to Iraq. The US supported Ethiopia's invasion of Somalia in 2007 because the Islamic Courts then controlling much of Somalia allegedly were aiding al Qaeda. Turkey has attacked Kurdistan within Iraq, allegedly to stop Kurdistan Workers Party (PKK) members who are using that land to launch terrorist attacks upon Turkey.

There are countless examples from history in which one state either actively or passively aids rebels from another state, helping them launch attacks on their own state. In the *Caroline* case in 1837, as discussed in the previous chapter, Canadian rebels were using the US as a sanctuary to attack then British-controlled Canada.[3] During the Vietnam War, the Viet Cong used neighboring Cambodia as a staging point for carrying out attacks against South Vietnam. A more recent example, the US involvement in Nicaragua is worthy of legal analysis.[4] President Ronald Reagan's administration saw Sandinista Nicaragua as the germ of another Cuba in Latin America. Although democratically elected, the Sandinista government began a program of nationalization that alarmed President Reagan and his inner circle. Thus began the most disturbing adventure in that administration: the illicit trade with Iran, which in turn armed the Contras—those Nicaraguans who opposed the Sandinistas—after the US Congress prohibited the administration from providing additional military assistance to the Contras. In any event, the Reagan administration, or more precisely, the CIA, trained, equipped, and financed the Contras to carry out a civil war against the elected Nicaraguan government. Nicaragua, in turn, aided the Farabundo Martí National Liberation Front (FMLN) to carry out an insurgency against a then-close ally to the US, El Salvador. In addition to heavily supporting the Contras, the CIA mined Nicaragua's harbors.

Aside from President Daniel Ortega's arguing Nicaragua's case before the UN Security Council, his country sued the US in the International Court of Justice (ICJ). The resulting case is complex. Although the ICJ addressed numerous issues, two issues are particularly significant. First, the Court established (or confirmed) the responsibility that an aiding state bears for helping private, irregular groups attack another state, and second, the Court set forth the criteria under international law of self-defense under which a state attacked by such groups may use armed force against the aiding state.

The *Nicaragua v. United States* case (*Case Concerning Military and Para-military Activities in and against Nicaragua*)[5] before the International Court of Justice raised some disturbing questions. In accepting the compulsory jurisdiction of the Court, the US had attached a reservation, refusing such jurisdiction concerning cases involving the interpretation of a multilateral treaty, in particular, the Charter of the United Nations. Nicaragua's complaint rested primarily on an alleged UN Charter Article 2.4 violation, the impermissible use of armed force by one state against another state. Yet the Court held that it was not using the Charter, but customary international law. The Court's arguments on custom running alongside, but presumably independent of the Charter are probably sound, but the US almost certainly would have added clarifying language if it realized it could have been hauled into the ICJ on a customary law ground virtually identical to the Charter.[6]

When the Reagan administration learned that the ICJ was still retaining jurisdiction despite the US's reservation, President Reagan withdrew the US from the compulsory jurisdiction of the court. The ICJ, nevertheless, kept jurisdiction over the case, as the Court's statute authorized.

In any event, the Court set the bar high for a victim state to demonstrate that another state's aiding a non-state actor amounts to an "armed attack" under custom and under Article 51 of the Charter. Initially the Court focused on Nicaragua's claim that by funding, equipping, supplying, and training the Contras, who then carried out attacks within Nicaragua, the US had illegally used force against Nicaragua and was responsible for all the actions of the Contras. US involvement in the Contras' operation against the Sandinista government was considerable. Not only did the US give the Contras arms, supplies, and training, but the US also selected the Contra leaders and gave them a salary.[7] Allegedly inspired by the so-called CIA assassination manual, the Contras carried out a series of operations on Nicaraguan soil, including the alleged "assassinations" or targeted killings of town and village leaders. The ICJ, however, rejected Nicaragua's assertion that the US was responsible for the Contras' acts: "For this conduct [United States' support of the Contras] to give rise to legal responsibility of the United States, it would in principle have to be proved that that State had *effective control of the military or paramilitary operations* in the course of which the alleged violations were committed."[8]

In addition to the control test, the *Nicaragua* case is the touchstone for much modern analysis of the concept of self-defense. In the case, the Court asked whether the US could legally justify its actions against Nicaragua under Article 51 of the Charter as a (collective) self-defense response to an armed attack committed by Nicaragua. The Court analyzed when and under what circumstances a state's sending "armed bands" to attack another state triggers the right of self-defense under customary international law. Concluding that Article 3 of the UN General Assembly's Declaration on Aggression constituted customary international law, the Court found that Nicaragua's assistance to rebels who were fighting the El Salvadoran government did not constitute an armed attack:

> [I]n customary law, the prohibition of armed attacks may apply to the sending by a State of armed bands to the territory of another State, if such an operation, because of its scale and effects, would have been classified as an armed attack rather than as a mere frontier incident had it been carried out by regular armed forces. But the Court does *not* believe that the concept of "armed attack" includes . . . *assistance to rebels* in the form of the provision of weapons or logistical or other support.[9]

Presumably, the ICJ was attempting to limit the right of self-defense out of a concern that a broad right might lead to greater violence. For example, if the

US's support for the Contras constituted an "armed attack," then Nicaragua would have the right to use proportionate armed force against the US.[10] Although tiny Nicaragua would have been unlikely to do so given the enormous military power of the US, one could easily imagine other scenarios, Pakistan–India for example, in which armed conflict could explode as a result of such a broad rule. A broad definition of self-defense, one advocated by the US and Nicaragua, would presumably have justified India using force against Pakistan for the 2008 Mumbai attacks. (If, as many experts believe, the Lashkar-e-Taiba are responsible for the 2008 Mumbai attacks, then India under the broad definition would be entitled to use force against Pakistan: The Pakistan Inter Services Intelligence (ISI) funded, armed, and trained that group, but there is little credible evidence at the time of writing that the Pakistani government ordered the group to carry out the attacks or "effectively controlled" the Lashkar-e-Taiba.[11])

The ICJ did not establish a blanket excuse for an aiding state: "Such assistance [by the state to the rebel group] may be regarded as a threat or use of force, or *amount to intervention* in the internal or external affairs of other States."[12] The rule prohibiting intervention is set forth in Article 2.7 of the UN Charter, stating that "[n]othing in the present Charter shall authorize the United Nations to *intervene* in matters which are essentially within the domestic jurisdiction of any state. . . ."[13] Thus the aiding state is responsible under international law for assisting rebel groups, and has an obligation to make reparation for the injuries suffered by the victim state. The ICJ held the US responsible under this theory.[14] The ICJ, however, underscored that unless the aiding state effectively controlled the rebel group, the victim state lacks the right under custom (and presumably under Article 51) to use armed force against the aiding state.

Nine years after *Nicaragua v. United States*, the UN Security Council's International Criminal Tribunal for the former Yugoslavia (ICTY), in *The Prosecutor v. Dusko Tadic*,[15] established a lower standard for imputing the acts of a terrorist or insurgent group to a state: "the overall control test." There, the Appellate Chamber of the ICTY had to decide whether the original state (the Federal Republic of Yugoslavia) is responsible for the acts of its former soldiers and the military force after they had formed in a neighboring emerging state (Bosnia), which broke off or seceded from the original state. In *Tadic*, the ICTY required that the state "ha[ve] a role in the organizing, coordinating or planning the military actions of the military group, in addition to financing, training and equipping or providing operational support to that group." Unlike the ICJ in *Nicaragua v. United States*, however, the *Tadic* court noted that to be responsible, a state need not "issue instructions [to the terrorist or rebel group] for the commission of specific acts contrary to international law."[16]

Well before September 11, 2001, the Security Council condemned the Taliban for serving as a haven state for al Qaeda: In 1998, the Council demanded in paragraph 13 of Resolution 1214 that "the Taliban stop providing sanctuary and training for international terrorists and their organizations [namely, Osama bin Laden and al Qaeda], and that all Afghan factions cooperate with efforts to bring indicted terrorists to justice. . . ." In 1999, the Council, acting under its chapter VII powers, "determin[ed] that the failure of the Taliban authorities to respond to the demands *in paragraph 13* of resolution 1214 *constitutes a threat to international peace and security*. . . ."[17] In this same resolution under chapter VII, the Security Council in an operational paragraph "insist[ed]" that the Taliban "cease the provision of sanctuary and training for international terrorists and their organizations. . . ." In the second operational paragraph, the Security Council "demand[ed] that the Taliban turn over Osama bin Laden without further delay. . . ." Two other pre-September 11 Security Council Resolutions under chapter VII condemned the Taliban regime and other factions for, among other things, serving as a safe haven for terrorist organizations.[18]

A strict reading of *Nicaragua* suggests that under the publicly available evidence the Taliban did not either on 11 September 2001 or on 7 October 2001 "effectively control" al Qaeda.[19] The Taliban did provide al Qaeda training bases. They permitted thousands of Jihadists to enter the country to attend the training camps. There is, however, little publicly available evidence that the Taliban ever directly funded al Qaeda or equipped their members,[20] let alone issued Osama bin Laden orders about the conduct of his organization's operations.

On the other hand, the Taliban repeatedly and openly defied the Security Council's chapter VII resolutions demanding that the Taliban cease serving as a safe haven for al Qaeda. The Taliban also defied a 1999 resolution requiring the Taliban to extradite Osama bin Laden. None of these pre-September 11 resolutions state or imply that a victim state may use force against al Qaeda or the Taliban. But may a state's defying the Security Council's demand to stop aiding a terrorist organization on the state's soil not constitute a sufficient degree of complicity with the terrorist organization such as to incur direct responsibility for the terrorist organization's use of force against another state?[21] By openly defying the UN Security Council, the foremost international body, did the Taliban adopt al Qaeda's actions as the Taliban's own? On the other hand, the Security Council is the appropriate organ to determine violations of its own resolutions, not a single state or a group of states.

The Taliban might also be considered responsible under the *Tadic* test. By letting al Qaeda set up training camps on Afghanistan soil, by permitting thousands of Jihadists from all over the world to enter Afghanistan to receive terrorist training at the al Qaeda camps, the Taliban "ha[d] a *role* in organizing . . . the military actions of the military group [al Qaeda]." Under the *Tadic* test, the Taliban did not have to give specific "instructions" or orders to al Qaeda to be responsible for its acts.

Proponents of the Taliban, however, could argue that it did not fund al Qaeda or provide it with training, weapons, or supplies. The Taliban "merely" allowed al Qaeda to operate training bases on Afghan soil. Thus, the Taliban could argue that they lacked "overall control" of al Qaeda even under the more liberal *Tadic* approach. The Taliban apparently did not directly "coordinate" al Qaeda's military actions, but rather "merely" helped them with logistics, a far cry from "effective control," but not amounting to "overall control" either.

Furthermore, *Tadic* dealt with an individual accused of a criminal offense, not a state that has allegedly used military force against another state in violation of international law. The ICJ, in *Nicaragua v. United States*, implied that a haven or otherwise aiding state will incur state responsibility for aiding an armed group operating outside its territory. Assistance alone, however, would not trigger Article 51 of the UN Charter or its customary international law analog. Consequently, the Taliban could argue that *Tadic* and *Nicaragua v. United States* can be reconciled to reach the conclusion that the Taliban's allowing a safe haven to al Qaeda does not justify the US launching an invasion of Afghanistan, toppling its government, inserting a new one in its place, and removing from its soil captured Taliban militia.

Lastly, proponents of the Taliban could argue that defiance of the Security Council does not necessarily indicate that the haven state controls or strongly supports the terrorist organization. For whatever reason, the haven state is merely taking the position that it will not accede to the Security Council's demand to expel Osama bin Laden and his organization. The Taliban regime might incur state responsibility for ignoring the Security Council's resolutions, but the Security Council did not authorize any state to use force against the Taliban. That would have required a separate resolution. The Security Council had ample opportunity to issue such a resolution, but chose not to do so. Consequently, proponents of the Taliban would argue that little should be deduced from the Taliban's disregard of Security Council resolutions.

12.2 Post 9/11 Legal regime

The devastating September 11 attacks shocked America even more than the Japanese bombing of Pearl Harbor. Al Qaeda's attack on the US that day shattered forever the myth that the oceans protected the US from such foreign bombardment. The attacks changed the thinking of most Americans, including policymakers on all sides of the aisle. Without for a moment forgetting the horror of state terrorism, the 7/7 attacks in London, the 3/11 attacks in Madrid, the 2002 Bali bombings, the 2003 Beslan School Massacre in Russia, the assassination of Benazir Bhutto in 2007, and the November 2008 attacks in Mumbai, among many others, have awakened the international community to the dangers that private terrorist organizations pose to public world order.

12.3 UN Security Council action

Reacting swiftly to September 11, the UN Security Council issued an unequivocal condemnation of the terrorist attacks three days later, called such attacks a threat to international peace and security, and "recognize[ed] the inherent right of individual and collective self defense under the UN Charter."[22] Less than three weeks later, the Security Council issued a far more detailed, policy-specific resolution on stopping international terrorism. Acting under its chapter VII powers, the Security Council adopted measures to stop financing of terrorist organizations, to ensure that individuals engaged in terrorism be prosecuted, and to require states to "afford one another the greatest measure of assistance in connection with criminal investigations" of terrorists. The resolution also prohibits states from "providing any form of support, active *or passive*" to individual terrorists or their organizations. The resolution adds that "all States *shall . . . deny safe haven* to those who finance, plan, support, or commit terrorist acts, or provide safe havens. . . ."[23]

In this resolution, the Security Council also established a "Committee of the Security Council to monitor implementation of the resolution."[24] Taking this unusual step presumably evidences the Security Council's resolve to insure that its resolution is followed. Article 25 of the UN Charter requires all member states to follow Security Council chapter VII resolutions, but the Security Council has often done little to states that have flouted the Council.[25]

The resolution is also notable for what it does not say. It does not say what consequences follow for a state that refuses to obey the resolution. If a state, for example, continues to serve as a haven state to a terrorist organization (but lacks effective control of that organization), may a victim state use armed force against the haven state? The US has argued for an affirmative answer to this question. In the preamble, the resolution does "reaffirm the need to *combat by all means, in accordance with the Charter of the United Nations*, the threat to international peace and security caused by *terrorist* acts." If the victim state's sole purpose is not to obtain territory or to engage in regime change, but to stop the terrorist organization from operating in the haven state, proponents of using armed force could argue that a narrowly focused, proportionate attack on the haven state's territory would, as a result of this resolution, be an authorized "means" tö "combat" terrorism and thus would not be "inconsistent with the purposes of the United Nations" under Article 51.

On the other hand, if the Security Council had so intended, it could have easily included an express authorization for victim states to use force against recalcitrant haven states. The "combat by all means" preambular paragraph quoted above begs the question, for it says states may engage in combat only "in accordance with the Charter of the United Nations." The question is, what does the Charter permit or perhaps more specifically what use of force, if any, has the Security Council authorized under its chapter VII powers? The resolution does little to affirmatively answer this question.

12.4　The dissent in *Nicaragua v. United States*, the emerging rule?

Even if the Taliban did not meet the *Tadic* test, the US should argue that in the post-9/11 world, the dissent in *Nicaragua v. United States* is sounder both as a matter of law and as a matter of promoting international world order. Also relying upon Article 3(g) of the UN General Assembly's Declaration against Aggression, the dissent argued that by funding, equipping, training, and providing safe haven for the FMLN Salvadoran rebels, Nicaragua was "substantially involved" with that organization and therefore should have been considered to have been responsible for their acts.[26] Likewise, the US could argue that by providing a safe haven for al Qaeda, by allowing them to establish training bases, and by permitting thousands of terrorist trainees to enter Afghanistan to attend al Qaeda's camps, the Taliban regime was "substantially involved" in al Qaeda's activities.[27] Furthermore, there is no question that on September 11, 2001 al Qaeda carried out an "armed attack" within the meaning of Article 51 of the UN Charter.

International terrorism threatens democracies and other states around the globe. Al Qaeda, for example, is said to operate underground in over 100 countries. Stopping such organizations is exceedingly difficult because of the clandestine nature of the organization and its operations. It is, however, far easier to identify states that aid and provide safe haven to such organizations. States should be deterred from doing so. Thus, the strict rule of "effective control" set forth in *Nicaragua v. United States* should be modified.[28] The "substantial" involvement test puts states on notice that if they significantly aid terrorist organizations, such states not only will be deemed responsible for the terrorist group's actions, but also may be subject to self-defense measures from the state attacked by the terrorist group.

The problem with the "substantial involvement" test, however, is its vagueness. "Substantial" is a weasel word like "reasonable." In proof contexts, some US courts, for example, have held that a "substantial" likelihood is less than a 50 percent probability, making even a 10 percent chance "substantial." A victim state could thus characterize any assistance a state gives a terrorist organization as "substantial involvement." For example, should a suspected haven state let one of its hospitals offer medical treatment to a "known terrorist," a "victim state" could plausibly claim that the "haven state," in providing medical assistance, is "substantially involved" with the terrorist organization and its acts. Giving victim states the right to use force on such a loose standard creates too broad a license to attack another state.

12.5　Legal limits on using force against haven states

If the haven or aiding state "effectively controlled" the terrorist organization or rebel group, and the terrorist organization launched an "armed attack" against the victim state, the victim state would be entitled under Article 51 of the Charter to make a proportionate use of armed force in self-defense. The victim state could presumably attack military targets in the haven state as long as the attack met the customary law requirements of proportionality and as long as the state had exhausted all peaceful means of resolving the dispute. Since the haven state would have effectively controlled the terrorist organization, the latter can be considered an organ of that state.

If, however, the haven state does not effectively control the terrorist organization, then a different rule should apply. If the haven state acts passively, letting a terrorist organization operate bases on its territory, but does not otherwise help that organization, and the terrorist organization has carried out an armed attack on the victim state within the meaning of Article 51, then, after exhausting all peaceful avenues, the victim state has a much narrower right of self-defense. It may target only the terrorists, not general military targets in the haven state.[29] Since in many cases these would essentially be targeted killing operations, the limits set forth in chapter 8 on targeted killings would have to be applied.

For example, President Clinton responded in such a manner to Iraq's plot and attempt to assassinate former President George H. W. Bush in Kuwait. As noted in the previous chapter, the Clinton administration ordered that cruise missiles be targeted at Iraq's Intelligence Services headquarters late at night to avoid civilian casualties.[30] Similarly, if Somalia's Islamic Courts had been harboring a dozen dangerous al Qaeda members who had been threatening continuing major attacks on the US, the US could have carried out a narrowly focused operation against the al Qaeda members. However, the US would have to have exhausted all peaceful remedies. Furthermore, the operation would have had to pose little danger to civilians. Under this test, however, the US could not invade or support the invasion of the country.

Professor Jordan Paust has, in essence, so interpreted the resolutions and *Nicaragua*. He criticizes the US use of force in Afghanistan as being too broad.[31] Thus attacking al Qaeda at Bora Bora would presumably be valid, but pursuing the Taliban as well goes beyond *Nicaragua* and *Tadic*. Jack Beard, on the other hand, argues that the close relationship between the Taliban and al Qaeda, the two UN Security Council resolutions, plus state practice simultaneous with the US's 7 October invasion demonstrate that the invasion comported with international law.[32] Beard points out that 36 nations offered the US assistance and 44 nations gave the US the right to overfly their territory.[33] He also notes that the Organization of the Islamic Conference (OIC) representing 53 Islamic nations almost unanimously condemned the 9/11 attacks. Furthermore, the OIC did little in opposition to the US invasion of Afghanistan.

12.6 Humanitarian intervention and the right to protect

Both authors largely overlook, however, the Taliban regime's gross violations of human rights, and the emerging norms of the Responsibility to Protect [one's own nationals] and humanitarian intervention. The Taliban decreed that Afghan women be barred from paid employment, that Afghan girls be banned from school, and that Afghan women be accompanied by an adult male and wear the cocoon-like burqa whenever leaving home. Amnesty International reports that "[s]cores of women were beaten" for failing to wear the burqa.[34] Amputations of feet and hands for theft became common; the accused were typically denied legal counsel and were adjudged guilty after a summary trial with no right of appeal.[35] Men were required to wear beards and, in many cases, forced by the threat of physical assault, to attend Friday prayers.[36] Thousands were reportedly detained for "un-Islamic" behavior.[37] Furthermore, the Taliban destroyed the magnificent, more than 1,000-year-old, towering Buddha statues as sacrilegious images of the infidel. In short, the Taliban constructed a totalitarian religious state.

Only three countries ever recognized the Taliban regime.[38] The United Nations General Assembly refused to permit the Taliban to occupy the Afghanistan seat at the UN, and the OIC likewise denied them the Afghan seat in the Organization of the Islamic Conference. The Security Council condemned the Taliban for denying women fundamental rights and for committing other human rights and law of war violations.[39] In a 1996 resolution directed primarily at the Taliban, the Security Council in an operational paragraph "[d]enounced *the discrimination against girls and women* and *other violations of human rights and international humanitarian law* in Afghanistan, and note[d] with deep concern possible repercussions on international relief and reconstruction programmes in Afghanistan."[40] The international support that the US received for invading Taliban Afghanistan may thus have derived not only from the world's revulsion at the 9/11 attacks, but also from the world's revulsion at the Taliban regime's gross human rights depradations.

12.7 Conclusion

The US invasion of Afghanistan on 7 October 2001, from a legal point of view, constituted a "perfect storm," which justified the use of armed force, with a few caveats. It is hard to fit the relationship between the Taliban and al Qaeda as the former "effectively controlling the latter." The available evidence is more complex and does not suggest a command–control operation. On the other hand, the Taliban openly defied Security Council resolutions requiring them in effect to surrender Osama bin Laden and to eject al Qaeda from the country. The Taliban did let al Qaeda train some 20,000 Jihadists from all over the world on Afghan soil. The Taliban created a totalitarian religious state, not only denying women and girls basic rights, but also repressing virtually the entire population. These three factors together, though not justifying the US's use of armed force, help explain why the US invasion garnered so much support in the international community.

To the extent that the US invasion of Afghanistan was justified by principles embodied in the Responsibility to Protect or the doctrine of humanitarian intervention, the greater the responsibility of the US and now NATO forces to pay the highest respect for human rights and humanitarian law. Unfortunately, the perception has been created that the US and NATO bombardments have been indiscriminate, causing significant civilian casualties.

The war in Afghanistan is further complicated by the role of the Pakistani tribal areas. Despite statements by some Pakistani leaders and efforts by the Pakistani army, the tribal areas remain largely under the control of warlords, some of whom are apparently sheltering the Taliban, al Qaeda and Ayman al-Zawahiri. Pakistan has been unable if not unwilling to control the areas. Thus, the US should be deemed to have the right to use "selective and proportionate" armed force in the tribal areas against al Qaeda and the Taliban. Yet, NATO attacks led by the US have engendered uproar in Pakistan, underscoring the wisdom of protecting civilians and proceeding cautiously in using armed force against the sovereign territory of a state that lacks effective control of a terrorist organization.

The megaterrorist event of 9/11, state practice, and the two post-9/11 Security Council resolutions have implicitly broadened the rule of self-defense to prevent such private organizations from endangering other countries and their people. Neither the resolutions nor evolving custom, however, generally authorize preventive war or unlimited use of armed force against haven states that lack effective control of a terrorist organization within their borders.

Notes

1   Lawrence Wright, The Looming Tower 165, 119 (2006).
2   A March 2002 NY Times article states that "an estimated 20,000 recruits passed through roughly a dozen training camps since 1996."
3   Timothy Kearley, *Raising The Caroline*, 17 Wis. Int'l L.J. 325, 328–29 (1999).
4   *See* Public Broadcasting Service, *War & Cambodia* (2003), *available at* www.pbs.org/independentlens/refugee/war_cambodia.html (last visited Feb. 19, 2009).
5   Case Concerning Military and Paramilitary Activities in and Against Nicaragua (Nicaragua v. United States), 1986 I.C.J. 14 (June 27).
6   The relevant language of the reservation is as follows:

> [T]he United States of America recognizes as compulsory ipso facto and without special agreement, in relation to any other State accepting the same obligation, the jurisdiction of the International Court of Justice in all legal disputes hereafter arising . . .
>   *Provided*, that this declaration shall **not** apply to . . . (c) **disputes arising under a multilateral treaty**, unless (1) all the Parties to the treaty affected by the decision are also Parties to the case before the Court, or (2) the US of America specially agrees to jurisdiction. . . .

United States Declaration of Aug. 14, 1946, 61 Stat. 1218, T.I.A.S. No. 1598, 1 U.N.T.S. 9 (emphasis added).

7   Case Concerning Military and Paramilitary Activities in and Against Nicaragua (Nicaragua v. United States), 1986 I.C.J. 14, paras. 100, 112 (June 27). (noting that "[a]ccording to the affidavit of Mr. Chamorro, who was directly

concerned, when the FDN (Nicaraguan Democratic Force] was formed 'the name of the organization, the members of the political junta, and the members of the general staff were all chosen or approved by the CIA;' later the CIA asked that a particular person be made head of the political directorate of the FDN, and this was done. However, the question of the selection, installation and payment of the leaders of the *contra* force is merely one aspect among others of the degree of dependency of that force.") *See also*, Leslie Cockburn, Out of Control: The Story of the Reagan administration's Secret War in Nicaragua, the Illegal Arms Pipeline, and the Contra Drug Connection 249 (1987).

8   Case Concerning Military and Paramilitary Activities in and Against Nicaragua (Nicaragua v. United States), 1986 I.C.J. 14, para. 115 (June 27).

9   *Id.* at 195 (emphasis added).

10 In the actual case, the Court was focusing on whether the United States had the right to use force under a collective self-defense rationale for Nicaragua's supporting the FMLN rebel group against the government of El Salvador.

11 The International Law Commission's Draft Convention appears to slightly relax the *Nicaragua v. United States* standard: "The conduct of a person or group of persons shall be considered an act of a State under international law if the person or group of persons is in fact acting on the instructions of, or under the direction or control of, that State in carrying out the conduct." The United Nations (2005), *Draft Convention on Internationally Wrongful Acts*, art. 8, *available at* http://untreaty.un.org/ilc/texts/instruments/english/draft%20Articles/9_6_2001.pdf (last visited Feb. 19, 2009).

Even if one were to consider ISI a rogue element of the government or some in the ISI rogue officers, Pakistan would still be legally responsible for their acts. See ILC's Draft Convention on Internationally Wrongful Acts: "The conduct of *any State organ* shall be considered an act of that State under international law, whether the organ exercises legislative, executive, judicial or any other functions, *whatever* position it holds in the organization of the State, and whatever its character as an organ of the central Government or of a territorial unit of the State." The United Nations (2005), *Draft Convention on Internationally Wrongful Acts*, art. 4.1, *available at* http://untreaty.un.org/ilc/texts/instruments/english/draft%20Articles/9_6_2001.pdf (last visited Feb. 19, 2009).

12 *Id.*

13 UN Charter, art. 2.7.

14 In its final judgment, the ICJ "[d]ecides that the United States of America, by training, arming, equipping, financing and supplying the contra forces or otherwise encouraging, supporting and aiding military and paramilitary activities in and against Nicaragua, has acted, against the Republic of Nicaragua, in breach of its obligation under customary international law *not to intervene* in the affairs of another State. . . ." Case Concerning Military and Paramilitary Activities in and Against Nicaragua (Nicaragua v. United States), 1986 I.C.J. 14, para. 292(3) (June 27).

15 Prosecutor v. Dusco Tadic, Case No. IT-94-1-AR72, Appeals Chamber Judgment (Oct. 2, 1995), *available at* http://www.mpil.de/shared/data/pdf/vrstraf0910_090911.pdf.

16 *Id.*

17 S.C. Res. 1267, U.N. Doc. S/res/1267 (Oct. 15, 1999). Note also that a year earlier the Security Council issued a resolution directed at the Taliban, which stated, among other things, that the Council was "[d]eeply disturbed by the continuing use of Afghan territory, especially areas controlled by the Taliban, for the sheltering and training of terrorists and the planning of terrorist acts, and reiterating that the suppression of international terrorism is essential for the maintenance of international peace and security. . . ." S.C. Res. 1214, U.N.

Doc S/res/1214 (Dec. 8, 1998). Two weeks later, the Security Council issued another resolution calling for a peaceful resolution in Afghanistan, particularly focusing on the fighting between the Taliban and the Northern Alliance, but also "demand[ing] the Afghan factions to refrain from harbouring and training terrorists and their organizations and to halt illegal drug activities. . . ." S.C. Res. 1193, U.N. Doc. S/res/1193 (Aug. 28, 1998).

18   On 13 August 1998, in condemning al Qaeda's attacks on the US embassies in Eastern Africa, the Security Council "[s]tress[ed] that every Member State has the duty to refrain from organizing, instigating, assisting or participating in terrorist acts in another State or acquiescing in organized activities within its territory directed towards the commission of such acts. . . ." S.C. Res. 1189, U.N. Doc. S/res/1189 (Aug. 13, 1998). *See also* S.C. Res. 1333, U.N. Doc. S/res/1333 (Dec. 19, 2000); S.C. Res. 1363, U.N. Doc. S/res/1363 (July 30, 2001). Both resolutions reaffirmed resolution 1267. U.N. S.C. Resolution 1333 in a preambular paragraph "{d}eplor{ed} the fact that the Taliban continues to provide safe haven to Osama bin Laden and to allow him and others associated with him to operate a network of terrorist training camps from Taliban-controlled territory and to use Afghanistan as a base from which to sponsor international terrorist operations. . . ." S.C. Res. 1333, U.N. Doc. S/res/1333 (Dec. 19, 2000).

In a preambular paragraph, U.N. S.C. Resolution 1363, {r}eaffirm{s} its previous resolutions, in particular resolution 1267 (1999) of 15 October 1999 and resolution 1333 (2000) of 19 December 2000, as well as the statements of its President on the situation in Afghanistan, [and] {d}etermin{es} that the situation in Afghanistan **constitutes a threat to international peace and security** in the region. . . . S.C. Res. 1363, U.N. Doc. S/RES/1363 (July 30, 2001), *available at* www.un.org/Docs/scres/2001/sc2001.htm (last visited Feb. 19, 2009).

19   *But see* Mary Ellen O'Connell, *Lawful Self-Defense to Terrorism*, 63 U. Pitt. L. Rev. 889, 901 (2002). Professor O'Connell relied mainly on the British White Paper issued on 4 October 2001 for the proposition that "the Taliban, Afghanistan's de facto government, developed such close links to the known terrorist organization al Qaeda that it became responsible for the acts of al Qaeda. With that responsibility came the right of the US and United Kingdom to take the fight to Afghanistan." *Id.* The White Paper stated, among other things, "Usama Bin Laden's Al Qaida and the Taleban régime have a close and mutually dependent alliance[.]" White Paper, *Responsibility for Terrorist Atrocities in the United States* (Oct. 4, 2001), *available at* www.ratical.org/ratville/CAH/linkscopy/page3554.html) (last visited Sept. 9, 2009). Others, however, have suggested that there were real tensions between the Taliban regime and Osama bin Laden, the former having initially agreed to expel bin Laden. *See, e.g.*, Jason Burke, Al-Qaeda 164–66 (2003). There of course may be reliable classified information that shows that al Qaeda was in effect an organ of the Taliban regime by 11 September 2001. The hard question is how much assistance must an aiding (haven) state provide a terrorist organization for a victim state to be entitled to use armed force against the aiding state. Regarding another question, Professor O'Connell indicates, however, that the US's continued bombing after the Taliban had fallen "may" have violated the proportionality principle of self-defense. O'Connell, *supra* at 904.

20   *See The Reach of War*, N.Y. Times, June 19, 2004, *available at* www.nytimes.com/2004/06/19/world/the-reach-of-war-intelligence-no-saudi-payment-to-qaeda-is-found.html (mainly discussing Saudi funding but also stating, "There is no convincing evidence that any government financially supported Al Qaeda before 9/11." It added, "Saudi Arabia has long been considered the primary source of Al Qaeda funding, but we found no evidence that

the Saudi government as an institution or senior officials within the Saudi government funded Al Qaeda"). *See* National Commission on Terrorist Attacks Upon the United States, The 9/11 Commission Report 64–67 (2004) *available at* www.9–11commission.gov/report/911Report.pdf (noting that bin Laden paid the Taliban and received primarily logistical support for his training camps but noting difficulties between bin Laden and the Taliban leadership). Peter Bergen, the Western journalist who interviewed Osama bin Laden, testified before Congress that [t]here was a fair amount of tension between Osama bin Laden and many Taliban leaders pre-9/11." Peter Bergen, Testimony before the House Government Reform and Oversight Committee, Mar. 5, 2009, *available at* 2009 WLNR 4214320.

> *See also* Rohan Gunaratna, Inside Al-Qaeda 61–62 (2002) (noting al Qaeda funded the Taliban but there is no indication of vice versa, and observing that al Qaeda did not profit with the Taliban regime on the sale of narcotics, the primary sources of al Qaeda funding being listed as wealthy Arab benefactors).

21 *See supra* note 11 for the UN International Law Commission's approach to state responsibility for the acts of private irregular forces.

22 S.C. Res. 1368, U.N. Doc. S/res/1368 (Sep. 12, 2001).

23 S.C. Res. 1373, U.N. Doc.S/res/1373 (Sept. 28, 2001) (reaffirming duty of states not to assist terrorist organizations).

24 Security Council Resolution 1267 issued in 1999 also established a committee to monitor and sanction individuals and entities. Denominated the al Qaeda and Taliban Committee, it has the power to freeze the assets of individuals and organizations. The Committee has been criticized for failing to accord individuals the right to a meaningful hearing and the means to challenge the accusations made against them.

25 Regarding violations of Security Council resolutions made under chapter VII, one commentator notes as follows:

> This begs the question of whether it matters that the Security Council brings these obligations within the U.N. legal framework. Resolution 232 of 1966 suggests that there is a particular set of sanctions for violating Security Council decisions when it states that "failure or refusal" by any of them to implement the present resolution shall constitute a violation of Article 25 of the United Nations Charter. In reality, there is no difference between the sanctions the Security Council will apply to a violation of Article 25 and a sanction in response to a 'regular' threat to international peace and security. Indeed, as Alfred Rubin notes, no provision in the U.N. Charter specifies the measures to be taken when a State violates Article 25, and so the moral-political order seems to be left to decide the appropriate sanctions on its own.

> J. Fry, *Dionysian disarmament: security council WMD coercive measures and their legal implications*, 29 Mich. J. Int'l L. 236 (2008). On some occasions, the Security Council has taken action, for example, its sanctioning Iraq and Libya. *See also, e.g.*, D. Kresock, *'Ethnic Cleansing' in the Balkans: the legal foundations of foreign intervention*, 27 Cornell Int'l L.J. 203 (1994), illustrating an instance where the Security Council imposed strict economic sanctions for an Article violation:

> By late February 1992, in response to the frequent violations of the initial cease-fire agreement between Croatia and Serbia, the Security Council adopted Resolution 743. Under Article 25 of the UN Charter, the resolution called for the development of a peace-keeping force to provide humanitarian

assistance in Sarajevo and supervise the withdrawal of federal troops from Croatia. However, despite the presence of UN Protection Forces, the situation in Bosnia continued to deteriorate and Bosnian Serbs increased their "ethnic cleansing" practices. By May, the Secretary-General determined the situation unfit for peace-keeping treatment. Instead, the Security Council adopted Resolution 752, which mandated that all parties in Bosnia observe the cease-fire agreement of 12 April and cooperate in peace-keeping negotiations. The resolution also required all parties to ensure safe conditions to facilitate the distribution of humanitarian aid in the region. When the parties in Bosnia failed to comply, the Security Council, attempting to force compliance, adopted Resolution 757 and imposed strict economic sanctions.'

Kresock, *supra* at 227. (citations omitted).

26 Case Concerning Military and Paramilitary Activities in and Against Nicaragua (Nicaragua v. United States), 1986 I.C.J. 14, para. 166 (June 27). (Schwebel, J., dissenting). The dissent also relied on the UN General Assembly resolution on aggression which defines aggression as including not only "invasion or attack" but also

(g) The sending by or on behalf of a State of armed bands, groups, irregulars or mercenaries, which carry out acts of armed force against another State of such gravity as to amount to the acts listed above, or its *substantial involvement* therein.

Definition of Aggression, G.A. Res. 3314 (XXIX), art. 3(g), U.N. Doc. A/res/ 3314 (Dec. 14, 1974), art. (emphasis added).

27 The dissent also argued that international law gave wide latitude to "victim states" to use force against states that provide safe havens to insurgent or terror-ist groups: "[I]nternational law imputed responsibility to a State knowingly serving as a base of such para-military activities, and gave the victim State rather wide liberties of self-defense against them." Case Concerning Military and Paramilitary Activities in and Against Nicaragua (Nicaragua v. United States), 1986 I.C.J. 14, para. 164 (June 27). (Schwebel, J., dissenting).

28 *See, e.g.*, M. Breger & M. Stern, *Introduction to the Symposium on Modifying the Law of War*, 56 Cath. U. L. Rev. 745 (2007) (arguing that the ICJ in Nicaragua, in the Oil Platforms case, and the ICJ judgment in the case of armed activities on the territory of the Congo (Democratic Republic of the Congo (DRC) v. Uganda), 19 December 2005, has too narrowly limited the right of self-defense of states engaged in "asymmetric warfare" with a terrorist organization).

29 *See* J. Paust, *Use of Armed Force against Terrorists in Afghanistan, Iraq, and beyond*, 35 Cornell Int'l L.J. 533, 540–41 (2002).

30 *See* D. Von Drehle & R. J. Smith, *U.S. Strikes Iraq for Plot to Kill Bush*, Wash. Post, June 27, 1993, at A1, *available at* www.washingtonpost.com/wp-srv/ inatl/longterm/iraq/timeline/062793.htm (noting that the 23 tomahawk cruise missile attack took place between 1 a.m. and 2 a.m.).

31 Paust, *supra* note 29 at 540–41.

32 J. Beard, *America's New War on Terror: The Case for Self-Defense under International Law*, 25 Harv. J.L. & Pub. Pol'y 559 (2002).

33 Beard notes that offers of assistance came from a large number of states: "Seven days after the U.S. had commenced its air campaign against Afghanistan, the Washington Post reported that thirty-six countries had offered the US troops or equipment, forty-four countries had allowed U.S. use of their airspace, thirty-three countries were offering landing rights, and thirteen countries had permitted storage of equipment." *Id.* at 571–72.

34 Amnesty International, Annual Report: Afghanistan (1997), *available at* www.

amnestyusa.org/annualreport.php?id=E0B7F15F8354548480256A
0F005BEA9C&c=AFG (last visited Feb. 2, 2009).

35   Amnesty International, Annual Report: Afghanistan (1996), *available at* www.
amnestyusa.org/annualreport.php?id=31C0FA8C8924880480256A
0F005BCC42&c=AFG (last visited Feb. 2, 2009).

36   Amnesty International, Annual Report: Afghanistan (1997), *available at* www.
amnestyusa.org/annualreport.php?id=E0B7F15F8354548480256A
0F005BEA9C&c=AFG (last visited Feb. 2, 2009).

37   Amnesty International, Annual Report: Afghanistan (1998), *available at* www.
amnestyusa.org/annualreport.php?id=8ABF006771A01C8080256A
0F005C0259&c=AFG (last visited Feb. 2, 2009).

38   Pakistan, Saudi Arabia, and the United Arab Emirates.

39   *See, e.g.*, S.C. Res. 1267, U.N. Doc. S/res/1267 (Oct. 15, 1999), which, among
other things, "[r]*eiterated* its [the Council's] deep concern over the continuing
violations of international humanitarian law and of human rights, particularly
discrimination against women and girls, and over the significant rise in the
illicit production of opium, and stressing that the capture by the Taliban of
the Consulate-General of the Islamic Republic of Iran and the murder of Iranian
diplomats and a journalist in Mazar-e-Sharif constituted flagrant violations of
established international law. . . ."

40   S.C. Res. 1076, para. 11, U.N. Doc. S/res/1076 (Oct. 22, 1996), *available at*
http://daccessdds.un.org/doc/UNDOC/GEN/N96/284/26/PDF/N9628426.
pdf?OpenElement (last visited Feb. 19, 2009).

13 Conquest, colonization, and the right of self-determination

The land of the Chechens consists of broad plains in the north gradually rising in the south to form part of the Caucasus, a mountain range higher than the Alps, spanning the Black Sea and the Caspian Sea. The Chechens have lived there for millennia.[1] Attila the Hun tried to subjugate the Caucasus peoples, including the Chechens, but was beaten back. Their Persian and Turkish neighbors to the south fought against the Chechens, but never were able to push the Chechens from their wild and rugged land that both protected and divided the Caucasus peoples. Then the Russians came.

Making initial thrusts in the 1700s, mammoth Russia began the "final stage" of its conquest of Chechnya, an area about the size of Connecticut, in the early part of the nineteenth century. Russia, however, "took five decades" to put down the Chechen "mountaineers."[2] The Caucasus were not inviting to an invader, even one as powerful as Russia. Covered by dense forests in ever-undulating terrain, the Caucasus were ideally constructed for ambuscade and for guerrilla warfare. Frustrated in their attempts to subdue the Chechens swiftly, the Russians opened a campaign of attrition: burning Chechen villages, destroying their crops, and killing men, women, and children, many of whom were innocent civilians. Like the American military's use of Agent Orange in Vietnam, the Russians cut down the Chechens' forests. After finally conquering the Chechens in 1859,[3] the Russians expelled about half of the Chechens from their own land.

Although beaten, the Chechens never fully gave in to the Russian empire, engaging in passive resistance until 1917.[4] Even after the Communists took over, the Chechens tried to "assert their independence," but this effort was put down. In 1944, Stalin engaged in "ethnic cleansing" of the Chechens, ordering his largely Russian troops forcibly to deport the entire Chechen population to Kazakhstan and Siberia, causing the death of over 100,000 Chechens from starvation and disease.[5] Furthermore, Stalin's troops burned alive some of the elderly Chechens who were too infirm to be transported. Among the victims was the grandmother of Chechnya's first modern president, Dzhokhar Dudayev.

In the Soviet era, Chechnya was one of the poorest areas in the USSR, with one of the highest infant mortality rates. Given this history, it "came as no surprise" that the Chechens began a separatist movement during Soviet President Mikhail Gorbachev's unanticipated push towards liberalization.[6] Similarly, it was hardly unforeseeable that the Chechens should resort to terror methods in the face of Russia employing its military might.

Many terrorist groups emerge for reasons other than nationalism and colonialism, which have little or nothing to do with the groups' rise. The Red Brigades, who carried out a reign of terror in Italy and kidnapped and killed the Italian Prime Minister, Adolpho Moro, fall into this category. The Red Brigades espoused a twisted left-wing ideology and apparently sought to install socialism or some form of communism in that country. The Baader-Meinhoff Gang of then West Germany had similar distorted left-wing roots. Neither of these groups can be said to have been responding directly to colonialism or reacting to violent conquest by a foreign nation.

Yet military and economic conquest often breeds terrorists. Highly advanced and expensive weapons technology advantages the state, giving rebels or resisters scant chance of prevailing on a traditional battlefield. Hence asymmetric warfare—what we would call terrorism—is the method of choice of many rebel or resistance leaders. More importantly, such conquest often drives segments of the conquered or colonized population to take extreme measures, to fight against what they perceive to be the gross injustice of conquest, colonization, and consequent national degradation and humiliation.

Conquering other peoples, annexing their land, looting their resources, treating them at best as second-class citizens on their own soil, stirred for most of recorded history few moral qualms, let alone legal ones. Historians often labeled such conquerors as "great." For example, Alexander the Great invaded and conquered most of the then known world, including Persia, Syria, Israel, Egypt, Turkey, Afghanistan, and Pakistan. Julius Caesar invaded and conquered Gaul, which included all of France and most of Switzerland and Belgium. He also invaded Britannia and conquered parts of Germania. Britain, Belgium, France, and Germany carved up virtually all of Africa among themselves. The Spanish, the French, the Dutch, the English, and the Portuguese sailed into North and South America, subjugating and, in some cases, wiping out the indigenous population, claiming with pride and moral presumption the land of the "uncivilized" natives for the conquerors' European countries.

In the last century, however, two streams of legal thought began to flow against the unfettered right both to attack other countries and to colonize them, streams that eventually joined to produce a revolutionary change in international law. The First and Second World Wars, and the calamitous death and destruction they caused, taught the world that unlimited use of military force could no longer be tolerated. These two conflicts and the human rights movement the latter inspired, also taught that one people may not put its boot on another people.

13.1 Prohibiting aggressive war

The Industrial Revolution of the nineteenth century not only brought tremendous advances in communications, machinery, and manufacturing, but also geometrically increased the destructive force of the world's weaponry. The US Civil War and nineteenth-century European conflicts resulted in mammoth casualty figures. The number of deaths and the severity of the wounds of surviving soldiers as a result of the progress of the Industrial Revolution prompted Henry Dunant to found the International Committee of the Red Cross in 1859 which led to the growth of humanitarian law, an attempt to soften the worst ravages of war. (In a battle between the Franco-Sardinian troops and Austro-Hungarian Empire's forces, Dunant witnessed the killing or wounding of approximately 40,000 troops in a single day.[7]) It was not until the First World War, however, that the massive death and destruction that modern technology had wrought became widely recognized.[8] That conflict left over eight and a half million dead, over 21 million wounded, and much of Europe devastated.[9]

After the "war to end all wars," the international community set up the League of Nations, an international organization aimed at preventing war. In a famous conflict with President Woodrow Wilson, the US Senate, led by Senator Henry Cabot Lodge, refused to give its advice and consent to the treaty establishing the League.[10] The harsh treatment the other allied powers insisted on meting out to vanquished Germany, the 1929 depression, and the US's isolationism are generally credited with giving rise to Hitler. Appealing to extreme nationalism, Hitler abrogated the Treaty of Versailles, rearmed Germany, and on September 1, 1939, invaded Poland, starting the Second World War. The League of Nations had failed its most important test.

The Second World War proved even deadlier than the First World War. It involved more countries, caused greater devastation, and inflicted more than five times the number of casualties. Europe and parts of Asia and Africa were laid waste; many of their cities, factories, bridges, and roads, if not destroyed, had been extensively damaged. Furthermore, approximately 25 million military personnel met their deaths in that war, and approximately 35 million civilians also lost their lives.[11] In comparison, not quite 3,000 people were killed on 9/11. That is, it would take approximately 20,000 September 11s to equal the number of persons killed in the Second World War.

The victorious Allies, including the US, recognized that a new international institution needed to be established to lessen the chance of warfare, if the human race were to survive. Less than a year after the war ended, the world community under the Allies' leadership crafted the United Nations Charter, creating the United Nations. The UN Charter's chief provision prohibits the use of armed force, and as noted in chapter 11, makes only two exceptions: self-defense and UN Security Council authorized military actions.[12]

The Charter was revolutionary. Although aggressive warfare was often condemned as immoral, it had not generally been considered illegal.[13] In arguing for Senate approval of the League of Nations, President Wilson stated that Article 10 of the League's Charter, guaranteeing each state's territorial integrity, created not a legal obligation, but only a moral one. The UN Charter's prohibition, contained in Article 2, is definite and mandatory. It requires states "to settle their international disputes by peaceful means" and declares that "[a]ll members *shall* refrain in their international relations from the threat or use of force against the territorial integrity or political independence of any state or in any other manner inconsistent with the Purposes of the United Nations."[14] This prohibition attempts to change over five thousand years of practice, where conquest was often the rule, not the exception. The Charter's language not only prohibits conquest, but also the use of any level of force against another state absent self-defense. Thus, it aims to prevent not only aggressive wars, but also conduct that might lead up to war.

Unfortunately, the UN Charter has not stopped war. Since 1945, the world has seen, in addition to international armed conflicts, an explosion of civil wars.[15] The Charter has, however, achieved considerable success in thwarting annexation. Although countries have sometimes argued for a broad interpretation of self-defense, few claim that the Charter permits one country to attack and take another country's territory.[16] In condemning Saddam Hussein's invasion of Kuwait in 1990, the UN Security Council declared, "[A]nnexation of Kuwait by Iraq under any form and whatever pretext has no legal validity, and is considered null and void."[17] That Iraq's 1990 invasion of Kuwait was so clearly an aggressive war to annex Kuwait in violation of the Charter unquestionably helped the US garner both Security Council authorization and a wide coalition of states, including Arab countries, to undo the aggression.[18]

13.2 The right of self-determination

By making aggressive uses of armed force illegal, the international community had begun to end, at least prospectively, the practice of conquest and colonization. If a country with colonizing designs may not use armed force except in self-defense, then it will have difficulty obtaining new colonies. Although some poor countries have signed concession agreements with multinational corporations that appear to give away nearly everything, it is unlikely that a country would agree to be colonized, absent extreme necessity or duress. Thus, the Charter essentially prohibits the formation of any new colonies. The Charter, however, did not abolish colonization. It did establish trusteeships for certain countries that were deemed "not ready" for independence, with the goal of helping them achieve independence, but achieving this goal was not mandatory.

Aside from Article 2 of the UN Charter, there arose another legal doctrine that has further hastened classical colonization's demise, namely, the right of self-determination. This right is traced back to the US and French revolutions in the eighteenth century. The doctrine rests on the notion that a people has the right to choose its own government. A more modern formulation of the right was made by President Woodrow Wilson, who actually coined the phrase "self-determination." Wilson believed that empire and colonization had contributed to the outbreak of the First World War. Fiercely resisted by the other Allies, Wilson advocated for the end of colonization and for the right of the countries who had been conquered in the War not only to free themselves from the past and present empires, but also to choose their own governments.

Many of Wilson's ideas were rejected by the other Allies after the First World War, but as with his support for an international organization like the League of Nations, his concept of self-determination later became a legal reality. Hitler's designs on much of the world and his attempt to conquer, colonize, and enslave other peoples reawakened the call not only for limits on countries' right to use armed force, but also for the Wilsonian ideal that each people had the right to determine its future and its government free from any overlord. These calls culminated in the drafting of the first Article of the UN Charter, which identified one of the UN's purposes as follows: "To develop friendly relations among nations based on respect for the principle of equal rights and *self-determination of peoples*. . . ."[19]

The precise meaning of this Article has been subject to debate. Those advocating the rights of the colonized argued that the Article meant that the colonizer had to leave and allow the people to set up their own governments. The empire states, like Britain, argued that it applied only to countries that had been conquered in the Second World War by Nazi Germany or by Imperial Japan. The text and drafting history of Article 1 suggest that it may be too vague to establish a specific right.[20]

Despite the arguably narrow meaning of Article 1, the colonized nations continued their demands for independence. Before the Second World War, nine colonial powers controlled 150 territories with 650 million people.[21] Then an unprecedented movement towards independence began to sweep the so-called developing world. From the start of the Second World War until 1980, the European powers relinquished most of their colonies: approximately 40 nations in Africa were declared independent, and during this time most of the colonies in the Middle East and Asia were likewise declared independent.

In 1966, two major human rights treaties were formed: the International Covenant on Civil and Political Rights and the International Covenant on Economic, Social, and Social Rights. Article 1 in both treaties is identical; it states: "All peoples have the *right of self-determination*. By virtue of that right they *freely* determine their political status and *freely* pursue their economic, social and cultural development."[22] This language was taken verbatim from the 1960 UN General Assembly resolution, Declaration on the Granting of independence to Colonial Countries and Peoples, which passed without a dissenting vote.[23] The drafting history of this Article indicated a much broader purpose, namely, to eliminate all forms of colonization of one nation by another. Both treaties have been widely ratified—167 nations have ratified the ICCPR and 160 have ratified the Economic Covenant, as of this writing.[24] Reinforced by state practice, the right of self-determination has been declared a *peremptory* norm of international law by some respectable scholars.[25]

Yet the right of self-determination has been fraught with problems of definition and application. Although the doctrine was relatively easy to apply to lands that had been conquered and colonized by countries far from the colonized state (classical European colonization), the right of self-determination has often not been applied to indigenous people whose land was taken by European settlers and others a century or more before. The doctrine has likewise generally not been applied to conquered peoples whose land was contiguous to and now within the conquerors'. (Chechnya, for example, lies next to Russia proper.) In other words, the doctrine generally is not intended to permit secession by minority groups or by those ethnic groups that may have occupied the same territory as sovereign nations in the past.[26] Furthermore, "[w]ho is the 'self' to whom 'self-determination' attaches? Is it Northern Ireland, Ireland, or the United Kingdom together with Northern Ireland? The present population of Taiwan (consisting of mainly Nationalist Chinese), the indigenous islanders, or Communist China? Gilbraltar or Spain?"[27]

Relying upon this right is also problematic when the conquering state sent masses of colonists to the conquered country for settlement. Prime Minister Margaret Thatcher notably invoked the right of self-determination to support the British military actions defending the Falkland/Malvinas islands against Argentinean attack. Yet the British had permitted Scottish immigrants to settle the islands after annexing them in 1833. Should the right of self-determination be used to justify keeping territory in the colonizer's hands, territory it had obtained through a war of aggression? On the other hand, if a great deal of time has passed after foreigners have settled in a new land and become the majority, can the right of self-determination be ignored?

Some of these problems are resolved by the legal doctrine of intertemporal law. This doctrine refuses to make retroactive international law, such as the UN Charter's prohibition on conquest: "[A] juridical fact must be appreciated in light of the law contemporary with it" and not in the light of the law today.[28] One can defend the doctrine on the grounds of finality and stability. There are approximately 5,000 separate ethnic or national groups in the world.[29] Currently there are a little under 200 countries in the world. (As of this writing there are 192 member states of the United Nations.) Creating 4,800 independent countries would not advance public world order, and, in many cases, retroactive application would cause upheaval. For example, retroactively applying the UN Charter prohibiting the use of force except in self-defense presumably would require at a minimum that the US return all the territories it took from Mexico in the Mexican–American War of 1846–1848.

Granted that before the UN Charter and the recognition of the right of self-determination, conquest, and colonization were legal.[30] The evils that the law now aims at preventing, however, obviously existed before the law was changed. Violence and national humiliation usually accompanied conquest and colonization. For example, Chief Seattle said, "Our children have seen their fathers humbled in defeat. Our warriors have felt shame, and after defeat they turn their days in idleness and contaminate their bodies with sweet foods and strong drink."[31]

Colonization was usually rooted in racism and in the colonists' unchallenged belief both in their racial superiority and in the "white man's burden." Jules Harmand, a French advocate of colonialism, exemplified the colonizer's sense of self:

> It is necessary then to accept as a principle and point of departure the fact that there is a hierarchy of races and civilizations, and that we belong to the superior race and civilization, still recognizing that while superiority confers rights, it imposes strict obligations in return. The basic legitimation of conquest over native peoples is the conviction of our superiority, not merely our mechanical, economic, and military superiority, but our moral superiority. Our dignity rests on that quality, and it underlies our right to direct the rest of humanity.[32]

Like cancerous discrimination long suffered by African-Americans and other minorities in the US, the scars of colonization are often long-lasting. Even those countries that no longer are in bondage to the colonizer often remain wounded by the colonial experience. As with institutional racial discrimination, it frequently takes several generations for a country to overcome colonialism's effects, assuming they are ever fully overcome.

Consequently, the lands of peoples who have been conquered and colonized in the last century and a half often possess especially rich soil for the growth of terrorist movements. Adding to the destructive colonial experience, many now independent states in Africa, the Middle East, and Asia have failed to adopt genuine democracy, depriving their people of avenues to express their grievances peacefully. Furthermore, many now independent states suffer from neocolonialism, a *de facto* reassertion of control by the former colonizer, by multinational corporations, or both. In addition, economic hardship experienced in many formerly colonized nations helps private terror organizations emerge.[33]

That these countries have suffered conquest and colonization does not excuse those who, partly in response, deliberately kill the innocent. By definition, terrorists engage in crimes against humanity, one of the most egregious crimes recognized by law, crimes that so erode societal security that they have transnational impact. The experience of conquest and colonization, however, should help guide governments that are attempting to stop terrorist organizations. Conquest and colonization often create an understandable reservoir of righteous resentment in the colonized or formerly colonized people. Governments, as both a moral and practical matter, should adopt counterterrorism policies that are sensitive to the colonial experience and fully respect the people colonized. Given the manner in which the colonizer treated the colonized, the most practical way of showing this respect is to follow the rule of law and to apply the law *equally*,[34] namely, to treat the colonized or formerly colonized people the same way the government officials would want themselves or their family members or their ethnic or nationality group to be treated.[35]

Unfortunately, governments dealing with terrorist threats sometimes demonize not only suspected terrorists, but also the ethnic or national group from which they have come. Such demonization and appeals to state security then implicitly provide the rationale for ignoring domestic and international law in carrying out counterterrorism efforts. For example, Russia has now established a state-sponsored campaign of discrimination against Chechens: "This discrimination has taken several forms: forcible evictions from residences; arbitrary identity checks, forcible entrance into premises, searches, detention and beatings; fabrication of criminal accusations; refusal to grant the status of 'forced migrant'; denial of the right to employment, health care and education; and refusal to grant sojourn or residence registration in many Russian regions. . . ."[36] Furthermore, Russian newspapers, newscasters, government officials, and soldiers routinely make racist comments about Chechens.[37]

These practices almost certainly make it easier to use counterterrorism tactics such as the following: Russia has assassinated four Chechen presidents since the fall of the Soviet Union. In addition, Russia has systematically tortured Chechens suspected of violence, carried out other extrajudicial killings, and adopted the practice of forced disappearance of Chechen suspects.[38] Russia also bombed Grozny, the Chechen capital, nearly to oblivion, killing thousands of innocent civilians, far out of proportion to any legitimate military objective.

Query whether these counterterrorism tactics, most of which violate international law, are likely to quell the anger of the Chechen people, provide security and stability in the long run, and promote public world order. Perhaps the bigger "battle" in the struggle against terrorist organizations and their adherents is not to capture every terrorist, every member of al Qaeda or its allied organizations, but to capture the hearts and minds of the world's 1.4 billion Muslims. Granted, religious-oriented terrorists rather than secular terrorists may look more to themselves for inspiration than to the larger community. Yet religious terrorists like most terrorists depend on the larger community for recruits, logistical support, and financing. Terrorist groups who lack sympathizers in the larger community have a hard time sustaining themselves.

The Bush–Cheney administration put the most weight on a military solution to the terrorist threat. This included the invasion and occupation of Iraq and Afghanistan, rough interrogation methods of captured suspected terrorists, including in some cases, waterboarding, the *incommunicado* and indefinite detention of "enemy combatants," extraordinarily rendering certain "enemy combatants" or terrorist suspects to countries that torture, the use of ethnic profiling against Middle Eastern looking people, and the enlisting of the local police for immigration enforcement (largely against Arab looking males). Seeming to ignore the treatment Muslim countries have had at the hands of the West for over two centuries, the Bush–Cheney policies have had the effect of inflaming much of the Islamic world against the US. Opinion polls in the Muslim world indicated that favorable opinion of the US had fallen to the nadir, to an unprecedented new low.

The consequences of losing the battle for the hearts and minds of Muslims are serious. Instead of isolating terrorist organizations, the Bush–Cheney administration's policies may have strengthened them by increasing their recruitment, financing, and acceptance within the larger Muslim community. Losing this battle also weakens moderate voices in Muslim communities around the world. Additionally, it means forfeiting the willing cooperation of Muslim countries, governments, and citizens in the struggle against terrorist organizations, cooperation that is critical if the US is ever to significantly lessen the threat of Islamic terrorism. Since these terrorist organizations operate clandestinely around the world, the US with all its military might can do relatively little if the people, police, and other governmental officials in the communities where the terrorists reside refuse to help.

When a country's people are frightened, they far more readily accept proposals put forward by zealous and often well-meaning governmental officials to take away freedoms in the name of greater security. Panicked people also tend to accept the arguments of governmental officials that domestic and international law can be violated or ignored. Yet resorting to force unchecked by law may create its own problems, causing a country to lose both moral authority and security. If the Obama administration and future American leaders learn this lesson as a result of the Bush–Cheney policies and practices, which often disregarded international law, the US and its people will be better equipped to meet the terrorist challenge. By helping to achieve international cooperation and by enhancing the moral and legal authority of the US and other countries subject to terrorist attacks, respecting international law may significantly advance both our short-term and long-term goals of reducing terrorism and keeping our country safe.

Notes

1   John Man, Attila: The Barbarian king who challenged Rome 112 (2006).
2   Vera Tolz, *Independence for Russian Minorities: War in Chechnya, in* The Collapse of the Soviet Union 210 (Leone Bruno et al. eds., 1999).
3   R. Williams Ayers, *Chechnya and Russia: A War of Succession*, 1 History Behind the Headlines: The Origins of Conflicts Worldwide 46–57 (Sonia G. Benson, Nancy Matuszak, & Meghan Appel O'Meara eds., 2003); Thomson Gale, *Gale Virtual Reference Library*, Vassar College Libraries, July 25, 2007, *available at* http://find.galegroup.com/gvrl/infomark.do?&contentSet=EBKS&type=

retrieve&tabID=T001&prodId=GVRL&docId=CX3410600014&source=gale &userGroupName=nysl_se_vassar&version=1.0.

4   Tolz, *supra* note 1, at 212. *See also* John F. Baddeley, The Russian Conquest of the Caucasus 130–31 (1908). The noted Russian nationalist and novelist, Aleksandr Solzhenitsyn, has stated that the Chechens were the only people not to bow to Soviet oppression: "[T]here was one nation which would not give in, would not acquire the mental habits of submission—and not just individual rebels among them, but the whole nation to a man. These were the Chechens." *Solzhenitsyn on the Chechens*, The Chechen Weekly, Sept. 4, 2003, *available at* http://jamestown.org/chechnya_weekly/Article.php?Articleid=2371616.

5   Svante E. Cornell, Small Nations and Great Powers 197–99 (2001) (estimating the violent deportations themselves and the destitution caused resulted in thousands of Chechen fatalities, causing "direct and indirect (from absence of growth) losses" to the Chechens of over 200,000 people (more than one-third of the population)); *see also* Tolz, *supra* note 2, at 212.

6   Tolz, *supra* note 2, at 212.

7   International Committee of the Red Cross, *Henry Dunant (1828–1910)*, ICRC.org, June 4, 1998, www.icrc.org/Web/eng/siteeng0.nsf/htm lall/57JNVQ (accessed September 9, 2009).

8   *How Far did Industrialization Revolutionize the Nature of Warfare from 1792 to 1918*, http://64.233.169.104/search?q=cache:Om-l8e6lwRcJ:www. ralphallen.org/New%2520school%2520web%2520site/elearninghome/ subject%2520areas/History%2520resources/history%25202/ASHistory_files/ war/1815-crimea/How%2520Far%2520Did%2520Industrialisation.doc+ weapons+%22industrial+revolution%22&hl=en&ct=clnk&cd=38&gl= us&client=firefox-a (last visited Sept. 9, 2009); The German Krupp armament firm made such progress in designing and manufacturing artillery that 70 percent of the casualties of the First World War came from artillery bombardment. *See How Far did the Industrial Revolution Go in Advancing Weaponry*, http://64.233.169.104/search?q=cache:Om-l8e6lwRcJ:www.ralphallen.org/ New%2520school%2520web%2520site/elearninghome/subject%2520areas/ History%2520resources/history%25202/ASHistory_files/war/1815-crimea/ How%2520Far%2520Did%2520Industrialisation.doc+weapons+%22 industrial+revolution%22&hl=en&ct=clnk&cd=38&gl=us&client=firefox-a (last visited Sept. 9, 2009).

9   *World War I*, 27 Funk & Wagnalls Encylopedia 419 (1986).

10 *Wilson and the League of Nations*, www.san.beck.org/GPJ21-LeagueofNations. html (last visited Sept. 9, 2009).

11 *World War II*, 27 Funk & Wagnalls Encyclopedia 447–48 (1986).

12 Some argue that there is another basis for the use of armed force, namely, humanitarian intervention. The NATO bombing of Serbia is generally justified on this basis. *See* chapter 11 for a more detailed discussion of humanitarian intervention.

13 Granted in 1928, the Kellogg-Briand Pact was signed, which purported to outlaw war. (40 countries became parties to this treaty.) The Kellogg-Briand Pact, however, consisting of a single page, was written in general language, and failed to include an exception for self-defense. *See Kellogg-Briand Pact*, Avalon Project, *available at* www.yale.edu/lawweb/avalon/kbpact/kbpact.htm (last visited Nov. 23, 2010). The Nuremberg Tribunals did rely on the Kellogg-Briand pact for the proposition that planning and carrying out an aggressive war was a war crime. This was the weakest charge in the indictment. (It is notable that Rudolf Hess, who was only convicted of conspiracy to carry out an aggressive war (and not for war crimes regarding the treatment of prisoners or the occupied population) was not sentenced to death. The other extenuating

circumstance was his apparent mental instability.) This issue remains controversial today, because the world community has thus far been unable to agree on
a definition of the crime of aggression.

14 UN Charter, arts. 2.3, 2.4 (emphasis added).

15 The drafters of the Charter, having just gone through the Second World War,
intended to prevent like conflicts and were not especially focusing on civil wars.

16 Notable exceptions include China's invasion and annexation of Tibet in 1950,
India's annexation of Goa in 1962, and Indonesia's annexation of East Timor in
1975. As Adam Roberts points out, only East Timor's annexation has been
reversed. *See* Adam Roberts, *Transformative Military Occupation: Applying the Laws
of War and Human Rights*, 100 Am. J. Int'l L. 580, 584 (2006). Roberts notes
the now established rule prohibiting annexation. *Id.* at 583. We will have to
see how the Russia-Georgia conflict is resolved. Israel's 1967 Six Day War with
neighboring Arab states demands a more complex analysis. Most international
law scholars probably agree that the bellicose language of some of the Arab
leaders, their refusal to speak with the Israelis, who were seeking dialogue, and
the Arab states' steps toward mobilization of their armed forces placed Israel
under threat of imminent attack, justifying the Israeli preemptive attack under
the doctrine of anticipatory self-defense. Security Council Resolution 242 states,
however, on the one hand, that Israel must return occupied territories and,
on the other, that all states in the region must "terminate all claims of
belligerency" and "respect the sovereignty, territorial integrity and political
independence of every State."

In its full text, the Resolution states that the Council:

> 1. *Affirms* that the fulfillment of Charter principles requires the establish-
> ment of a just and lasting peace in the Middle East which should include
> the application of both the following principles:
>   (i) Withdrawal of Israel armed forces from territories occupied in the
>   recent conflict;
>   (ii) Termination of all claims or states of belligerency and respect for
>   and acknowledgement of the sovereignty, territorial integrity and
>   political independence of every State in the area and their right to live
>   in peace within secure and recognized boundaries free from threats or
>   acts of force; . . .

S.C. Res. 242, U.N. Doc. S/RES/242 (Nov. 22, 1967), *available at* http://
www1.umn.edu/humanrts/peace/docs/scres242.html. Some argue that Israel has
the obligation to withdraw from all the occupied territories, including East
Jerusalem. *See, e.g.*, John Quigley, *Sovereignty in Jerusalem*, 45 Cath. U. L. Rev.
765, 776–76 (1996). Some argue that, based on the drafting history of Security
Council Resolution 242, Israel does not have the legal obligation to withdraw
from "all" territories it took in the 1967 war. *See* David M. Phillips, *The
Unexplored Option, Jewish Settlements in a Palestinian State*, 25 Penn St. Int'l L. Rev.
75 (2006) (citing Eugene V. Rostow, *Correspondence*, 84 Am. J. Int'l L. 717, 720
(1990)); Shimon Shetree, *Negotiations and Agreements are Better than Legal Resolutions: A Response to Professor John Quigley*, 32 Case W. Res. J. Int'l L. 259, 265
(2000). Under either interpretation, SC 242 envisions a reciprocal process, in
essence, land for peace.

17 S.C. Res. 662, art. 1, U.N. Doc. S/res/662 (Aug. 9, 1990).

18 Conspicuous by its absence from US justification for its invasion of Iraq in 2003
was any claim that Iraq had invaded another country or had used or threatened
imminent attack of another country, let alone that the US was in danger of such
an attack. *See* chapter 11 for a more detailed discussion of this point.

19 UN Charter, art. 1.2 (emphasis added).

20   *See* Burns H. Weston, Richard A. Falk, et al., International Law and World Order 562 (4th edition 2006) (quoting Daniel Thurer, *Self-Determination*, 8 Encyl. Pub. Int'l L. 470, 471 (1985)).

21   Ruth Gordon, *Saving Failed States: Sometimes a Neocolonialist Notion*, 12 Am. U. J. Int'l L. & Pol'y 903, 953 (1997) (citing Yassin El-Ayouty, United Nations and Decolonization 4 (1971)).

22   International Covenant on Civil and Political Rights art. 1.1, Dec. 16, 1966, 993 U.N.T.S. 171, *reprinted in* 6 I.L.M. 368 (1967); International Covenant on Economic, Social, and Cultural Rights art. 1.1, Dec. 16, 1966, 993 U.N.T.S. 3, *reprinted in* 6 I.L.M. 360 (1967) (emphasis added).

23   G.A. Res. 1514, at 66, U.N. GAOR, 15th Sess., Supp. 16, U.N. Doc. A/4684 (Dec. 14, 1960).

24   The UN General Assembly in 1970 passed another resolution, strengthening the right of self-determination, Declaration of Principles of International Law Concerning Friendly Relations and Cooperation Among States. *See also* UN General Assembly Declaration on the Rights of Indigenous Peoples, (143 in favor, 4 against (Australia, Canada, New Zealand, United States), 11 abstained, Oct. 2, 2007, *available at* http://daccessdds. un.org/doc/ UNDOC/GEN/N06/512/07/PDF/N0651207.pdf?OpenElement (last visited Sept. 9, 2009).

25   *See* Antonio Cassese, Self-Determination of Peoples 134–35 (1995).

26   The UN General Assembly Declaration on the Rights of Indigenous Peoples, likewise denies the right to secession: "Nothing in this Declaration may be interpreted as implying for any State, people, group or person any right to engage in any activity or to perform any act contrary to the Charter of the United Nations or construed as authorizing or encouraging any action which would dismember or impair totally or in part, the territorial integrity or political unity of sovereign and independent States." UN General Assembly Declaration on the Rights of Indigenous Peoples, G.A. Res. 61/295, art. 46.1, U.N. GAOR, U.N. Doc. A/Res/61/295 (Sept. 13, 2007), *available at* http://daccessdds.un.org/doc/UNDOC/GEN/N06/512/07/PDF/N0651207. pdf?OpenElement (accessed September 9, 2009). But *see* Kosovo's Declaration of Independence, Jure Vidmar, *International Legal Responses to Kosovo's Declaration of Independence*, 42 Vand. J. Transnat'l L. 779 (2009).

27   Michla Pomerance, *Self-Determination Today: The Metamorphosis of an Ideal*, 19 Israel L. Rev. 310, 311 (1984).

28   S. James Anaya, *The Capacity of International Law to Advance Ethnic or Nationality Rights Claims*, 75 Iowa L. Rev. 837, 839 n.6 (1990) (quoting Island of Palmas (*Netherlands v. U.S.*), 2 R. Int'l Arb. Awards 829, 845 (1928)).

29   *See* Anaya, *supra* note 28, at 840.

30   One could argue that the law was changing before the advent of the UN Charter in 1945. The Kellogg-Briand Pact was, after all, agreed upon in 1928. The US and the Western European countries, for example, refused to recognize the Soviet Union's conquest and annexation of the Baltic states in 1940. *See* Anaya, *supra* note 28, at 839. As noted earlier, Wilson had advocated after WWI both for the right of self-determination and for the prohibition of war except in self-defense. Yet 1945 marks the clearest point forbidding the use of armed force for conquest. The right of self-determination did not fully ripen until the 1960s with the two Human Rights covenants and with state practice, namely, the European countries permitting the vast majority of their numerous colonies to become independent. That right, however, still does not reach some peoples, like the Chechens, who still suffer from conquest and colonization.

31   *Chief Seattle Message*, The Power of the People 6, 7 (Robert Cooney & Helen Michalowski eds., 1977).

32   Gordon, *supra* note 21, at 933 n.153 (quoting Edward Said, quoting Jules Harmand).

33   I do not mean to suggest that economic deprivation alone causes terrorism. Osama bin Laden, after all, was the son of a multimillionaire. His right hand, Ayman al-Zawahiri, is a physician. National humiliation seems to be a greater factor than economics. Nonetheless, it probably is easier to recruit from those experiencing economic hardship.

34   *Cf.* Committee on the Elimination of Racial Discrimination, General Comment 21, UN Doc. A/51/18, Annex VIII A, p. 125–26 ("Governments should be sensitive towards the rights of persons belonging to ethnic groups, particularly their right to lead lives of dignity, to preserve their culture, to share equitably in the fruits of national growth and to play their part in the Government of the country of which they are citizens.")

35   Of course governments dealing with a terrorist threat could resort to military repression so familiar to the nineteenth-century empires headquartered in Europe and Russia. The human rights revolution that arose because of the Nazi atrocities in the Second World War has raised the consciousness of the world community and of peoples who have gone through colonization. Even a repressive communist regime, the Peoples Republic of China, has felt compelled to retreat somewhat from its repression of Tibet, a country it illegally invaded and annexed in 1950.

36   *See* Mary Holland, *Chechnya's Internally Displaced and the Role of Russia's Non-Governmental Organizations*, 17 J. Refugee Stud. 334, 337 (2004).

37   *Id.*

38   Tarik Abdel-Monem, *The European Court of Human Rights, Chechnya's Last Chance?*, 28 Vt. L. Rev. 237, 252–57 (2004).

Glossary

Actus Reus an act that, when carried out with the required *mens rea*, constitutes a crime.

Casus Belli an act that justifies or is used to justify a war or armed conflict.

Civil Law System one patterned after the Roman system. Usually used by countries in continental Europe and former colonies thereof. All laws are codified, the judge acts as both the finder of fact and the applier of law, and juries are not usually used. The international tribunals borrow some procedure, court rules, and tradition from this system.

Common Article 3 provides substantive rules governing non-international armed conflict and procedural mechanisms inviting parties to internal conflicts to agree to abide by the rest of the Geneva Conventions. Common Article 3 prohibits torture and requires humane treatment in the context of armed conflict. It applies to armed conflict *not* of an international character, binds all parties (including insurgents), and applies to all detained persons, regardless of status. According to the International Court of Justice, Common Article 3 is now used as a general yardstick against which all treatment of enemy combatants is measured and is called "Common Article 3" because it appears in all four of the 1949 Geneva Conventions.

Common Law System patterned after the English court system. Use is generally limited to the UK and its former colonies. Some laws are traditional and judge-made, then codified. Others are established by the monarchy or legislature then interpreted and applied by the judges. Juries and case precedent are an integral part of the system. The international tribunals borrow some procedure, court rules, and tradition from this system.

Customary International Law "international custom, as evidence of a general practice accepted as law." Statute of the International Court of Justice, art. 38(1)b. A US authority defines custom as follows: "Customary international law results from a general and consistent practice of states followed by them from a sense of obligation." Restatement (Third) of Foreign Relations § 102(2) (1987).

De facto "in fact."

De jure   "at law," or under law.

Dicta   a statement made by a judge in a legal opinion that does not pertain to the substance of the case's decision, but is general commentary on a given topic. In Anglo-Saxon jurisprudence, dicta is less meaningful than the holding of a given case.

Human Rights Law   a system of laws that establishes the minimum rights an individual should be afforded, regardless of where they live and their government's policies.

International Humanitarian Law (IHL)   governs the conduct of warring parties in transnational armed conflict and civil wars; also, "the law of war," "humanitarian law," "the law of armed conflict."

Jurisprudence   the philosophy of law; a system or body of law.

Lex Specialis   a legal interpretive rule that can be used to indicate which rule should be applied when there is more than one that can possibly be applied to the given facts.[1]

Mens Rea   in common law jurisprudence, a person's culpable mental state *and* the probability of harm they understood their action to cause. For one to be guilty of a certain crime, it must be proven that they had the required *mens rea* at the time of the crime—that the person was, for example, aware of the fact that their action had a high probability of causing another harm. In civil law jurisprudence, the equation is a bit more complex, but generally serves the same purpose of gauging the alleged criminal's state of mind and intent at the time of the crime.

Treaty   An agreement between one or more nations that creates binding legal obligations. There are many names given to treaties including agreement, bilateral or multilateral agreement, convention, accord protocol, exchange of letters, charter, and statute, for example.

UN Security Council Chapter VII Powers   the Security Council's ability to control, regulate, and initiate responses to threats to peace, breaches of peace, and acts of aggression. Under these powers, the response may be peaceful or involve armed force. Security Council Resolutions issued under chapter VII are binding on all member states under Article 25 of the UN Charter. Security Council Resolutions issued under chapter VI are only recommendations.

Note

1   *See*, Koskenniemi. International Law Commission Study Group on Fragmentation, Fragmentation of International Law: Topic (a): The function and scope of the lex specialis rule and the question of 'self-contained regimes:' An Outline, http://untreaty.un.org/ilc/sessions/55/fragmentation_outline.pdf.

Index